The Troubled Trinity

The Troubled Trinity

GODOY

AND THE

SPANISH

MONARCHS

Douglas Hilt

THE UNIVERSITY
OF ALABAMA PRESS
TUSCALOOSA AND LONDON

Copyright © 1987 by
The University of Alabama Press
Tuscaloosa, Alabama 35487
Manufactured in the United States of America

Library of Congress Cataloging-in-Publication Data

Hilt, Douglas.
  The troubled trinity.

  Bibliography: p.
  Includes index.
    1. Godoy, Manuel de, príncipe de la Paz, 1767–1851.
  2. Carlos IV, King of Spain, 1748–1819.   3. María
  Luisa, consort of Carlos IV, King of Spain, 1751–1819.
  4. Spain—History—Charles IV, 1788–1808.
  5. Statesmen—Spain—Biography.   I. Title.
  DP200.8.G7H55   1987   946'.058'0924   [B]   86–7017
  ISBN 0-8173-0320-0

British Library Cataloguing-in-Publication Data is available.

To Marquita,

    and to all who,

    despite human frailties, seek after

        Enlightenment

Contents

Illustrations

Preface

Despite the voluminous literature on the Napoleonic period, to this day Manuel Godoy, the Prince of the Peace, remains unjustifiably a neglected figure. The de facto ruler of Spain from 1792 to 1808 and the French emperor's main political adversary south of the Pyrenees, he is summarily dismissed in most standard accounts as the paramour of a meretricious queen. Otherwise reputable historians have trouble marshaling their facts when dealing with Godoy. Geoffroy de Grandmaison, for example, has him a mere ten years younger than Queen María Luisa (in fact the age difference was sixteen years), and consigns him to an early grave in Rome in 1823, oblivious to his subsequent move to Paris, where he died as late as 1851.[1] A nineteenth-century English visitor to Spain reported unequivocally that, "after an exile and obscurity of thirty-six years, he was recalled to Madrid in 1844 by Christina, the widow of Ferdinand VII,"[2] a half-truth at best.

Today, Godoy is often simplistically vilified as a *persona de mala fama,* the venal royal favorite who single-handedly precipitated the French invasion of 1808 and thereby the horrors of the Peninsular War. When alluded to in non-Spanish histories, he is usually given a cursory paragraph to the same damning effect. Most historiographers are content to depict him as the stock villain, the *parvenu par excellence,* and to reiterate what others in turn have themselves dutifully repeated.

If Godoy has long been neglected abroad, that is certainly not the case in Spain. The bibliography dealing with his life and times is impressive by any standard. One obstacle is that the bulk of the material is written in Spanish or French. Often the original source has long been out of print and only rarely has it been translated into English. Even so, as Serrano Poncela points out, this is not the principal problem:

> Among fourteen direct biographies and several historical testimonies dealing with the reign of Carlos IV, we can only find two that are decidedly favorable, and though it seems that the moment has come to examine his [Godoy's] character objectively, the scholar has not appeared who is willing to carry out the task. Yet the fact is that Godoy finds himself on the

threshold of an intractable Spanish problem which is as real today as it was a hundred and fifty years ago, so that his disputes, seemingly anachronistic, are still very much alive.[3]

The only extensive biography of Godoy originally written in English remains that of Edmund Basil D'Auvergne, an early-twentieth-century work that sought to rehabilitate the oft-maligned minister. This revisionist attempt followed a series of self-serving memoirs penned by Godoy's numerous enemies during the reactionary reign of his chief antagonist, Fernando VII. Subsequent studies were even more vindictive, culminating in the diatribes of the *erotomaníaco* (the term is Francisco Martí's) Marquis de Villa-Urrutia. In the biography of the German writer Hans Roger Madol, conjecture—none of it flattering to Godoy or Queen María Luisa—is readily pressed into service to fill in any lacunae.

More recent historians have endeavored to strike an objective balance. Among these are Jacques Chastenet, in France, and the Mexican scholar Carlos Pereyra, as well as Juan Pérez de Guzmán, Manuel Izquierdo Hernández, Carlos Seco Serrano, Francisco Martí, and others in Spain and elsewhere. Except for Chastenet's biography (in J.F. Huntington's lively translation), none of these authors is accessible in English. Their work is characterized by impartial research and sound scholarship; any writer dealing with Godoy is greatly indebted to them.

No account of Godoy's turbulent career can completely ignore his close relationship with María Luisa. The amatory affair itself was in all probability of brief duration, and by no means unique in the illaudable annals of court dalliances. Nor was Godoy the first royal favorite to assume dominant power; he follows in a long and by no means always dishonorable line.

It was the cynical undermining of his vulnerable position by his opponents—admittedly aided by Godoy's imprudent Sybaritic life-style—that lent credence to the stories of unbridled licentious conduct by the nation's rulers. Alcalá Galiano, a youthful observer of the royal couple and their favorite, wrote that "it was generally agreed that Carlos IV was good, but weak and foolish; the Queen was regarded as a bad woman, and the Prince of the Peace as a monster." This view was all too typical. Propagated by the unscrupulous supporters of Fernando, the heir apparent, rumor soon became reality in the public mind.

Within the larger disaster resides another. The twenty-year reign of Carlos IV and María Luisa (1788–1808), far from being the extended bedroom farce of common belief, at the outset had the potential of accelerating the germinal programs initiated under Carlos III. Godoy himself was an enlightened product of the *siglo de las luces,* a liberal anxious to free Spain of obscurantism. The progressive minds of the day—including Jovellanos, Cabarrús, Meléndez Valdés, Moratín *hijo,* and Goya—supported his policies, if not his morals. Regrettably, many of these highly civilized men failed to distinguish between Godoy the reformist minister and Godoy the unreformed roué. Spurned by his natural allies, he was forced to depend on the discredited royal couple for his entire support. When their fragile authority crumbled in the face of Napoleon's duplicity, the game was up.

The present work makes no claim to being a definitive biography of Godoy, which would imply that the last word has been said on the subject. As Christopher Herold has pointed out, such biographies are tantamount to the coup de grace, a second and final burial for which Godoy is not yet ready (unless, in a literal sense, it is in Spanish soil). Moreover, the same problems that he was unable to resolve persist today. The subterranean forces of *las dos Españas,* held in check by the moral authority of the first Bourbon kings in Spain, finally erupted coincidentally with the French Revolution. In vain, Godoy attempted to reconcile the progressive with the traditional, the liberal with the conservative, offering himself as a synthesis of the two Spains. It was a hopeless endeavor. Caught between the relentless opposing pressure plates, he sought to bestride the fault line and hold the nation together. He failed, just as the subsequent Carlist wars, the Generation of '98, the Civil War, and the Franco regime also failed to solve the dilemma.

As this work is intended for the non-Hispanicist as well as for the specialist, all quotations have been translated into English. Early nineteenth-century Spanish (especially diplomatic dispatches couched in florid phraseology) presents some ticklish problems; how close ought one to adhere to the convoluted original? *Traduttore, traditore.* Hispanic place-names and first names have been kept in the original; those of other nations appear in their anglicized form, following the usual quite arbitrary practice. As poetry has a flavor and spirit of its own, both the original Spanish and a literal prose translation are given. Any failings in the English renditions are, of course, entirely my own.

In a work of this nature, I should be remiss not to acknowledge the help received from many sources. Manuel Rodríguez cast a critical eye over my translations of the poems and lent much-needed support over a long period. Thanks are due to Carlos Rojas for valuable advice, and to John Dowling for providing helpful information. Dorothy Joiner assisted in garnering material, and Joseph Tyler gave cheerfully of his time. I wish to thank Malcolm MacDonald and Judith Knight of The University of Alabama Press for their encouragement and enthusiasm. I am indebted to Robert Ferris for his useful suggestions as copy editor and for pardoning my stubborn British idiosyncrasies. As always, the assistance given by my wife was invaluable; without her many hours of unstinting toil, my task would have been immeasurably more difficult. My thanks to all, but this in no way implies guilt by association. Any errors or other shortcomings are mine alone, and not to be attributed to the innocent.

D. H.

Chronology

1748   *November 11.*   Future King Carlos IV of Spain born in Pórtici, near Naples.

1751   *December 9.*   Future Queen María Luisa of Spain born in Parma, Italy.

1759   Carlos III becomes king of Spain.

1765   *December 9.*   Wedding of Carlos and María Luisa.

1766   Outbreak of *motín de Esquilache* with street riots in Madrid.

1767   *May 12.*   Birth of Manuel Godoy in Badajoz.

1784   *August 17.*   Godoy joins First Brigade of the *Compañía Española* as bodyguard.

       October 15.   Birth of future Fernando VII.

1785   Manuel Godoy presented to Princess María Luisa.

1788   *December 14.*   Death of Carlos III. His son, Carlos IV, and María Luisa ascend the throne.

1789   *May.*   Godoy promoted to colonel of the Royal Bodyguards.

       July 14.   Storming of the Bastille, outbreak of the French Revolution.

       November 26.   Godoy made a Knight of the Order of Santiago.

1791   *February.*   Godoy elevated to *mariscal de campo*.

1792   *February 28.*   Floridablanca dismissed from office.

       May–July.   Godoy created Duke of Alcudia, admitted as a Grandee of Spain and Councillor of State.

       November 14.   Aranda dismissed, Godoy appointed First Secretary of State at the age of twenty-five.

1793   *January 21.*   Louis XVI guillotined.

       March 7.   War with France.

       May 23.   Godoy promoted to captain-general.

1794   *March 10.*   Birth of Infante Francisco de Paula, reputed to be Godoy's son.

1795   *July 22.*   Treaty of Basle ends war with France.

       September 4.   Godoy created Prince of the Peace.

1796   *January 18–February 15.*   Carlos IV and María Luisa guests of Godoy in Badajoz.

July 27. Treaty of San Ildefonso signed with France.

October 18. Spain at war with England.

1797 *February 14.* Defeat of Spanish fleet off Cape St. Vincent.

September 16. Godoy marries María Teresa de Borbón, the monarchs' niece.

1798 *March 28.* Godoy relieved of post as First Secretary of State.

1799 *November 9.* Napoleon comes to power through coup d'etat of 18–19 Brumaire.

1800 *October 1.* Second Treaty of San Ildefonso signed with France.

October 7. Birth of Carlota, daughter of Godoy and María Teresa.

1801 *March 31.* War of the Oranges against Portugal. Godoy appointed commanding general.

June 6. Treaty of Badajoz ends war. Godoy promoted to generalissimo.

1802 *October 4.* Marriage of Fernando to his cousin María Antonia of Naples.

1803 *October 19.* Treaty conceding subsidies to France.

1804 *December 12.* Spain declares war on England.

1805 *October 21.* Battle of Trafalgar.

1806 *January 21.* Death of Fernando's first wife, María Antonia.

October 6. Godoy's manifesto to the Spanish nation.

1807 *January 13.* Godoy appointed admiral-general and also elevated to rank of *Alteza Serenísima.*

October 27. Treaty of Fontainebleau signed; however, French troops had already entered Spain to attack Portugal on October 17.

Late October–November. Escorial affair. Fernando attempts to remove Godoy but fails.

1808 *January 25.* Escorial defendants acquitted, but sent into provincial exile by Carlos IV.

March 17. *Motín de Aranjuez,* Godoy's house attacked by mob.

March 18. Carlos IV deprives Godoy of his titles in effort to save him.

March 19. Godoy discovered, nearly lynched, and finally imprisoned thanks to Fernando's intervention. Carlos IV abdicates in favor of his son, who is proclaimed Fernando VII.

March 23. French army under Murat's command enters Madrid.

April 10. Fernando sets forth from Madrid to meet Napoleon.

April 21. Godoy released from imprisonment at Villaviciosa, leaves for Bayonne.

April 27. Godoy and Napoleon meet for the first time.

May 5. Napoleon pressures Fernando to abdicate in favor of his father.

May 6. Carlos IV in turn cedes Spanish crown to Napoleon.

May 9. *Reyes* and Godoy set out for exile in Compiègne.

September 20. They leave for Marseilles, where they remain four years.

1812 *July 16.* The exiles arrive in Rome, residing first in the Borghese Palace, later at the Barberini.

1814 *March 22.* Fernando returns to Spain as king.

October 1. Carlos recognizes his son as Fernando VII.

1818 *February 2.* Godoy informed of Austrian decision to withdraw offer of a diplomatic post.

March 18. Death of Luis, son of Godoy and Pepita Tudó.

1819 *January 2.* Death of Queen María Luisa in Rome.

January 19. Death of King Carlos IV near his birthplace in Naples.

1828 *November 24.* Death of Godoy's wife, María Teresa.

1829 *February 7.* Wedding of Godoy and Pepita Tudó.

1832 Godoy and Pepita leave Rome, settle in Paris.

1833 *September 29.* Death of Fernando VII.

1834 Pepita deserts Godoy, returns to Spain.

1836–37 Godoy's *Memorias* published in a French translation.

1844 *April 30.* Godoy's remaining property in Spain restored to him.

1847 *May 31.* Godoy regains most of his former titles, also given permission to return to Spain. However, he is too old and infirm to travel.

1851 *October 4.* Death of Manuel Godoy, Prince of the Peace, in Paris.

The Troubled Trinity

INTRODUCTION

The story of Manuel Godoy is told against the richest of backgrounds. It is the age of the French Revolution and Napoleon, of Goethe and Beethoven, of Goya and David, classicists vying with romanticists, an era of impassioned, talented men and women. The roll call is endless: Byron, Schiller, and Madame de Staël; Haydn and Schubert; Géricault and Blake; Talleyrand, William Pitt, and Czar Alexander I—to make the most cursory of selections. It is a world of challenging ideas and reevaluations, the beginning of industrialization and new processes, of scientific experimentation and radical political thought. Above all, it is a time of movement, whether of armies, social patterns, or economic innovations.

Viewed in this agitated setting, the isolated figure of Godoy may seem trivial by comparison. It is a deceptive appearance. The Spain of the late eighteenth century was still a major world power whose possessions reached from Italy to the two continents of the New World and as far as the Philippines. Under the Bourbons, the country had benefited from an economic and military resurgence. No longer decadent or in visible decline, Spain at the death of Carlos III (1788), if not yet the promised land, at least was very much a land of promise.

The disturbing events of 1789 in the sister Bourbon monarchy to the north did not cause undue alarm at first—after all, Spain and France were united in a Family Pact, and Floridablanca and Aranda were statesmen of acknowledged ability. This time, however, it was no passing crisis, but an upheaval of transcendent significance. The troubled aftermath of the French Revolution and Napoleon's seizure of power give Godoy's sixteen years at the helm a crucial importance. To dismiss him as merely another in a long line of royal favorites is to ignore a unique historical reality.

Within Spain itself, Godoy had to contend with a situation that differed markedly from that of previous favorites. Following Carlos III's enlightened reign, it was optimistically assumed that the institution of the *privado* had been laid to rest. The country had slowly become accustomed to ministerial rule by men at least outwardly qualified to hold high position. What counted was that aspiring ministers had served a lengthy apprenticeship at home and abroad before assuming office. In the public mind, advanced age came to be equated with wisdom and trustworthiness.

These factors were totally absent in the astonishing rise of Manuel Godoy—or so it appeared to the vast majority of Spaniards. An untried guardsman fresh from the provinces, barely twenty-five years of age, yet recently created Duke of Alcudia, a grandee and councillor of state, a recipient of the Great Cross of Carlos III, and promoted to lieutenant general—his rapid ascent to the position of First Minister aroused widespread hostility from the outset. Godoy's flagrant accumulation of wealth and titles as well as his dominance over the purblind Carlos IV and especially over the sensuous María Luisa allowed only one conclusion: the *privado* and the queen were lovers.

Many of the anecdotes regarding Godoy were fabricated by proficient scandalmongers at court, then maliciously passed on to a wider receptive audience and generously amplified with each retelling. Like some medieval *canción de gesta,* a modicum of fact was transmuted into folklore and ultimately, in grossly exaggerated form, accepted as incontrovertible truth.

On one point there can be little argument. Godoy was an opportunist in the literal sense of the word: he saw his chances and he took them. At the same time, like many a former *valido,* he perceived realities that often eluded his superiors in social station. An upholder of the Enlightenment, he was more closely attuned to the changing tides of his age than were the conservative traditionalists. Like Napoleon, progressing from the periphery of his country to its center, he seized and created openings whenever the occasion presented itself. Both men by their own admission were children of fortune, impelled forward by the inner momentum of the arriviste. Perhaps this similarity of background enabled Godoy to be the first official in Spain to penetrate Napoleon's true intentions in 1808 while other gentlemen of rank continued to believe in the emperor's protestations of friendship.

One essential difference between the two leaders is immediately apparent. Whereas Napoleon enjoyed despotic power—provided he could maintain it by repeated victories and by cowing his domestic opponents into submission—Godoy was precariously dependent on the continued favor of the *reyes* for his authority. He saw himself as but one member of a ministerial government (albeit the *primus inter pares*) acting under the king's directives.

This exculpatory leitmotiv runs its questionable course through the deposed favorite's *Memorias,* an extended paean to the regal magnanimity of Carlos IV and his gracious consort. It could hardly be otherwise. Lacking any constituency of his own—social, political, or military—Godoy was entirely beholden to his sovereigns. No matter that the relationship was often strained to the breaking point, the bond somehow always held. When Carlos and María Luisa went into exile, their *querido* Manuel dutifully accompanied them and remained at their side until their deaths.

The *Memorias* have long been the subject of spirited debate. Menéndez y Pelayo, the eminent nineteenth-century Spanish literary critic, accepting the popular myth that Godoy was semiliterate, rashly concluded that he was therefore incapable of writing his own memoirs. More temperate research has since prevailed, and, though the discreet editorial hand of Esmenard and possibly those of the abbés Siccard and Sicilia may be discerned, there is no question that Godoy is the principal author.[1] His imprint pervades every page of the voluminous text: an impassioned advocacy of his views and a forthright refutation of those of his critics, on the whole a magnanimous outlook (Escoiquiz and Caballero, his chosen villains, are two notable exceptions), and an underlying reproach to his countrymen: "If only you had listened to me, none of this would have happened."

Internal evidence indicates that preparatory work on the *Memorias* dates from about 1812, the beginning of the years in Italian exile. Remarks made by the royal couple as well as use made of confidential material known to have been in their possession point to an early formulation. From the outset, the *reyes* were aware of Manuel's project and of its significance. On one occasion, the king admonished him: "Although the defense will be written in your name, your cause is mine, and my cause is yours; if you say something it is the same as if I were to speak; if you defend yourself, I am the one you are defending."[2] In a real sense, Godoy's memoirs are also those of King Carlos IV and Queen María Luisa.

The favorite unexpectedly profited from his monarchs' entreaty that he not publish his memoirs during Fernando's lifetime. Perhaps they sensed that the sturdy *Extremeño* would outlive their tormented son. "You cannot defend yourself," Carlos said, "without striking out at him and causing him pain, however you go about it."[3] The long wait was not easy for Godoy, who in exile found himself vilified in countless speeches and articles, often with Fernando's knowledge and covert encouragement. Even so, Manuel tells his readers, "Out of love for my monarchs and devotion to their children I shall remain silent regarding many deplorable things."[4] His loyalty and patience gave him the opportunity to peruse the reminiscences of Escoiquiz, Cevallos, and Caballero among others, as well as the accounts of Juan Llorente, Muriel,[5] the condes de Toreno and Rovigo, in addition to the versions of French historians. In the copious footnotes appended to the *Memorias,* Godoy delights in correcting factual inaccuracies and even the occasional solecism, whether in Spanish, French, or Italian. Nor is he at all averse to comparing his years in office with parallels drawn from world history: Frederick the Great, Catherine the Great, Godoy . . . well, why not? Modesty is no impediment to his remembrance of times past.

Godoy's later access to official French documents in the national archives in Paris and the reproduction of key passages in their entirety give the *Memorias* a deceptive impression of objectivity. The technique is a familiar one: lengthy excerpts from unimpeachable sources (often irrelevant to the matter in hand), buttressed by exhaustive lists of scientists and scholars who presumably benefited from his policies and who, by specious inference, were his allies. The very prolixity of the work—four volumes originally published in 1836 in Esmenard's French translation under the author's supervision—helps conceal many omissions and the occasional fabrication.

Perhaps it is easier to say what the *Memorias* are not. The modern reader, surfeited with intimate autobiographies more suited to the confessional, may be surprised—disappointed even—by the expanse of unrevealing prose. Mention of Godoy's royal wife is brief (which, given the facts of his political marriage, is understandable enough), but one might conclude that his larger family—Pepita Tudó, their children, his parents, uncles and brothers—barely existed. Of his childhood there is scarcely a mention: no cherished memories, no boyish scrapes, just a few names of teachers and subjects studied. The biographer searches in vain for germinal clues that might illuminate some future action. Predictably, there is not the slightest hint of scandal; we are still in the circumspect nineteenth century in matters of personal conduct. Any revelation of impropriety, whatever the beneficial effect upon the sale of the work, would have vitiated the very purpose of its publication. For Godoy, the good reputation of his late sovereigns outweighed any financial gain. Proud Spaniard that he was, he preferred honorable poverty to infamy.

The biographer is faced with a formidable challenge. To the end, Godoy's real character remains tantalizingly elusive. He arrives too soon, and is quickly on his guard; no shared confidences, even within his family; no close friends; no extended travels. Godoy is not a literary figure whose works provide limitless analytical material and psychological insights. He is rather the reverse: the more he says, the less he tells, bearing out Talleyrand's *bon mot* that "speech was given to man to disguise his thoughts." Like the impassive exterior of his walled home, the true character of a Spaniard can often prove mysterious to an outsider. The Prince of the Peace, despite the outer finery of his uniforms and titles, consistently withheld his private personality from the public gaze. To penetrate this defensive wall, to reach into the inner emotional man, is no easy task.

Not surprisingly, Godoy's true self—Manuel as distinct from the Prince of the Peace—is revealed far more spontaneously in his personal correspondence, notably with the childishly uninhibited María Luisa. And what a character he shows himself to be! Alternately arrogant and humble, intimate then guarded, bluntly matter-of-fact one moment yet solicitous the next, grammar and spelling thrown to the winds (so much for the elaborate facade of the *Memorias*), the letters offer us a fascinating insight into an engaging personality.

At the same time, it becomes clear that his relationship with the *reyes* was vastly more complex than his detractors' oversimplifications would have one believe. For the truth is that Godoy—*privado*, lover, statesman, and soldier—was a man of uncommon attributes in an uncommon age. A firm believer in *las luces*, he deserves to be brought out of the shadows and into the light.

1

CARLOS AND

MARÍA LUISA

On the night of November 17, 1792, the French ambassador in Madrid was highly agitated. Jean-François Bourgoing had, of course, followed the alarming news from Paris with apprehension; first the attack on the Tuileries, where King Louis XVI and his family were housed, then the massacre of the Swiss Guard, and finally the mindless slaughter in the streets.

Strangely enough, such oppressive thoughts were not uppermost in Bourgoing's mind that cold November evening. He was about to forward a dispatch to his superior in Paris, not the usual dry report, but a communiqué replete with scandalous innuendo, this time bolstered by irrefutable fact. Bourgoing put pen to paper:

> During the night it was decided that the position of Secretary of State be given to the Duke of Alcudia. You know, Citizen Minister, who and what the Duke of Alcudia is. Four years ago he was a simple soldier in the bodyguards, Manuel Godoy by name, but his advancement has been so rapid thanks to the favor of the king and especially that of the queen that in less than two years he was named Commander of the Bodyguard, Lieutenant-General, and moreover has been decorated with the Great Cross of the Order of Carlos III; he is a Grandee of Spain, member of the Council of State, and the possessor of immense wealth. In such critical circumstances it is hardly conceivable that a young man without experience, without knowledge of foreign countries, could be appointed to the most important ministry; a man, moreover, whose attentiveness towards the

queen leaves him so little free time. Such a choice surprises as much as it offends everyone.[1]

The diplomatic corps was collectively shocked at the news of Godoy's appointment to the highest office. The Russian ambassador, Zinoviev, haughtily dismissed him as being "without talent or background, in whom no elevated sentiments are to be found, only greed and ambition."[2] Zinoviev's Prussian colleague, Sandoz Rollin, of a more generous disposition, found Godoy to be "frank, affable, and accommodating, knowing that the favor he enjoyed was without a solid base."[3] By December, Bourgoing had partially reversed himself, discerning that "this young minister has some judgment and good intentions, but his extreme inexperience and lack of aptitude for public affairs cannot be gainsaid . . . He tries to make as few personal enemies as possible. He gives several proofs of humanity and of kindness, and he corrects many injustices. In general the favorite inspires more jealousy than hatred."[4] Such contradictory assessments of Godoy's character and abilities were to characterize his entire career.

Neither King Carlos IV nor Queen María Luisa entertained the slightest doubt as to the unique genius of their *querido Manuel*. In an early letter, the queen confided to him that "you are the only friend we have or will have, you are the redeemer of this monarchy . . . believe me, we are and always will be your only friends, we beg you always to be ours, don't go away, don't leave us."[5] Yet, outwardly there was nothing extraordinary in the appearance of the twenty-five-year-old Manuel Godoy to justify such an effusive encomium:

> The truth is that he was no more than five feet four inches tall, little above the average, and that his features were not that regular, his mouth being too large, although his teeth (which he kept all his life) were very fine. His nose was too long and wide, his eyes were brown and disproportionate to the arch of his thick reddish eyebrows, his forehead rather narrow and flattened . . . His most handsome feature consisted of a golden and thick head of hair, and in the radiance of the blushing whiteness of his skin.[6]

The key to Godoy's character obviously does not reside in externals. To understand the deep emotions he inspired one must look elsewhere.

The long history of Spain is strewn with *favoritos, privados, validos,* all names for royal favorites responsible to no one but the king. Like Godoy, most were drawn from the ranks of the *hidalguía,* the minor nobility, and were used by the Crown as a counterpoise to the powerful landed grandees. Thus, the long reign of Juan II of Castille (1406–54), a weak monarch often at the mercy of factious nobles, was only rendered possible by the firm hand of Álvaro de Luna. It is entirely possible that one of Godoy's ancestors fought under Luna. In the previous century, a Godoy had risen to become the Grand Master of the Calatrava order and a staunch supporter of the monarchy. The fate of Luna is significant; finally, he overplayed his hand, was arrested, and died on the scaffold.

A more colorful *privado* was the dashing Andalucian, Beltrán de la Cueva, the favorite of the impotent Enrique IV and his second wife, Queen Juana. *Mirabile dictu,* the queen was soon with child. For an age steeped in miracles, the nobles were ungallant enough to discern the work of Beltrán de la Cueva rather than the hand of God. Similarly, three and a half centuries later Godoy was to be reviled as the alleged father of two of the infantes.

Of Godoy's predecessors, Francisco de Sandoval y Rojas, later raised to the rank of Duke of Lerma, was surely among the most avaricious. As the *privado* of Felipe III, he ruled Spain as de facto First Minister from 1599 to 1618. During the seventeenth century, the position of *privado* acquired recognized status and, for all its shortcomings, may be regarded as a forerunner of later First Ministers.

Beyond a doubt, the Conde-Duque de Olivares, the *privado* of Felipe IV and chief minister from 1621 to 1643, must be accorded the palm among favorites. The bearer of a unique double title, his is the most resplendent honor bestowed by a Spanish monarch until that of the Prince of the Peace was conferred upon Godoy. This talented statesman prefigures Godoy in many respects: capable and intelligent, unswervingly loyal and anxious to enact reforms, yet impelled to flaunt his wealth amid crushing poverty, and ultimately ending in disgrace and failure.

There was even a minor dynasty of favorites when Luis de Haro, the nephew of Olivares, succeeded his uncle in 1643. Like Godoy, he disliked the appellation of *privado,* preferring to be judged on his own merits. Of an unheroic nature—he led his army in headlong flight at the Battle of Elvas against the Portuguese—Haro nevertheless retained the position until his death in 1661. In sharp contrast, Godoy emerged victorious in the War of the Oranges against the same enemy, only to be driven from office a few years later.

Upon the arrival of the French Bourbons in Spain, a change in the status of the *privado* gradually becomes apparent. The foreign favorites—

the French Princesse des Ursins, the Italian cleric Giulio Alberoni, and the unscrupulous Dutch adventurer Jan Willem Ripperdá—whatever their failings and eventual fate, on the whole served their adopted country well. Increasingly, the favorites gave way to men of the caliber of Carvajal and Ensenada, who were rightly regarded as ministers and not as *validos*. When Carlos III ascended the Spanish throne in 1759, the age of the court favorite appeared to be at an end.

Carlos's reign began inauspiciously. A stranger in his own country after two decades of rule in Naples, the new king distressed his proud subjects by appointing a covey of Italians to leading positions. Among the latter was the luckless Marqués de Esquilache (originally Squilache). Enlightened minister though he was, he had acquired scant understanding of the Spanish character or traditions. His reforms, ranging from the introduction of street lighting to the imposition of the French-style short cape and tricorn hat, met with popular opposition, instigated by a dissatisfied segment of the nobility. In the following reign, Godoy was to find himself embroiled in a similar situation.

The *motín de Esquilache* of 1766—the bloody street rioting forever associated with the minister's name—may be regarded as a precursor of the Aranjuez uprising that dethroned Carlos IV forty-two years later and sent the royal family and Godoy into exile. Soon the Madrid rabble was out of control, pillaging Esquilache's house just as their descendants in turn were to ransack Godoy's mansions after his fall. Carlos III fled to the royal palace at Aranjuez, thirty miles to the south of the mutinous capital, and by coincidence also the scene of his son's discomfiture in 1808. The nomination of Count Aranda, a native-born grandee and an outstanding soldier and statesman, finally pacified the unruly *populacho*. Nine months later and considerably wiser, Carlos III returned to Madrid.

Except for the first few months, Carlos III was a widower during his entire reign (1759–88). His wife, Queen María Amalia, was only thirty-six at the time of her death—"the first trouble she has given me in twenty-two years" was her husband's laconic epitaph—and by all accounts he never touched a woman again, setting an austere standard of moral conduct against which some in his family (notably his son's wife María Luisa) were found sadly wanting. By general consent, Carlos III is considered the best king to have ruled over Spain, a fact that only discredits his son further by comparison.

If the reign of Carlos III is remembered as the apogee of enlightened despotism in Spain, it is attributable in large measure to the talents of

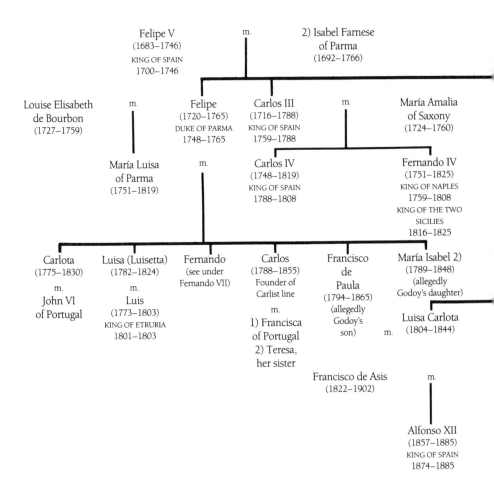

Felipe V
(1683–1746)
KING OF SPAIN
1700–1746

m.

2) Isabel Farnese
of Parma
(1692–1766)

Louise Elisabeth
de Bourbon
(1727–1759)

m.

Felipe
(1720–1765)
DUKE OF PARMA
1748–1765

Carlos III
(1716–1788)
KING OF SPAIN
1759–1788

m.

María Amalia
of Saxony
(1724–1760)

María Luisa
of Parma
(1751–1819)

m.

Carlos IV
(1748–1819)
KING OF SPAIN
1788–1808

Fernando IV
(1751–1825)
KING OF NAPLES
1759–1808
KING OF THE TWO
SICILIES
1816–1825

Carlota
(1775–1830)

m.

John VI
of Portugal

Luisa (Luisetta)
(1782–1824)

m.

Luis
(1773–1803)
KING OF ETRURIA
1801–1803

Fernando
(see under
Fernando VII)

Carlos
(1788–1855)
Founder of
Carlist line

m.

1) Francisca
of Portugal
2) Teresa,
her sister

Francisco
de
Paula
(1794–1865)
(allegedly
Godoy's
son)

m.

María Isabel 2)
(1789–1848)
(allegedly
Godoy's daughter)

Luisa Carlota
(1804–1844)

Francisco de Asis
(1822–1902)

m.

Alfonso XII
(1857–1885)
KING OF SPAIN
1874–1885

Genealogical Table

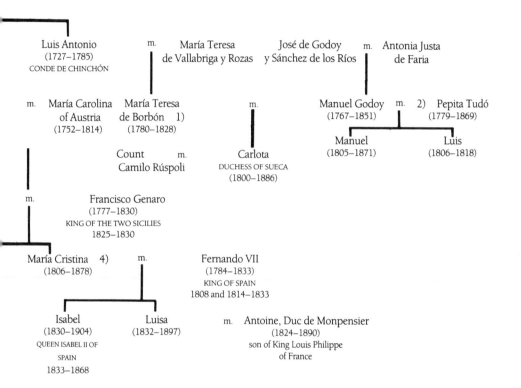

Luis Antonio
(1727–1785)
CONDE DE CHINCHÓN

m.   María Teresa
       de Vallabriga y Rozas

José de Godoy   m.   Antonia Justa
y Sánchez de los Ríos   de Faria

m.   María Carolina
     of Austria
     (1752–1814)

María Teresa
de Borbón   1)
(1780–1828)

m.

Manuel Godoy   m.   2)   Pepita Tudó
(1767–1851)   (1779–1869)

Count   m.
Camilo Rúspoli

Carlota
DUCHESS OF SUECA
(1800–1886)

Manuel
(1805–1871)

Luis
(1806–1818)

m.   Francisco Genaro
       (1777–1830)
       KING OF THE TWO SICILIES
       1825–1830

María Cristina   4)   m.
(1806–1878)

Fernando VII
(1784–1833)
KING OF SPAIN
1808 and 1814–1833

Isabel
(1830–1904)
QUEEN ISABEL II OF
SPAIN
1833–1868

Luisa
(1832–1897)

m.   Antoine, Duc de Monpensier
     (1824–1890)
     son of King Louis Philippe
     of France

ministers such as Aranda, Campomanes, and Floridablanca. The king him-self, divested of his regalia as in the famous hunting portrait by Goya, was a mortal of middling intelligence and devoid of any real creative imagina-tion. No matter: to his subjects these shortcomings were more than offset by his piety and unblemished life. He had chosen his ministers wisely, and on his deathbed exhorted his successor to continue them in office. Dutifully, his son agreed—at least for the immediate future. Beyond that, he had ideas of his own that were to shape the destiny of Spain.

Spain, in the final two decades of the eighteenth century, despite the progressive ideas of the Enlightenment, remained an absolute monarchy. At the highest level, all officials, whether legislative, judicial, or ecclesiastic, owed their authority directly to the Crown. In the case of advisers and ministers, they served solely at the king's pleasure and were beholden to no other constituency. Each major region had a central administration presided over by a *capitán general,* while at the municipal level the *corre-gidores* (royal representatives) were the main officeholders. The *Cortes,* the ancient legislative assembly, over the years had been reduced to a mere cipher and were rarely convened; in actual practice, the majority of the population had little if any say in government.

During the course of the century, the *Consejos,* the State Councils, such as those of Castilla, the Indias, the Inquisition, and the *Hacienda* (Exche-quer), had acquired considerable importance. The Council of Castille, the supreme tribunal of the kingdom, exercised direct control over the judi-ciary, always, of course, as an extension of the king's authority. Justice tended to be slow as it worked its way cumbrously through the system. Despite these and other shortcomings, there was virtually no opposition to the concept of absolute monarchy; republican sentiment was all but un-known, and the vast majority of Spaniards were unwaveringly loyal to Crown, Church, and Country.

On September 21, 1789, King Carlos IV and Queen María Luisa entered Madrid in triumph. The *motín de Esquilache* had faded to the most distant of memories as the capital was given over to eight days of festivities. The ominous rumblings in Paris were a world away as Masses were celebrated and the Cortes de Castilla convened to confirm the succession of the four-year-old Fernando as Prince of Asturias. "What a singular contrast with the French National Assembly which was in session at the same time!" Sandoz-Rollin exclaimed in wonder. "Here, all the members of the Cortes kneel with heads uncovered when the King enters."[7]

It had been an agonizingly long wait for the new monarchs. For twenty-three years, Carlos and his fretful wife had sullenly endured the imposed tedium of court life. Living in the shadow of a venerated widower, they had been expected to conform to rigorous etiquette and to the strictest of moral standards. Nor is it accurate to say that they had served a useful apprenticeship—far from it in actual fact. The ascetic Carlos III had long ago formed a poor opinion of his son's abilities. Not only did he exclude him from council discussions, however trivial, but also from the perusal of all but the least important state documents.[8] The heir apparent was rarely entrusted with any responsibilities; in later years, he in turn saw no reason to treat his son Fernando any differently.

Carlos had been born in Pórtici, just to the south of Naples, on November 11, 1748. His formative years were spent at the Court of the Two Sicilies; seventy-one years later, reduced to pitiable exile, he returned to the scene of his birth to breathe his last. But this is to anticipate the narrative. In 1759 young Carlos accompanied his father, now King Carlos III of Spain, to Madrid. The eleven-year-old boy was proclaimed Prince of Asturias, the traditional title given the heir to the throne. Strictly speaking, under the rules of primogeniture, he should not have assumed the title for he was the second son. However, his elder brother, Felipe Pascual, was so feeble-minded that Carlos III freely acknowledged "the notorious imbecility of my royal first born" and took measures to have him removed from the succession.

The Prince of Asturias grew up to be a ruddy-faced, well-built (if a little overweight), sluggish young man who possessed many of the Bourbon facial features—especially the bulbous nose and protruding jaw—but also with many of the kinder characteristics of the family. Totally without affectation, he was considerate of others and generally well intentioned. He was certainly never the credulous fool or the pliant dupe of Godoy as depicted by his detractors. The key to his nature lay more in his mental laziness rather than in any supposed congenital debility. Lethargic he undoubtedly was, but this is a far cry from the dullard of popular legend.

María Luisa is an altogether more engaging personality. A *leyenda negra,* doubtful by definition, has irreparably been attached to her name, which itself is inaccurate. Luisa María Teresa always signed herself Luisa, and was never called anything else by her family. If further proof be needed, one of Spain's proudest ships was later christened the *Reina Luisa María Teresa.*[9] Strict accuracy after two centuries of mistaken nomenclature borders on academic pedantry and so will be dispensed with.

Like that of her future husband, María Luisa's childhood was spent in

Italy. She was born in Parma on December 9, 1751, the daughter of Felipe, the younger brother of Carlos III, and of Luisa Isabel de Bourbon, the eldest daughter of Louis XV of France. With her brother Fernando she shared the celebrated French philosopher Condillac as private tutor. The vivacious princess, quick witted and cheerful by nature, gained only moderately from the learned abbé's teachings; a command of spelling and grammar eluded her to the end.

At the age of thirteen, María Luisa was affianced to her Spanish first cousin Carlos, three years her senior, and immediately insisted on the consideration due to the future Princess of Asturias. One day, in a fit of childish pique, she taunted her brother: "I'll teach you to respect me, because one day I'll be Queen of Spain and you'll have to be content with the dukedom of Parma," whereupon Fernando replied: "In that case I'll have the honor of slapping the Queen of Spain," and forthwith boxed the royal ears.

On June 29, 1765, María Luisa left her native Parma and sailed from Genoa to Cartagena to become the First Lady of Spain in the absence of a reigning queen. After some minor indisposition of the princess, the wedding was finally celebrated on December 9, her fourteenth birthday. From the beginning, she found herself under constant surveillance, even in the most intimate moments; it was the duty of the *camaristas* to watch over their royal charges both day and night.[10] Just as vexatious was the suffocating court protocol insisted on by her austere father-in-law, who seemed as cold and forbidding as the granite of the Escorial royal residence in the Castillian countryside. Four months after the wedding, the Esquilache riots broke out—hardly an auspicious omen.

During the first five years of marriage, the bride suffered at least three miscarriages, and it was only in September 1771 that a lengthy succession of accouchements began that extended until the birth of Francisco de Paula Antonio in 1794. None other than Pepita Tudó, Godoy's longtime mistress and second wife, estimated that María Luisa was with child some twenty-four times, including several miscarriages, stillbirths, and the seven children who survived beyond infancy.[11]

But the repellent image of the future queen, the grotesque-featured matron who stares vacantly from Goya's canvases, still lies in the future. Chastenet, quite openly hostile toward María Luisa, asserts that "she has not yet become the lascivious pander, with the fleshy face, the provocative air and the flesh at once sullied and on offer, of Goya's later portrait—not that she took offense at it; but here already is a passionate, unsatisfied woman, bursting with ill-restrained desires."[12] This, surely, is to overstate the case. In fact, the early portraits by Mengs and Paret reveal an attractive young woman of considerable charm.

The positive impression of the two artists is further corroborated by eyewitness reports. As late as 1782, Bourgoing could still attest that "the Princess of Asturias, whose courtesy, wit, and graces have an irresistible charm, spends her whole time in her suite of rooms, her only pleasures being conversation and music."[13] The most remarkable testimonial is that of Escoiquiz, now remembered chiefly as Fernando's scheming tutor and Godoy's bitter enemy:

> She was of an ardent and voluptuous nature with a figure, if no longer beautiful, yet still attractive. She possessed an extraordinary liveliness and grace in her movements, a disposition that seemed kind and affectionate, and an unusual ability to win hearts. This had been perfected by a fine upbringing and the cultivation of social graces . . . Although only fourteen at the time of her marriage, it was precisely this background which allowed her to wield a decisive influence over a young husband of Carlos' character, completely innocent and totally ignorant when it came to love, brought up like a novice and only seventeen, simple and upright, kind to the point of being weak.[14]

The canon's later judgments were to be far less charitable.

At first there was no breath of scandal, and, if the abstemious Carlos III at times disapproved of his daughter-in-law's levity, her fecundity met with his royal approbation. His joy was only marred by the untimely deaths of the infant princes; it seemed that the princesses alone were destined to survive the crucial early years. Not until October 1784 was a son born who enjoyed better prospects of attaining adulthood. The boy was christened Fernando, and in due time he became the worst king the Spanish nation has ever been called upon to endure.

Russian ambassador Zinoviev was shocked to see María Luisa at the age of thirty-eight with the unhealthy complexion and false teeth of an old woman. Madame Junot, who met the queen in 1805, when María Luisa was fifty-one, more charitably observed: "She seemed to me to be still a fine woman, though she was then growing stout and was getting a double chin, like Catherine II, which imparted a matronly appearance to her countenance. She, nevertheless, wore a *coiffure à la grecque* with pearls and diamonds, plaited along with her hair, or rather her wig."[15] Many eyewitnesses commented on her ill-fitting dentures. Yet, to the end of her life she retained her faultlessly proportioned arms, of which she was inordinately proud. Nor did her good-natured vivacity desert her, as is attested to by those who knew her well and not merely by repute.

Unfortunately, as her beauty waned, so did her public reputation. Many observers claimed to discern an increase in her sexual appetite inversely proportional to the diminution of her physical attractions. Escoiquiz, as if to make up for his earlier lapse into kindness, now damned the princess thoroughly as some latter-day Messalina:

> She combined a mind that was naturally vicious and incapable of affection, selfishness carried to an extreme, a cunning astuteness, an incredible gift for hypocrisy and pretense, and a talent completely ruled by her passions which continuously sought means to satisfy them. She considered any really useful or serious work as an insufferable torture. The ignorance which resulted from this lack of application barred any path towards improvement, and ended in the misfortune of her husband and their subjects. She was thus obliged to entrust the reins of government to a totally inexperienced favorite. As long as he [Godoy] knew how to take advantage of his complete ascendancy over her, in the absence of true love this ensured the dominion of vice over her corrupted soul.[16]

For his part, the abbé Muriel was determined not to be outdone by his fellow divine in his condemnation of María Luisa. She might have become a fitting ruler "if, like other queens, she had been upright, well brought up, and had good sense; but unfortunately she was ruled by the passions and weaknesses of her sex, and possessed none of its virtues." Nor is that all: "She had scandalous love affairs, obscene flirtations, already during the lifetime of Carlos III. The solicitous vigilance of this monarch proved ineffective." What could the saintly king do, faced with the "whims of her female vanity?"[17]

The ultimate authority on María Luisa's supposed lustful appetites is the Marqués de Villa-Urrutia. To him, she was "a woman of excessive temperament, whose appetites were not satiated by her lovers, and whose ardor was not slaked by the passage of the years." The marquis accounts for this by noting that she was born "with special aptitudes and robust appetites, which marriage aroused but could not satisfy because her inherited blood, fervid and excited, which coursed through her veins demanded more than the conjugal duty of a gentle husband."[18] Such arrant nonsense is only too typical. María Luisa was not a saint—she was far too irrepressible for that—but neither was she the perennial sinner nor her husband the doltish *marido cornudo* so often portrayed.

Carlos is no villain; villains require energy. Rather, he sought refuge in a simple piety and undemanding pursuits. Above all, he hated to make decisions, which accounts largely for the unchanging routine of his daily life. He was happiest when nothing untoward happened: no surprises, no displays of emotion, no upsets. The prince was openly despised by his father; their sole common interest was a love of the hunt, a euphemism for the daily battues that were little more than the organized slaughter of thousands of deer and wild boar.

For all that, the heir to the throne was basically well intentioned. Apart from a crude bonhomie that manifested itself in some one-sided backslapping of servants and stable hands, Carlos was considerate of others and content with his simple life. During inclement weather, he busied himself with repairing watches and working as a carpenter and plumber. A gargantuan meal in the evening, a game of cards during which he invariably fell asleep, and off to bed. Sometimes he would play the violin in a string quartet, with the other musicians discreetly attempting to anticipate the capricious royal tempi. On one occasion, a fellow participant ventured to tell Carlos that he must take three bars rest, whereupon he was informed in Italian, *"I re n'aspettano mai!"* ("Kings never wait").[19] How dare Boccherini and Haydn dictate to a prince?

Carlos seems to have been totally blind to the possibility that his wife might find amatory distractions elsewhere. Rumors that the skittish princess no longer contented herself with admiring glances had reached the ears of the old king, but apparently not those of her trusting husband. When Carlos smugly remarked to his father that it was his princely good fortune that royal spouses were removed by their exalted station from carnal temptations, the king sighed wearily before uttering the memorable rebuke, *"Carlos, Carlos, ¡qué tonto tú eres! Todas, si todas, son putas."* ("Charles, Charles, how stupid you are! All of them, yes, all of them are whores.")[20]

The implications of María Luisa's uncorroborated *liaisons amoureuses* have engaged the attention of every Hispanicist dealing with the period. Opinions range from complete exoneration on the one hand (notably Pérez de Guzmán and Izquierdo Hernández) to the vilifications of Villa-Urrutia, on a par with the defamatory catalog published in Riga in 1797 that purported to be an authentic list of her lovers. Even D'Auvergne, generally of an impartial disposition, states flatly: "She was the kind of woman to whom a succession of lovers—preferably two or three at a time—is an absolute necessity."[21] María Luisa has been the victim of a bad press, to use Pereyra's phrase, both during her lifetime and to the present day.

It would be equally foolish to deny even the mere possibility of an extramarital affair. Many detached scholars, such as Richard Herr, have postulated that María Luisa, in accepting the attentions of a *cortejo,* was no more than following a practice widespread among the aristocracy.[22] Gabriel Lovett—certainly no sensationalist—concludes, "that Luisa and Godoy were lovers must be accepted in the light of circumstantial evidence."[23] Given the paucity of facts, no definite conclusion is possible.

How much Carlos knew—or even cared—will likewise never be known. The Duque del Infantado once heard the prince expatiate on women and the dangers of their fickleness in a southern clime. Carlos found comfort in the fact that "we crowned heads, however, have this chief advantage above other people, that our honor, as they call it, is safe; for suppose that queens were as much bent on mischief as some of their sex, where could they find kings and emperors to flirt with? Eh?"[24] If Carlos's muddled perception is amusing, that of some of his critics is less so. At least two of them[25] have baselessly implied or openly stated that his attitude can only be explained in one way: he was a homosexual. This is gross speculation without a scintilla of supportive evidence.

Had Carlos confined himself to his innocuous pastimes, he could have claimed total innocence when at last he became king. This is not quite the case. Unfortunately, when finally aroused from his complaisant frame of mind, he revealed a devious temperament hitherto unsuspected. In 1781 the Prince of Asturias initiated a subversive intrigue against his father that prefigures the troubles he was to have with his own son Fernando a quarter of a century later.

In his lethargic way, Carlos resented the arrogance with which Count Floridablanca, a commoner elevated to the nobility, exercised his authority as First Minister. The latter's chief political rival and personal adversary, the prominent Freemason and pro-French libertarian Count Aranda, had appropriately been transferred to Paris in 1773 as the Spanish ambassador. The antagonism between the two men was of long standing.[26] Carlos now saw the opportunity to undermine the haughty First Minister (and indirectly his own father), while at the same time gaining the friendship of Aranda. The correspondence that ensued bordered on sedition, a harbinger of Fernando's later disastrous approach to Napoleon. On March 19, 1781, Carlos wrote to Aranda:

> I wish to ask you for some advice which must remain a secret between the two of us. You know how corrupt this machinery of the monarchy is, and how little one can count on the present ministers. I should like you to

draw up a plan for what ought to be done in the event—which God forbid—that my father be no more. Give me a list of men who strike you as being best suited as ministers and for other positions . . . You may rest assured that no one will ever know about it, and that I shall remain eternally grateful to you and always be your true friend.

Carlos.[27]

A month later, Aranda replied with the recommendation that a *ministro confidente* be appointed; doubtless he had himself in mind. Quite unwittingly, his advocacy of a confidential minister helped prepare the way for Godoy's astounding career.

Subsequent letters, if anything, were even more compromising than the first. On July 15 Carlos warns Aranda that "if our correspondence were to come to light, it would mean the end of everything . . . I dissemble in everything as much as possible, because there is no other way."[28] Vague reference is made to underhand business directed against them, even of a conspiracy, but no names are given. Soon Aranda's letters descend to petty ad hominem attacks on Floridablanca; in the light of these unseemly squabbles, it is small wonder that Godoy was later preferred to either of these geriatric grandees.

All the carefully hatched schemes of Carlos and Aranda eventually came to naught. Quite possibly, Floridablanca through his spies had become aware of the incriminatory letters and had warned Carlos regarding his impolitic behavior. The First Minister now entered into a lengthy correspondence, not with the heir apparent, as might be supposed, but with María Luisa. The princess was in trouble, serious enough to necessitate the help of the man she and her uxorious husband had hitherto most disliked.

As far as can be ascertained, the correspondence began in January 1782 and continued for about a year. Certain letters are missing, and several events alluded to remain a mystery. From the outset, Floridablanca sought to reassure the distraught princess:

> Have no fear that the public will become displeased with either yourself or the Prince if you follow the path of treating them with propriety and not allowing yourselves to be dominated by evil people . . . The only ones who speak disparagingly are a few mischief-makers, servants, courtiers, or soldiers, but even these keep it to themselves, fearing the populace, which is all for the King and his children, the Prince and Princess of Asturias . . . If only all would do the same, but there is much gossiping and imprudent and false talk. May God discover the cause of these troubles . . . [29]

The First Minister invariably counsels *la paciencia, el disimulo, y la conducta* as the most efficacious defense. Meanwhile, he will try to unravel some business regarding a mysterious guardsman, a topic no doubt first broached during private conversation. This shadowy figure assuredly was not Godoy—the date is far too early—or his elder brother Luis, who supposedly preceded him in the royal *alcoba*.

In August a crisis arose. Somehow, the king and Fray Joaquín de Eleta, his personal confessor, were hot on the trail. To forestall any embarrassing disclosure, Floridablanca not only suggested that María Luisa write to Father Eleta, but even included a rough draft that not surprisingly contained some acerbic thrusts at Aranda.

The letter is extremely long and can only be quoted in part, enough, however, to convey the flavor of the whole:

> Father: I find myself in a very bad situation, full of worries and exposed to further ones, without knowing how to extricate myself because there is a group of people aiming at vexing me and sowing discord between me, the King, and the Prince . . . For a while it seemed they were going to leave us in peace, everyone, I mean Papa and us and the royal brothers, we were relaxing, when the malcontents began to write anonymous letters with such filthy language and threats that I dare not repeat them . . . Now they have spread the rumor around Madrid, as they already have around the palace, that a guardsman, whom the Prince and I heard sing, had left for this very reason . . . They have the effrontery to threaten me and speculate whether the guardsman will return or not. In that case, everyone will know and talk about his departure, just as they do now with other things and with gossip that is ruining my reputation, the Prince's, and even that of my children, which would expose me to arguments with my husband, were he not so honorable and God-fearing.[30]

María Luisa's letter is a cavern of conjecture—poorly lit, of uncertain dimensions, and full of mocking echoes. The details are tantalizingly imprecise. Clearly, long before Godoy's appearance, a powerful party at court had sunk its claws into her reputation and was loath to release its prey.

It required a further highly emotional letter to elicit a reply from Father Eleta. He assured her that she was highly esteemed by all and that the king in private conversation had never alluded to any of the points raised in either of the two letters. In defense of the princess, one must admit that the puritanical surveillance at court would have proved a dismaying obstacle to any casual *amorío*. María Luisa's outbursts are more comprehensible as the anguish of a woman falsely accused than of one fabricating a cover-up. The exact truth will probably never be known.

Increasingly, the Prince of Asturias and his wife concluded that the Old Guard—specifically Aranda and Floridablanca—were more concerned with factional bickering than in devoting themselves to the interests of the heirs apparent. Their displeasure contained a large measure of frustration, unworthily directed against two men who, despite their childish vendetta and other human failings, had repeatedly shown themselves to be patriots and loyal servants of the Crown. The idea of a *ministro confidente* beholden to no one but themselves began to germinate in the minds of the royal couple, now approaching middle age and bored with the tedium of court life, punctuated only by the equally depressing succession of pregnancies and births. Often joy and Te Deums were shortly followed by the intoning of *requiescat in pace* as yet another royal infant was laid to rest. Children died aged three, six, and again three years. The cruelest blow was the death within a month of one another of twin boys barely a year old. Only with the birth of Fernando on October 15, 1784, did a male child show any prospect of attaining manhood.

King Carlos III was also visibly grieved by a melancholy sequence of deaths among the older members of the family. The cheerless procession began with the loss of his brother, the Infante Don Luis, whose daughter María Teresa was destined to marry Manuel Godoy. Some relief was afforded by the birth of a brother to Fernando, Carlos María Isidro, at Aranjuez in March 1788; had one known that here lay the future cause of the Carlist civil wars, the rejoicing would have been considerably muted. Toward the end of the same year, Death the Leveller again laid his icy hand on the royal family. A smallpox epidemic snatched away Mariana Josefa, the Portuguese wife of the king's fourth and favorite son, Gabriel, followed a week later by the death of their infant child, and a mere four days afterward by that of the recent widower. Don Gabriel was a talented scholar and musician, and quite possibly Carlos III had considered altering the succession in his favor.[31]

The elderly king was brokenhearted, but, methodical monarch to the last, he prepared his will and besought his eldest son to uphold the Catholic faith and to retain Floridablanca in office. Having received assurances on both counts, the moribund made his last confession and kissed the holy relics of San Isidore and San Diego de Alcalá before rendering his soul up to God. The ancient cry went up, *El rey ha muerto, ¡viva el rey!* A reign had ended, and an uncertain new age was about to begin.

2

THE DAZZLING

ASCENT

There is also another Spain, far removed from the glitter of the capital. This is the rural Spain of the *Quijote,* a vast expanse of high plateau flecked with dusty whitewashed villages and ancient towns, provincial by geography and outlook, *castizo* to the core in its cultural isolation, yet to many the repository of *la España eterna.*

One of these peripheral regions is Extremadura, which borders a province in Portugal bearing the same name. In 25 B.C. the Romans established a strategic garrison town of 90,000 men at Augusta Emerita, today's Mérida, and made it the capital of Lusitania. Despite Extremadura's past glories, the province historically has been an exporter of native sons. The name derives from the Latin *terra extrema et dura,* equally applicable to the harsh climate and to its sturdy inhabitants. Among the latter may be counted Hernán Cortés, Francisco Pizarro, and Vasco Núñez de Balboa. Seared by the summer sun and whipped by freezing winds in winter, small wonder that this barren land should have produced far more than its share of the *conquistadores.*

It also produced Manuel Godoy. He was born in the frontier city of Badajoz on May 12, 1767, that is to say, two years before Napoleon. The family on both sides was of old Christian stock, the Godoy branch tracing its ancestry back at least to a Don Pedro Muñiz de Godoy, Grand Master of Calatrava and Santiago, Captain General of the Portuguese Frontier, who died heroically on the field of battle at Valverde in 1387.[1] In later life, Manuel boasted that his name was a contraction of *"Godo soy"* ("I am a Goth"), implying that his origins extended back still further to the Visigoth period before the Arab invasion of 711.

The paternal grandparents originated in Castuera, a small country town lying about thirty miles east of Mérida and a like distance north of Fuenteovejuna, the scene of Lope de Vega's play of the same name. For reasons unknown, they settled in Badajoz with its imposing Moorish castle and granite bridge over the Guadiana River. There they built the modest house on the Calle del Teniente Coronel Yagües, where Manuel was born. They also brought with them the family coat of arms, which they prominently displayed in the patio.

Godoy's father, Don José de Godoy y Sánchez de los Ríos, was a colonel in the local militia. On June 19, 1757, aged twenty-six, he married Doña Antonia Justa de Faria, of aristocratic Portuguese lineage, and a year younger than her husband. Six children were born of this union, two girls and four boys, of whom Manuel was the next to youngest. The entire family would be handsomely taken care of by the brother who was to succeed so well. His sister Antonia became the Marchioness of Branciforte, the wife of a grandee of impeccable background if questionable honesty; on April 21, 1792, she was given the sash of the Damas Nobles de María Luisa, an order created for the wives of the elite.[2] Another sister, Ramona, married the Count of Fuente Blanca, thereby acquiring an equally impressive title.

The eldest brother, José, was destined for the church, and eventually was appointed a canon in Toledo. Luis chose a military career, soon reaching the rank of Captain-General of Extremadura and by 1794 that of Lieutenant-General of the Royal Armies. In addition, he was made a Knight of the Order of Santiago, and as a lagniappe received the Grand Cross of Carlos III. The youngest brother, Diego, in the opinion of many was the most talented in the family, rather like Lucien Bonaparte. Besides accumulating the usual titles and honors, Diego, eventually the Duque de Almodóvar del Campo, Colonel of the Spanish Guards, Grandee of Spain, and Knight of the Order of Calatrava, also proved to be a brave soldier. He fought valiantly against the French at the Battle of Trullas in September 1793, and later at Ceuta when it was besieged by the Moors. For his prowess he was also promoted to lieutenant general.

But to return to the infant Manuel. On May 18, 1767, six days after his birth, he was baptized Manuel Domingo Francisco in the fortress-like cathedral of Badajoz. Other than the sparse account in the *Memorias,* little is known of his childhood and education. We are told of no illuminating anecdotes, no boyish escapades, no lifetime friendships formed at school or at play. Yet, surely there must have been all of these. Manuel's relationship with his family seems to have been happy enough; in later life, he was conspicuously free of tensions and inhibitions. His memoirs are distinctly pre-Freudian, revealing little about the child or adolescent. A perfunctory introduction, a list of teachers and subjects, and after two or three pages the reader already finds himself *in medias res* in Madrid.

The few details relating to Manuel's formative years are all devoted to his education, a typically eighteenth-century approach. His teachers were enlightened men, and he later recalled their names with gratitude and affection. Throughout his political life, he retained a keen interest in furthering public instruction, being one of the first in Spain to discern the merits of Pestalozzi's innovative methods. Contrary to the aspersions of his detractors, Manuel received a broadly based liberal schooling that exemplified the progressive traits of *las luces*. He proved to be a good student, and from the age of eight to sixteen he mastered the basics of mathematics, philosophy, and *letras humanas en toda su extensión*, with emphasis on ancient history.[3]

Godoy's critics remained undeterred; a royal favorite—especially one from a backward province—must needs be unschooled and ignorant. Muriel could affirm without hesitation that "Manuel Godoy's education was not polished; there is evident proof of this, both in his official writings as well as in his correspondence."[4] It was Godoy's practice as First Minister to make copious notes in the margins of state papers. Not only do these testify to his diligence, but also to his command of the written language. To seize on spelling and grammatical errors in his letters betrays a basic unawareness on the part of the carping critic. In the late eighteenth century, the Spanish language, like its practitioners, was vigorous but often undisciplined. The works of other writers of the period are characterized as much by orthographic individuality as strict accuracy, but because of their lesser notoriety they have escaped the censure meted out to Godoy.

The years up to 1788 are lacking in verifiable fact. It would seem, however, that Colonel Godoy had good connections and secured the admission of Luis into the royal bodyguard. The appointment was impressive, as was the uniform with its dashing bandolier and trim of crimson and silver, all of which helped conceal what was little more than genteel poverty. When Manuel was seventeen, he followed his elder brother's footsteps to the capital, and, after presenting a letter of introduction to a *camarista* at court, on August 17, 1784, joined the First Brigade of the *Compañía*

Española, thanks to an opening left by a cadet who chose to go to Mexico.[5] The young soldiers lived in comfortable quarters within the barracks, which certainly did not hamper their amatory adventures. As a young man, Manuel was reputed to be muscular and agile, a good rider and dancer as well as an agreeable conversationalist. Those who knew him remarked on his outgoing nature; neither then nor later in life could he be characterized as introspective.

In Madrid, he became friendly with the Joubert brothers, from whom he learned some French and Italian. Typically, no further details are given; the two men are briefly mentioned, then disappear from the narrative forever. Godoy's studies and military duties kept him so busy, we are assured in his memoirs, that he had little time for anything else, least of all for practicing the guitar. This defensive remark appears aimed at tale-bearers who, having cheerfully confused him with the mysterious guards-man of an earlier date, bruited it about that he had once serenaded the enraptured María Luisa with songs of love. Of these early years, the only fact not in dispute is that he returned to Badajoz on leave from January to June 1786 before rejoining his brigade.

Although the *Memorias* simply ignore the next four years, gossip and rumor have amply filled the vacuum. The chronology of the period 1788–92 is clear enough in matters of promotion and the acquisition of honors and titles, but perplexingly incomplete as to the reason why. Likewise, Manuel's first meeting with the royal couple has been shrouded in surmise and outright fabrication. The simplistic explanation has Luis preparing the way for his brother in the *alcoba real,* only to be banished from court when an infuriated Carlos III discovers the scandalous behavior of his son's wife. If this is true, then only the timely death of the old monarch saved Manuel also from being posted to the provinces. Blanco-White, that garrulous apostate, has it on good authority (as usual, unnamed) that Luis continued to send love letters to María Luisa, using Manuel as an intermediary. In this beguiling version, Manuel has now graduated to the flute, using it like some lascivious Pied Piper as a "signal which drew the Princess to a private room."[6]

This palpable nonsense is by no means an isolated case. D'Auvergne believes (or rather, imagines) that the young man approached this succubus with apprehension, "but the voluptuous and love-sick princess was able to bring tremendous pressure to bear on him. To resist her entreaties meant instant disgrace . . . "[7] In a variation on this unoriginal theme, a *camarista* offers her services as a go-between.

In another reported incident, Godoy was one of four guards bearing a crucifix in a Good Friday procession through the streets of Madrid. The anecdote has him cause the religious image to dance in sacrilegious fashion as it was borne aloft, either to indicate his objection to the assignment or merely to distract the bored princess. When the priest leading the cortege turned round to remonstrate, he received the impudent reply: "Father, is it our fault that Jesus Christ feels like dancing on the day of His funeral?"[8] One can hardly think of a ploy less likely to recommend Manuel in a country where religion is taken so seriously. Nor is the incident of Godoy that same afternoon tossing up acorns (an Extremaduran tidbit) to an amused María Luisa on the balcony any more convincing.

Exactly how and when the young guardsman first met the princess, soon to become queen of Spain, is uncertain. However, on September 12, 1788, Luis wrote the following letter to his parents:

> Manuel, on the road from La Granja to Segovia, fell from the horse he was riding. Full of courage he mastered it and regained his saddle. He has been bothered for two or three days, complaining about his leg, though still going about his ordinary duties. As he formed part of the escort of Her Serene Highness the Princess of Asturias, both she and the Prince have shown a lively interest in what happened. Brigadier Trejo told me that today he [Manuel] will be summoned to the palace as Don Carlos wishes to make his acquaintance.[9]

Manuel must have created a most favorable impression, for on December 30—that is, barely a fortnight after the accession of the new *reyes*—he was promoted to adjutant in the palace service.

At least there is unanimity that Godoy came to dominate María Luisa within a brief span. More difficult to ascertain is whether the attraction was primarily physical, merely a passing flirtation, or maternal on her part, and exactly what his feelings for her might have been. Certainly the middle-aged matron was captivated by this assured young provincial, sixteen years her junior, witty, charming, and above all, attentive. Most chroniclers have readily assumed that they became lovers, and indeed a short-lived affair cannot be entirely dismissed as idle chatter. Whatever the truth, their relationship quickly deepened:

> The wonderful lover became a cherished son as well, for whom nothing could be too much; he was her hero, whom she would always look on as the superior of everyone else, Napoleon included; he was her counselor, the guide from whom she never swerved, whose opinions would to the very end receive a blind acceptance.[10]

Izquierdo Hernández, on the other hand, basing his opinion in part on a psychological study by the noted essayist Ortega y Gasset, indignantly rejects any insinuation of a liaison. He holds that María Luisa's unbounded admiration for what she regarded as *the* great figure of the age precluded any physical attachment: "In Luisa de Parma's eyes Godoy was a great man, and this is a further reason to reject any sexual hypothesis regarding his favor at Court."[11] The writer's purpose is praiseworthy, but there is as much danger in this type of speculation as in the uncritical acceptance of court anecdotes.

At first, María Luisa was discreet, even reticent, about her new admirer. For seven years, she had been the object of surreptitious attacks, and she was now determined to lend dignity to her position as queen. Many observers remarked on her decorum during the first months of the new reign. One can only conclude that Escoiquiz was motivated by malice when he wrote, "Hardly had that good and mourned monarch [Carlos III] closed his eyes when María Luisa, now placed on the throne and free to behave as she wished, gave free rein to her passions."[12]

A more accurate portent of her future role was her conspicuous presence by the new king's side at his first reception for the accredited ambassadors and ministers of state. Much to the chagrin of those diplomats who had anticipated an extended bacchanalia in reaction to the stern dictates of the late ruler, the official period of mourning imperceptibly merged into a routine of unrelieved dreariness. Eight months after the accession of the new monarchs, the Russian ambassador, Zinoviev, complained:

> Never has the court been so lugubrious. It is everywhere penetrated with suspicion. There are no more large assemblies. Everyone avoids appearing at court for fear of falling into disgrace on a bare suspicion. The diplomatic body seems to be shunned. The queen understands quite well that it is the principal occupation of diplomatists to observe all that is passing at courts and thereby to fathom their intrigues. She is by no means expansive with them. She receives foreigners only twice a week, whereas formerly she would receive them every day. We could remain invisible for months together without on that account being any worse received.[13]

In the background, Godoy continued his modest ascent, modest, that is, only by his own later vertiginous standards. Already by May 1789 he had attained the rank of colonel in the cavalry division with a corresponding promotion in the Royal Bodyguards—he was barely twenty-two at the time—and, accomplished horseman that he was, hurdled the intervening steps to become a lieutenant general a mere two years later.[14] So far, his promotions had been mainly confined to his chosen career in the army. On November 27, 1789, he was dubbed a Knight of the Order of Santiago (Spain's national saint, the warrior figure of Saint James). The required *pruebas de nobleza,* a careful check into his background and the purity of his blood, revealed that "in many years there has not been a more perfect proof of nobility."[15]

María Luisa was not alone in her esteem for Manuel. Carlos reportedly enjoyed many a game of chess with his friend and bodyguard, and an indication of the royal couple's growing dependence on Manuel was his appointment in March 1791 as Gentleman of the Bedchamber. When the Grand Cross of Carlos III was conferred by the king on August 25, 1791, few doubted that a star was in the ascendant.

Carlos IV, in accordance with his late father's wishes, had unenthusiastically retained Floridablanca as his First Minister. During the first week of March 1789, riots in Barcelona were occasioned by a sudden rise in the price of bread. Seven of the instigators were hanged—a bad omen for the new reign.[16] A violent rising in Galicia resulted from an ill-considered new tax levy, and again severe military measures were required to subdue the rioters.

From the outset of the French Revolution, Floridablanca had perceived that the lives of his liege's French cousins were in danger. The account of their escape of June 21, 1791, ending with the ignominious capture of Louis XVI and his family at Varennes and their demeaning return to Paris, brought tears to the eyes of Carlos and María Luisa. The imperious First Minister chose his moment ill-advisedly to demand that the National Assembly make itself responsible for the safety of the captive king. Bourgoing, the new French ambassador, *un homme intègre, conciliant, bien élevé,*[17] a Hispanophile with a most persuasive manner, had little difficulty convincing the distressed monarchs that Floridablanca's demarches were imperiling the lives of the French Bourbons.

On February 28, 1792, three days after Bourgoing's arrival in Madrid, the First Minister was dismissed from office—surely no coincidence. In the best cloak-and-dagger tradition, he was aroused in the middle of the night, shown the royal decree, and packed into a waiting carriage. At first, he was allowed to return to his native Murcia, but in July he was rearrested on a trumped-up charge and transferred to the northern fortress of Pamplona, where he remained until 1794. In perfect character to the end, he accepted his fate with equanimity.

The precise reasons for Floridablanca's fall, other than those enumerated, are in dispute. True, he had previously opposed the granting of the estate and title of Duke of Alcudia to Godoy as being illegal, and tried to bring the matter up in the Council of State. Nevertheless, evidence is scant that either María Luisa or Godoy was involved in the decision. In fact, it was Godoy who later secured the release of the fallen minister from his irksome confinement. Unquestionably, Floridablanca had been too brusque toward the French revolutionary leaders and, more surprising for one of humble origins, had failed to gauge the temper of his own people. A new minister was required to remedy these two shortcomings.

Godoy had not remained idle. By now, having emerged from the shadows, he was recognized as the decisive influence over the untried monarchs. To the courtiers and ministers, his domination of the queen was deplorable, but only to be expected, given her generally accepted meretricious nature. What occasioned widespread consternation was Godoy's total ascendancy over the king, who seemed to share his wife's boundless regard for the provincial upstart. During a hunting party, Floridablanca had the temerity to interrupt the carnage and inform Carlos in general terms of the queen's infatuation for the young soldier. The minister's admonition failed disastrously. Carlos confided everything to María Luisa, who played the mortified *grande dame* to perfection. Turning her pronounced pregnancy to advantage, she threatened to return to her relatives in Parma if her husband dared listen again to such scurrilous talk. Carlos dutifully obeyed, not knowing—or apparently caring—that the consensus at court had designated Godoy as the unborn child's father. Floridablanca bowed to the inevitable and, like his rival Aranda, sought by every means to ingratiate himself with the *privado,* even presenting him with a set of valuable chandeliers and a crucifix of Italian lapis lazuli.

Godoy's preeminent position was evident to all. At first, an attempt had been made to conceal his successive advancements by promoting fellow officers en bloc, sometimes literally by the dozen. Thus, in February 1791 no less than twenty-four lieutenant generals and forty major generals were created, in the opinion of the skeptical Zinoviev for the sole purpose of raising Godoy to the rank of *mariscal de campo* (a general commanding a division). Soon, even this transparent pretense was dispensed with, and scarcely a month passed by without some new honor. In October, Godoy received from the queen the ostentatious gift of a magnificent coach adorned with his own monogram, significantly surmounted by a crown, the impressive equipage being drawn by six matching horses. Nor had he been forgotten by the *madrileños.* One wit released a dog in the streets of the capital with a sign affixed to its collar stating: "I belong to Godoy, I fear nothing." Failing to find the original culprit, the police did the next best thing and clapped the offending canine into the *calabozo*.

Despite Floridablanca's opposition, Godoy was raised to Duke of Alcudia on April 21, 1792; in July of the same year, he was admitted as a Grandee of Spain and a Councillor of State. The favorite was rising so rapidly that many feared he would succeed Floridablanca without delay. But the more immediate problem was to ensure the safety of Louis XVI and Marie Antoinette, now in peril of their lives. Since their abortive flight attempt, the members of the royal family were little more than prisoners of the National Assembly. On a personal level, Carlos had scant affection for his French cousin. Supposedly, Louis had thought it hardly necessary to send a letter of congratulation on Carlos's accession, "for the poor man is a mere cypher, completely governed and henpecked by his wife."[18] As might be expected, word got back to the target of the barb.

This, however, was no occasion for pettiness. Like most monarchs, Carlos IV felt that the very foundations of the royalist principle were endangered. By now as alarmed as his stolid nature would allow, he needed a First Minister with influential connections in Paris who in turn might intercede on behalf of the august captives. Count Aranda was the obvious choice. Never mind past differences: this was the time to take advantage of the Aragonese's free-thinking philosophy.

The count was now seventy-four years old, and not even the acquisition of a young wife barely a quarter his age could rejuvenate him. A quarter of a century earlier, as president of the Council of Castilla under Carlos III, Aranda had terminated the *motín de Esquilache* in statesmanly fashion by instituting necessary reforms. The expulsion of the Jesuits from Spain shortly afterward was in part attributed to his alleged anticlericalism and to his being a Freemason, though the actual reasons were far more complex.[19] He was widely considered to be the head of the *partido aragonés,* the faction from Aragon that "distinguished itself . . . in the form of opposition to the reigning dynasty and through the demand for the return of local privileges [*fueros*] taken away by the Bourbons."[20] Thus, though he had faithfully served king and country, an inherent tension existed between the elderly count and the court.

Now, more than ever, Aranda was the victim of an inner paradox of his own making. On the one hand, the born aristocrat and monarchist, the upholder of vested traditions; on the other, the anticlerical, liberal Freemason in open sympathy with many of the declared aims of the French

Revolution. Not surprisingly, he decided on a compromise course of moderation (his political enemies were quick to call it appeasement) and immediately relaxed the more repressive measures of his predecessor.

Less than two months later, France declared war on Austria. Prussia
joined in the fray, and Aranda was faced with the dilemma whether to lend
Spain's support to the royalist forces massing on France's borders, or to
persist in his gamble on conciliation. He hoped that the untried French
revolutionary armies would be defeated on the eastern frontier by the
advancing Austrians and Prussians, thus obviating the need for Spanish
participation. His hopes proved ineffectual; on August 10, the Swiss Guard
was slaughtered, Louis XVI deposed, and shortly thereafter the Republic
declared. The ensuing September massacres, the emergence of the Jacobins,
and the defeat of the allied armies at Valmy merely underscored the bankruptcy of Aranda's Panglossian policies. When the gray-haired ex-general
offered to lead the Spanish forces in person, his quixotic suggestion was
met with derision from all sides.

Aranda could hardly have been surprised when he was summoned to
the Escorial on November 14, 1792, and ushered into the royal presence.
The king with the queen at his side—María Luisa possessed a great flair
for the dramatic occasion—gently informed the septuagenarian that, in
view of his advanced age and the burdensome demands of his office, it had
been reluctantly decided to replace him with a younger man. In marked
contrast to the abrupt dismissal of his predecessor, Aranda was allowed to
remain as president of the *Consejo de Estado* as a token of his monarch's
esteem. The ministerial change was announced officially the following day:

> By my Royal Decree of February 28 of the current year, I graciously
> appointed Count Aranda to serve provisionally in the post of my First
> Secretary of State. In consideration of his advanced age and the fact that
> his service to me has been fittingly carried out: I have decided to release
> him from the temporary post he is occupying, while letting him retain all
> the honors which are his by right . . . To succeed him in the said position
> as my Secretary of State, I have named the Duke of Alcudia for the
> confidence I have in him, who will also retain the office of Sergeant-Major
> of my royal bodyguard.[21]

Godoy's accession to the rank of First Minister at the age of twenty-five
can only be surpassed in precocity by that of his contemporary William
Pitt. If the Duke of Alcudia was widely considered to be too young for such
a demanding post—Spain, unlike England and France, still administered

a vast, undiminished overseas empire—then Aranda at seventy-four was clearly too old. Muriel, on the scantiest of evidence, believed that María Luisa's unbridled passion for Godoy was the principal cause for the downfall of Floridablanca and Aranda.[22] The fact is that both senior statesmen had failed, and their dismissal would have occurred in any case. Even so, Godoy's appointment to the highest office stirred widespread resentment. The Prussian ambassador, Sandoz-Rollin, observed, "The grandees are furious, but they are at Godoy's feet."[23] They were to remain there for the next sixteen years.

Godoy's abilities were totally unknown. He had never ventured abroad, and was unacquainted with the greater part of his own country. It has been suggested (quite erroneously) that the sole purpose of the Aranda ministry was to complete Godoy's apprenticeship. Some malevolent observers even assert that the discomfiture of Floridablanca and Aranda was welcome to the king and queen, inasmuch that Godoy would appear decisive by comparison. Undoubtedly, the *reyes* were tired of the two contending factions at court, but they hardly wished their own appointed ministers to fail when the life of their own flesh and blood was at stake. In all likelihood, the decision to make Godoy their trusted confidant evolved slowly and was not the result of any premeditated scheme:

> Carlos IV and María Luisa needed a vigilant, active, and self-sacrificing person, who, without making it obvious, would lead them by the hand in their actions. Aranda had failed to meet their need, and they had found the right man in the lowly guardsman, whom they placed in the necessary surroundings, so that he could provide them the services they needed.[24]

Godoy's appointment evoked cries of anger and outrage. The institution of the *valido* had prematurely been consigned to the past, and even then (with the possible exception of Queen Juana and Beltrán de la Cueva in the fifteenth century) none had dared share the royal bed, as was now widely believed. Bourgoing complained bitterly that "the young Duke of Alcudia is well-intentioned, but is drunk with his limitless power. One can say that he plays with the Crown, which passion placed in his hands."[25] For a brief time, the real possibility of a popular uprising existed, but the general resentment failed to coalesce around a national leader.

If María Luisa and Godoy were despised, the king was regarded with a pity tinged by the ridicule Latins reserve for the duped husband who, by inaction, lends his tacit consent. Richard Herr pithily states, "The idea that

Spain was being governed by an empty-headed lover, a lascivious Queen, and cuckold King broke the spell that Carlos III had cast over his people."[26] It was common gossip that the favorite had even found a pliant confessor named Múzquiz to ease the queen's guilty conscience. The truth is that María Luisa was far more superstitious than religious, as her correspondence amply proves. Her real confessor, of course, was Manuel Godoy.

To the end, he remained the *choricero* (sausage-maker) in the eyes of his fellow countrymen, a disrespectful allusion to a specialty of his native Extremadura. The royal couple and their First Minister were derisively referred to as *la santa trinidad en la tierra,* a designation that originated in all innocence with María Luisa, who once impulsively blurted out the unfortunate epithet. Demonstrating the peculiar blindness of myopic admiration, the king and queen seemed oblivious to the sullen exasperation that surrounded them. All that mattered was that they had their *querido Manuel* to turn to and direct the nation's destinies.

Understandably enough, Godoy had a far different perception. In his *Memorias,* he dismisses Floridablanca and Aranda with perfunctory politeness, the one reacting too much and the other too little to the challenges facing Spain from without. To Godoy, they were a pair of outworn anachronisms to be humored, a superannuated Rosencrantz and Guildenstern quite out of touch with reality. To be sure, he tosses in some complimentary remarks at set intervals—he even admits his indebtedness to Floridablanca in a footnote inserted as an afterthought[27]— but it all seems entirely pro forma. The royal couple had sensed the ministers' inadequacy to cope with the threat from the north, and desperately sought an adviser of their own:

> The proximity of the two kingdoms made them constantly fear that the conflagration could spread to their own realm; they looked all around, they lacked confidence in themselves, and did not know where to place it; they desired enlightenment, but feared deception; they craved for virtue, but feared the whims of vanity and pride; the dangers were increasing, and they perceived the threats to all of Europe emanating from France . . . Troubled and uncertain in their power of decision, they conceived the idea of finding a man and making him an incorruptible friend, the product of their own hands, one who would be closely united to the royal house, and who would keep vigil over them and the kingdom without fail.[28]

One can only surmise what Godoy's emotions must have been. Why should he succeed where far more experienced men had failed? What precedents were there to turn to as a guideline? Perhaps there weren't any.

The first task of the young minister was terrifyingly clear: hardly had he assumed the reins of government when the Convention in strife-torn Paris announced that "Citizen Louis Capet" was to be tried for treason. Time was running desperately short.

3

PRINCE OF THE

PEACE

Godoy's predicament was unenviable. Hard on the "miracle" at Valmy, the French revolutionary armies repulsed the Austrians and the Prussians as far as the length of the Rhine. Clearly, war against France was not to be embarked upon lightly. At no time was this more evident than during the winter of 1792. As an army officer—albeit not an avowed militarist despite his love of insignia—Godoy was aware that the Spanish army was ill-prepared to undertake an arduous campaign; equipment and supplies were lacking, the means of transportation untested, and the military leadership suspect after years of inactivity. Had the decision been his alone, Manuel would undoubtedly have counseled against hostilities.

But the very raison d'être of his appointment was to succeed where his cautious elders had failed. The church had long castigated Aranda as an atheist—worse still, a Protestant—unfit to lead the nation in a crusade against the godless sansculottes.[1] Secretly, Godoy shared Aranda's view that the French forces were better motivated and imbued with a superior ideology. The most he could do was to temporize in the hope that some unforeseen event would render intervention unnecessary—in other words, precisely Aranda's attitude.

Such an evasive policy could not last for long. Louis XVI's life hung in the balance, and, though in the past he had frequently made disparaging remarks at the expense of his lethargic cousin, this was no time for petty recrimination. The Spanish unofficial agent in Paris, Ocáriz, was given carte blanche to employ whatever measures were necessary—including the efficacious bribery of selected deputies and the offer to exchange hostages—to save the king. It was hoped that an acceptable compromise could be reached, war averted, and Godoy acclaimed a statesman of the first order.

Yet, the pressure to declare war mounted inexorably. Recent émigrés gave lurid eyewitness accounts of the September massacres and of the degrading treatment accorded the royal family. Both the Russian and Prussian envoys in Madrid openly voiced their contempt at Godoy's vacillation; even Carlos IV in private questioned the hesitancy of his protégé. The expectation had been that the youthful First Minister, energetic and resolute, would jettison the timorous policies of his venerable predecessors and forthwith open hostilities. Instead, he trusted that the disbursement of liberal *pots-de-vin* in the Convention would result in an affirmative vote for the king. Regrettably, most of the deputies were still afflicted with revolutionary rectitude (it soon wore off, but too late for Godoy).

It was now the last week of December. The king's trial was imminent. To gain a much-needed respite, Ocáriz approached Lebrun, the French foreign minister, with a personal plea from Carlos IV. At the same time, Godoy broached the matter to Bourgoing, who, like Lebrun, was a moderate and amenable to reason. If the case were presented factually and unemotionally to the Convention, there was guarded optimism that a compassionate majority would prevail.

Lebrun relayed Carlos IV's communication to the president of the Convention with a curiously worded note of his own, which stated in part:

> Citizen President, when I received the two notes . . . I knew that the Duke of Alcudia had not withheld from the Plenipotentiary of the French Republic [Bourgoing] that one of the powerful motives of the Catholic King in bringing about this friendly step was the power to influence favorably the fate of his cousin, the ex-King.[2]

Lebrun had sought to steer a middle course, but his awkward words were seized on by Thuriot, a proficient rabble-rouser. "Away with the influence of kings!" he shouted. "How dare the Spanish despot threaten us!" A handful of deputies dissented, pointing out that far from threatening the infant Republic, Carlos IV and Godoy had, in fact, been most anxious to reach a compromise. But who wished to listen to pleas for moderation in this new Age of Unreason? In vain, Ocáriz made one last appeal; by the narrowest of margins, Louis XVI was sentenced to the guillotine.

The news of the execution reached Madrid on January 31, 1793. The court went into deep mourning, as did the entire city in a spontaneous gesture of commiseration. On hearing of his cousin's death, Carlos reportedly commented: "A gentleman so ready to find fault with others did not seem to have managed his own affairs very well."[3] A long memory and an unpleasant vindictiveness are two traits in Carlos's character frequently overlooked by those who have accepted at face value the good-natured bonhomie he affected so convincingly.

The reaction throughout the country was entirely predictable. Down to the humblest parish priest, the church renewed its strident clamor for a Holy War against the regicides; now, because of the sacrilegious murder of the Most Christian King, the Spanish nation was united as never before. And yet, to the dismay of his compatriots, the *privado* still refrained from declaring war.

His reasons are not far to seek. According to him,[4] the number of men under arms barely amounted to 36,000 effectives when he assumed power in 1792. Only the navy was up to required strength. Although he no doubt exaggerated somewhat so as to impute later battle losses to previous administrations, his firsthand inspections had convinced him that war was to be avoided, if at all possible. When Bourgoing, from his refuge in the French embassy, requested an unofficial meeting, his demarche was readily accepted.

The meeting was cool but correct. Godoy stressed that war could be averted only on two conditions: first, Queen Marie Antoinette and her two children were to be assured of their safety; and, secondly, the Convention must renounce the doctrine of furthering revolution and subversion abroad. As a private citizen, Bourgoing expressed his fullest sympathy, but, in his capacity as French ambassador, he was unable to accede to Godoy's stipulations. On February 19, 1793, Bourgoing received his diplomatic passports with the telling inscription: *Pour le ci-devant ministre de Sa Majesté très Chrétienne.* On his journey to France, he barely escaped the wrath of the crowd in Valencia.

The National Convention in Paris finally declared war on March 7 with the gratuitous barb that "the intrigues of the Court of St. James have triumphed in Madrid, and the Papal Nuncio has sharpened the daggers of fanaticism in the states of the Catholic King."[5] The hope was expressed that the Spanish Bourbons would soon be unseated from their throne. Despite such provocation, Godoy waited until March 27 before announcing hostilities.

That the war was genuinely popular cannot be doubted for one moment. Had Godoy persisted in his covert opposition, he would have been swept out of office. It might well be argued that the outbreak of war was his salvation inasmuch as it diverted the nation's attention elsewhere. As so often during his career, he bowed to the inevitable. Inflated language aside, his summation of his predicament is accurate enough: "In the hour of danger, when there was nothing positive, only evils, terror, consternation, collapse, whirlwind, confusion, and volcanoes erupting, I was placed—O God!—at the helm of state . . . Fate condemned me to navigate the ship of state with a meager tiller in the most difficult period in the annals of Europe."[6] More often than not, he was to find himself bailing out the ship of state rather than piloting it.

Entirely beholden to the Crown, Godoy had no political faction or geographical power base on which to depend; the reformers and intellectuals were wary of his intentions, the aristocrats despised him wholeheartedly, and the officer corps dismissed him out of hand as a bemedalled peacock. The king's informal calls on him in the morning to supervise Manuel's levee and their walks together through the gardens of the Aranjuez palace only served to increase the suspicions of the favorite's detractors. Royal honors, such as the bestowal of the Order of the Golden Fleece, did little to enhance his stature, and his appointment as Secretary to the Queen in February 1793 was greeted with knowing sneers. Nor did it help that his servants were now entitled to wear the royal livery, all of which merely confirmed in the public mind that the *choricero* was bent on becoming part of the reigning family. With unabashed nepotism, he arranged for his brother-in-law, the Marquis of Branciforte, to be appointed as viceroy to Mexico, where he shamelessly enriched himself during his three years in office. Clearly Godoy's hopes for survival hinged entirely on a successful outcome to the war.

The beginning was propitious. Enthusiasm for the jihad proclaimed from plaza and pulpit alike was contagious while France was decried as a *pueblo sin rey, sin ley, y sin Dios*. Precious silver objects were melted down, and church orders vied with one another to make the greater sacrifice (the archbishop of Toledo alone raised six million reales). In Catalonia, a popular *levantamiento* was declared, throughout the country new municipal taxes were raised without the customary protest, and the aristocracy—which now included Godoy—hastened to equip whole regiments at their own expense. Even the smugglers of the Sierra Morena descended from their mountain fastnesses to make a contribution. An unexpected windfall was gratefully accepted by the Spaniards when some richly laden French merchant ships put in at Cádiz, unaware that the two nations were now at war. Significantly, the National Convention was hard pressed to raise five million francs, while in Spain the voluntary contributions of Carlos's loyal subjects exceeded twelve times that amount. If religious zeal and fighting spirit were all that counted, the war was as good as won.

Godoy was not entirely immune from the fervor that gripped the country. In one reckless moment, he offered to lead the army like a rejuvenated Aranda across the Pyrenees in person, only to be dissuaded by the affrighted royal couple. Undaunted, he proposed to strike a decisive blow at the enemy by means of a daring joint Anglo-Spanish landing in Normandy and a quick seizure of Paris. The plan came to naught, and the favorite's military role was confined to supervising a minor change in the infantryman's uniform and following the campaign from a safe distance. Even so, on May 23, 1793, shortly after his twenty-sixth birthday, he was promoted to captain-general and received a gratifying raise in pay. Well aware of the rumors and scuttlebutt, he prevailed upon the king to create twenty-four lieutenant generals and thirty-two major generals to keep him company.

In the field, General Ricardos immediately advanced into France on the eastern flank. At first, all went well. The carmagnoles were routed at the Battle of Masdeu, Bellegarde was taken, the engagement at Truillas won (in which Manuel's brother Diego played a heroic part), and by the first week in November the Spaniards were threatening Perpignan. At the outset of 1794, this was the only foreign army to remain on French soil.

If the progress on the central and western fronts was less spectacular, on balance the first year of war had generally been in Spain's favor. Yet, despite a succession of victory bulletins, it was evident that the campaign had deteriorated into one of attrition with little prospect of ultimate victory for either side. Already the "widow Capet" had followed her late husband to the scaffold; no amount of fighting would restore the royal martyrs to life.

In Paris, Robespierre was calling for the creation in Catalonia of a "sister republic" under French protection, a euphemism for incorporation. With less subtlety, but with the same end result in mind, General J. F. Dugommier advocated the annexation of the province on the specious grounds that the Catalans were non-Spanish by heritage and sentiment; how that made them

Frenchmen was never explained. More to the point, such a territorial acquisition would provide "a new boulevard between Spain and France, safer than the Pyrenees,"[7] not to mention the agricultural and commercial wealth of the area. This southern extension of France's boundaries was no mere revolutionary whim; in later years, both Talleyrand and Napoleon were to covet the Ebro River as France's new frontier, much to Godoy's consternation.

The favorite also had to contend with other irritants. General Ricardos—admittedly able and patriotic—owed his command to Aranda and not to Godoy, whom he viewed with the ill-concealed scorn of the professional soldier. For Manuel, there were also domestic crosses to bear. On March 10, 1794, the queen gave birth to the Infante Francisco de Paula, and within hours an irrefutable resemblance to the *privado* was discerned by those who would not have it otherwise. The same month, Ricardos was killed in action; a few days later, his replacement suffered a like fate. At this crucial moment, Aranda decided to strike against Godoy.

The clash came on March 14, the setting the *Consejo de Estado*. Showing minimal respect for the king, the elderly Voltairean was determined to use his incumbency as president of the council to present his own views. He argued that the war was indefensible because it interfered in France's internal affairs, thus establishing a dangerous precedent; on a more somber note, he intimated that a Spanish defeat—a heretical thought in itself—could undermine the very foundation of the monarchical system.

Aranda's speech was not only tactless and repetitive, but ignored the reality that it was the Convention which had forced war on Spain. Godoy, in fact, had thus far shown an exemplary restraint that belied his inexperience. He claims—and his account up to this point is corroborated in its essentials by Muriel[8]— that the king listened impassively to Aranda's jeremiad.

At this juncture, the two versions part company. Godoy protests that he, too, seeks peace, but not on any terms. The present French government is an oppressor of its own citizens, and under the terms of the Bourbon Family Pact, Spanish intervention is legitimate—indeed, an obligation. This action is no irresponsible caprice on the part of the king and his chief minister; the entire Spanish populace supports this view. Who, if not Spain, Godoy asks rhetorically, can deal with a Robespierre, a Saint-Just? Having exhausted the subject (and no doubt his listeners—the speech continues for eight pages in the *Memorias*), Godoy took his place to await the king's pleasure.[9]

All in all, an impressive peroration, but there are grounds to believe that it was never given and is no more than an oratorical exercise composed many years later in exile.[10] Muriel—no friend of the favorite or María Luisa but basically accurate in factual matters—has the Duke of Alcudia turn to the king with the heated words: "Sire, this is a discourse which merits punishment, and its author should be brought to trial and judges named to censure him, as well as various other people who have formed a society and adopted ideas in conflict with service to Your Majesty, which is a disgrace. Severe measures are necessary."[11] Less flattering to Godoy, perhaps, but infinitely more human.

If the *privado* had hoped to elicit some token of penitence from the doyen of the council, he was doomed to disappointment. Aranda taunted him with being young and inexperienced, to which Godoy riposted: "It is true that I am only twenty-six, but I work fourteen hours a day which no one else has done before; I sleep four hours, and except for eating, I attend to the service of the state."[12] In reply, Aranda made the acerbic observation that any further discussion was pointless. In a display of mock deference, he bowed to the king and lamented: "What's the use? Anything I were to add would be to no purpose; Your Majesty has given unmistakable signs that he approves everything said by his minister. Who dare displease Your Majesty by taking the opposite tack?"[13] The impassive king was stung sufficiently to close the session with a curt, "That's enough for today," and cut the count's stumbling apology short with the stinging rebuke, "With my father you were stubborn and insolent, but you never went so far as to insult him in the Council." Two hours later, Aranda was arrested for lese majesty, bundled into the usual waiting carriage, and was driven off to provincial exile in Jaen, some two hundred miles to the south of Madrid.

Although Godoy, by inaction, could have sealed his rival's fate, he insisted that the charges leveled against the disgraced diplomat be restricted to those arising from the tempestuous session of the *Consejo*. Aranda was sentenced to confinement in the Alhambra palace in Granada (not the most arduous of prisons, as Washington Irving rhapsodically testifies in his tales), where he remained for a year. Again Godoy intervened; Aranda was then allowed to return to his native Aragon, despite the war and that province's close proximity to France.

On April 4, 1794, Floridablanca was released from the fortress of Pamplona, where he had been sent on Aranda's orders. Godoy goes out of his way to emphasize that the venerable minister was accorded all his revenues and privileges. If Manuel had sought to win an ally through his humanitarian gesture, his hopes were dashed forthwith. Floridablanca never forgave the upstart who had usurped his office. Following the French invasion of 1808, he heaped the entire blame for Spain's suffering on Godoy's shoulders.

Meanwhile, the war dragged on. Despite the unremitting exhortation of the clergy to efface the apostate enemy, Godoy was often reminded of his precarious isolation. One day he received the anonymous gift of a French prayer book that contained an outline of the Rights of Man; the revolutionary arm reached far indeed. Spanish reverses now far outnumbered advances. Cases of desertion and of abandoning arms, hitherto rare, became more frequent. The grotesque disciplinary measure of stripping the offender of his uniform before his comrades and then seating him back to front on a burro with a distaff in his hands predictably failed to raise morale.[14] Such was the lack of reserves that the humiliated soldier was immediately returned to the ranks.

Godoy feared that Aranda's dire prophesies of a full-scale invasion might yet come to pass. Already the French had crossed the Pyrenees in force, captured San Sebastian in the west, and were advancing into Catalonia on the eastern flank. An ominous portent was the abject surrender of the fortress-city of Figueras. Though well stocked with supplies to withstand a lengthy siege *a la española,* it fell without offering even token resistance. The timorous commandant and three senior officers were condemned to death by a court-martial, but Carlos, on the advice of Godoy, commuted the sentence to expulsion from the service and exile.[15]

Manuel, drawing on his already well-developed instinct for survival, knew it was time to sound the chamade. Peace talks were initiated in secret through the intermediary of the Prussian ambassador, Sandoz-Rollin. Godoy proposed to the French that the infant dauphin ascend the throne of his fathers as Louis XVII; in a magnanimous gesture, King Carlos IV would graciously allow the National Convention to establish itself as a Republic on the island of Santo Domingo. Not surprisingly, Godoy avoids mention of this in the *Memorias.*

Both sides were acutely aware that England had most to gain from the unresolved conflict. Yet, Spanish *pundonor* remained a formidable barrier to the signing of any peace treaty. Nor for that matter could the French be absolved from all blame. An incident earlier in the year had convinced Godoy that they were quite capable of undermining his position at home. A bizarre pedagogue named Juan Bautista Picornell had planned a rising to take place on February 3, the day of San Blas. Apparently influenced by the French constitution of 1793, he and his associates proposed replacing the monarchy with a democratic republican form of government; Godoy's removal was but incidental in the far more ambitious design.

Picornell's gifts as a translator of subversive French works were far superior to his modest abilities as a plotter. In quick order, the ringleader and his companions were betrayed and arrested. The discovery of incriminating documents, which in turn led to further arrests, clearly indicated a complot of embarrassing proportions. Any evidence, such as the following ribald pasquinade aimed at Godoy and the queen, had to be handled with extreme care:

> The Frenchman today treats
> the Spaniard as a coward
> for allowing the nation
> to be governed—by whom? Godoy.
> But how can I admire him
> if the queen aroused him
> with her lustful desire—O rage!—
> and pulled him out of the barracks
> so as to have sex with
> Señor Duke of Alcudia?[16]

Understandably, this and other satirical squibs were suppressed before they could do further damage. As it was, Picornell's charge that the king spent huge sums to "aggrandize and maintain Godoy in a state of luxury superior to the revenues of the wealthiest potentate"[17] was embarrassing enough.

Picornell and his codefendants stubbornly refused to admit their guilt, but to no avail; all were condemned to the garrote. The verdict was sent to the king for approval, but Godoy added a note that "this is not the opportune moment for enactment." Picornell's sentence was mitigated to life imprisonment and "perpetual exile among the savages" in Panama, and the others were packed off to other insalubrious penal colonies in the West Indies. While it is true that Godoy instinctively recoiled from bloodshed, on this occasion a subtle hint from the French seems to have been the decisive factor.

Picornell did not end his days in a fetid cell. He escaped from prison only to resume his career as a revolutionary in the New World. As a result of his seditious writings, he was sentenced to death in absentia. In 1798 began a perigrination around the Caribbean that later took him through Mexico, Venezuela, Texas, Cuba, then Philadelphia, and on to Paris. Finally, in 1814, this "conspicuous enemy of Godoy," as he termed himself, wrote to Fernando VII from New Orleans begging to be forgiven and to be allowed back into his native land:

> This, Sire, is the hapless Picornell, who at the beginning of 1795, carried away by love and the renown of his nation, tried to attack the arbitrary power of the Prince of the Peace who was threatening the throne of His Majesty and the Queen of Spain. If only one could have deposed the ambitious favorite by means of a quick and wise measure, and immediately convened the Cortes to remedy the grave ills and pernicious abuses from which the people were suffering![18]

But Fernando had not forgotten that the conspiracy had originally been aimed at the monarchy as well as at Godoy. The royal permission to return was therefore withheld; like the *privado* against whom he had schemed, Picornell was destined to spend the remainder of his life as a wandering exile.

In Basle, the continuing negotiations, so close to success, were ensnared on one inflexible point: the fate of the dauphin and his sister. Spain's offer to provide exile in a newly created Kingdom of Navarre for the young "Capet" was totally unacceptable to the French, who rightly foresaw the danger of a royalist focal point. Yet, Godoy's suggestion, dismissed by his critics as the chimera of an unfledged mind, was certainly no more fanciful than later subdivisions of the map of Europe by Napoleon that were hailed as masterstrokes.

This seeming impasse was resolved by the sudden news from Paris that the dauphin had died. The dispatch of June 8, 1795, stated merely: "This morning the Convention was informed of Capet's death, which did not arouse much attention; on the other hand, the capture of Luxembourg has caused great excitement. Capet had been ill for some time . . ."[19] The timing of the prince's death was opportune for Godoy, to say the least. However suspect, it removed the one remaining obstacle to a successful outcome. On July 22 the Treaty of Basle was signed in the house of Peter Ochs, a leading member of the Helvetian Republic. For Spain, the cessation of hostilities was vital; Bilbao and Vitoria had fallen before the enemy advance, causing Godoy to confide to Iriarte, the Spanish negotiator in Basle, "We need peace, whatever the price." More ominously, he added that "peace is the only sweet drink [*jarabe*] that can wash away the calumnies of the faithless vassals of the King; there are many of them, and they are on the increase"[20]—a surprising admission of domestic discontent. Blanco-White, that inveterate cynic, observed, "The French armies, having received reinforcements, would soon have paid a visit to Carlos at Madrid if his favorite minister, with more address than he ever discovered in his subsequent management of political affairs, had not concluded and ratified the peace of Basle."[21]

Yet, the cost to Spain was minimal. Of all France's enemies, the Spanish Bourbons suffered the least, enabling Godoy to boast that the "glorious peace did not cost Spain a single tree of her soil."[22] The defensible border of the Pyrenees was confirmed, the only territorial loss being that of the eastern half of the malaria-infested island of Santo Domingo. In 1802 a French expeditionary force was ravaged in neighboring Haiti as much by yellow fever as by the rebellious natives. Godoy concluded that Spain was well rid of the pestilential colony.

Under the generous terms of the treaty, all prisoners were to be repatriated within two months. The French agreed to withdraw their troops unconditionally and, as a gesture of good faith, to return the border fortresses intact. Spain was given custody of the dauphin's strong-willed sister Marie-Thérèse, "the only man in the family," as Napoleon was later to observe. There is no verifiable basis for the report that the still-unmarried *privado* had ambitious plans linking himself with the princess.[23] In fact, much to Manuel's relief, she decided to settle in Austria.

In Madrid, the announcement of peace was greeted with acclaim, the initial fervor for the crusade having long since yielded to disillusionment. During the course of the war, Godoy had been held responsible for every setback. Now it was known that the treaty was considered by many in Paris to be far too lenient. Somehow, Godoy had outwitted the *franchutes,* always an occasion for rejoicing. Such was the wild jubilation convulsing the nation that even the *choricero* enjoyed a brief moment of genuine popularity.

On August 25 the infantas María Amalia and María Luisa Josefina were married off amid the usual pageantry. In the general exultation, the original purpose of the war was entirely forgotten. Few paused to reflect that the French Bourbons had been virtually eliminated, the Revolution firmly established and in effect acknowledged by Madrid, and that the Pope and the church's very existence were being threatened in Italy by the brilliant young General Bonaparte.

If some reflective Spaniards harbored such Cassandran thoughts, their misgivings were quickly drowned in a veritable deluge of rewards, promotions, honors, and titles. No one was forgotten: Aranda was forgiven his trespasses, Jovellanos and Cabarrús (of whom more later) were received back into official favor, and several officials who had failed in their duty during the war were granted amnesty. And what of Godoy, the genius who had wrought these wonders? Assuredly the grateful monarchs had no intention of overlooking their *querido Manuel*. On September 4, 1795, the following official court announcement was made public:

> Don Carlos, etc. Inasmuch as the good fortune of my subjects and the conservation of my realm cannot be assured without peace, which I have just concluded with France, and my solicitude would not have attained the level which I deem necessary for the continued welfare of this monarchy if you, my First Secretary of State and the Cabinet, Don Manuel de Godoy, Duke of Alcudia, had not carried out punctually and efficiently the task I entrusted to you, and in the conduct of which were so worthy of the true ancient nobility and the consequent love with which you serve me . . . I feel obliged to procure for you a monument which will show my appreciation for posterity; by a decree signed by my royal hand on the fourth of this month, to be published in the Council on the fifth, the next day, I have determined to award you the title of Prince of the Peace.[24]

Godoy's fragile acceptance among the common people evaporated upon his elevation to such vertiginous heights. To most Spaniards, the accolade of Prince of the Peace was doubly offensive: those outside the reigning family must never be accorded the title of royalty; and to the devout it appeared blasphemous to thus arrogate Christ's epithet. Furthermore, the wealth that accrued from Godoy's new estates was enormous, especially at a time when the nation had been called upon to make such sacrifices. A final touch: in the future, he was to be preceded on state occasions by a herald bearing the twin-faced image of Janus, emblematic of foresight and the wisdom of the past. In one respect, the symbolism was hardly appropriate. Manuel, at twenty-eight, had no intention of looking back.

4

THE FRENCH

ALLIANCE

The brief period of euphoria following the Treaty of Basle marks the true apogee of Godoy's career. To his contemporaries, his power seemed to be further confirmed by the victorious General Bonaparte's recognition of the Prince of the Peace as the leading figure in Spain. Yet, from September 1795 on, it is downhill, *cuesta abajo*, for the favorite, all outward distinctions to the contrary. An insistent paradox begins to intrude: the stronger he appears in the public eye, the weaker he is in reality. He is increasingly dependent on his native wits to survive, and finally is caught in a trap that all but costs him his life.

Once peace with France had been concluded, Manuel turned his attention to domestic matters, which included the cares of the royal family. For some time, the queen had contemplated a journey to Seville to pray at the tomb of San Fernando. She fervently believed that the saint had answered a mother's prayers by watching over his young namesake during a near fatal illness. Fernando's recovery was greeted with an effusion of thanks by the entire nation. As queen and mother, María Luisa was determined to fulfill her sacred vow.

On January 4, 1796, in the depths of the bitter castilian winter, the royal party left the palace of the Escorial. In addition to Manuel, the group consisted of Their Majesties, the two recently wed infantas and their husbands, and Fernando, the Prince of Asturias, as well as the accompanying retinue. On the way to Seville, the king and queen paid Manuel the signal honor of staying at his home in Badajoz, not for a mere day or two, but for an entire month (January 18 to February 15). Ostensibly, the purpose of the visit was the opportunity for the royal couple to meet with their eldest daughter, Carlota Joaquina, who was married to the Prince of Brazil, the future King John VI of Portugal.[1] But few doubted the true reason for the unprecedented sojourn. The house had been refurbished, and Godoy's father, the old colonel, now elevated to president of the local Board of Finance, played the attentive host. Carlos and María Luisa were delighted in their good-natured way, but failed to note the first signs of smoldering resentment in Fernando's attitude.

Just eleven years old at the time, the heir to the throne was indignant that Manuel (as he was instructed by his parents to address the favorite) should share the royal title of prince. Izquierdo Hernández speculates that Fernando's character underwent a fundamental change precisely during this visit:

> The Prince of the Peace was in command on that *jornada*. With his pompous strutting about as a prince—superior, arrogant, domineering, active, energetic, and full of strength—he imposed himself on everyone. The mistrust of Fernando turned into envy, into hatred, and for the first time the idea occurs in his timorous mind that this man could snatch the crown away from him, the only one who by divine right may wear it . . . All his rancor towards the Prince of the Peace stems from this foreboding, and not from the supposed concubinage with his mother, an incomprehensible idea for a child of eleven.[2]

Debatable as this last statement may be, Fernando certainly never shared his parents' adulation for their *querido* Manuel. The latter's initial unawareness of Fernando's hatred is testimonial either to the child's ready dissimulation or—just as likely—to the myopic vanity of the *privado*.

Back in Madrid, the Prince of the Peace had to face a new reality. The French ambassador, Pérignon, was the same general who in the final months of the war had driven the Spanish armies across the border. As a diplomat of the new Republic, he had taken an oath vowing "eternal hatred to those of royal rank." To everyone's vast relief, he arrived in the Spanish capital on April 12, 1796, *"avec une branche d'olivier à la main et une couronne de laurier sur la tête"* (with an olive branch in his hand and a crown of laurel on his head).[3] When Pérignon appeared at court to present his credentials, the two-year-old Francisco de Paula, who was considered by most of those present to have been fathered by Godoy, ran toward the startled envoy. Before he could be restrained, the youngster, in a gesture possibly indicating his own confusion regarding his father's identity, entwined himself around the ambassador's legs with cries of "Papa! Papa!" Quite unperturbed, Pérignon patted the infante's head and exclaimed, "Charming!"—making the transition from general to diplomat with unruffled dignity.

His republican background notwithstanding, Pérignon soon felt at ease at the Bourbon court. In a matter of weeks, he was on excellent terms with Godoy, even allowing himself to be the target of some heavy-handed banter regarding his correct title. Revolutionary representatives had been instructed in Paris to insist on the apellation "Citizen" while serving abroad, but Pérignon showed not the slightest objection when addressed by Godoy as "Your Excellency." Such pleasantries, however, were not the main purpose of his mission to Madrid. France had shown herself conciliatory, indeed most generous, at Basle; it was now Spain's turn to reciprocate.

Godoy was the first to admit that England, and not France, was his country's historical enemy. Since 1704 Spain had repeatedly attempted to wrest Gibraltar back from the English; the Great Siege of 1779–83, launched by Franco-Spanish floating batteries, was still a fresh memory to many. Just as insufferable to Godoy, at times the Mediterranean took on the appearance of an English lake to be commanded with impunity. In the Americas, the British continued to foment trouble in the Spanish colonies and to disrupt trade with the mother country. Furthermore, the traditional foe meddled openly in Portuguese affairs under the pretext of an ancient treaty. Godoy, himself of Portuguese ancestry on his mother's side, deemed such foreign interference a personal affront. His own intrusion in later years was, of course, quite a different matter.

The result of the new rapprochement with France was the signing of the Treaty of San Ildefonso on July 27, 1796, and its ratification the following month. Godoy attempted to limit the terms of the treaty to the protection of Spain's boundaries, but, some trivial concessions aside, Pérignon's views prevailed—an unpromising auspice of future dealings with the French. In case either party were drawn into war, its ally undertook to provide fifteen ships of the line and to furnish an army of 18,000 infantrymen, 6,000 cavalry, and supporting artillery. The heart of the treaty was the secret eighteenth article, which stipulated:

> As England is the sole power from whom Spain has suffered direct grievances, in the event of actual war the present alliance will only go into effect against her, and Spain shall remain neutral with any other powers which are at war with the Republic.[4]

It was further understood—or misunderstood—that Spain would bring pressure to bear on Portugal to close her harbors to English ships. The optimistic assumption was that the *reyes* could influence their headstrong daughter, Carlota Joaquina, married to the heir to the Portuguese throne. Filial obedience, alas, was not a salient characteristic among the Bourbons.

Godoy has been severely criticized for the treaty and its consequences. A French diplomat reported at the time that the Prince of the Peace was "a young man avid for glory, but who only seeks it in grand and brilliant feats. He is dazzled by declarations of war, peace treaties, alliances, and even commercial agreements. This is all that interests him, and the rest he leaves to subordinates as being unworthy of his attention."[5] In later years, Floridablanca and others were to castigate the fallen favorite as the *autor infame* of the Treaty of 1796, which allegedly caused immeasurable harm culminating in Napoleon's invasion.

For his part, Godoy stressed that the treaty originated in the council and was fiercely debated at every point. But, if he sincerely believed that Spain was secure from any future French attack or could remain neutral in a European conflagration, he revealed the innocence of his years. San Ildefonso was the inevitable outcome of the Treaty of Basle; the French did not advance credit indefinitely. As Godoy quickly discovered, this was no marriage between equals. Two months after the signing of the treaty, King Carlos found himself drawn by his possessive partner into an unpopular war with England.

Certainly, the protracted conflict was not the unmitigated chain of disasters for Spain so often recorded by English historians. Nelson's fleet was obliged to leave the Mediterranean for a year and a half, Corsica was abandoned to a French expeditionary force (much to Bonaparte's personal satisfaction), and the war at sea was by no means always one-sided. Had secret English peace feelers met with a more sympathetic response from the Directory—as usual, the Spaniards were not consulted—Godoy might conceivably have been hailed a second time as an outstanding statesman and peacemaker, thus justifying his grandiloquent title.

Two series of events dashed any such hopes. On February 14, 1797, the Spanish fleet suffered a decisive defeat off Cape St. Vincent. True, the English failed in their attempts to capture Caracas and Puerto Rico, and were beaten back at Tenerife (where Nelson lost an arm) and at Cádiz. Such was the elation of the *gaditanos* that, amid three days of festivities, it was decided to appoint Godoy a *regidor perpetuo* (lifetime magistrate) of that city.[6] Yet, nothing could be done to prevent Trinidad from falling into enemy hands, a similar fate that befell Menorca when the English fleet returned to the Mediterranean in 1798.

A second blow to Godoy's hopes was the coup d'etat of Fructidor (September 4, 1797) in Paris. An incipient royalist plot was uncovered and suppressed, putting an end to the immediate ambitions of the Comte de Provence, the self-styled Louis XVIII. Godoy was uneasy about the generous allowance paid to the cause of "Louis XVIII" at the insistence of Carlos. Quite mistakenly, the Directory regarded the subvention as convincing testimony to the favorite's duplicity. In the eyes of the Directory, he had now become an untrustworthy ally to be removed from power at the earliest opportunity. Pérignon's secretary, an ardent republican and anticlerical Freemason named Mangourit, was instructed to send confidential reports on Godoy to Paris behind the ambassador's back. Finally, Manuel felt impelled to remonstrate to Pérignon through official channels that "you have some secretaries who are really mischievous; Mangourit has made some scandalous remarks, among others, that the present King will be the last to reign in Spain; he has vilified the Queen in letters sent to Paris; he has written against me and you, Ambassador, and against your officers."[7]

On a personal level, Godoy had no special liking for the émigrés, though he considered it politic to consult periodically with the Duke d'Havré, the representative of the Comte de Provence in Madrid. Manuel went so far on one occasion as to invite Pérignon and the duke to the same banquet—whether as an oversight, an exercise in tolerance, or out of sheer impishness is not clear.

If France remained largely terra incognita to Manuel, he was well acquainted with Portugal from his childhood. As a boy, he had listened to his mother's Lusitanian accents; and the border, such as it was in those days, was but a league or two along the highway from Badajoz. Spain's Iberian neighbor was a frustrating enigma: linked to the Bourbons by close ties of marriage, she yet persisted in upholding her traditional friendship with England despite apparently irreconcilable differences of religion and culture. Surely, the Directory reasoned, King Carlos could bring pressure to bear on his son-in-law to close all Portuguese harbors to the English in accordance with the terms of the Treaty of San Ildefonso. With its customary solicitude, the Directory offered to send an army of 30,000 men to ensure compliance.

Carlos and Godoy viewed the prospect of French armed intervention with dismay. A land campaign directed against Portugal would necessarily require passage across Spanish territory. In a typically confused letter to

Amigo Manuel, the queen alternately praises his military prowess while fearing the worst: "People are right to believe that you are the only one who can command an expedition of this sort, and believe me we will do you justice and make use of you, but praise be to God that there won't be any such war, and if there is, God keep the French troops from coming, as we cannot admit them or allow them to pass through our realm."[8] Keeping the *franchutes* out of Spain would henceforth be Godoy's main preoccupation.

In the case of Portugal, another factor was involved. Carlos IV had no wish to deprive his own daughter, however recalcitrant, of her inheritance. And, just in case the Spanish king might waver in his paternal resolve, the Portuguese Crown conferred upon Manuel the Order of Christ and the title of Count of Evoramonte, together with some lucrative estates that formerly had been in the possession of his mother's ancestors. The French embassy in Madrid placed the additional revenue accruing to the Prince of the Peace at between 200,000 and 300,000 francs. For his part, Godoy assured the ruling pentarchy in Paris that the moment was not opportune for a military venture against Portugal. As usual, he is at no loss for words in his account of the bloodless victory: "I am not relating this triumph so as to boast; I considered it a duty, and in doing so subordinated material considerations to Castillian honor; I merely refer to it so as to prove that the alliance between Spain and the French Republic was not one of servitude."[9]

Portugal was not the only foreign dilemma facing Godoy and the *reyes.* By coincidence, a parallel situation prevailed in the Duchy of Parma, in northern Italy. Recently, the third daughter of the Spanish sovereigns, the Infanta María Luisa Josefina, had married her cousin Luis, the sickly epileptic heir to Duke Fernando of Parma, the brother of María Luisa. To confuse matters further, Carlos IV's brother, also named Fernando, was the reigning King of Naples. General Bonaparte's open intimation that he would redraw the map of the peninsula once he had settled accounts with Pope Pius VI and his Austrian allies served as warning that such redistributions would result in fewer principalities and a concomitant territorial gain for France.

Godoy would have his readers believe that he was anxious to measure his mettle with the Corsican *condottiere.* Emboldened with retrospective courage, he flings down the gauntlet: "By chance was it not possible to fight such a man in time? When there was still time and he only dared imagine himself ruler of Europe, I wanted to engage him."[10] No historian or biographer has found the slightest evidence to support this braggadocio.

Godoy's record is generally one of caution. Neither then, nor at any other time for that matter, did the First Minister make a determined effort to join any of the various alliances formed against France. Save for the minor dissonance, he was content to provide a discreet obbligato to the swelling theme proclaimed in Paris. Even so, he found himself thrust center stage by Napoleon, invariably at times not of his own bidding.

Such an incident occurred in 1797. Emanuel de Rohan, Grand Master of the Order of the Knights of Saint John of Jerusalem and Sovereign of Malta, lay gravely ill. The Directory, stirred less by Christian piety than by the island's strategic location in the Mediterranean, sent a cajoling letter to Godoy that was delivered personally by Pérignon. They were collectively of the opinion that the Prince of the Peace was uniquely suited to fill the expected vacancy. The proposal seems to have originated from Bonaparte in a memorandum to the Directory dated May 26, 1797:

> The island of Malta is extraordinarily important to us. The Grand Master is dying, and his successor will be, it seems, a German. It would require five or six hundred thousand francs to have a Spaniard named. Would it not be possible to drop a hint to the Prince of the Peace that here is something that should interest him?[11]

Godoy found the offer intriguing, and at first naively believed that the post could become hereditary. Accordingly, he wrote Pérignon that "as Minister of His Catholic Majesty I must consider the religious opinion of the Spanish people, and I cannot all of a sudden associate myself with the project of appropriating the domain attached to the Papal See; but if the matter has been well thought out, I shall support its fulfillment in all good faith."[12] In other words, he could make himself available.

The money to secure the election presented no problem. Carlos, convinced that Manuel richly deserved an ecclesiastical honor, was prepared to fund the enterprise himself; apparently the king had no idea that the Grand Master was expected to reside on Malta. On closer investigation, the vows of chastity decreed by the Order of the Knights appeared to be an insurmountable obstacle. Since his early days as a guardsman, Manuel had acquired a steadily growing reputation as a dedicated philogynist. Recently his attentions had been devoted to an attractive Andalucian half-orphan girl named Josefa Tudó. Neither the first nor the last of a long succession of his mistresses, she was apparently a main cause of his domestic troubles with the queen. Though María Luisa reproached him with neglect and temporarily had turned against him, he was reluctant to forsake his position as First Minister. Despite a noticeable corpulence brought on by Lucullan banquets, unlike Sancho Panza, he was not yet ready to settle down and become governor of an island; in any event, the post went to Ferdinand von Hompesch, Rohan's former page.

Many observers at court discerned the hand of an embittered María Luisa in the Malta affair and believed that she, in fact, had fomented the scheme to rid herself of the ingrate *privado*. Not a tittle of evidence has been adduced to support such a conclusion. Certainly, Manuel's relationship with the queen had become tempestuous and marked by frequent spats, both in private and in public. No longer was he so deferential; his open familiarity, often bordering on unmannerliness, seemed to many onlookers more apposite to the self-assured lover than the dutiful attendant. On one occasion, attested to by reliable eyewitnesses, he went so far as to slap her face in anger. The king turned round and asked, "What was that noise?" only to be reassured by his blushing wife, "Nothing, a book that Manuel has dropped," whereupon the trio resumed their walk as if nothing untoward had happened.[13]

It was natural that many of those who plotted against the hated *choricero* should regard the slighted queen as a potential ally. The problem was twofold, however. Just when María Luisa appeared to be won over, Godoy would mend his fences with an effusive reconciliation. Worse still, she had the distressing habit of leaking details of any conspiracy to him through the agency of a third party.

An early palace intrigue that failed for just such reasons involved the Conde de Teba, the son of the Countess of Montijo. The declared aim of this particular cabal was the restoration of a medieval type monarchy dominated by the aristocracy. More serious was the Malaspina affair, which posed the greatest threat to Godoy since Picornell's stillborn uprising. The plot was hatched by an unlikely quartet straight out of a comic zarzuela. In the leading role was a born conspirator, Antonio Despuig y Dameto, the archbishop of Seville. Together with the Countess of Matallana, a Padre Gil, and Antonio Valdés, the minister of marine (whom Godoy termed *mi excelente amigo* even in later years), he made a concerted attempt to remove the favorite from office. The queen's supposed resentment toward Manuel was the key to the machination. Why not fight fire with fire? Somehow her notorious weakness of the flesh must be exploited to save Spain from further moral degradation. All that was needed was to find the right man for the task.

Alejandro Malaspina was a handsome officer of Italian background serving in the Spanish Navy, a romantic combination that would assuredly win the susceptible queen's heart—or so it was thought. He had returned some eighteen months previously from a scientific voyage around the world, bringing back valuable botanical specimens from the Pacific, ironically a project much favored by Godoy, who wished to expand the tropical gardens in Sanlúcar de Barrameda.[14] Malaspina was a simple soul easily persuaded by the *intrigantes* that the country was in grave danger and that it was his patriotic duty to supplant Manuel in the queen's bedchamber. Whether he performed this sacrifice on behalf of his adopted land is not certain. What is clear is that he set about collecting every bit of scandal he could find about the favorite, determined to present it to King Carlos as a devastating indictment of the First Minister's lubricity. Not unexpectedly, someone (perhaps the queen) spoke out of turn, and the scheme was laid bare. The countess was banished from court, Father Gil consigned to a *casa de corrección,* and the ingenuous Malaspina imprisoned until 1803, when he was sent into permanent exile. Broken in health and spirit, he died shortly afterward. As for the archbishop, he was left free to intrigue further.

Godoy, assured that the death sentence and torture would not be applied, remained indifferent as to his opponents' fate. On all sides, problems and pressures were mounting; the relatively carefree years of his early successes had given way to growing threats to his position. Conspiracies could be thwarted or deflected, but what of institutions such as the church? To most prelates, the need to rid themselves of this notorious philanderer was obvious; he had not attended Easter Mass for eight years (the Inquisition kept detailed records of lapsed laity) and only the Lord knew when he had last confessed. Finally, the persistent archbishop of Seville, aided this time by the archbishop of Ávila and Father Rafael Músquiz, the undemanding confessor whom Manuel had personally selected for the queen—so much for gratitude—prepared to denounce Godoy to the Holy Office as *un gran pecador*. The trap was ready to be sprung when Cardinal Lorenzana, the inquisitor-general, declared his unwillingness to involve himself in a case with political overtones.

Godoy's clerical enemies refused to give up. A communication was dispatched to the Vatican deploring Lorenzana's dilatoriness. The archbishop of Seville declared the situation intolerable and urged that the case against the Prince of the Peace be initiated without further delay. His Holiness fully agreed; papal orders were immediately issued to have Godoy formally indicted by the Inquisition. Somehow Bonaparte intercepted the documents in Genoa and, realizing their potential nuisance value, forwarded copies to Pérignon, in Madrid. The ambassador artfully disclosed their contents to Godoy, who bided his time.

Because of the incursions of the French, the Pope had been obliged to surrender his claims to Bologna, Ferrara, and the Romagna, in addition to paying a huge indemnity. On March 14, 1797, the inquisitor-general and Godoy's two principal accusers were delegated to bring "spiritual consolation" to Pius VI and to remain in the Eternal City for that laudable purpose. The pontiff's reaction on seeing the trio is not recorded. A thoughtful touch, no doubt inspired by Manuel, was the leniency shown toward the queen's confessor, who remained at his post. Lorenzana's inclusion among the reluctant wayfarers was due, ironically, to his meddling in government matters, if we are to believe Godoy.[15] More surprising still, Muriel voiced his approval of the First Minister's conduct, "as the aggression came from the archbishops; the vengeance of the Prince of the Peace did not offend the decorum of the latter and was, above all, far from being cruel."[16]

So far, Manuel had prevailed on every occasion, but the persistence of plots and rumors of imminent disgrace merely underlined the precariousness of his position. Whether, as Pérignon believed, Godoy was forced to turn to the French for support, is debatable. Far more likely was a growing awareness of the *privado* that he needed men of recognized stature in his government to lend it an aura of respectability. The suggestion had originated from the Frenchborn banker Francisco de Cabarrús, who in one forthright moment reminded Godoy of the sad fate of Álvaro de Luna. Though a gifted favorite, he had failed to bring prosperity to the country and had died ignominiously on the scaffold. Manuel had no inclination to see history repeat itself.

His first selection was a man of vast experience who enjoyed a somewhat inflated reputation as an efficient administrator. A native of Seville, Francisco de Saavedra was renowned for his integrity and patriotism. Unluckily, he was of weak physical constitution and often lacked the will to resist demands made by those less honest than himself. Although no admirer of Godoy, Saavedra accepted the ministry of finance on November 21, 1797.

Perhaps Godoy's single greatest domestic coup was to enlist the cooperation of Gaspar Melchor de Jovellanos, a close friend of Cabarrús and a man of many talents. In the public mind, Jovellanos was regarded as the very antithesis of the overweening, hedonistic First Minister: that is, moral, diligent, and responsible. Godoy's desperate need to include Jovellanos in his administration may be seen from his effusive welcome: "My friend, you are now in the inner five; the Ministry of Justice has been designated yours, and the nation will receive the benefit of your talent. Ignorance will be banished, and the judicial processes will not be debased under the cover of force or of parties wishing to suppress innocence. Come as soon as possible . . ."[17] The truth was considerably more muted; both men were wary of one another, and the appointment was not without inherent risks on both sides.

Jovellanos, an enlightened educator and jurist, a gifted writer and a humanist to his very marrow, was among the few leading figures to discern merit in Godoy's reformist policies. In 1794 he had founded the *Real Instituto Asturiano,* in his native Gijón. By emphasizing practical needs, such as the applied sciences, modern languages, and manual skills, he implicitly pointed out the glaring deficiencies in Spanish higher education, still the jealously guarded preserve of the church. Only with much difficulty had Godoy persuaded a highly reluctant Carlos IV to lend the royal patronage to the pioneering project.

The following year saw the publication of Jovellanos's *Informe sobre la ley agraria (Report on the Agrarian Law),* which, despite its innocuous title, was a thoughtful attempt to rectify abuses and suggest remedies to raise productivity. Without Godoy's active support, the work probably never would have seen the light of day; in a public display of gratitude, Jovellanos dedicated the report to the progressive First Minister. Immediately the *Informe* aroused the enmity of the church and other large landowners, in no small measure owing to criticism of the pernicious practice of the *mayorazgo,* or property held in entail. On a more personal level, Manuel appreciated the strictures directed against the *Mesta,* the powerful sheep-raisers' association; as a youth, he remembered watching helplessly as vast flocks of sheep trampled destructively over agricultural land in his native Extremadura. Predictably enough, the Inquisition denounced the author of the *Informe* as a subversive, but, thanks partly to Godoy, the inquiry was temporarily suspended.

In all probability, Jovellanos would have been content to spend his remaining years furthering the *Instituto,* far from the petty intrigues and moral laxity of Madrid. Then, to his great surprise, he learned on October 16, 1797, that he had been appointed ambassador to the Court of Czar Paul I, in St. Petersburg. Once more, Godoy intervened, offering Jovellanos instead the more appropriate position of minister of justice. In the *Memorias,* a passing mention is made of an "enemy" (unspecified, but presumably Caballero, whom with another minister, Cevallos, Godoy characterizes as *"mis enemigos capitales"*) who wanted the liberal educator out of the way. Godoy counseled Jovellanos to feign acceptance of the diplomatic post, and then, when the "enemy's" back was turned, prevailed upon the king to name him minister instead. Owing to Jovellanos's many foes at Court, it was no easy task: "How many attempts and efforts it took me to have the King nominate him Minister!" Manuel sighs almost audibly.[18]

In truth, the moralistic Asturian was not always easy to get along with. An altercation with the lighthearted queen was all but inevitable. On one occasion, she asked Jovellanos to favor a certain candidate for a church prebend. The minister denied the request flatly, pointing out that the applicant had not qualified himself at any of the universities. "At which of them," asked María Luisa, "did you receive your education?" "At Salamanca, Madame." "What a pity they forgot to teach you manners!" was the royal rejoinder.[19] Undeterred by this minor setback, Jovellanos later forwarded a remonstrance to Godoy, in which he primly reminded him of his public and moral duties.

Whatever Godoy's influence over the king might have been, it never extended to complete freedom in making cabinet appointments. And yet, apparently in direct contradiction, the Council of Castile was obliged by royal decree to submit legal decisions to the favorite for his approval, an unprecedented humiliation. In an unusually vigorous rebuttal the council denounced the decree's author—presumably Godoy—as a "base seducer who, for the common good, should have been confined long ago to the furthest corner of the universe" and complained that their function as a tribunal should not be judged "by a vassal."[20] If Godoy was the dictator his detractors take pains to depict, he was certainly a most tolerant one. But the reality was far more complex.

Whereas Carlos and María Luisa both regarded him almost as a son, their support was often lukewarm when it came to political decisions. At times, the king exhibited a curious, and by no means always beneficent, ambivalence towards his *amigo Manuel*. Many a time a caustic remark was sufficient to convince those present that the *privado* had fallen from the royal favor, only to see him reassert himself once the king's tantrum had blown over. He often felt exasperated, knowing that his rivals received secret encouragement from the very monarch who relied so heavily on him. He sincerely wished to be done with it all on more than one occasion, but each time the king rejected his petition to resign office. Unable to step down or govern effectively, Godoy struggled on as best he could.

Faced with such obstacles, his achievements are all the more remarkable. His performance as First Minister is noteworthy precisely because his power was never absolute. Even if a generous allowance is made for the vainglorious boasting that occupies entire pages—even chapters—of the *Memorias,* the residue is still most impressive. Francisco Martí places Godoy "at the crossroads of revolutionary and conservative tendencies: a reformer in education, economics, and religious matters, and a stabilizer in the political and social realm."[21] Yet, when Spain's progressive ministers of the Enlightenment are listed in standard histories, the name of Manuel Godoy is frequently omitted.

The institutions founded largely because of Godoy's patronage date from the very beginning of his administration and proceed unimpeded during the course of two costly wars. It has been asserted, quite erroneously, that his policies marked a reaction to the advances made during the reign of Carlos III. The exact opposite is the truth. Already in 1793, Godoy encouraged the founding of the First Veterinary College, followed by the establishment of the Royal Medical College two years later. At his instigation, hospitals and workshops to manufacture surgical instruments sprang up around the country. His most cherished project was the School for the Deaf and Dumb, in which connection he is said to have learned the rudiments of sign language in order to communicate with the hard-of-hearing Goya. Manuel's interest in the natural sciences found expression in the magnificent botanical gardens near the Duchess of Alba's estate in Sanlúcar de Barrameda, at the mouth of the Guadalquivir. Such was the insensate fury of the mob after Godoy's fall in 1808 that it vented its anger by destroying the collection of exotic plants he had introduced—guilt by association carried to an irrational extreme.

Under Godoy's aegis, even that most Sisyphean of labors, the overhaul of the university system, was undertaken in one particularly optimistic moment. The reforms effected were modest for a host of reasons. Despite the conservative cast of most of the faculty at Salamanca, the university nevertheless had acquired a reputation for producing dissidents such as Picornell and, to a lesser extent, the poet Meléndez Valdés, who for a time was a professor of literature. Godoy himself appears to have been of two minds. On the one hand, he permitted the publication of the increasingly outspoken *Semanario erudito y curioso de Salamanca,* and limited censorship to topics pertaining to religion and the monarchy. Yet, at the same time, he forbade the appearance of *El Académico,* much to the displeasure of Meléndez Valdés and others who generally supported the favorite.[22] His inconsistent attitude as often as not reflected some twist or change in domestic politics.

In contrast to many liberal thinkers of the period, Godoy's humanitarian instincts were not confined merely to abstract theories. As First Minister he was in a position to act, to use his influence on behalf of luckless individuals. An illuminating incident is recounted by Lord Holland, who had met Godoy during a sojourn in Spain. A young Englishman named Powell had been taken prisoner while serving with Miranda's rebellious army in South America. As a mercenary, he was sentenced not to death, but worse: life imprisonment in the fetid fortress of Omoa. His father, the chief justice of Canada, hurried to England to seek the help of Lord Holland, who had on occasion corresponded with the Prince of the Peace. Armed only with a personal letter from the English nobleman, the unhappy father made his way to Spain, even though hostilities between the two countries had broken out. Not only did Godoy receive him at Aranjuez and listen to his story, but to the father's surprise—and boundless joy—undertook to secure the young man's release. Manuel personally obtained an order signed by the king and, as a further act of kindness, also provided the chief justice with a passport and passage on a frigate leaving from Cádiz for the West Indies.[23]

Such individual attentions were little known and seldom reported, in contrast to the innumerable exaggerated reports of Godoy's venality. Whatever else he may have been, he was no propagandist or demagogue; his innocence of public relations would dismay the modern officeholder. At no time did he make a serious attempt to seek a better rapport with the common people. Being of relatively humble background himself, he had no desire to be reminded of his modest origins. His imposing array of titles notwithstanding—indeed, largely on that very account—Manuel felt a growing sense of isolation. Hounded by the Inquisition, despised by the populace as an upstart and the queen's lover, denied the *tú* by which the nobility addressed one another, by 1797 he found his position seriously imperiled:

> The nobles hated him for his improvisation; the people because they preferred to suffer under a deified lord rather than under one of their own number raised to the nobility. Amid all these hatreds it was difficult for him to advance, but his policies were more attuned to the times and were more innovative, more generous than those of the aristocrats stuffed with vanity and litanies, and far more decent than those of that coterie of brutal sutlers, ignorant clergy, and despicable lackeys who [later] surrounded Fernando VII.[24]

Fernando. In the light of later events, the very name conjures up images of cruelty and moral depravity, much of it merited, a fair part not. Such a judgment during the first part of Godoy's career is, however, entirely prochronistic. His pressing need had been to find a suitable tutor for the difficult young prince. Fernando had already tried the patience of a succession of religious teachers, but the selection of a more permanent preceptor could no longer be delayed. In keeping with the benign neglect of the *reyes,* the responsibility for finding the right man naturally fell to their reliable Manuel.

On October 3, 1796, the following brief note in his own handwriting was sent to Don Juan de Escoiquiz: "The King appoints you the Prince's teacher of geography and mathematics." So far, there is no dispute; even Escoiquiz admits that Godoy introduced him to the monarchs: "The favorite praised me highly, and the Queen, saying that my appointment was due to him, commanded me to inform him frequently of the progress made by the Prince." The first divergence appears when the tutor claims that Godoy sought "a docile man who, placed close to the royal youth, would act as a dependable spy. He didn't know me . . ."[25] Few would argue the last point. Manuel had other important matters to attend to, and, despite later disclaimers to the contrary, the search had been a cursory one at best. His hasty decision was to have the direst consequences, nothing less than a brush with death and over forty years in exile.

5

A ROYAL BRIDE FOR

MANUEL

No single error in judgment was to pursue Godoy as remorselessly as his selection of Escoiquiz. Both antagonists have left us their memoirs purporting to describe the same events. Two facts, heatedly denied by the respective authors, immediately become clear. First, Escoiquiz sought the position with every means at his disposal, not shunning crass adulation, and owed his nomination entirely to Godoy. Secondly, the Prince of the Peace was delighted with the choice he had made. Although hedged with retrospective qualifiers, his enumeration of Escoiquiz's abilities seems factual enough; after all, to admit that he had engaged an incompetent would have been to acknowledge gross dereliction of duty. Having been instructed by the king to engage an ecclesiastic as tutor for the Prince of Asturias, Godoy interviewed several candidates:

> When it became known what was being sought, one of the aspirants to the honor was Canon Escoiquiz. His presence, his outward bearing, and his conversation inclined me towards him. Escoiquiz had often visited my house and seemed to have allied himself to the Enlightenment . . . I checked into reports, and his were the most advantageous. He was regarded very highly by the most respected people at Court in matters of art, science, taste, talents, moderation, prudence, fine feelings, and decorum. They added the fact that this meritorious man was being persecuted on account of his knowledge and was being oppressed by his chapter of the cathedral. This persecution, as it was referred to in all good

faith by those who extolled his learning, his gifts and morals, was one more reason to incline me in his favor.[1]

One may question whether the selection process was quite that thorough. War with England had been declared the same month in which Godoy made the fateful appointment, and no doubt military considerations were uppermost in his mind.

From the beginning, Escoiquiz set about the task of commending himself to the favorite. His dual position of canon and chaplain afforded him plenty of time to pen several memoranda to Godoy; it is not for nothing that in colloquial Spanish a *canonjía* has come to mean a sinecure. Escoiquiz's tracts had definite political overtones that in part reflected the ideas he had picked up at the *tertulias* held by Manuel, who now had his own impressive house in Madrid. The canon's assiduous flattery culminates in a public announcement to the effect that "the extraordinary preoccupation of running the war has not prevented his Excellency, the Duke of Alcudia in his capacity as First Secretary of State and protector of public education, from attending to the promotion of such an important project."[2]

Not many historians have written kindly about the canon; if anything, he has suffered more grievously at their hands than has Godoy. One of the few to attempt a partial exoneration is Francisco Martí, who believes that Escoiquiz was motivated as much by loyalty to his pupil and a desire to restore a higher moral tone to the nation's rulers as he was by personal ambition. Certainly, as Fernando's tutor, he played a decisive role in the impressionable prince's upbringing. Whether at court or elsewhere, the bookish cleric was well cast as the *éminence grise*. But such positions do not afford lifetime tenure. On his charge's return to Spain in 1814 as *el rey deseado,* Escoiquiz found himself first ignored and then exiled, most appropriately, to the city of San Fernando. Finally, he settled down in Ronda, where he recorded his memoirs shortly before his death in 1820. In old age, he had little choice but to swallow his pride and overlook his ex-student's ingratitude. Without Fernando, and indirectly Godoy, he was nothing, and he knew it. Understandably, his recollections concentrate almost entirely on his years as the prince's tutor.

Not a word of reproach escapes the canon's lips on the subject of Fernando; quite the contrary. Escoiquiz sees himself as chosen by Providence to defend the Prince of Asturias—and by extension Spain—from the depravations and ambitions of a venal favorite bent on arrogating all power for himself. On one family occasion, Escoiquiz confided to his assembled relatives that, "in this unhappy kingdom in which a favorite rules everything," there was one position more than any other in which he might serve his country. With unwitting irony, he informed them that as Fernando's preceptor he would "fill him with the best thoughts and teach him so that his reign will make Spain fortunate."[3] Tragically, Fernando learned far too well from his designing mentor.

Despite the strained posturing, Escoiquiz's memoirs contain several illuminating passages. Not only was he an eyewitness to many of the events described, but in some cases also a participant. On the subject of Godoy, he is biased to the point of grotesque distortion. In the face of the "tyrannical oppression of Godoy," he asks rhetorically, "Who was the first to fling himself forward to fight this monster, to reveal his infamies, to attack him face to face, to accuse him as a tyrant and traitor in the eyes of the world . . . to overthrow the colossus and save the august Prince and his beloved homeland by running the imminent risk of losing his life on a scaffold as a traitor?"[4]

Such fantasy can readily be disproved by referring to official correspondence. Godoy, of course, had no reason to recall Escoiquiz with affection, but the favorite's version of the same events is in its main thrust corroborated by other witnesses. The canon not only actively sought the post of tutor, but continued to flatter the *privado,* terming him—correctly as it so happens—the "born defender of the branch of public education." On New Year's Day 1798, Escoiquiz dedicated a laudatory *Oda Genetlíaca (Astrological Ode)* in twenty stanzas to Godoy. With all due deference, the poet placed him above the Greek heroes, praise that even Manuel might have found excessive. The work has been lost to posterity, but Moratín and others who read it unhesitatingly damned it as a neoclassical vapidity. Even following Godoy's temporary fall from power, Escoiquiz continued to hymn the glories of the man who "opened so many doors to my hopes." Like numerous others at court, the tutor was uncertain how to assess Godoy's first dismissal and whether it presaged his own. Yet, even as he was eulogizing the favorite, he became cognizant of hitherto unsuspected possibilities for himself and his royal pupil.

Almost certainly Manuel was slow to realize that Escoiquiz was poisoning Fernando's mind against him. In all probability, it had been a gradual process. At first, the canon shared tutorial duties with other pedagogues, and thus would not have exercised full control over the prince. One can only surmise that the conversations between teacher and pupil became more confidential and less academic as time passed. Whether or not Fernando "resented the exclusion and isolation imposed by Godoy, who systematically kept him from knowing matters of state"[5] is conjectural; Godoy fiercely denied the charge and asserted just the opposite. At what precise point he began to suspect the canon's machinations is uncertain, though it may well have coincided with his own short-lived removal from office in 1798. Thus, his appraisal of Escoiquiz's baleful influence on Fernando is a synthesis of several years:

> To take possession of the mind of his disciple at a tender age, to make it conform to his mold, to inspire him with distrust for all men, to arouse his ambition, to flatter him and create difficulties which would always require his advice and help, to prepare his domination over the boy in the future, and to acquire a powerful influence over the parents for the time being—such was the plan of Canon Escoiquiz.[6]

Godoy, usually magnanimous in outlook, could not refrain from castigating the meddlesome cleric as the *"ángel de las tinieblas"* ("angel of darkness") and commenting that "his only talent was intrigue and the art of deception." Escoiquiz, who neglected few opportunities to criticize the favorite's morals, was himself living in a blissful state of *barraganería* (concubinage), and had produced two children out of wedlock. Instead of imparting a like measure of human warmth and understanding, he chose to inculcate an implacable hatred upon the mind of his impressionable young student. Godoy avers that "Prince Fernando never learned to love but only how to mistrust and fear. He feared in his adolescence, he feared in his youth, and he went through life fearing and suspecting, without ever believing in the honesty of any man, not even Escoiquiz himself."[7] A later historian has seen little reason to quarrel with this judgment:

> [Fernando's] lack of culture, the permanent distrust, his liking for coarse people and things, his cowardice and the absence of any political program other than the maintenance of his personal absolutism—these constitute the dominant traits in Fernando VII, and if one has to judge by the results, one cannot doubt the disastrous influence of his tutor.[8]

Preoccupied with foreign policy and facing the open hostility of ministers such as Caballero and Cevallos in the council, Godoy failed to perceive that the real danger to his position lay much closer at hand, indeed, within the very family to whom he owed everything. And then, quite unexpectedly,

Manuel gave his enemies new grounds to fear the worst: he was about to became related to his royal benefactors by marriage. This was all the court gossips needed. Was it possible the *choricero* now aspired to the very throne of Spain? Perhaps Fernando's inchoate fears were not so foolish after all.

There was also the matter of Josefa Tudó. Pepita, as her friends called her, was generally regarded as Godoy's common-law wife, even, it was rumored, his secret spouse. María Luisa resented his lack of propriety and inattentiveness, while the church deplored a relationship that flouted the sacred institution of matrimony. Nevertheless, for excellent reasons that require no elucidation, Godoy's enemies hesitated to point the finger at one living in an irregular union. A less perilous course was to denigrate the character and background of the powerful minister's *querida*. Accordingly, Pepita was reviled as lacking in intelligence and social distinction, an object he had "picked up from the gutter" merely to satisfy his "depraved taste."[9]

The truth, as so often in this narrative, was the exact reverse. Pepita was the daughter of a distinguished, if impecunious, artillery officer whose lineage was strikingly similar to that of Godoy's own family. Twelve years younger than Manuel, she had been born in Cádiz on May 19, 1779. Accompanying her to solicit a pension at San Ildefonso were her widowed mother, Doña Catalina, and her two sisters, Magdalena and Socorro. Pepita was introduced to the Prince of the Peace by the *Bailío* Valdez, minister of marine, at one of the former's weekly public audiences, which always attracted a throng of petitioners. The favorite was quick to notice the striking eyes and sensuous lips of this southern beauty, and they soon became lovers. Two sons, Manuel and Luis, were born of this *amorío*. Godoy set himself up openly as the defender of the family's honor, and once warned off one of Socorro's admirers with the admonition *"Soy protector de esta familia, es bien público"* ("It's well known I'm the protector of this family").[10] Had Manuel and Pepita regularized their relationship from the outset, many of the later calumnies—including the damaging charge of bigamy—might well have been avoided. Instead, he embarked on a course that led to grief for all concerned.

To be fair, the idea of marrying into the royal family did not originate with him, nor can he be said to have evinced much enthusiasm for the project. Following the Maltese fiasco, Carlos IV and María Luisa had concluded that it was time for Manuel to marry and settle down. The queen had also been shocked one evening to discover Manuel and Pepita enjoying an intimate supper in the Escorial, and feared for a moment that they were already married. Speed was therefore of the essence. Quite obviously, the future wife of the Prince of the Peace must be of the aristocracy, so why not one of the royal blood? A diligent search was undertaken, during which a few tarnished skeletons tumbled out of the Bourbon closet. One such rapscallion was none other than the Infante Luis, the younger brother of Carlos III of venerated memory.

From his youth, Luis had been destined for the church, and on that basis his life was assumed to be as chaste as that of his widowed brother, the king. One day, he was unable to participate in the morning hunt owing to a mysterious illness; closer investigation revealed that he was suffering from a disreputable disease totally unbecoming a high churchman. Worse was to follow, for "later it was divulged that His Highness was keeping three chorus girls of the lowest type in the royal palace."[11] An ecclesiastical career was now presumably out of the question, and so a morganatic marriage was arranged with a lady of the minor nobility, Doña María Teresa Vallabriga y Rozas. Three children were born of this union, a son, Luis María (who became a cardinal and archbishop of Seville and Toledo), and two daughters, María Teresa and María Luisa. By the terms of a royal ordinance dated March 23, 1776, it was decreed that the issue of the marriage would have no claim to a royal title other than the courtesy of being addressed as "Your Excellency."

In the summer of 1783, Goya stayed four weeks with Don Luis at his country estate, and painted a charming family group in an informal setting. Demonstrably, the artist took an immense liking to the unpretentious domestic circle, especially the young daughter María Teresa. A delightfully curious child, she peers over Goya's shoulder, her head coyly bent to one side, her large, expressive eyes directed straight at the viewer. A second canvas of María Teresa, painted the same year, is less successful. The formal pose with her Pekingese at her feet lacks the spontaneity of the previous likeness, and seems to presage an early unchildlike seriousness.

Fourteen years had passed since that carefree summer in the country. And then suddenly came the official court announcement: Their Majesties were pleased to bestow the hand of their seventeen-year-old cousin in marriage to the Prince of the Peace. With some truth, Manuel claims he was merely obeying his sovereign's wish in that "Carlos IV gave orders for the celebration of this marriage in such a way that between his order to me and his notification to the Council no time elapsed at all. I obeyed him in this matter with the same loyalty and submission as in all the other acts of my life."[12] This is one of the rare references to his wife contained in the *Memorias;* Pepita is passed over in complete silence. In any event, the wedding took place on September 16, 1797. To signify the royal approval, the king graciously allowed the bride to avail herself of the titles her father had enjoyed before his regrettable lapse. Manuel had now officially gained entrée into the royal family.

The news of his marriage was the subject of widely differing interpretations. Pérignon regarded the union as Godoy's "strongest defense against his numerous enemies. He has gained it through his devotion to Their Catholic Majesties and his services rendered to the Crown.[13] Others viewed his latest advancement far less charitably. The *choricero* was stigmatized in many quarters as a bigamist, though no evidence, then or since, has ever been adduced regarding a previous marriage to Pepita. Typical of the many pasquinades that made the rounds is the following:

> To call you Your Excellency or rather Your Highness,
> public opinion has not yet determined,
> doubting, great sir, whether you are married,
> and who exactly is your wife.[14]

The general consensus was that somehow or other Godoy had successfully wormed his way into the ruling house. Escoiquiz assiduously nurtured the nascent fear in Fernando's mind that it was now the intention of the *valido* to usurp the succession to the throne. The prince's tutor sincerely believed, as did many others, that Godoy had married above his station as part of some diabolical stratagem. How could the family of the Infante Don Luis (he had died in 1785 and been buried in a humble church) possibly countenance such a *mésalliance?* In fact, the relatives of María Teresa de Borbón considered the match extremely advantageous. The bride wrote to the queen: "I know, Madame, how much I owe my husband; it is to him that all my relatives owe the good fortune which they presently enjoy, I myself more than anyone else, for my entire happiness consists of loving this husband and being his; that is the strongest reason I could have to sacrifice myself, were that necessary, on behalf of Your Majesties who have granted me such a husband."[15] How spontaneous the above letter was will never be known. It does, however, stand in marked contrast to María Teresa's later condemnation of her husband.

It would be fruitless to deny that Godoy enriched himself outrageously and often tactlessly in the course of his meteoric career. It is equally true that none of his relatives or friends ever had reason to complain of his munificence. Manuel accumulated huge sums and disbursed them with equal abandon. He rescued María Teresa's younger sister from penury by providing an annual pension of ten thousand gold pesos; her brother, besides being able to style himself infante, also received the lucrative archbishopric of Toledo. As a special royal favor, the remains of the Infante Luis were transferred with all due pomp to the royal mausoleum at the Escorial. The recipients of such tangible consideration were fulsome in their gratitude to Manuel, but, like so many others, they showed no hesitation in repudiating their benefactor in later years.

And what of María Luisa? Why had she not only sanctioned but even encouraged the marriage? The queen's ill-wishers, to whom a *liaison amoureuse* with the favorite was one of the few certainties in life, were either nonplussed or else regarded it cynically as yet another devious ploy on the part of the presumed lovers. Or perhaps it was all a royal maneuver designed to detach *la Tudó* from Manuel's embrace. That the queen could have been motivated by maternal goodwill did not occur to any of them.

The marriage was a disaster from the outset. Manuel's unwillingness to divorce himself from the company of Pepita, and the attention devoted to the *reyes* and matters of state meant that little was left for his young bride. Her disappointment and resentment would only intensify with the passage of time. Goya's masterful psychological portrait of María Teresa heavy with Godoy's child reveals all the pent-up embitterment she must have felt toward her husband. Gone is the sprightly innocence of a happy childhood as the dejected countess stares blankly into the middle-distance.

Naturally, no such dismal thoughts were contemplated that autumn wedding day in 1797. Carlos and María Luisa naively assumed that, once married, Manuel would remain faithful. This he was, unfortunately, not to his wife, but to Pepita with whom he continued in unashamed cohabitation. The Prussian ambassador, Rohde, was indignant that "after he had drawn the dowry of five million reales, Godoy had the effrontery to return to *la Tudó* immediately, with whom he now lives more intimately than ever. He has brought her to live in his house."[16] Other than the size of the dowry, Rohde's complaint was true enough. At least the favorite refused to play favorites with his ladies; as his wife now had the right to be addressed as the Countess of Chinchón, he later insisted that Pepita likewise be raised to the nobility with the title of Countess of Castillofiel. More remarkably, the queen in time seems to have accepted the ménage à trois with cheerful good grace, and in later years regarded Pepita, Teresa, and the resultant offspring with genuine motherly affection.

From this domestic scene, Godoy's attention was soon diverted elsewhere. For some time, it had been felt in Paris that Pérignon was far too close to him and that the situation warranted investigation. Already a Mademoiselle Jeanne Riflon, a *modiste* of dubious repute, had found her way to Madrid as an agent of the Directory. Before long, she was receiving gifts and visits from Manuel, and through him was introduced to the king and queen at court. She quickly became mistress of the situation as well as of both Ambassador Pérignon and the duc d'Havré. With complete candor, she could report back to Paris that "Pérignon has offered to serve as my mentor and zealous protector in Madrid."[17] Overnight, state secrets and delectable scandal filled the air, to the French envoy's intense mortification. Jeanne was sent packing, but only after complaining bitterly about his ingratitude: "After receiving from you proofs of boundless confidence, you who were always my first choice at night!"[18] The ambassador was now the laughing stock of Madrid.

For Godoy, it was a serious matter. Though Talleyrand had come to regard him favorably, the Directory was angered by the Prince of the Peace's laggard prosecution of the war against England. Pérignon was recalled in disgrace on October 1, 1797, and replaced by Truguet, *"jeune beau, élégant, poli et très causant"* ("elegant young beau, polite, and with much to say")— just the qualities to impress the queen, who was undergoing yet another of her recurrent huffs with Manuel. Truguet, a Jacobin ex-minister of marine as well as a friend of Barras and also of Saavedra, might indeed have been attentive when flattering the ladies, but as an ardent revolutionary he expressed himself forthrightly even during a formal audience with the king. Cabarrús had already warned Godoy that the new ambassador was ill-disposed towards him as First Minister, and was bent on securing his dismissal. When Truguet presented his credentials to Carlos IV wearing *pantalón y botas* instead of the prescribed diplomatic attire, a pained shudder ran down every well-bred courtier's spine.

This was merely the beginning. Having first assured the bewildered monarch that he, Truguet, would raise His Most Catholic Majesty to the "level of the luminaries of the century"—he failed to specify how it was to be done with such unpromising material—he launched into his main theme:

> Sire, the Executive Directory of the French Republic, desirous to maintain and further strengthen the alliance which unites our two nations, has appointed me Ambassador to Your Majesty's Court. The security of the alliance is based not only on our common interests, but also on our sacred and solemn pledges; it is also founded on the virtues of Your Majesty and the political talents of the First Minister at his side.[19]

The latter remark was only the opening salvo at Godoy. The favorite was further disconcerted by Truguet's insistence that all émigrés on Spanish soil be disciplined and the war extended to Portugal should that nation continue to lend assistance to the English. His speech at an end, Truguet turned his back on the king—an unheard-of breach of etiquette—and stalked out of the chamber.

In the face of these insulting demands, Godoy fell back on his usual temporizing tactics. He had been reduced to the status of a French vassal, barely surviving on sufferance and on the implicit condition that he comply with orders from Paris. Out and out evasion was no longer possible, only a humane approach to what had to be done. The émigrés were ordered confined to the island of Mallorca, amid mutterings from the local inhabitants, who knew they would be called upon to bear the financial brunt. Godoy suffered a further setback at the hands of his supposed allies when the Directory refused to accept Cabarrús's credentials as Spanish ambassador on the specious grounds of his French birth.

The Prince of the Peace hoped he could still wield influence through his unofficial representative in Paris, Eugenio Izquierdo. A native of Navarre and at one time director of the Library of Natural History in Madrid, Izquierdo was frequently entrusted by Godoy to carry out delicate assignments. Manuel praised his friend as "sagacious, very capable, and cautious in all types of negotiations";[20] when Izquierdo was expelled from the French capital on the pretext that he was a spy, it was more than a personal rebuff to the favorite. Simply put, the Directory had no further use for either Spaniard.

All appeared lost when Truguet insisted on a private audience with the king, during which he insolently demanded that the *privado* be dismissed. The revolutionary envoy had openly boasted that he himself had made "noticeable inroads on the Queen's heart; this will in time serve the turn of the Republic,"[21] and he must have assumed that likewise the king would offer little or no resistance. Like so many others, Truguet had formed his assessment of Carlos by lending credence to palatine prattle; the royal streak of stubbornness, resentment, contrariness—call it what you will— that smoldered beneath an impassive exterior merely required such an affront to kindle into flame. To the ambassador's astonishment, the king loyally stood by his First Minister and roundly scolded the boorish diplomat.

Even so, Godoy's usefulness to the Crown had become gravely impaired. Carlos, unnerved by his own uncharacteristic display of decisiveness, soon reverted to the more congenial role of vacillating monarch. He began to pay heed to the biased counsel of Saavedra, "an excessively weak and malleable man" (Pereyra's phrase) and especially to Caballero, that scoundrel for all seasons. The assertion by Madol that at this critical point Saavedra had become María Luisa's lover is no more than scurrilous conjecture. Godoy's first dismissal from office, though contradictory in many details and capable of diverse interpretations, resulted from an accumulation of factors and not from any single bedroom intrigue.

By 1798 Spain's economic position had become critical. Revenue had steadily fallen far short of covering the nation's expenses, seriously aggravated by two prolonged wars. The struggles against France and England cost the treasury respectively 2,300 and 4,800 million reales, amounts by no means covered by loans, new taxes, and other desperate measures. To finance the war against the Convention, Carlos IV issued *vales reales* (promissory notes) to the value of 963 million, and for the war against England another 796 million. The *vales* quickly lost their face value, with resulting accelerated inflation. In September 1798 the king signed the decree authorizing the sale by auction of property belonging to charitable institutions in return for an annual payment of 3 percent of the amount received.[22] As a result, many of the poorer monasteries and churches found themselves in financial difficulties, for which Godoy was duly blamed.

Another problem was that the war against England lacked the enthusiastic popular support of the earlier war against revolutionary France. The *donativos patrióticos* and the *préstamos voluntarios,* the patriotic gifts and voluntary loans, were consequently made far less willingly. In a circular soliciting loans dated April 24, 1798, Saavedra confessed that great harm had been done to the public treasury by substituting the *vales reales* for coin of the realm.[23] There were also other abuses. In Godoy's census of 1797, the number of *hidalgos* had declined to an estimated 403,000, some 4 percent of the total population; two years later, the Crown again had recourse to selling titles to raise money for the war.[24]

The war with England and near-national bankruptcy may well have been the main causes of Godoy's undoing. Given Spain's situation, the crisis was all but inevitable, no matter who was First Minister. Richard Herr believes that "a less impulsive first secretary than Godoy might have postponed open hostilities, but the Anglo-Spanish struggle was basically a product of Spain's industrial renaissance and the French Revolutionary wars, not the levity of an untried statesman."[25] Nevertheless, the Duke of Alcudia was reviled as the *Duque de la Alcuza* (Duke of the Oil Cruet), one of the kinder epithets bestowed on Godoy.

A contributory cause may well have been an inadvertent *lapsus linguae* on his part. In a letter welcoming Jovellanos to the post of minister of justice, he allegedly had used the words "Come then, my friend, and take your place in our executive directory." Such phraseology was redolent of Republicanism, and Caballero wasted no time in drawing the offensive wording to the king's attention. In vain, Godoy protested that it had been maliciously miscopied from the original draft, which clearly stated the monarchical form of government. Carlos remained unconvinced, and María Luisa showed no inclination to spring to Manuel's defense. His last support was about to collapse.

The queen had indeed been badly treated by the disrespectful *valido*. He had insulted her to her face, humiliated her in public with cutting remarks, and at times quite forgotten their respective stations in life, treating her as an equal or even an inferior. Whether she wished to see him deprived of his official position is not clear; in all likelihood, she had little idea herself as to what she hoped to accomplish. María Luisa was not by nature an underhanded woman. From the scant evidence available, it does seem that the slighted queen unburdened herself to Saavedra and, more surprisingly, to Jovellanos.

There is a Jansenistic vein in Spanish Catholicism from which Jovellanos was not exempt. Cabarrús had given his moralistic friend vivid descriptions of the supposed nocturnal relationship between Godoy and María Luisa. One evening, against his better judgment, Jovellanos attended a dinner given in the First Minister's home. To the host's right sat his wife of a few weeks, and unashamedly to his left sat Pepita. His hand quivering, Jovellanos recorded the indignation in his diary: "My mind could not bear it. I neither ate nor spoke, I couldn't calm my feelings. I took to my heels, I remained at home all evening, troubled and downcast, wishing to do something, yet wasting time and intelligence."[26]

Admittedly, Jovellanos was exasperated by the lax morality surrounding him, but this is a far cry from instigating Godoy's ouster. Most likely he followed a middle course, in keeping with his character. A Spanish historian concludes: "I don't think that he would have taken part in an intrigue fomented by those at Court, but neither would he have defended him in the Council presided over by the king where the crisis was resolved."[27] Without too much difficulty, Carlos was persuaded that Manuel must go; the only questions were how and when. Did the king suddenly turn hostile towards the favorite? Muriel holds that "Jovellanos and Saavedra were opposed to a tragic end for the *valido* and took a stand against having a harsh punishment meted out to him as the king himself had come to wish."[28] As a compromise, Jovellanos favored exiling Godoy to the Alhambra, à la Aranda, without further delay. He was overruled by Saavedra who felt that dismissal from office was sufficient ignominy. A document to this effect was drawn up and presented to Carlos for the royal signature, but in typical fashion that irresolute monarch kept the order in his pocket for a week as he agonized over Manuel's fate.

The climax came on March 28, 1798, following a stormy meeting of the council, over which the king presided. In a studied attack, an emboldened Saavedra proposed a reduction in military expenditures by disbanding some army camps close to the Portuguese border, an area in which the favorite had always shown a special interest. Godoy was stung into protesting the foolishness of such an economy while the threat of an English advance through neighboring territory still remained. Saavedra refused to yield, secure in the king's support. "No," Carlos stated unequivocally for once in his life, "these camps serve no purpose," whereupon the meeting was adjourned.

Godoy immediately recognized the hopelessness of his position, and requested the king to relieve him of his portfolio. Though he had heard the same request many times previously, now Carlos acceded without hesitation, if without enthusiasm. Familiar habits were hard to break, and none was more deeply ingrained than having Manuel run the country for him. The document of dismissal bore every mark of Carlos's consideration for a loyal minister:

> Mindful of the repeated requests you have made to me, both orally and in writing, to be relieved of your posts as Secretary of State and Sergeant-Major of my royal bodyguard, I have granted your repeated petitions, excusing you from the said two positions . . . You will retain all your honors, income, emoluments and right of access to the Court which you now possess. Remain assured that I am extremely satisfied with the zeal, love, and ability with which you have fulfilled everything under your authority. I shall always be extremely grateful to you as long as I live, and I shall always give you unmistakable proof of my gratitude for your singular services.
>
> Aranjuez, March 28, 1798
> Carlos. To the Prince of the Peace.[29]

Taking his leave from the king, Manuel embraced his successor, Francisco Saavedra, and handed him the keys of office. Few among those present doubted that Godoy would return in some capacity or other. In later years, he recalled his first ministry with justifiable pride:

> Many, many people lamented my retirement, but not one of them shed tears for any harm suffered at my hands to his reputation or possessions. I never wronged anyone, not even my enemies. The fortresses and castles did not confine a single victim; there were no state prisoners. Even the Inquisition kept its jails empty; peace reigned everywhere.[30]

An exaggeration undoubtedly—self-composed testimonials are inherently suspect—but there is an imposing amount of truth for all that. If Godoy is judged dispassionately on his merits as a minister of state, the resultant evaluation is generally favorable. Herr states that "far from being the incompetent paramour many saw in him, Godoy shunned the reaction of Floridablanca and navigated resolutely along the paths charted earlier by Carlos III and Campomanes and more recently by Aranda."[31] Another historian describes Godoy as "an indefatigable worker with an exceptional assiduity which no one can deny,"[32] and places him in the company of Walpole, Pitt, Choiseul, Kaunitz, Patiño, and—one of life's gentler ironies—Floridablanca.

In fact, Godoy's situation had become intolerable. Sadly, he was never trusted by anyone; the progressives questioned his will to continue *las luces,* the traditionalists doubted his competency, the masses detested his lack of moral rectitude, and even the king and queen wavered in their constancy. Few Spaniards knew precisely what they expected of their leaders, but they were nearly unanimous in what they did not want, and that was Godoy. It is all the more remarkable that the favorite performed as well as he did. In her troubled history, Spain has suffered far worse.

6

ENTR'ACTE

Saavedra's ministry was of brief duration. His health had always been precarious at best, and now the exertions of his office forced him to relinquish his duties one by one until he felt unable to continue. In contrast to Godoy's diligence, a noticeable letup occurred under Saavedra; papers remained unsigned, memoranda unread, and daily business unattended to. In August 1798 he tendered his resignation to the king, and only agreed to remain at his post until a successor was chosen. Then, in the same month, Jovellanos took to his sickbed with a mysterious malady and was similarly obliged to give up his cabinet position. In the public mind, such a coincidence naturally required an explanation, which was readily forthcoming: the two ministers had been poisoned, either by the queen or the *choricero*—perhaps even by both. Only the latter point was in dispute.

Godoy's continued presence at court, his direct access to the monarchs, a self-assuredness that verged on conceit—few doubted that his dismissal was a classic case of *reculer pour mieux sauter*. It is improbable that he was in any way instrumental in Jovellanos's political misfortunes, let alone his illness. Exhausted in spirit and body, the minister of justice gave up the futile struggle on August 15 and returned to his beloved institute, in Gijón, to await events. His term in office had lasted barely nine months.

Jovellanos's successor was none other than José Antonio Caballero. Carlos could hardly have made a less fortunate choice. From all accounts, the new appointee was one of those *leguleyos*—pettifogging lawyers—

whose insatiable chicanery is the mainstay of many a Galdosian novel. In addition, he was a drunkard, adulterer, extortioner, and, to round out the picture, a proficient wife-beater. Godoy's earlier description of Escoiquiz is a lyrical panegyric compared to his portrait of Caballero:

> This man given to drink, of ignoble figure, with a short and fatty body, of very limited and crass intelligence, a jaundiced color, of evil visage, his face lacking in luster just like his spirit, blind in one eye and half blind in the other, had the good fortune to enter the judiciary through the influence of an uncle . . . That fox sneaked into power, that new agent of perdition opposed to everything that is good, who never in his whole life conceived in his heart a single generous feeling.[1]

Several paragraphs follow in the same vein. As a portrayal, it would seem a gross caricature, but other verbal likenesses offered by contemporary writers are hardly more charitable. The new *Ministro de Gracia y Justicia* seems to have been that *rara avis,* the perfect villain, down to the last detail. One wag noted that he was neither *graciable, justiciero,* nor even *caballero.*

Why did Carlos IV appoint *aquel hombre de Satanás* (that man of Satan)? Surely, far better qualified men were available. To ascribe Caballero's alarming influence over the king solely to an adulatory tongue is a partial answer at best. His main asset in the king's eyes was his overt dislike of Jovellanos, with whom the *reyes* had never felt at ease. There were also other reasons. Like María Luisa, the king felt irritated at times by Manuel's lack of deference and was not averse to elevating a counterweight at court. In a temperamental outburst, Carlos reportedly had threatened the *privado* with banishment before withdrawing his pronouncement.

No doubt some of these considerations also played a part in the choice of a new First Minister to replace the ailing Saavedra. But, again, the decision was unfortunate. The court tattlers were quick to spew forth their venom: María Luisa, to teach Manuel a lesson, had shamelessly advanced the cause of her latest *amante.* Mariano Luis Urquijo admittedly looked the part. A native of Bilbao, handsome and witty, he was also a man of considerable diplomatic experience far beyond his thirty years. Alquier, Truguet's successor as French ambassador, uncritically accepted the latest rumors and found him "vain, insolent, with haughty and peevish manners, vindictive, and above all very deceitful."[2] Urquijo had become the lover of Godoy's sister Antonia, the Marchioness of Branciforte, newly returned from Mexico, where her husband had served as viceroy.

Godoy's fall from grace and Urquijo's elevation to power momentarily disconcerted Escoiquiz in his ambitious schemes. At first, he was hesitant, believing (as did most courtiers) that the favorite would resume office within a matter of weeks. In January 1799 Fernando's other teacher, the bishop of Ávila, conveniently died, and to the canon's vast relief was not replaced. (For a brief period Godoy's uncle, General José Álvarez de Faria, had charge of the prince's military training; Fernando never became a soldier or took to riding.) Now that Godoy was in apparent disfavor, here was an opportune time for Escoiquiz to advance his own interests at court. Accordingly, the litterateur dashed off two treatises for the royal perusal, the first outlining the evils besetting the kingdom, which he unhesitatingly attributed to the *privado;* and the second enumerating the qualities expected of a good administrator—suspiciously a mirror likeness of the author. If Escoiquiz is to be believed (and here the inferential evidence is strongly in his favor), it was the queen herself who had suggested the project during their several meetings at the palace of Aranjuez. Escoiquiz had no reason to believe that his memoranda had not been well received.

Suddenly, by a royal decree dated January 20, 1800, he was informed that he had been relieved of his duties as tutor to the Prince of Asturias and was instead to take over the vacant canonry in Toledo. He attributes the edict to the queen: "I had noted a new indifference in Her Majesty towards me,"[3] but more likely he had overreached himself by proposing that Fernando be given a seat on the council as part of his regal preparation. Not even Escoiquiz alleges that Godoy had a hand in sending him away from "Babylon," his derisive epithet for the court. His exile in no way prevented him from sending insidious dispatches to Fernando during the next seven years and from preparing the groundwork for the *partido fernandino.*

And Godoy—had he indeed fallen into disgrace or was he still the real power behind the throne? His own appraisal of his position during this two-year hiatus (1798–1800) is less than completely candid:

> Those who have affirmed that my retirement from the leadership and the Court showed a lack of esteem that I owed to Carlos IV are misleading themselves. Others who have written that my resignation was only for the sake of appearances and that during my retirement I continued to direct the affairs of government or influence their course are also deluding themselves.[4]

He expresses the wish that his correspondence with both monarchs might one day be published, as it would exonerate him of "ruling in secret by letter." And he regrets that, while writing his memoirs, he did not have access to this material, adding that "my enemies and assassins who have it in their possession have not published any of it, abundant proof that they did not find anything with which to damage me."[5] He insists that he eschewed politics during this period inasmuch as it would have been improper to "disturb the King's mind and to obstruct the conduct of government." In brief, Godoy disclaims all responsibility for any measures taken by Saavedra and Urquijo during his *villeggiatura*.

Fortunately, a large portion of his correspondence with Carlos and María Luisa has been preserved. The uninhibited spontaneity of the interchanges is in cheerful contrast to the ponderous self-vindicating tone of the *Memorias*. A far more appealing Manuel emerges, in turn overly forward, then abruptly mindful of his dutiful position. At times he is clearly distraught and apprehensive about the future, yet always solicitous and moved by the afflictions of the royal couple as mortal beings rather than as deities removed from the human condition.

The exchange of confidences provides close insight into the true relationship between María Luisa and Manuel. Whatever its origins might have been, the affinity by now was more suggestive of older friend and trusty companion than anything else. Delightfully frank and woefully ungrammatical, the hurried notes—which is what many of them are—enumerate the queen's intimate ailments in unabashed detail; Manuel is the family doctor who prescribes efficacious remedies for anything from the common cold to difficult menstruation. Other letters are devoted to the fickleness of the weather and people in general; the progress of Goya's portraits; the condition of the queen's favorite horse, Marcial; an occasional swipe at the Duchess of Alba; a dissection of the new French ambassador, Alquier, with his *"muy mala cara"* ("his nasty old face"), the extended pregnancy of Manuel's wife and the royal wish to be the child's godparents—hardly subjects brought up with one in disgrace. Nor, one might add, the language of love.

There is also a more serious side. Perhaps to Godoy's surprise, Carlos had finally relieved him as First Minister, a post that could only bring him "new vexations and sorrows." Manuel soon discovered that, contrary to the assurances of the pastoral poets, the life of solitary contemplation was less than idyllic, especially when enemies lurked behind every rock and tree. In a revelatory letter to the queen dated September 26, 1798, he strikes a Romantic pose:

Madam:

A man who is pursued by envy and hated by the unjust cannot rest where their shots may wound him. I know what those people are thinking and saying about me, the very ones who used to obey and fear me, I know to what level of authority they have risen. Is my vigilance then foolish? I am at home everywhere; solitude and ruined walls will afford me pleasure. I want nothing to do with violence, nor have anyone concern himself about me. And so, if Your Majesty knows what I should do and bears feelings of good will towards me, please tell me and I shall obey. Manuel will never do anything else; Manuel, that man who so often has pleased Your Majesties, would not wish to inconvenience you for one moment, but will always remain the same faithful and loyal grateful servant of Your Majesties.

Manuel.

May God cure your sore throat, take care it is not like the bad one you had at the Escorial.[6]

It has become commonplace for historians to accuse the favorite of irresponsibility, of reckless military adventures abroad to bolster his crumbling position at home. Typical is the assertion by Buisman that "Godoy, a favorite of [Carlos's] wife, plunged the country into ruin through senseless wars and a corrupt administration."[7] Godoy's own position is revealed in a letter dated October 19, 1798, and intended only for the king's eyes:

Sire:

Let us take care that the course of foreign affairs not occupy us entirely, for it is not in the true interest of nations, but only gives the appearance of greatness . . . War does not exclude the implementation of useful projects; let the agricultural plan which I instituted continue; may Academies and Military Colleges be founded, as they are urgently needed to contain insubordination and to wage war; reestablish factories, and then commerce will flourish. There is nothing we need from abroad as everything brought to us is harmful. Let us reduce the clergy to the fitting rank of their station, let us separate the social classes so that the hierarchies do not become confused; let us renew the sumptuary laws, punish vice with the rigor of law, remove the rod of justice from corrupt and venal hands, and discipline the judges. Finally, Sire, let us cast off this lethargy so that your name will become immortal, let us do nothing that is merely superficial. Wars are of no concern if we build a solid defense here at home, if the earth is bountiful and our hearts are nourished on the sound precepts of religion; that being so, we need fear no enemy.

Manuel.[8]

These insights as to the true needs of the nation are farsighted enough to be still pertinent today. In his advocacy of strength from within, the stimulation of domestic industries, and an honest judicial system, Godoy is firmly in the tradition of Campomanes, Floridablanca, and the majority of enlightened ministers of the Crown. To this day, he has been denied the credit that is rightfully his.

Another subject to receive frequent attention was the clergy. One group of *eclesiásticos*—no names are given—seemed determined to challenge the royal authority in a temporal matter. For that reason, on August 22, 1799, the queen found herself writing to *amigo Manuel* in great secret on instructions from the king. The prelates were attempting to collect "some of our best revenues, to tie our hands, to make themselves fearsome and more like kings than the king himself . . . With this Bull they will subject us to the Pope and put an end to royal privileges. Don't show this letter to anyone . . ."[9] The allusion to the clerics is something of a mystery, for no trace of any such open challenge to the Crown's rights has been unearthed. Was the threat more imagined than real?

Two days later, María Luisa again alludes to the *papel insultante de los clérigos* for a brief moment before getting down to the main business, that is, her constricted throat, bothersome hot flashes and stomach pains, constipation that requires a poultice, and *mi corazón afligido,* all pointing unmistakably to an early end (in fact the queen lived for another twenty years), but God's will be done, Marcial is trotting magnificently and wants to gallop—all in the same sentence! A week later, having made a miraculous recovery—no doubt thanks to a *pegadito en el estómago*—the queen assures Manuel that he will always be "our true and faithful friend in whom we have no doubts and who in turn need never doubt that we are and will ever remain the same."[10] The uninhibited disclosure of bodily ailments and the ensuing frank discussion was a common topic, even in royal circles: "In those days, sexual problems were regarded quite differently than nowadays, and for that reason there is nothing strange in Luisa of Parma relating her physiological intimacies to the Prince of the Peace."[11]

Their correspondence still leaves many questions unanswered. Often the genesis of events alluded to by both parties remains exasperatingly obscure, no doubt having originated in some private conversation. Moreover, Godoy and the monarchs were frequently separated from one another for several days. This necessitated further caution for they now feared that not even the couriers were entirely to be trusted. Following an ancient tradition, the entire court journeyed from one royal residence to the next with the same regularity as the change of the seasons. Madrid was avoided by Carlos and María Luisa whenever possible, partly because it rekindled memories of the Esquilache riots, but also because of an understandable lack of affection for the reeking capital and its *seis meses de invierno y seis meses de infierno* (six months of winter and six months of hell).

It thus fell to Manuel to inform the *reyes* of what was transpiring in the metropolis. From his opulent city residence, he brought the latest news out to the surrounding circle of country palaces—Aranjuez, San Lorenzo (El Escorial), and San Ildefonso (La Granja, which María Luisa hated from the beginning)—each at a distance of some twenty-five miles from the Puerta del Sol, in the heart of the capital. In the absence of the monarchs, it was only natural that Godoy's public audiences should in time have acquired the trappings of a court: the unvaried protocol, the formal attire, the long receiving line, the exchanged pleasantries with the fortunate few singled out by the Prince of the Peace, the granting of special favors—all more reminiscent of a royal levee than a reception held by a former minister. Granted that he was extraordinarily vain in outward display, but on these occasions his solicitude toward others and his desire to be informed of what was happening in the country fully matched his *amor propio*. Without Manuel, Carlos and María Luisa would have been entirely dependent on the likes of Caballero and other fair-weather sycophants.

In contrast to the weighty ceremonial of the Madrid assemblies, the letters are extremely informal, though not without serious overtones. Once, after telling Manuel the story of a woman who stabbed her lover and then poisoned her husband, the queen assures him that he is *demasiado bueno* toward those who have schemed against him. She adds, "We shall always defend you from your enemies (they are few, but a rotten lot) as we are and always shall remain your true friends." Later, she mentions anonymous assailants, "dogs which bark but do not bite," and candidly admits that "for certain there are many discontented people and if something were to happen we would be the first three victims." Manuel counters that "misery, dissatisfaction, and superstition are the enemies attacking us, and the weapons we are trying to fight with are insufficient and merely serve to encourage the vices themselves; one has to look well ahead . . ."[12]

A note of impending catastrophe is struck in his remarkably prophetic letter written probably sometime in May 1800. It is a strange amalgam of emotion and tortured syntax:

Madam:
If I were to say that Your Majesties were unaware of my qualities, if I were

to suspect that you had forgotten the labors with which I have served you, then indeed Your Majesty would wish me to know the difference between the appreciation with which you honor me and what the people in the kingdom are doing to me. But this, Madam, is not my apprehension. It is the force and violence, I see the kingdom agitated, I detect an unchanging apathy in those who govern, I fear that Your Majesties do not know what is happening, yet I fear even more if you know and do not make changes. The voice of the people fills me with terror, and I am afraid of the vigor of the people when they refuse to acknowledge authority. My humble person, Madam, would be in danger were such an unfortunate event to transpire, only the confidence which reasonable men have in me and the respect which the common people have in my justice might perhaps deflect their energies to shield me. On the other hand, ambition, greed, and unruliness could excite them against the wealth they believe I possess, and one way or another I could easily end up being burnt at the stake. Perhaps I could better serve Your Majesties at some distance, and that was my wish, but if you do not consent, I shall remain until you think otherwise.[13]

These fears must have been broached orally in what, one suspects, was a very frank discussion, and perhaps too dangerous to be committed to writing. The queen's colloquial effusions cannot disguise the fact that the *reyes* felt their rule threatened: the repeated use of key words such as "violence," "enemy," "discontent," "victims," "terror," and "unruliness" is indicative of a widespread malaise that affected the very future of the Spanish monarchy.

Amid all the talk of plots and poultices—often in the same breath—something else had supposedly happened: María Luisa had taken on a new lover. It seems that, during a stay in Caracas, Saavedra had become acquainted with a young soldier named Manuel Malló (or Mallo), who eventually found his way to Madrid. This nonentity from Popayán (now a city in Colombia), presumably thanks to Saavedra, had been introduced to the queen and, so malicious tongues had it, became her lover. Little is known about Malló. D'Auvergne calls him "little more than a proper noun,"[14] though given his one minor claim to posterity, "improper" might be more appropriate. Apparently the queen and Manuel continued to discuss their most personal problems by day; once the evening meal was over, they went their separate ways.

An oft-repeated episode is illustrative of Godoy's continued close relationship with the royal couple during this period of supposed disgrace. Malló had suddenly acquired conspicuous wealth, which he flaunted for all to see; only the gullible king remained ignorant of its source. One day,

Carlos observed the popinjay from Popayán being driven in an ornate carriage drawn by four superb horses. "Manuel, who is this Malló? Where does he get his money?" he asked in all innocence. To which Godoy artfully replied, "Malló hasn't a penny of his own, but they say he's kept by some toothless old woman who robs her husband to enrich her lover." Whereupon the king roared with laughter and turned to his wife: "What do you think of that, eh, Luisa?" "Oh, it is probably only one of Manuel's little jokes," she is said to have replied with a brave smile.

In a further embellishment to the foregoing anecdote, a distraught María Luisa requires the services of Manuel to retrieve some incautious love letters that the ungentlemanly Malló refused to surrender. In an adventure worthy of Don Juan Tenorio, Manuel succeeds in his task, only to retain them so as to blackmail his royal mistress should the need arise. None of this silliness is alluded to in the correspondence, much less in the *Memorias*, for the simplest of reasons: it very likely never occurred.

Another incident is related by that accomplished mischiefmaker, Charles-Jean-Marie Alquier, the new French ambassador and possessor of the *muy mala cara* already mentioned. Not one to disappoint his expectant superiors in Paris, he regaled them with choice tidbits such as the following:

> The evening before the departure, just as the King had retired for the night, there was a scene at half past nine. Malló did not like the idea of the journey, and as you can easily imagine, he hated the Prince of the Peace. When he was ordered to undertake the journey with the Court, he replied in the most insolent tone: "No, I'm not going on the trip!" "I order you!" the Queen shouted. "No, I'm not going. You're a harlot, a wicked woman."[15]

Like Pantalone in the Commedia dell'arte, the king rushed out of his bedroom on cue to find out what was going on, only to be assured that it was all the fault of some foolish servant girl and that he could safely return to his slumbers. Alquier, fearful that he might have shocked Talleyrand (an unlikely event), hastens to add: "These scandalous happenings and terrible anecdotes will seem incredible to you perhaps. But I give you my word of honor that they are true."

Manuel continued to bide his time, confident in his appraisal of the political realities and the queen's ultimate loyalty. To no one's surprise, Malló was eventually banished from court. Meanwhile, as Urquijo had persisted in adding to his enemies by simultaneously infuriating both the church and the French, it became evident that Godoy's return could not be delayed much longer. He now presented himself at court quite openly with the full approbation of the king.

The birth of Manuel's first child on October 7, 1800, had already stirred intense speculation among the foreign emissaries. María Teresa's pregnancy—her third—had been long and difficult, and yet another miscarriage was feared. The queen, in her letters to Manuel, makes frequent mention of the royal wish to be the child's godparents. Naturally, as an experienced mother, she cannot refrain from offering practical advice. As Manuel's wife is a *muger* [sic] *de temperamento ardiente,* a steady infusion of quinine should prove an efficacious remedy. Whatever the treatment, María Teresa finally gave birth to a girl, who was christened Carlota.

The diplomats were not only shocked by the *reyes* making a special journey from the Escorial to Madrid in celebration of the event, but even worse was the spectacle of the infant being baptized in the royal palace by the inquisitor-general. Alquier, who as a deputy had voted *la mort* for Louis XVI, was nevertheless incensed by the breach in court etiquette:

> The Queen, having lived openly and shamelessly, for all Spain to see, with the Prince of the Peace both before and after his marriage, having, besides, had by him two children whose paternity none disputes, quits her Court and goes out of her way to invite and defy all eyes at a religious ceremony whose glamour puts the final touch to the unheard-of distinctions lavished by her on her lover. The decencies are all forgotten; the venerable customs of the monarchy are violated, and the forms set aside for marking the births of the Royal Family are brought into use when the child born is a stranger to the royal blood.[16]

The regicide-diplomat was notorious for his love of scandal and his antipathy toward Spain;[17] nevertheless, many historians have accepted his lively *récits* concerning the queen and Manuel at face value.

By inference, it would seem that Fernando, now aged sixteen, must have remonstrated with his parents on their return to the Escorial against their attendance at the christening of Godoy's daughter. Manuel also appears to have inadvertently contributed to the family altercation, for on October 13, 1800, three days after the baptism, the queen wrote him: "We told Fernando what you had told us in your letter, and we added that he was always to esteem, appreciate, and love you the way we do, and the King added how much you deserved it, and then I told him [Fernando] that he must always esteem and love your relatives, especially your wife and your children."[18] On October 16 María Luisa reassured Manuel that "the King and I will always make sure that Fernando shows you all the appreciation and confidence you deserve, and that he will always continue the friendship of his parents, the King and I, towards you should we no longer be here. While we live we are and always will be your true, sincere, and constant friends, the King and Luisa."[19] Incredibly, the queen remained totally oblivious to the growing danger posed by Fernando and his adherents in the world beyond the confines of the royal palaces.

Admittedly, Lady Holland as well as Alquier and others at court had claimed to note an "indecent likeness" between some of the infantes and Manuel, but by the time her ladyship arrived in Madrid such talk was already rife. It had been damaging enough to portray the queen and Godoy as lovers; even worse, two of the infantes had been positively identified—at least in the public mind—as the illicit fruit of this union. Now that passions have cooled, certain basic questions suggest themselves. If María Luisa was deceiving her husband from an early date, how can *any* of the infantes—including Fernando—be certain of their royal blood? Yet no writer has ever intimated that a single child born prior to the birth of María Isabel on July 6, 1789, was fathered by any other than Carlos. Of María Luisa's fourteen children to survive the first few days (ten, including a set of twins, were born between 1771 and 1788), the paternity of none is questioned except those attributed to Godoy. On what basis are the children born in 1791 and 1792[20] acknowledged to be legitimate (even though these are precisely the years of Godoy's remarkable rise to power) but not Francisco de Paula Antonio, born on March 10, 1794? Was it because María Isabel and Francisco de Paula survived and the two intervening ones did not? By some inexplicable omission, Manuel's brother Luis was never deemed the procreator of Carlos María Isidro, born in 1788 and destined in later life to plunge Spain into the prolonged strife known as the Carlist wars. Even a cursory study reveals the inconsistency of the allegations brought against Godoy and the queen.

What, for example, of Brigadier Juan de Pignatelli, supposedly a well-established recipient of María Luisa's favors prior to Manuel's arrival? The soundest perspective is that of Carlos Pereyra:

> The simplicist doesn't realize that it is all in the realm of conjecture and does not take into consideration the thousand possibilities in behavior hidden from public view. One can only discuss in a guarded way whether María Luisa was a saint or a depraved woman. Godoy may not have been her lover at all, perhaps he might have been for a day, a month, a year, or all the years that elapsed from his arrival at Court to the death of María Luisa. It is the same case with Malló . . .[21]

In other words, we simply do not know. The best guess—the word is used advisedly—is that all the queen's children were legitimate, and that her affairs, if any, were furtive flings of the moment.

One illuminating incident should lay the whole matter to rest. Many years later, during the exile of the *trinidad* in Rome, María Luisa encouraged a match between her son Francisco de Paula, and Manuel's legitimate daughter, Carlota. Even if one concedes the Bourbons' dangerous predilection for inbreeding, a consanguineous marriage between half-brother and half-sister would never have been countenanced. Just as convincing (perhaps even more so) is the fact that Fernando took María Isabel's daughter María Cristina as his fourth wife; had he reason to believe that his betrothed was Godoy's granddaughter, he assuredly would never have entered into such a union. Persuasive evidence is also provided by Goya's brush. The "indecent likeness" seems to have escaped the painter's attention; but then it is always possible that he was not endowed with the penetrating insight of his illustrious superiors at court.

Be that as it may, the artist was certainly indebted to Godoy. Whether the latter had any hand in Goya's promotion to *Pintor de Cámara* in April 1789 is most unlikely; the date is still too early. Within a brief span, however, the two men struck up an acquaintanceship based as much on a shared enlightened outlook as any deep intimacy. Their mutual regard extended to long walks together and the occasional outing in the First Minister's carriage. Goya, in an undated letter to his close friend Martín Zapater, testified to the consideration of the *privado*:

> Martín *mío*: The day before yesterday I arrived from Aranjuez and that's why I haven't answered you. The Minister [Godoy] was kind enough to devote his attention to me, taking me with him on a coach ride and professing the greatest expressions of friendship one can possibly make; he allowed me to eat with my cloak on as the weather was so cold, he learned to speak through sign language, and he stopped eating so as to converse with me. He wanted me to stay until Easter and to paint a portrait of Saavedra (who is his friend) and I would have been delighted to do it but I didn't have a canvas or a shirt to change into, and I left him unhappy and came home.[22]

Some time during 1795, Goya had become friendly with the Duke and Duchess of Alba. After the death of the duke in 1796, Goya spent several months at the Alba estate in Sanlúcar, near Cádiz, comforting the bereaved widow in agreeable fashion. In between tempestuous lovers' spats, he painted two full-length portraits of the strong-willed duchess, which, though brilliant technically, are somewhat lacking in vivacity. Goya was now over fifty, gruff, taciturn, and still quite unsophisticated despite his years at court; the duchess, nearly twenty years younger, yearned for more dashing company. The affair was over, and the saddened artist returned to Madrid and his long-suffering wife amid his gloomy innermost thoughts.

Artistically, the result was the powerful series of engravings known as the *Caprichos*. The eighty etchings form a sequence of biting satire, underlined by Goya's mordant comments that accompany each scene. Grotesque and hallucinatory, they are a devastating summation of Spain's social and political sicknesses. Godoy had once boasted that his name signified *godo soy* and that therefore his ancestry stretched back to the Goths. The king lent his support to this contention by declaring that "it is evident that Manuel is closely related to us," to which María Luisa remarked, "I knew that long ago."[23] Goya's comment in the *Caprichos* is considerably less charitable, notwithstanding his friendship with Godoy. One of the etchings (number 39 in the series) portrays a donkey diligently studying his genealogy; the caption reads: *Hasta su abuelo* ("As far back as his grandfather"). Another scene depicts the same donkey taking the pulse of a prostrate man (Spain perhaps?) with the caustic question, "*¿De qué mal morirá?*" ("What sickness will he die of?") implying, à la Molière, that the patient is in danger of succumbing to the doctor.

Just how Goya hoped to transmute the prophetic visions of the *Caprichos* into a financial success remains a mystery. He laboriously reproduced some three hundred sets of the eighty plates, and on February 6, 1799, they were offered to the public. The result was a commercial disaster of the first order. During the four years that the etchings were on sale, only twenty-seven sets were sold. One might imagine that Manuel was piqued by the unkind cut he had suffered from Goya's burin. Not only had he been held up to public ridicule—hardly a novel experience—but also the moral environment of his ministry had been implicitly castigated. Yet, he chose to overlook the slight and even to help Goya out of his predicament. On Godoy's advice, the king agreed to purchase the original plates for the Royal Printing Office. Furthermore, thanks to a good word from Manuel, the misanthropic artist was appointed First Painter to the King in 1799, the year of the *Caprichos*. Petty rancor was not one of Manuel's failings; possessing a goodly share of other vices, he could afford to be generous of spirit.

There might also have been a very practical reason. In celebration of Godoy's recent marriage, Goya had partially redecorated the favorite's mansion in Madrid. The work consisted of four circular allegories entitled *Commerce, Agriculture, Industry,* and *Science,* displayed at the main entrance; the fourth of these has been lost. In addition, two large paintings, *Spain, Time, and History* and *The Allegory of Poetry,* were commissioned for the library. None of these works is considered among the artist's happier achievements.

In his new court position, Goya embarked on a series of portraits of the royal family, which by extension included Manuel and his wife. At about the same time as his masterful study of the dejected María Teresa, Goya painted her husband on horseback, striking a heroic attitude. Unfortunately, this equestrian canvas has been lost, the greater the pity, for it was generously praised by those who viewed it. Goya refers to the projected painting in a letter to Zapater dated August 2, 1800: "I am making a sketch of the Duke of Alcudia on horseback. He wrote me saying he would send for me and arrange for my lodgings at the royal palace [at Aranjuez] as I would need more time than I thought. I assure you this is one of the most difficult subjects a painter can face. That's the way I feel."[24] No further explanation is offered; instead, a caricature of Godoy seated with his legs crossed is appended for Zapater's amusement. Some critics have discerned in this and in Goya's withholding of Godoy's title of Prince of the Peace an oblique attack on the *privado.* But, at the same time, the artist hastened to assure Zapater of Godoy's personal interest, going so far as to enclose a message from the favorite with his own note attached: "Here is a letter that proves it. I do not know if you will be able to read his writing, which is worse than mine. Do not show it to anyone, don't say anything about it, and send it back to me."[25]

The surviving portrait shows a dissolute Godoy, bedecked in full-dress uniform in a most unmilitary pose, his bulky frame recumbent in an ornamental chair against an incongruous battlefield setting (the date is 1801, the year of the brief War of the Oranges). The angle of the body is awkward, the features are lax, not an ounce of energy stirs in the swollen limbs. A middle-aged acedia has set in, the inexorable cumulation of years of self-indulgence. Undoubtedly it is an accurate physical likeness. One senses the overtones of brutish insensitivity toward his wife; yet, when all is said and done, only half the man emerges. There is no hint of the energetic administrator, the considerate friend, the enquiring mind hidden behind the fleshy exterior.

Just previously, Goya had twice captured the seductive form of the *maja* on canvas, first au naturel and then demurely garbed in a diaphanous

"¡Hasta su abuelo!" (As far back as his grandfather!) (Goya, 1797: Museo del Prado, Madrid)

"¿De qué mal morira?" (What sickness will he die of?) (Goya, 1797: Museo del Prado, Madrid)

ensemble straight out of the harem. One hoary legend may be dispensed with immediately: the shapely contours do not belong to the Duchess of Alba, and indeed, the head and body may well be total strangers to one another.[26] Other critics have speculated that the model might have been one of Godoy's mistresses on the tenuous grounds that both paintings were in his possession at the time of the Aranjuez uprising. Granted, the subject was dear to his heart, but to link him with the original *maja,* however delectable that lady may have been, is sheer supposition. Both versions were listed in an inventory of Godoy's artworks taken on January 1, 1808;[27] three months later, the mob showed admirable discernment and spared them.

The years 1799–1800 saw a veritable deluge of royal portraits issue from Goya's brush. María Luisa, when not complaining about the weather and her concomitant ailments, followed the progress of the portraits as they unfolded. She was as much concerned as to how her horse Marcial, a present from Godoy, would fare on canvas as about herself. To Manuel she wrote on September 24, 1799: "Yesterday it rained very hard, so I have not been able to ride these last two days. Goya is painting me full-length dressed in a mantilla, and they say it is turning out very well. Then he is off to the Escorial and will do me on horseback, as I want him to paint Marcial."[28]

The equestrian portrait is one of Goya's workaday efforts, proficient rather than inspired. María Luisa's mouth is reduced to a smirk, the pose is strained as if the rider were bestriding a stone statue or some lifeless studio animal. No wonder; "I spent two hours and a half raised upon a platform reached by five or six steps," she complained to Manuel, "wearing my hat, my neckcloth, and wool dress so that Goya could go on with what he was doing, and they say it is going well." On October 19 she pronounced herself satisfied with the result: "The portrait on horseback has been completed in three sittings, and they tell me it is even more like me than the one with the mantilla."[29] Typically, the queen was mainly worried throughout lest the flies cause poor Marcial to bite into his bit; her own portrayal was incidental.

A few weeks later (and innumerable colds, headaches, and bleedings as well), the talk was once more of royal portraits. On April 22, 1800, María Luisa wrote to *amigo Manuel:* "We are so glad you are well, also your wife, let's hope that everything will turn out all right. We are also glad that she is being painted." The reference was to María Teresa's labored pregnancy and to the magnificent psychological study underway. The queen contin-

Queen María Luisa on Horseback (*Marcial*) by Goya, 1799. (Museo del Prado, Madrid)

ued: "If Goya can do ours there [i.e., in Madrid] in similar fashion it would be just as well as this way it will free us of bother."[30] The remark is puzzling, given María Luisa's well-known antipathy toward the capital. At all events, the grumpy First Painter to the King made his way with his paraphernalia to Aranjuez, for on June 9 the queen wrote Manuel from that Arcadian retreat: "Tomorrow Goya is beginning another portrait of me, all the others are completed, and all are very natural."[31] Then on June 14 comes the news that "Goya has finished my portrait which they say is the best of the lot; he is working on the King's in the Casa del Labrador, and I believe it will turn out just as well."[32] From the queen's brief description, the one of her appears to be a different painting from those previously alluded to, in which case it may well be lost; that of the king, a stiff, full-length portrayal appropriately in hunting attire with gun in hand, has survived. Such was the royal pleasure that Manuel was given a copy of the latter painting as well as one of the mantilla study of the queen.

Just how worthy was Manuel of such esteem on the part of the *reyes?* In particular, how faithful was he to the queen's cause in her extended tiff with the Duchess of Alba? A curious undercurrent runs through the correspondence between María Luisa and Manuel that indicated all was not well. A Spanish scholar posits the question: "What kind of relationship was there between the favorite and *la de Alba?* Certain phrases recorded in letters copied later on make one suspect that, like the majority of men, he was a skirtchaser *[mujeriego]* and not indifferent to her; but it suited his purposes to conceal his feelings, knowing the enmity María Luisa felt towards her."[33] The queen had every reason to suspect Manuel's allegiance in matters of the heart and did not hesitate to remind him of his obligation to her. Thus, in an undated letter from Aranjuez, she informs him: "*La de Alba* took her leave of us this afternoon; she dined with Cornel [Lieutenant General Antonio Cornel, minister of war] and went off; she's reduced to a skinny piece of flesh. I don't think what happened before would happen to you now, and I also believe that you really regret it."[34] If the allusion to past transgressions is obscure, the warning is crystal clear. On April 30, 1800, a triumphant announcement is made: "This evening *la de Alba* has probably left, just as crazy as in her first bloom of youth."[35]

Getting rid of the temperamental duchess was not quite that easy. From her estate in Andalucia, she must have sent the queen a particularly offensive note some time during August. The exact contents are not known, nor does it seem that the duchess was the original author, to judge from a postscript in a letter sent by the queen to Manuel on September 4: "Today I am sending you a letter which I received yesterday from *la de Alba,* so that you can see what this woman is really like, even though this note doesn't seem to be her work, she and her friends are one and the same."[36] Manuel replied the very next day in language that is uncharacteristically and, one might add, suspiciously harsh: "I am returning *la de Alba's* letter, she and all her supporters ought to be buried in a huge pit. Cornel, who has taken sides with the Alba woman since his love affair with her, has no right to exist."[37] In his unsettled, and perhaps guilty, frame of mind, Godoy became convinced that Cornel was in league with Urquijo and others to cause him mischief: "But this and everything else would not concern me if only they would leave me in peace and stop talking about me, or if Cornel through his love affair with the Alba woman would not take advantage by telling her that I'm the one who caused her banishment from the royal palaces: Your Majesty knows what happened at Aranjuez."[38] Unfortunately, we do not, and probably never will.

Squabbles aside, the new century witnessed some amazing artistic creativity in Aranjuez with the royal family as the cynosure. By any standards, the most striking work that Goya painted in this memorable year was *The Family of Carlos IV.* The focal point of the spacious canvas is the dominant figure of the queen. No longer the regal, if somewhat rigid presence Goya had painted earlier, María Luisa comes closest here to the unkind depictions of malevolent court observers. Her coarse features are merely heightened by her frippery, her blowsy complexion in stark contrast with the angelic faces of the children, whose hands she is holding. The original sketch, now in Munich, was even less flattering than the completed version; one art historian compares María Luisa to a fishwife.[39] To her right stands the king, his dull expressionless face in juxtaposition to the glittering baubles that bedizen his ample chest. Completing the central group are the two infantes generally ascribed to Godoy's paternity.

The final canvas is a montage of separate sketches and groupings of royal children and other relatives assembled during the course of an entire year. Although most critics dwell on the supposed degeneracy of the royal family and hint at social satire, the simplest explanation, that Goya painted what he saw, warts and all, is as acceptable as any. One key member of the family is missing: Don Manuel Godoy, the Prince of the Peace, and cousin by marriage to the king and queen of Spain. His absence is understandable; more pressing matters required his immediate attention.

The Family of Charles IV by Goya, 1800. (Museo del Prado, Madrid)

7

THE POWER

OF THE PEN

On November 9, 1799, an event occurred in Paris that was to prove decisive for Spain. Through the coup d'etat of 18–19 Brumaire, Napoleon Bonaparte stumbled into power, owing in large measure to the presence of mind of his younger brother, Lucien, and the strong-arm tactics of Joachim Murat, his future brother-in-law. Far from feeling gratitude towards his rescuers, France's new ruler saw in them mortifying reminders of his momentary weakness. His resentful attitude surfaced later in Spain, where both Lucien and Murat were to play leading parts.

From Madrid, Godoy followed the distant turmoil with keen interest. He had little reason to mourn the passing of the Directory, for he held that corrupt quintet largely responsible for his current predicament. Strictly speaking, after his dismissal from office, nothing remained to Manuel save his wealth and titles. His royal kinship aside, theoretically he was once more an ordinary citizen with no say in the formulation of governmental policies. Bonaparte was not deceived for a moment. Having assured himself of Godoy's continued predominance, the First Consul shrewdly presented him with a suit of precious damascened armor. Urquijo, still nominally First Minister, had to be content with copies of Virgil and the Bible, a book with which he was none too familiar, along with the incongruous accompanying gift of a case of pistols.

But what of the *reyes,* didn't they count for something? This regrettable oversight was soon rectified by the bestowal of munificent gifts: hunting guns for Carlos (significantly, he was kept waiting for them until May 1802) and for María Luisa a breakfast service and some exquisite dresses from Mademoiselle Minette, the famous couturiere. The latter inspiration was directly attributable to Alquier, who slyly ordered "the most dazzling ensembles, such as a lively brunette of twenty would order." Bonaparte's reaction was that "We must insist on the necessary decorum so that the whole thing does not become ridiculous."[1]

For his part, Carlos was determined not to be found wanting. He personally supervised the selection of a commensurate offering. Sixteen magnificent horses of fiery Arabian blood, each accompanied by a groom arrayed in the Bourbon livery, were dispatched to Paris. The attendants were under strict orders not to mount the steeds for fear they might be unduly burdened. Carlos's sole request was that the members of the escort be allowed to attend Mass on feast days en route. Bonaparte graciously assented, whereupon the grateful monarch exclaimed: "I recognize there the act of the First Consul! I know that he is a Catholic like me, and rejoice that we are of the same religion."[2] For the first time since the revolution, the Bourbon fleur-de-lis was seen on the streets of Paris.

Had Carlos been fully cognizant of the facts, his enthusiasm might have been tempered. In the haggling that preceded the signing of the Concordat with the Vatican, Bonaparte at one point had threatened to end the matter by becoming a Calvinist and sending Murat's troops into Rome. When Manuel ventured to express his doubts to the king, he was told: "You don't know either the French or Bonaparte. It's clear to me they're behaving very well in Milan. They know how to respect religion!"[3]

Now that religion had indeed become the latest fashion in Paris—Chateaubriand was about to publish the moving Atala episode from his *Génie du Christianisme*—Urquijo's dismissal from office was virtually assured. A relentless critic of the church, he had encouraged the translation of a Portuguese exposé that purported to recount a compendium of Vatican villanies. The papal nuncio in Madrid protested in the strongest of terms, whereupon he was handed his papers and requested to leave the country. Like Bonaparte, the cleric was well aware where the true power resided and went directly to the Prince of the Peace. Godoy found himself in a delicate situation:

> The Nuncio came to me with tears in his eyes, begging me to write the King and plead in his favor. I only saw one objection to taking that step, and that was the fear that people in Spain might think I was doing it so

as to undermine the Minister [Urquijo] in order to supplant him, and that an act of piety and civility which I advised the King to take against the decree which had uprooted the Nuncio might be attributed to my ambition. However, of my own volition I decided to write the King without impugning the policies of the Minister or entering into opinions, only interceding and requesting Carlos IV to revoke the Order and return the Nuncio to favor . . . Urquijo never forgave me those steps which prevented his gaining an evil triumph.[4]

Nowhere is Godoy's overall predicament more apparent than in his position vis-à-vis the church. Yet, his moderation here, as elsewhere, did not spare him from unmerited aspersions from parish priest all the way to the Supreme Pontiff. One minor incident is illustrative. In obedience to the recommendations of a papal commission, Godoy put an end to the insalubrious practice of burial within the confines of church buildings. A modest advance, in all conscience, but the favorite was in an especially vulnerable position to enforce reforms because their very provenance made them suspect to the faithful. He had been decried from the pulpit as a disbeliever, an ally of the godless French and—most damaging of all— as a bigamist who had defiled the royal family. And now he was bent on depriving the common people of a Christian burial within hallowed ground! Few conceded that the space inside the church walls had become exhausted, that the new proposals originated from the clergy, that the surrounding cemetery was also sacred soil—anything to do with the hated *privado* must be rejected.

Such concerted hostility seriously weakened Godoy's sphere of action. Like most progressive Spaniards, he regarded the Inquisition with repugnance, having himself but barely escaped its chill embrace. Had he done away with the *Oficio Santo,* his stock would have risen immeasurably in the eyes of succeeding generations. He knew, however, that largely due to misplaced national pride, the venerable institution still enjoyed genuine popularity among the people; any attempt at reform—much less abolition—was fraught with danger. All he could do was to encourage the appointment of more liberal-minded officials to that baleful anachronism.

Many of the tribunal's potential victims, such as a hapless Moroccan Jew who had come to Spain to visit the grave of his forefathers, were spared by a royal decree that required the *Oficio Santo* to obtain the king's assent before initiating proceedings. Manuel made sure that such permission was rarely forthcoming. Thanks to his intercession, many elderly Jesuits were permitted to return to the land from which they had been expelled in 1767 following the Esquilache riots. He also arranged for several Jews to settle in Cádiz, admittedly for a financial consideration from which he siphoned a generous share; even so, his action demonstrated considerable political courage.

Unquestionably, many of Godoy's efforts at reform—political, social, and religious—find an echo in the writers of the day. As might readily be expected, their voices were anything but unanimous in their assessment of the *privado*; in most cases, effusive praise was just as suspect as unbridled vituperation. Yet, all allowances having been made—on occasion quite literally in the form of a generous remuneration to the panegyrist—many literati were undoubtedly attracted to Godoy on his own merits.

One such was the dramatist Moratín. Many years later, he unstintingly expressed his gratitude to the fallen favorite, acknowledging that "what he was he owed to him."[5] Leandro Fernández de Moratín was indeed immeasurably indebted to Godoy. The leading playwright of the late neoclassical period, his trenchant wit and scathing attacks had brought him into inevitable conflict with the official censorship. His play *El viejo y la niña* was at first banned, and only Godoy's personal intervention (at the age of twenty-three and while still in the ascendant) enabled it to be performed in 1790. Two years later, Godoy provided the dramatist with a stipend of 30,000 reales to undertake a four-year educational tour through Europe to assist in his chosen career. From Paris and London, Moratín sent the First Minister gratuitous advice concerning Fernando's education; like Escoiquiz, he was angling for the post of royal tutor. On his return to Spain, Moratín was appointed by Godoy as Secretary for the Interpretation of Languages and later Director of Theaters, undemanding sinecures that allowed him to concentrate on his literary work.

Essentially a pessimist, Moratín was a sensitive introvert who abhorred violent revolution. In Paris, he had witnessed the severed head of the Princesse de Lamballe borne aloft on a pike by the crazed mob. Small wonder, then, that he vigorously defended the moderate policies of Godoy to his *contertulios* (members of the same social circle). Soon, he was dedicating paeans to *el apuesto cumplido garzón,* the "genteel, accomplished youth," as he termed Godoy, wondering whether "justice could ever be done to the greatness of his worthy name."[6] It certainly was not for want of trying, as the following ode dedicated to the favorite amply demonstrates:

Power is not assured by violence,
nor does the horror of torture sustain it,
nor armed troops of horse;
where love was lacking, force is in vain.
You know this, sire, and by your actions
you set an example. You protect
hidden virtue and innocence. If merit
has been overlooked, you reward it;
under your shelter literature flourished,
you applaud zeal and pardon error,
you received the recompense for your judgments
in the inner pleasure your heart feels.[7]

No poet was more assiduous in his praise of Godoy than Juan Meléndez Valdés. By coincidence, both men hailed from the same part of Extremadura. Shortly before his arrival in the capital in 1797, Meléndez dedicated the three-volume revised edition of his poems, not to his close friend Jovellanos, but to the Prince of the Peace. The latter was quick to respond, averring, "I cannot read Meléndez without feeling a sort of divine balsam which penetrates me, delights me, and which fills soul and body."[8] The poet, not content with extravagant flattery, even "translated into rich verse the conversations we held on more than one occasion,"[9] according to Manuel.

Godoy's extraordinary elevation and preposterous title had aroused much soul-searching among Meléndez's liberal friends, both at Salamanca and in Madrid. Undismayed, the poet sprang to his defense with an ode boldly entitled *Al Príncipe de la Paz sobre la calumnia*. No longer can the bard sleep in peace; his "placid dreams" have been dispelled by the "horrible monster of malicious slander." He finds himself mocked for his "honest frankness," but then so is his *príncipe amado*. Nor has the Prince of the Peace been spared from the injurious effects of *la negra invidia*:

And here, the unfortunate who in his right hand
holds the aggregate of power, I see
my prince's breast wounded also
by the arrow of heinous slander;
he gives to the people the sweet peace
they desire anxiously with tears,
yet this blessed peace is a transgression
with which stupid ignorance rebukes him.[10]

A voice from heaven assures the troubled poet that the struggle is not in vain; encouraged by God, Godoy and other enlightened men are urged to continue their beneficent task.

Meléndez's hope, of course, was that Godoy would prove to be God's chosen instrument. In the *Epístola al Príncipe de la Paz,* he besought him to strike at the hydra-headed Inquisition:

> Do not tolerate it, sire, but with your power
> cast out the monster which in its envy
> wages impious war on holy truth.[11]

As in the moving *Oda contra el fanatismo,* also addressed to Godoy, the poet passionately denounced the *Oficio Santo* as a travesty of God's will on earth. It is safe to assume that he would never have dared dedicate either work to the *privado* had he not been assured of his attitude.

Another eulogist was the ardent nationalist Juan Pablo Forner, who died in 1797 at the age of forty-one. Besides some *octavas* addressed *Al Príncipe de la Paz* in which he discerned "light reflected from God" in Godoy's administering hand—not even María Luisa in her first rapture claimed as much—he ventured the hope that

> Perhaps your renown,
> by lightening my load,
> will live on in history
> through all eternity.[12]

Equally outrageous is the interminable *Canto Heroico,* dedicated to Godoy on the occasion of the Treaty of Basle. Even this effusive praise appears modest compared with the extravagant *A un caballo del excelentísimo Señor Príncipe de la Paz,* in which Godoy's horse takes on divine attributes, presumably by osmosis through the saddle.

A fair number of Spain's literary figures were far less favorably disposed toward the favorite. One of these was Manuel José Quintana, Meléndez's literary disciple at Salamanca but in general lacking his master's gifts. When the name of Godoy cropped up in their *tertulias,* the two friends simply agreed to disagree rather than engage in corrosive disputes. With other acquaintances, Quintana was less reticent. In a letter to Lord Holland following the overthrow of the *valido* in 1808, he wrote: "The nation, in effect, got on its knees before him, the women sacrificed their virtue to him, the men their honor and dignity. When he averted his glance it was enough to raise up or prostrate a person; he disposed of the treasury, the provinces, declared war and concluded peace. As if with all his talents and dexterity he could have let one pardon the scandal of his elevation!"[13] Even so, Quintana, a man of strong moral character, did not hesitate to hymn the success of the Balmis scientific expedition in a fitting ode, though it had set sail with Godoy's encouragement.

The majority of Manuel's critics deemed it advisable to remain anonymous, certainly those who committed themselves to writing (Quintana contented himself with sharp verbal attacks in congenial company). The most popular theme, of course, was the generally accepted intimate relationship between queen and *privado*. Scurrilous pasquinades, such as the following, enjoyed a gleeful circulation:

> He joined the Royal Guard
> and turned a big somersault.
> He went in with the Queen
> and still has not come out.
> And his omnipotent power
> comes from knowing how to . . . sing.[14]

(In the original Spanish, *cantar*, to sing, is substituted for the understood *joder*, to have intercourse.)

Some of the jibes adopted a threatening tone:

> As he looked around his house
> he was the Prince of the Raisin [pun on *Pasa/Paz*]
> He's the one who rules Spain and the Indies
> underleggedly [presumably even worse than underhandedly].
> He's a mischievous creature whose tail
> will finally have to be cut off.[15]

None of these *coplas de ciego* (vulgar ballads) can claim the slightest objectivity, let alone any literary merit. Yet, their effectiveness as propaganda can be seen by Espronceda's later designation of the queen as *una impura prostituta*, clearly a repetition of the standard calumny he had heard from his elders. Godoy had been the target of ribald doggerel practically from the first meeting with María Luisa. In addition to the scandalmongers at court, a steady stream of visitors from abroad was quick to heap scorn on him, largely on the basis of hearsay.

One of these beratements issued from the pen of William Beckford, the highly eccentric English author of the oriental novel *Vathek* and the architect of the amazing Fonthill, with its 260-foot tower. A notoriously licentious character himself, he saw fit to comment in a letter dated December 2, 1795: "A train of eager, hungry dependents, picked out of inferior and foreign classes, form the company of the Duke of Alcudia. Notwithstanding his lofty titles, unbounded wealth, solid power, and dazzling magnificence, he is treated by the first class with silent contempt and passive indifference."[16] If Beckford at least strove for a semblance of objectivity, no such attempt is discernible in the onslaught of his compatriot Richard Ford, a later visitor to the Iberian Peninsula: "Godoy, like a foul beast of prey, was always craving, always swallowing, and yet always gaunt, needy, and hungry; he plundered without scruple, and spent without advantage."[17] In between, both in time and sentiment, came Lord Byron, who similarly never made the acquaintance of the Prince of the Peace. The poet spent less than a month in southern Spain during the summer of 1809 (the year following Godoy's exile) and set salacious gossip to verse in his *Childe Harold's Pilgrimage:*

How carols now the lusty muleteer?
Of love, romance, devotion is his lay,
As whilome he was wont the leagues to cheer,
His quick bells wildly jingling on the way?
No! As he speeds, he chants "Viva el Rey!"
And checks his song to execrate Godoy,
The royal wittol Charles, and curse the day
When first Spain's queen beheld the black-eyed boy
And gore-faced treason sprung from her adulterous joy.[18]

To an English-speaking reader, Godoy is known, if at all, through this one stanza; immorality and immortality are often closely bound.

Byron and the others, of course, were merely repeating the common talk of the tavern and marketplace. The source of much of this "information" emanated from the court, either by word of mouth, as in the case of the *partido fernandino,* or in the numerous dispatches of accredited diplomats. Later assessments of Godoy were augmented by the reminiscenses of more detached observers, such as Alcalá Galiano and Blanco-White, both native Spaniards. It is well to remember that these youthful eyewitness accounts are seen through the interpretative veil of later years.

No admirer of Godoy, Alcalá Galiano nevertheless mitigated his repugnance by restricting his opinions to those incidents he had personally observed. Godoy's mansion in Madrid had immediately become a focal point for *pretendientes* (office seekers) and fortune hunters of both sexes, and, even during his brief period out of office, his audiences continued to be held:

> The powerful Prince of the Peace spent his life alternating between Madrid and the royal residences. Here [in Madrid] he held court once a week; and not unjustly it was called his court, because it far more resembled the court of a king than that of a minister, even though it had little in common with the way the sovereigns of Spain would receive their subjects.[19]

Friends and foe agree, if on no other point, that Godoy was easily accessible; the debate revolves around the type of person he received. Alcalá Galiano offers his readers a vivid description of public receptions he witnessed:

> A staircase, built at tremendous expense and distinguished more by its opulence than by its good taste, led to various drawing-rooms. In one of them, long and comparatively narrow, was the greater part of the gathered assembly which nevertheless extended so far as to fill two or three smaller rooms. The people who formed the crowd were of very differing classes and background, most of them brought there by some special solicitation; some, but not many, just to witness an amusing spectacle; quite a few who had no wish to be conspicuous by their absence and cause ill will. Both sexes, in nearly equal proportion, on some days nearly turned it into an uproar. As no entrance permit was required, one could see, though not that many, ladies of doubtful reputation or even worse. There was never missing a prostitute or two, though only the highest, or let's say, the wealthiest of that awful breed. And, sad to relate, even though the wickedness has been exaggerated—there was enough of it!—there were enough ladies who by birth and social position were deserving of respect who went there to show off their personal charms to enter the good graces of that all-powerful man, selling their virtue in exchange for favors. If not that common, it was not infrequent for mothers to take their unmarried daughters to that obscene market and even husbands bringing their wives.[20]

The moment the Prince of the Peace appeared, the hubbub immediately subsided and everyone stood in line waiting to be presented. In a more compassionate moment, Alcalá Galiano admits that many of the incidents related by *la voz popular* in its blind hatred of Godoy are grossly overdrawn, though undeniably containing a kernel of truth. What seems certain— many eyewitnesses attest to the fact—was Manuel's extraordinary ability to recall not only the faces of the petitioners but also the concern which brought them there. Nevertheless, no sooner was the reception over and the crowd had dispersed, than the very persons who moments earlier had begged the assistance of the *privado* were the first to damn him mercilessly once out of earshot.

It is again to Alcalá Galiano that we are indebted for the most perceptive description of Godoy at the height of his influence. The date is not precise, but it must have been soon after the turn of the century. It is no longer the brash, confident First Minister but the more disillusioned, wary soldier-statesman of Goya's portrait:

> Don Manuel Godoy, whose advancement at first was entirely due to his physical attractions, was tall, well-built though certainly not corpulent, very broad-shouldered to the point of carrying his head somewhat low, red-haired and very fair-skinned, something unusual in a native son of Extremadura whose inhabitants with few exceptions reflect in their faces the sunburnt pasture-grounds where they were born and spent their youth. A very vivid ruddiness glowed in the whiteness of his cheeks which the malice of his enemies ascribed to makeup; but even people who certainly are no friends of his allow is a gift of nature. He was dressed in the uniform of a Captain-General but with a blue sash which distinguished him as Generalísimo. He held in his hand his baton and his cocked hat with a white plume. His features were gentle but with little expression. In his speech he was neither very stiff nor relaxed, with few signs of a talented mind. At times he did aspire to wit, but without hitting the mark, only producing some effect because a more or less forced smile greeted his jokes with seeming approval.[21]

Another Spanish chronicler was that most engaging figure José Blanco y Crespo, usually known as Blanco-White, the name he later adopted in his voluntary English exile. He remarked on Godoy's lack of affectation, noting that "very different from the ministers who tremble before him, he can be approached by an individual in the kingdom without an introduction, and in the certainty of receiving a civil if not a favorable answer."[22] Blanco echoes the sentiments of other writers who benefited from Godoy's support of the arts:

The Prince of the Peace, who had received a much better education than most unprofessional gentlemen in Spain, continued to the last a friend to improvements in literature; and had it not been for the total demoralization of the country and the court intrigues which frequently endangered his power and made him confine his attention to his own safety, he would have been a most effectual patron of knowledge.[23]

Many years later, Godoy also briefly considered permanent exile in England. The man responsible for extending the invitation was Henry Richard Fox, Lord Holland, an impassioned liberal who befriended Blanco-White in his own home for several years. He was one of the comparatively few Englishmen familiar with the Spanish language and literature, and during the course of various stays in the peninsula had evinced a keen understanding of the people. Although deploring some obvious lacunae in Godoy's basic knowledge—in the First Minister's notes the *Villas Hanseáticas* were transformed into *Islas Asiáticas,* and he had held the post for some time before discovering that Prussia and Russia were not one and the same—the English lord was generous in his description of Manuel:

> His manner, though somewhat indolent, or what the French term *non-chalant,* was graceful and attractive. Though he had neither education nor reading, his language was at once elegant and peculiar; and, notwithstanding his humble origin, his whole deportment announced, more than that of any untraveled Spaniard I ever met with, that mixture of dignity, politeness, propriety, and ease, which the habits of good company are supposed exclusively to confer. He seemed born for a high station. Without any effort he would have passed, wherever he was, for the first man in the society.[24]

As frequently happened, those who came to know Godoy personally and not merely by repute were favorably impressed by his many praiseworthy qualities, even while acknowledging his shortcomings.

That incorrigible tattletale, Ambassador Alquier, was in an excellent position to observe Godoy during his period out of office. By coincidence, Urquijo's dismissal and Alquier's recall to Paris took place almost concurrently. The ambassador judged the moment opportune to deliver a telling Parthian shot at Godoy:

> In no way at all did I wish to leave Madrid without first having seen the Prince of the Peace. It is enough merely to listen to this man to convince oneself that he owes his tremendous eminence entirely to shameful procedures and has followed a path where it is very rare to come across a man with honor and talent. If one excepts the beginning of every ordinary and unimportant conversation, which he can conduct fairly well for a few minutes, there is nothing to equal the infinite poverty of his ideas, the complete emptiness of his thoughts and, above all, the profound and shameful ignorance which he reveals in everything he says. With an exceptional lack of skill he talks about that which, in his opinion, can heighten the impression of his importance. When he can think of nothing else to do than shake hands, he tells lies with the most ridiculous and outrageous effrontery.[25]

The ambassador's petty rancor is difficult to understand. At that time, Godoy held no official position, and Alquier was therefore under no diplomatic obligation to pay his respects. The meeting was at the ambassador's request; as usual, Manuel willingly acceded.

Alquier's specialty, of course, was the supposed relationship between the queen and the favorite; by now such talk was a staple topic for gossip in every chancellery in Europe. Occasionally, Alquier offers a personal insight:

> The Queen does not love anyone, not even her lover, whom she profoundly despises without trying to disguise it. In the long line of her favorites, the Prince of the Peace is the only one who has managed to subdue this empty and frivolous creature. Even now his influence is still tremendous, and he always gets his way. But this subjection can neither be attributed to love nor habit. The Prince knows this astute woman very well and what he has to fear from her. He has fettered her in such a way that he need never again fear her vengeance; she, on the other hand, lives in perpetual fear of his revenge. Whatever the procedure he used to achieve this end, it is certain that the chain is very strong. The details of their relationship are entirely without interest. Never has another woman been treated with such insulting scorn and subjected to such acts of violence which no drunken soldier would allow himself with a besotted prostitute. He has never concealed from her his passing love affairs. He wants her to know about them, and he derives pleasure from torturing her pride with the ill fame of his numerous infidelities.[26]

Largely on the basis of these "facts," Napoleon and Talleyrand concluded that Spain was a house of cards; all the French need do was to blow at the opportune moment.

Of greater interest is Alquier's highly pictorial account of a public reception held by the *privado*:

> The assembly rooms, antechambers, and corridors were full of women; there were two hundred—no, three hundred—who converged from all parts of the kingdom. Believe me, I am not exaggerating [Alquier's standard disclaimer]. They entered one after the other. When a girl came in with her mother the latter was never admitted into the presence of the Minister. The petitioners always emerged blushing and with rumpled dresses which they would smooth down in full view of everyone. Finally the foreign ambassadors made their way through this assembly to the reception room. The women were received in a boudoir, the doors of which remained open allowing one to see a big sofa during the audience. The Prince was pleased with himself and would tell what had just happened. He was not sparing for details, names, praise or criticism, and he would complain about the distaste he felt for this grab bag of offers and pleasures that came too easily. The clerks came in for what fell from the Prince's table. This scene was repeated every night no more than twenty steps from the Queen's suite. She would shout and threaten, only in the end to admit defeat.[27]

This description contrasts with that of the young Alcalá Galiano, who noted, among other differences, a more or less equal representation of the sexes. Fortunately, Alquier was not the sole foreign representative to commit his impressions to writing.

The Prussian ambassador Rohde, despite his indignation at Godoy's marital waywardness, nevertheless managed to separate the public from the private man. Perhaps reflecting the character of his homeland, the tone of Rohde's dispatches is altogether more serious; his superiors wished to be informed rather than amused. For this reason, his overall view, though lacking Alquier's immediacy, probably comes closest to being a fair assessment of Godoy's work habits. Even so, his account must be treated with caution:

> He rises early and talks a little with his equerries and household staff. At eight o'clock he goes to the riding stables at his country house where the Queen comes every morning at nine to watch him mount his horse. This exercise lasts until eleven. The King has the habit of joining in when he returns from the hunt. At the Prince's house there are already quite a few

people waiting to confer with him on various matters. All of them are disposed of in a quarter of an hour so as to make time for his toilette which he carries on in the presence of half a dozen ladies of the upper class while some musicians offer a concert. At one o'clock he returns to the Palace where he has his office and bedroom so as to be present at the Queen's luncheon in his capacity as Gentleman of the Chamber. After the meal he goes down to his own suite which is directly below that of the Queen. There he dines alone, but is immediately joined by the Queen who uses a secret staircase as soon as the King has gone off to the hunt again. In these secret meetings the Queen and Godoy decide what proposals to lay before the King. Round about seven Godoy visits the King to confer with him, at eight he descends again to his room, but not without encountering in his anteroom some thirty or forty women of every class and social position who pester him with their petitions. These visitors keep him busy for at least two hours, and only from about ten o'clock to midnight is he able to get down to work with his office clerks.[28]

Rohde certainly strives to be more temperate than Alquier, but cannot entirely be trusted on that account alone. Nevertheless, he is generous in his appraisal of Godoy's abilities and character:

But I must add that he is very punctual in everyday matters; he answers those letters the same day which do not require much reflection regarding their content. Moreover, he is very intelligent and fair-minded, and whenever his mind is distracted so that he cannot pay much attention to the matter at hand, he makes up for it to a certain extent with a strength of character for those difficulties which could come as a result. This firmness of character does him honor and will keep him for the longest time possible in his present political career.[29]

As with Alquier and Alcalá Galiano, a revealing self-portrait of the observer also emerges. In each case, Godoy stirred such deep emotions that any analysis of him could not help but be hopelessly subjective. Rohde is plainly confused, torn between sneaking admiration for a fellow hard-worker and efficient bureaucrat, and his repugnance for a statesman given to licentious living at the expense of his nation's fair name.

This was the same predicament in which Jovellanos had found himself. The Asturian soon had cause to regret that Godoy was temporarily out of power. As the result of a secret denunciation, the *Instituto,* in Gijón, hitherto under Manuel's protection, came under official investigation. On March 13, 1801, Jovellanos was arrested at his home and escorted incommunicado to Barcelona and thence to solitary confinement on the island of Mallorca. A dignified petition to the king was, in all probability, intercepted by Caballero, his successor as minister of justice.

Godoy later made a halfhearted attempt to improve the lot of his former ministerial colleague. Certainly he did not try very hard; he knew the *reyes* regarded Jovellanos as a dangerous innovator, bent upon the destruction of holy religion, and he felt that the ex-minister might well have had a hand in his own removal from office. Casting the blame on Caballero's shoulders, Godoy states rather lamely that, "When I found out these things and could talk to the King about them, the harm was already done."[30] Possibly so; but Manuel was no longer the confident rising official who without a moment's hesitation had interceded with the king to have the young English prisoner released.

The same Lord Holland who related that incident approached Nelson in 1805 with a view of freeing Jovellanos. In his reply, the admiral (obviously unaware of his lordship's acquaintance with the Prince of the Peace) could not refrain from a direct attack on Godoy:

> I have long deplored his [Jovellanos's] lot, would to God I could make that infernal Prince of Darkness change place with him, but it is very difficult in any way to try to be useful to him and would only hasten probably his death if it is known that an Englishman took an interest about him. Therefore we must look for the speedy downfall of the P.P. as the most likely mode of delivering Don Gaspar.[31]

Less than six weeks later, the author of this letter found a hero's death on the deck of the *Victory*. Jovellanos remained a prisoner at Bellver until April 5, 1808, when, in one of history's happier ironies, he was released on orders of Fernando during his initial brief period as king. However, this is to anticipate the present narrative, to which we must return.

8

THE WAR OF THE

ORANGES

Throughout most of 1800, Urquijo clung on as First Minister. Doubtless, the post was Godoy's for the asking, but his earlier bold resolve had given way to wariness; the fruit must fall of its own weight. The *reyes* were not so fortunately placed. Urquijo's "Jansenism" and lack of tact, at first a mild irritant, became insufferable; on a day-to-day basis the king sought out the reassuring counsel of his *buen amigo* Manuel, who, in all but name, was now once more in effective control. Even so, on occasion the favorite was quite content to remain in the background when he disapproved of the matter at hand.

Such an event occurred that summer. Bonaparte, whom Carlos had extravagantly hailed as *mi grande y bien amado amigo*,[1] had sent General Berthier to Madrid, not as ambassador, but as his special representative. Obviously something was in the wind; Bonaparte did not dispatch his chief of staff for nothing. On October 1, 1800, a second Treaty of San Ildefonso was signed by Urquijo and Berthier (Manuel, perhaps with an eye to the judgment of posterity, henceforth avoided affixing his signature to documents of dubious propriety whenever possible). Both King Carlos and Queen María Luisa took the leading part in the secret negotiations; it is unlikely that Urquijo or Godoy had much enthusiasm for the ignominious affair. Not surprisingly, the lure of further Italian domains lay at the root of the problem. The first two articles of the treaty stipulated that the First Consul would create a new principality out of Tuscany for the monarchs' daughter, Luisetta (christened María Luisa Josefina) and her sickly husband Luis, the heir apparent to the Duchy of Parma. In return for the throne of Etruria, as the new enclave was to be called, Spain pledged to retrocede to France the vast Louisiana Territory, which she had acquired barely forty years previously. As if that were insufficient, Spain also agreed to furnish six men-of-war of seventy-four cannon each. The future disposition of the Duchy of Parma was left somewhat vague.

In retrospect, the exchange of territories was a disaster for the Bourbons, but at the time the agreement had much to commend it. Carlos and María Luisa, both born and raised in Italy, were overjoyed to exchange the Mississippi swamplands for the homeland of Dante and Petrarch, which had the ancient city of Florence as its centerpiece. Then there were also family considerations that went beyond the acquisition of a new throne. A Bourbon kingdom in the north would serve as a corrective to Carlos's pro-English brother, Fernando, the King of Naples, who provided a convenient naval base for Nelson. But, more importantly, Carlos was dealing with the Bonaparte of the Concordat, the restorer of religion and order, who solemnly promised that were France ever to surrender Louisiana it would revert back to Spain.

The real criticism of the treaty, though, goes far beyond any of the above considerations. Godoy claims, with partial truth, that he was aware of Bonaparte's ultimate designs from an early date: "From a single skein were born a thousand of his colossal projects, without his concerning himself regarding the means, however unjust or violent they might be, so that he could implement his policies."[2] This presupposes that those who had dealings with Bonaparte were always his victims, never his collaborators. Often this was simply not the case. The *reyes,* in their unseemly haste to provide a throne for their daughter, were totally insensitive to the protestations of María Luisa's brother, also named Fernando, the reigning Duke of Parma, who bitterly resented being deposed with the concurrence of his own family and compensated elsewhere. Revealing myopic naiveté, the queen in a letter to Manuel railed at her brother's inflexibility: "What an egoist he is! His only concern is with his own good pleasure and his own sacred purposes; he refuses to submit to the smallest inconvenience or to be in anyone's debt for anything. What a man!"[3] In other words, the hallowed principle of legitimacy was to be jettisoned in favor of expediency, backed, of course, by assurances from the First Consul.

Both the king and queen were anxious to make amends for past mis-understandings with their powerful neighbor. France's new ruler regretted that in the months following Godoy's dismissal in 1798 relations between the two countries had undeniably deteriorated. Under Urquijo, "the most arrant of Jacobins,"[4] in Bonaparte's estimation, religion had been imperiled, and cooperation between the two governments had reached its nadir. Obviously, such a regrettable state of affairs would require prompt attention.

In the south of Spain, the irreligious First Minister was faced with an incursion that no army could repel. The plague, regarded by many as proof of divine wrath, had crossed over from Morocco, ravaging the province of Andalucía and especially the cities of Cádiz and Seville, claiming some 80,000 victims in a space of three months. In an astounding letter to a friend, Manuel could assert without hesitation: "Urquijo has given strict orders to find out and punish those who talk about the cause of the plague, as everyone knows that he is the one who introduced it."[5] Had the queen penned such nonsense, no additional comment would be needed. The insensate remark, though not typical of Godoy's feelings toward his adversaries, is indicative of a hardening attitude. The generosity of spirit of his younger years is now a thing of the past.

Events were also stirring in the north of Spain. In deep secrecy, an important personage and his retinue had crossed the Pyrenees from France on an extraordinary mission and had already reached the city of Vitoria. The stranger was none other than Lucien Bonaparte, who had become a political embarrassment to his brother in Paris and so, in effect, had been packed off to Spain in semidisgrace. In Vitoria, he had the notion of opening the diplomatic pouches destined for Alquier. Several of the dispatches contained sarcastic references by Talleyrand as to Lucien's swarthy appearance and lack of ability. Leaving his travel companions behind, Lucien hastened with all speed to the Escorial, where, breathless and still in his riding costume, he presented himself to a startled King Carlos on December 6.

Godoy's first reaction was distinctly unfavorable, tinged with the fear that Lucien, like Bourgoing and Truguet before him, had come to demand basic changes in Spain's political leadership that might mean perhaps his own ouster. Manuel was quick to warn the queen of this and other dangers: "He [Lucien] seems to be very eloquent, and his pleasing manners in his relationship with others will effect prodigies with the subversive sect that is still in Madrid."[6] Two days later, Manuel saw cautious grounds for optimism: "Your Majesty will see the harm this Frenchman is bringing us, although thanks to the incident with the mail I think he will perhaps change his behavior and rather wish to seek his revenge and sell out his brother and the others in the government"[7]—a prophetic observation on Godoy's part. Shortly afterward, a reaction seems to have set in. Manuel confided that "the description of the new ambassador is very, very bad" and that "a Frenchman, after all, is always a Frenchman,"[8] a remark not intended as a compliment.

Contrary to their expectations, upon personal acquaintance Manuel and Lucien got along famously. Soon they were on a first-name basis and exchanging confidences; as Pereyra noted, "It was a miracle they didn't say 'tú' to one another."[9] Within a matter of weeks, Godoy could write to José Nicholás Azara, the elderly Spanish ambassador in Paris, that Lucien "enters my house without prior notice or without giving thought to the hour, quite openly and without being restricted by etiquette."[10] For his part, Lucien was able to report home: "Here I am heaped with favors; I have broken the etiquette barrier. I am received when I wish and in private; I discuss matters with the king and the queen. The Prince of the Peace, far from being alarmed, is delighted."[11] On an individual basis, he found Manuel to be "a man of exceptional handsomeness without in any way lacking in personal dignity. He has an open intelligence, in contrast to what his enemies have maintained . . . in brief, he has shown moderation while at the height of his extraordinary power, and all he has done is to defend himself against his foes."[12] In later years, Lucien still held his friend in the highest regard: "The number of enemies which his extraordinary favor and esteem in the eyes of his sovereigns has attracted will not deter me from saying that in my eyes the Prince of the Peace was always amiable, obliging, sincere, compassionate, very chivalrously disposed toward the ladies, himself courageous and much better informed than his detractors would like to admit, and finally that I felt as much friendship towards him as he himself showed on every occasion."[13]

Lucien, at twenty-six already a widower, immediately set about the task of finding a wife, not for himself (he was enjoying life too much for that), but, incredibly, for his brother, the First Consul, who was happily married to the barren Josephine. Enjoying Manuel's tacit support, Lucien visualized himself as a royal marriage broker. For a while the pair contemplated the Infanta María Isabel, barely thirteen years old and generally assumed to be

Godoy's daughter, as a suitable replacement. According to Lucien, the queen, upon consultation, was elated at the prospect of her favorite child marrying so august a figure. In a note to his brother, Lucien reported the conversation he had held with María Luisa, adding, "From all this I am convinced that the trust placed in me by the Queen has as its object the wish to find out if you advise her to commit her daughter or to hold back."[14] The First Consul was furious and fulminated, "If I were contemplating a second marriage, I should not go to a house in ruins to look for my descendants."[15] Now an official Catholic, he had no intention of seeking a divorce, much less a marriage arranged by his scapegrace brother and his accomplice, the Prince of the Peace.

Lucien was not in the least disconcerted. He pronounced the king to be "a flower of the old Castillian integrity; religious, generous, trusting, too trusting in fact, as he judges those around him in accordance with his own character."[16] Carlos was quick to return the compliment and was soon addressing Lucien with the familiar "tú" hitherto reserved for the grandees. When the Marquis of Santa Cruz (whose wife had meanwhile become Lucien's mistress) dared remonstrate, the king brushed his objections aside with the comment, "What would you have me do? This young man is so friendly and personable that I cannot bring myself to treat him differently from the rest of you!"[17] Carlos even went so far as to present Lucien with a pair of shoes he had made with his royal hands. As was only to be expected, the young man got on just as well with María Luisa, who cherished the hope that her daughter might yet become the First Lady of France. In a letter to Manuel dated May 12, 1801, she let slip that she had again broached the matter with Lucien: "He spoke about Francisco Antonio [the Infante Francisco de Paula] saying how robust he was; we spoke about María Isabel, I told him how happy I should be if the marriage was confirmed. He replied: '*Peut-être, il ne faut pas se presser*' ['Perhaps, but we should not be in a hurry']."[18]

If the *reyes* were charmed by the attentions of the French envoy, they were equally disenchanted by the continued presence of Urquijo, whose graceless manner had become all the more boorish by comparison. On December 7, 1800, Godoy, recently hailed by Pope Pius VII as a *columna de la fe* (pillar of the Faith), was present at the Escorial to attend his brother-in-law's investiture as a Prince of the Church. As a signal honor, María Teresa's brother Don Luis María de Borbón, at the age of twenty-eight, was to receive his cardinal's hat from the king himself. His remarkable elevation was due considerably more to Manuel's interest in his career than to any theological erudition. Unfortunately, this well-intentioned action merely incurred the jealousy of the Marquis de Branciforte who, it will be remembered, had married Manuel's sister Antonia before amassing a considerable fortune as viceroy in Mexico. He had always detested his benefactor, and now, as Godoy entered the palace, he pointedly remained seated as the gathered company rose to pay their respects to the Prince of the Peace. Manuel was livid, and caustically asked a nonplussed María Luisa whether she had sanctioned such an affront. The queen in turn demanded an explanation from an embarrassed Urquijo, who, as a close friend of the offending marquis, was held equally responsible. Finally, Branciforte was confronted with his outrageous conduct, but, far from apologizing, he merely offered to resign as commander of the military guard.

The matter clearly could not rest there. In the highly ritualized world of Spanish court etiquette, the insulting gesture was tantamount to a slap in the face, not only to Manuel but also to the king. As Branciforte belatedly tendered his formal resignation, Carlos fixed him with a regal stare and directed: "Keep that paper in your pocket, and don't talk again of resigning. I order you to go immediately to the Prince of the Peace and ask his pardon. If you do not do so, and if I learn of similar conduct again, I shall order your execution."[19] Apparently, Manuel was less than satisfied with the apology of his contumacious relative; that same night he bitterly complained to Urquijo, who was not in the best of health.

The dismissal of the ailing anticleric was now imminent. A letter from the Pope to King Carlos protesting his First Minister's hostile initiatives in Rome signaled the end of Urquijo's usefulness. Carlos, as irresolute as ever and perhaps shamefaced at having endorsed many of Urquijo's measures that were designed to protect the royal interests, was finally prodded into action by an unlikely quartet, consisting of the queen, Godoy, the papal nuncio, and the vulpine Caballero.

Carlos was visibly disappointed when Manuel declined to assume the mantle of the banished minister, but nevertheless appreciated his assistance in finding a successor. The favorite presented a long list of possible candidates to the king, who commented on each one in turn before passing on to the next. Without giving the matter much thought, Manuel casually mentioned Pedro Cevallos, a name that unexpectedly caught the king's attention. When asked his opinion, Manuel observed, "He's my cousin by marriage." Carlos beamed ecstatically. "So much the better! I can then count on him not to reject your advice!"[20] On this basis, Cevallos was appointed First Minister, and for the next seven years served as a compliant facade, even going so far as to forward the state correspondence to Godoy, the effective power behind the throne.

In his peculiar nonofficial position as supreme minister, Manuel soon had important matters to attend to. Seen from Bonaparte's perspective, the situation in Portugal had remained a constant irritant that now had to be excised one way or another. The view from Lisbon was quite different. Somewhat naively, the Regent Juan and his wife, Carlota, the grotesquely proportioned daughter of the Spanish *reyes,* assumed that the close family affinity would assure their protection from any Spanish invasion as it had in the past. Placing their faith in kinship and geography, as well as in English assurances, they had continued to defy the First Consul's demands that the Atlantic harbors be closed to France's enemy. For his part, Godoy, as a rule so anxious to avoid hostilities, could not resist what promised to be an easy campaign as outlined by Lucien. It seems that as early as 1801 the *privado* had envisioned part of Portugal as a realm of his own, to which he might retire. Now that Bonaparte was redrawing the map of Europe, might he not find a modest kingdom for the Prince of the Peace as an act of gratitude?

Carlos vacillated until the very last moment before declaring war against Portugal on March 31, 1801. Even following the official announcement in the *Gaceta,* the correspondence between the monarchs and their loved ones in Portugal continued uninterrupted. The king poured out his soul to Lucien: "Don't you see, dear Ambassador, how distressing it is to be King and for political reasons to be obliged to wage war against one's own daughter?"[21] In the leisurely fashion of yesteryear, the armies on both sides had to be mobilized and drilled before they could assume their battle positions, an operation requiring two months. Finally Manuel took his leave of the queen and left for the front: "I go, Madame, full of anxiety and hope; I intend to gain a victory, but this enterprise entails a great sacrifice. I bid Your Majesties farewell, it is the same as separating the soul from the body . . ."[22]

Incredibly, despite his total lack of experience in the conduct of war, Godoy had been appointed field commander of the Spanish forces. The plan of attack called for three armies: the northernmost one of 20,000 men under the Marquis of San Simón, mainly as a general reserve; a southern force of 10,000 under General José Iturrigay based in Ayamonte and poised to invade the Algarve; and the Prince of the Peace, heading the main force of 30,000 quartered in Badajoz to strike through the center. Though necessarily unstated, the hope was that the Portuguese would have no stomach for the fight and that the war would be over before the French could intervene.

These were undoubtedly some of the most carefree weeks in Godoy's life, far from the daily bureaucracy and petty jealousies of the capital. Bedecked in his splendid uniform of commanding general, Manuel poured out his heart to María Luisa:

> To the devil with files of paper when I am on the point of making the enemy listen to reason at the cannon's mouth. Never shall I be able to live in the future without soldiers; the sight of them thrills me and I was born never to leave them. I cannot express to Your Majesty what pleasure swells my heart. I have but one regret: ah, how happy should I be if my Sovereigns were here! All is agitation, warlike bustle and rousing fanfares! And all that, Madam, intoxicates the imagination. Let me never hear talk again of political intrigues—never Madam, for the love of God! and may I be sent to the ends of the earth with my troops! I want never to leave the colours. May Your Majesty deign to let me serve her with the sword for no shorter time than I have served her with the pen![23]

María Luisa was visibly thrilled to receive such a stirring letter from her brave soldier at the front. At the same time, she blanched at the thought of her beloved Manuel coming to any harm, and, like any solicitous mother was not sparing in her admonitions, though clearly proud that he was fighting for king and country:

> Do not imperil yourself too much. Do not tire yourself. Do not take that worthless horse on the campaign, Manuel, take a tame one . . . Ah, Manuel, what battles my imagination conjures up! I believe they are all justified. I already see you at the head of our troops . . . Merely on opening your letters I feel I can see you with the puffed-up [Portuguese] lion at your feet, acceding to whatever conditions you choose to impose, I don't know how to express my feelings . . . Cover yourself with glory so that our children and grandchildren will know all about it.[24]

As to the war itself, there is little to relate. From his headquarters in Badajoz, Manuel boasted to the king: "I hope that within six days Your

Majesty will be master of what I offered you. Rest assured that I do not fear 80,000 English and Portuguese with the army at my command."[25] No wonder; at that very moment the English were engaged in peace pourparlers with the French and had no intention of sending an expeditionary force to the peninsula. Some local resistance aside, the war was all over within a matter of days. Under Godoy's direct command, the main Spanish army attacked and captured the border fortresses of Elvas and Juromenha on May 20, and after a spirited battle the fortified town of Arronches also fell to the invading troops. The Portuguese soon realized the hopelessness of the situation and sued for peace.

Godoy's detractors have seen fit to ridicule his conduct of the war, mainly on the basis of an oft-repeated incident. During the assault of the Elvas bastion, situated a mere ten miles or so from Manuel's birthplace, a soldier while under fire plucked two branches from an orange tree and presented them to Godoy as his commanding general. Manuel, impressed by the gallant gesture, sent the unusual war trophy to the queen in Madrid— hence the name of "War of the Oranges." The feat (with certain embellishments) was announced to the nation in the *Gaceta extraordinaria* of May 24: "The troops, who attacked the moment they heard my voice as I reached the vanguard, made me a present of two orange boughs from the gardens of Elvas which I in turn now present to the Queen."[26] In the course of his campaigns throughout Europe, Napoleon looted entire art galleries and museums as the spoils of war; his legend remains intact, whereas Godoy's ingenuous action has merely earned him further contempt.

Nor was he spared criticism during the actual military operation. Some military officers at court considered Godoy to be a drawing-room general and stated their opinion quite openly. The chief of these tormentors, General De Wite, goaded María Luisa into wishing aloud, *"Ojalá le diesen un balazo en la lengua"* ("I hope he gets a bullet in his tongue").[27] In truth, Godoy had run a considerable risk in leading the Spanish armies; had the Portuguese resisted and a stalemate ensued, his career might well have ended then and there.

Lucien was able to report to his brother in Paris that "the Prince of the Peace attacked without auxiliary troops and kept ours in reserve in case of extreme need. His plan has been a complete success and has spared our valiant soldiers a few tiring days."[28] This, of course, was not what Bonaparte wished to hear; if he had his way, the impudent Portuguese would have been given a sound drubbing, the Atlantic ports occupied by the French, and England's ally rendered harmless for all time. Yet, amazingly, aided by Lucien, Manuel chose to defy the First Consul's known wishes. By now he was working hand in glove with Lucien, whom Napoleon was soon to term a "thief, scoundrel, and traitor."[29] The cooperative tone was established from the beginning of the offensive when Lucien counseled his friend to "throw money at the poor Spanish officers. Overwhelm with attentions and presents those who approach you. Money is of no use unless it's for fame."[30]

It was not long before Lucien had convinced Manuel that a peace settlement could be turned to their own pecuniary advantage. In a confidential letter to the *reyes* on June 1, Manuel makes a lame attempt to express his disapproval of such a base proposal: "Lucien has been ordered to demand fifteen million pounds [from Portugal] for his government but he started off asking for thirty. When I pointed out to him the enormity of this sum, he came down to twenty-five and said to me, 'Fifteen for the government and ten for us.' I didn't appreciate at all what he had said, but when he repeated it to me, I told him: 'Well, my friend, if the government only receives fifteen million, you ought to be content with five and so only ask for twenty.' Then he added: 'And you? One has to take advantage of such opportunities, they don't come along every day.' "[31] The queen was suitably horrified and exclaimed, "These millions of the French Ambassador! What a scandal! And the pity is that it must be hushed up!"[32] With a touch of unconscious irony, the king wrote to Manuel: "I've seen the note you sent the Queen about Lucien from which one can see his despicable way of thinking and that he will sell his brother and all the French to serve his own interests. If he'd been dealing with Urquijo he would have succeeded!"[33]

There seems little doubt that, scandal or no, Manuel received his share of the iniquitous transaction. In his memoirs, he protests mightily against any such insinuation and vehemently refutes two anonymous articles which claimed that he had enriched himself immoderately as a result of the peace treaty: "Let him speak out who can affirm that I was interested in as much as a single drachma."[34] Unfortunately, there is also a letter to Lucien on record (May 16, 1801), written shortly before the outbreak of hostilities, in which Manuel threatens the Portuguese with all sorts of dire consequences "if they do not satisfy their debt towards the two of us."[35] The weight of evidence points conclusively to a concerted plan on the part of the two intrigants.

To clinch the deal, a peace treaty had to be signed as quickly as possible.

On June 6 two hasty preliminary agreements were concluded in Badajoz; Pinto de Souza signed on behalf of Portugal, and Manuel and Lucien for their respective countries. Except for a sizable indemnity, the terms were not onerous: Portugal ceded the border town of Olivenza and some adjoining territory to Spain, a part of Guiana went to France, and the Lisbon government pledged to deny her harbors to English ships. Neither Carlos nor the First Consul had any notion that a peace treaty had been signed without their having been consulted, and that soon they were to be presented with a *fait accompli* outlining their contractual obligations.

Just before the document was signed, however, for a moment all had seemed lost. As he had feared, Lucien received an urgent dispatch from Talleyrand insisting on a military occupation of Portugal as part of any settlement. Lucien instructed Manuel to antedate the treaty by one day and to have King Carlos sign it without delay. With an aplomb worthy of Talleyrand himself, Lucien bemoaned the fact to all within earshot that the First Consul's instructions had arrived a day too late. If only he had known . . . Meanwhile, Godoy in a letter to the king showed that he was also not without a certain duplicity:

> Sire: Both amazed and full of rejoicing I enclose for Your Majesty the peace treaty which we finally concluded last night on my return from Campo-mayor. I know that there are not many examples in history which can compare with the time, manner and circumstances in which this task was completed . . . This peace presumes more than appears on the surface. France tried to deceive us. The idea was not to enlarge Spain but to sacrifice her forces by making conquests which she would then have to cede. The inconsistency of France's government parallels that of Ambassador Lucien . . . His mail left yesterday afternoon, but he is subject to the treaty. The poor man considers himself lost, even doubting whether the treaty will be ratified, but he signed it. As soon as I have the honor of talking to Your Majesties I shall inform you in detail concerning what happened during the negotiations; but let it suffice to say that you cannot trust France in anything or ever think that the French will be friends other than in their own self-interest. My openness with Lucien has enabled me to discover his real nature. I know him, and I venture to say that even without the great advantages we derive from the treaty we ought to conclude peace and throw the French troops out of the Kingdom.[36]

Such forebodings were furthermost from the *reyes'* minds as they set out for Badajoz to celebrate the successful outcome of the military venture. As the carriages rumbled westward, Carlos and María Luisa could barely contain their admiration for Manuel's astuteness, not to mention his bravery under enemy fire. A luxurious tent had been pitched on the outskirts of the city so that the monarchs could rough it in the midst of their battle-scarred veterans. Carlos especially was thrilled to hear the huzzas of the drawn-up troops and the sound of cannon fired in his honor. The highlight was a troop review, while the king and queen sat in a triumphal carriage pulled by grenadiers selected from each battalion. After the ceremony incorporating Olivenza into Spain, Carlos sought to bestow the city on Manuel and raise it to a dukedom. The favorite declined—he did not wish it to appear that the war had been fought solely for his benefit—and accepted instead the title of Duke of Albufera. Two standards were added to his coat of arms by royal decree, and as a personal gift he received a sabre encrusted with diamonds (which was lost in Aranjueż in 1808).

All too soon, it was time for the *reyes* to return to "the center of gossip and shelter of scoundrels, that Babylon of Madrid," as the queen wrote Manuel in terms reminiscent of Escoiquiz. "Life is much sadder now that we are going back than when we were coming out here."[37] Then, accompanied by the entire cabinet, the royal couple set out along the dusty roads to cross the high castilian plateau in the full summer heat, tired but delighted by the reception accorded them.

Manuel and Lucien remained in Badajoz to await the inevitable fulminations from Paris. In a sarcastic observation to Talleyrand, the First Consul commented, "You should know that the Prince of the Peace, who has captured nine fortresses and taken part in heaven knows how many battles, has adopted the tone of a Suvarow with our ambassador."[38] Lucien had once suggested to his brother that he send his portrait to Godoy as a testimony of his esteem. Already at that time, the request had evoked the retort, "I shall never send my portrait to a man who keeps his predecessor in a dungeon and who uses the methods of the Inquisition. I can make use of him, but all I owe him is disdain."[39] Informed by Lucien, Manuel was greatly irritated both by the tone and inaccuracy of Bonaparte's remark. The result was his intemperate note of July 26 that amounted to an ultimatum, if not a *casus belli*. Without mincing words, the Prince of the Peace made it abundantly clear that "His Catholic Majesty will regard the entry of French troops exceeding the number of 15,000 as a violation of his territory as determined by the treaty, and by the terms of the same treaty he wishes these 15,000 men to withdraw as soon as possible, as the purpose of the war has been achieved."[40]

Upon receipt of Godoy's presumptuous letter, Talleyrand found himself the object of the First Consul's tirade, which culminated with an ominous threat: "I have read the note of the General Prince of the Peace; it is so ridiculous it does not deserve a formal reply; but if this Prince, bought by England, is going to drag the King and Queen into his dispositions against the honor and interests of the Republic, then the final hour of the Spanish monarchy has sounded."[41] When Azara, the Spanish ambassador, later attempted to mollify Bonaparte, he was taunted with the biting question: "Are your monarchs tired of reigning, that their minister dares to provoke me thus?"[42] Somehow, the ambassador and Talleyrand succeeded in abating the Corsican's fury; the disrespectful favorite could be dealt with in good time. Pocketing his considerable pride for the moment, the First Consul ratified the Treaty of Badajoz (with a few minor amendments) on August 27. Godoy had emerged victorious in the first confrontation between the two headstrong leaders; for Spain it was to prove the costliest of triumphs.

The leisurely conquest of Portugal terminating in an inconclusive peace treaty did little to improve Godoy's stock in the estimation of his fellow countrymen. Many noted the irony that the Prince of the Peace had involved Spain in her third war in less than a decade with the distinct promise of future conflicts. With unrestrained delight, the satirists reached for their gall-tipped pens:

> Prince, duke, count
> now he is all, and hopes
> to be King of the Algarve,
> but he will be what Fate has in store.
>   For Providence now heeds
> the weeping and lamentation
> which, through your guilt, you have debased.[43]

This pasquinade, in addition to others no less contemptuous, was later found in a collection of drawings belonging to Fernando. Included among them were some decidedly ribald caricatures of his parents and their *privado*. Apparently the heir to the throne had once commissioned some thirty-five of these sketches made by painters resident at the royal palace in Aranjuez; the most indecent contribution was the work of none other than the great Goya.[44] The accompanying verses were, if anything, even more insulting than the depictions of the *santa trinidad* as the king, queen, and knave in a pack of cards. Fernando's dislike of his parents and the *privado* was hardly one-sided, though María Luisa would never have conceded as much. In her letters to Manuel, more in sadness than in anger, she assigns the entire blame to her eldest son, who "does not have his father's kindness of heart, nor mine, though it pains me to say so."[45] There is no hint of hypocrisy; she sincerely believed herself to be the best of mothers.

María Luisa chose the occasion of Manuel's military glory to commit a grave psychological blunder. She suggested—tantamount to an order— that Fernando write a personal letter to the victorious general to express his thanks and admiration for his valor. The youth complied dutifully, but was careful to emphasize the relationship between his parents and Godoy. In his note to *"querido Manuel,"* he slyly pointed out that the advantageous peace was "above all for Papa and Mama," and that "certainly the love, fidelity, and loyalty which you feel for Their Majesties is well known,"[46] once again drawing attention to the favorite's complete dependence on the monarchs. Godoy was quick to realize the implication, for in a letter to the queen dated a week later he complained that "the letters of the Prince are worse than mediocre because he pays too much attention to the fact that I love Your Majesties and that I am loyal to you, so he hides, for his part, any merit he might discern in my affection, gratitude, and loyalty."[47] On both sides, mutual dislike was now giving way to implacable hatred.

Manuel was about to be separated from a good friend. He and Lucien, notwithstanding the proverbial distrust among thieves, had come to understand and appreciate one another. Napoleon was considerably less impressed; Lucien had consistently disobeyed orders, acted on his own initiative, and enriched himself outrageously. For their part, the *reyes* had become increasingly disillusioned with a man whose unseemly greed stood in sharp contrast with castilian probity (Manuel, of course, was exempt from such strictures). On November 12, 1801, Lucien took his hasty leave, exchanging an embassy adorned with young mistresses for a carriage filled with old masters. Rumor had it that the frame of a portrait of Carlos IV was crammed with diamonds; the painting itself was left behind in Madrid. Such was Lucien's fear of being arrested for misappropriation of national treasures—many of the artworks had hitherto been housed in the Retiro gallery—that he only felt safe once he had crossed the frontier. In later years, he continued to correspond with Manuel, using a secret code in which the First Consul was referred to as Achmet, Talleyrand as Ali, Saint-Cyr as Omar; Godoy styled himself Gustave.[48]

The government now found itself embroiled in a regional conflict that had all the potential of serious civil strife. Contrary to the advice of Godoy and Cevallos, the king appointed Don Antonio Cornel (who will be remembered in his dual role as minister of war and lover of the Duchess of Alba) as commanding general of the restive domain of Valencia. One of his first acts was to rescind the ancient *fuero* exempting the local population from militia service, and order the formation of six new army corps. The Valencians rose as a man to maintain their rights. Caballero and Cornel strongly urged the king to send in an army of 12,000 and to mete out salutary punishments. Not to be outdone, María Luisa, drawing on blurred memories of the Esquilache riots, preposterously blamed "the wicked Italians they have here, they're all English" as the prime motivators, as well as "the monks and the Jesuits who were in Valencia, can't they be behind all this? After all, they were the ones who caused the tumult in 1766."[49]

Fortunately, Carlos chose to overlook his consort's wondrous logic and had the good sense to place Godoy in command of the volatile situation. Manuel pointed out that Valencia was not trying to break away from Spain, as many ministers averred (in past wars, volunteers had proudly flocked to the colors in large numbers), and in a memorandum to the king he vigorously advocated the retention of the status quo ante: "If Your Majesty approves of this idea, he will naturally disapprove of what has been done in Valencia and will make public that he is not thinking of establishing militia of any type either in that, or in any other *reino*."[50] In the September 5 issue of the *Gaceta,* the king gave his unqualified approval to this proposal, and on November 12 issued a general pardon with a handful of exceptions. Godoy had but recently been elevated to the supreme rank of generalissimo and awarded a sabre of honor; for once the honor was fully justified.

Civil war had been averted, only to be succeeded by a new and potentially more severe crisis; the king lay gravely ill, felled by a stroke variously diagnosed as an attack of angina pectoris or apoplexy. For years he had insisted that the heating of the royal residences be kept to a Spartan minimum (one of the few instances that María Luisa and Manuel pleaded in vain), and every morning he went off to the hunt clad in the same garments whatever the weather. As to illness in the family, when he was informed that one of the infantes was in such poor health that his life was despaired of, Carlos replied, "Well, what do you expect me to do?" plainly annoyed that the hunt had needlessly been interrupted.[51] And now the king, seemingly oblivious to maladies that afflicted others, had finally been laid low.

While his life hung in the balance, the baseless report was circulated that the queen and Godoy had extracted a codicil from the moribund naming them as joint regents. This canard gained credence through a decree, also of November 12, which proclaimed that henceforth all documents signed by the king were to be countersigned by Godoy. The timing could hardly have been worse, yet to regard it as a devious ploy on the part of the *privado,* let alone as an attempt to usurp the succession, is absurd in light of his fear that the king's death would leave him without a protector. If anything, he went to the opposite extreme, bewailing that "the absence of Your Majesty would once again darken this century for us and there would be no end to wars."[52] In a less emotional vein, Bonaparte directed Gouvion Saint-Cyr, Lucien's replacement as ambassador, that "if the King were to die to declare publicly that France will only recognize the heir-apparent as King of Spain,"[53] a gratuitous slap at Godoy. By now the king's doctors were desperate and, rather than admit their ineptitude, ordered their royal patient to be bled, that time-honored therapy when all else had failed. Just in time, María Luisa sent the whole lot packing, and on her own initiative concocted an old housewife's remedy based on a generous supply of pippin apples, which soon had Carlos on his feet again.

His illness brought two insistent facts into sharp focus. Fernando was now seventeen and no longer a child to be kept in his place. More ominous still, the First Consul had dared intervene in Spain's internal affairs. On December 1, 1801, he notified Saint-Cyr: "I wish you to relay to Their Majesties my extreme displeasure regarding the unjust and inconsistent conduct of the Prince of the Peace. During these last six months this minister has not been sparing either in insulting notes or dangerous démarches; everything he could do against France, he has done. If this system continues, tell the Queen and the Prince of the Peace that this will end in a thunderclap."[54] The *reyes* disregarded Bonaparte's missive as no more than an outburst of momentary anger, which, like the storm alluded to, was more noise than substance and would soon blow away, once again leaving serene skies.

At no time did Manuel enjoy the royal favor more than during this period. Quite unabashedly the king could write to him in his own hand: "We are never happier than when you are with us, you know the natural feeling I have for you, and so I'm determined not to leave this afternoon until we've seen one another and can relax." And the queen admitted to Manuel: "The King stuck his head out of all the windows to catch sight of you, but you weren't there."[55] No testimonial summarizes the relationship as forcefully as does her letter of February 11, 1802:

No one has served us so well or sacrificed himself for us and our happiness as well as that of the Kingdom as you have, *amigo* Manuel. Neither has anyone destroyed and ruined this monarchy as have those two scoundrels Jovellanos and Saavedra, who don't deserve the name of minister, as well as that intruder Urquijo. These are the ones who wanted to enhance themselves and come up in the world and in public opinion by discrediting you. Through their wicked behavior they have only succeeded by contrast in uplifting yours which is so good. They have completely lost their reputation with their knavish tricks. I only wish that such monsters had never existed as well as the one who proposed them with such knavishness, that awful Cabarrús![56]

The *santa trinidad en la tierra* erred in one vital respect: far from entering a prolonged era of peace, they were enjoying a mere lull before the storm that was destined to sweep them all away.

9

FAMILY SQUABBLES

The accumulated tensions of the war, Bonaparte, the specter of rebellion, the king's near-fatal illness—some minor distraction was desperately needed. When it came, it was peculiarly Spanish. On May 11, 1801, a week before the Spanish armies under Godoy's command entered Portugal, the famous veteran torero Pepe Hillo was gored to death in Madrid. Goya, in his series of etchings which form the *Tauromaquia,* has vividly recreated the scene. So in her inimitable manner has María Luisa. In a lengthy letter to Manuel, she provides her own dramatic rendition of the fatal event:

> I forgot to tell you in my last letter about the misfortune that befell Pepe Hillo who was killed by a single thrust from the bull without the final sacraments being administered in time. At the moment of taking aim at the bull with his sword, it gored him, lifted him up by the breastbone which is in the chest, split his stomach, threw his liver up in the air, cut his colon in two, broke four ribs on one side and six on the other, left all his blood in the ring, and for some time he was held suspended on the horns. Many people left the bullring, and as for me, *amigo* Manuel, who do not like bullfights, what's going to happen now?[1]

The queen's description is remarkable, not only for its graphic detail—entirely in keeping with her obsession for medical minutiae—but all the more so as she was in Aranjuez at the time and did not actually witness the misadventure. The national preoccupation with the incident also reveals the attitude of many fellow countrymen toward Godoy. A later historian observes: "Please pardon us Spaniards for this digression from a matter as important as a war, but the death of that famous torero had far greater repercussions in Spain than the war against Portugal, at that time ridiculed by the people and thenceforth by the historians."[2] In fact, the whole question of the *corrida* was to cause Manuel endless vexation at a time when he could least afford any further diminution in public support.

It is therefore all the more surprising that he urged the king to issue a decree banning all bullfights. Had the favorite been the unprincipled opportunist so often depicted by his adversaries, he would never have involved himself in such a politically unprofitable area. His opponents harbored no scruples on this score whatsoever. In 1808 both Fernando VII and the French—whatever their private feelings—hastened to reinstitute the *corrida* amid wide public acclaim. Godoy's controversial action, then, requires a closer look. The Bourbon rulers and their ministers in the eighteenth century, enlightened men for the most part, viewed the bullfight with repugnance. Carlos IV, despite his obsession for the hunt, was no exception. As early as 1790, he had issued orders forbidding the running of the bulls in the streets, from whence the *corrida* originally received its name. Even so, bullfights in the Plaza Mayor in Madrid and elsewhere continued to be held to celebrate royal weddings and other joyous occasions. The consternation that greeted the total prohibition is therefore all the more understandable.

Four years after the death of Pepe Hillo and following lengthy debate in the council, the royal decree was signed and put into effect, making Godoy generally more hated than ever. Some thirty years later, he looked back on his action:

> The abolition of the bullfights and the killing of young bulls also dates from 1805. Many people grumbled, but all those of sound judgment and moderate habits applauded. Even though I played a leading role in the adoption of this reform, it was not the result of a caprice on my part . . . When my enemies assumed full power they reestablished these bloody spectacles and converted them into daily sustenance for the crowd. They were granted in return for the liberties and all the rights which the heroic people of Spain had earned with their blood. No one was given bread; bulls were offered instead. The unfortunate common people thought they had been well requited![3]

As he foresaw, within a few brief years it was all circus and no bread. No matter; his suppression of the *corrida* was seen as an insufferable affront by the populace. No ruler of Spain has since repeated Godoy's grievous error.

Pepe Hillo's untimely death was followed a year later on July 23, 1802, by that of the Duchess of Alba, barely forty years old. Her end was as controversial as her life, giving rise to the usual speculation of foul play. In recent years, the smoldering rivalry between *la de Alba* and María Luisa had grown in intensity; on one famous occasion, the duchess committed the unpardonable sin of dressing her ladies-in-waiting in the identical latest Parisian fashion as the queen herself, much to the latter's mortification. Another anecdote on altogether shakier ground tells of the duchess inviting the entire court to celebrate the completion of a new wing to her palace in Madrid. The climax to the evening was a dazzling display of fireworks. Carlos was delighted to behold the initial "C" light up the evening sky, followed by an "L" in honor of the queen; suddenly joy was transformed to rage as the letter "G" burst between the royal characters to form an impudent celestial monogram.[4]

Shortly thereafter, a large section of the duchess's palace went up in flames, not once, but twice, raising the suspicion of arson. The names of the queen and Godoy were on everyone's lips, though in fact he and Lucien had tried in vain to effect a reconciliation between the disputants. Having twice restored the damage, the duchess is said to have put the torch to her curtains herself, "as I do not wish to leave others the pleasure of setting fire to my palace; I'll take care of that myself."[5] Whatever the truth, the city of Madrid bought the palace in 1805 and presented it to the Prince of the Peace.[6]

The actual cause of the duchess's death has remained obscure to this day. But those with little taste for subtleties that tax the brain preferred the tried and true: "'Twas the *choricero* and the royal strumpet who had poisoned her." The death of *la de Alba* called for an official investigation to quell the attendant rumors. Ordinarily, the case should have been handled routinely by the minister of justice, José Caballero. But, instead, Carlos entrusted the inquiry to Manuel, who could hardly be termed a disinterested party. The king's instructions to him, far from shedding light on the matter, merely led to further obfuscation. In a letter dated July 30, exactly one week after the death of the duchess, he unburdened himself to Manuel:

> As I suspect the rectitude of the physicians who were present during her illness, I have ordered an inquiry to discover if her death was due to natural causes and the result of her illness. This examination, which I believe is

indicated for reasons counter to nature, has produced various other results; the Justice of the Peace, who was entrusted with the case against those suspected in the inheritance of her goods, has been able to ascertain that papers had been removed from the safety box of the Duchess by disloyal servants the very moment she expired . . . I don't know to whom I can entrust the enquiry; there are several aspects to be considered; some could well pertain to a natural secret, others to my estates, and others to her property . . . I therefore entrust you with this matter; discharge it as you see fit in accord with my peace of mind and decorum. Appoint people to conduct the inquiry in any way you wish, and inform me afterwards. I trust your well-known zeal.

Carlos.[7]

The ambiguously worded letter raises some disconcerting questions. Did Godoy dictate, or at least suggest, the content to the king—to put it simply, did he in effect nominate himself chief investigator? What exactly are "reasons counter to nature"? And why, in a manner reminiscent of Macbeth, cast criminal blame on the servants as those responsible for the theft? The duchess was widely known for her egalitarian impulses and generosity; only someone vitally interested in challenging her will—perhaps even in having it revoked—would go to such extraordinary lengths and risks. Suspicion inevitably centered around the queen and Godoy as potential beneficiaries of an amended will:

> With María Cayetana's body still unburied, the Queen intimated to the legal authorities concerned that the Duchess's will—which incidentally included a bequest of 3,500 reales a year to Goya's son Javier—must obviously be set aside as fantastic and inoperable. Her Majesty's hard black eye was in fact on two items in the inventory; a set of pearls valued at 384,000 reales and a diamond ornament valued at 300,000. These she intended to buy. Though the Spanish crown jewels included far more magnificent and historic gauds, the pleasure of flaunting a detested rival's jewels was invincible.[8]

If the details of the transactions that followed are obscure, the outcome is abundantly clear: Godoy, either through an indirect purchase or a gift from the king, acquired the *Venus of the Mirror*, by Velásquez; the *School of Love*, by Correggio; and a painting of the Virgin, by Raphael. Even more mysteriously, by 1803 both versions of Goya's *Maja*, previously known to have been in the duchess's possession, found their way into Manuel's growing art collection. Esquerra del Bayo ventures the opinion that the duchess had a secret *gabineto reservado* in her palace where the more unconventional paintings were displayed to a select audience.[9] Unanswered—and unanswerable—is the question whether Manuel knew of this inner sanctum and, if so, what measures he took to acquire the portraits.

Godoy figures curiously in another work executed by Goya. In 1804 the artist painted Don Alberto Foraster, an elderly army officer, on a canvas that had been used eleven years earlier by an obscure Portuguese painter named José Caetano de Pinho e Silva. The 1793 work was none other than a portrait of the youthful Manuel in his days as Duke of Alcudia. A recent cleaning of the Goya portrait has revealed the presence of the underlying work, which was further examined by X-rays and infrared photographs. In Pinho's rendition, Godoy's pose is awkward, and the subject was clearly unimpressed with the final result, noting that "the head is very massive and the face rounder than mine, but as for the rest it is all right."[10] One can only conclude that Manuel was unconcerned as to the fate of the finished work, and that Goya simply reused the canvas as a matter of economy.

The Goya-Godoy puzzle does not quite end there. In his memoirs, Manuel proudly reproduces one of those defiant responses that he periodically hurled at overbearing French ambassadors: "For the public welfare I love peace, but I shall never sanction a law which might offend my king."[11] The retort itself is not so remarkable as his assertion that he had the words inscribed at the foot of a portrait which Goya had just completed. Presumably the object was to render the aphorism of the *valido* immortal. If so, it failed; no trace of this work has been found.

An avid art collector, Manuel also had an eye for the advantageous purchase, as evidenced by a list of paintings acquired legitimately from the heirs of the Duchess of Alba. Among them were a portrait of Anne Boleyn, a study of Martin Luther contemplating Death, and a Velásquez canvas of a farmer with a fox at his feet. Apparently, Manuel was his own workman when it came to hanging up his collection, as one can infer from a letter to the queen dated March 17, 1805: "Madame, I've been constantly on the go from seven o'clock this morning. No sooner did I finish my task at two thirty than I began my meal, and since then I haven't stopped hanging up and taking down pictures. It's eight o'clock now, and at this moment I'm putting down my hammer and ladder."[12] Time to attend to the ladies, if we are to believe his detractors.

It was also time to attend to matters at court. The king had nearly succumbed the previous year; Fernando was now a young man of eighteen, and might well ascend the throne at any moment. About this time, Lady Holland had a private audience with the king and queen. She noted, "The Queen's manner is uncommonly gracious. She shows great readiness in making conversation, and taste in choosing her topics; all she said was flattering, obliging, and well-expressed. The King was quite a *bon homme,* and his great talents lie in the skill of a *garde de chasse.* The Queen called her favorite child, the Infante Don Francisco, a pretty, lively boy, bearing a most indecent likeness to the P. of the Peace. She enumerated the children she had, and those she had lost, 22!! 6 only remaining. 'My eldest son whom you are going to see you will find ugly, he is the counterpart of myself.' "[13] Such disparaging comments, from his mother no less, could hardly have bolstered the self-esteem of the wretched Prince of Asturias. Yet, whatever Fernando's physical and emotional shortcomings, a royal wedding could not be postponed much longer.

On this point, the sovereigns and Manuel were apparently divided. As to Fernando's lack of worldly experience there was no disagreement; the debate centered entirely on the timing of a prospective marriage. According to Godoy, the king admitted his son's shortcomings quite frankly:

> "I can see it very well; Fernando is backward. But do you think that waiting a few years before getting married will help him acquire what is lacking?"
>
> "Sire," I replied to the King, my heart pounding, "the study of the outside world, a study which instead of boring him might arouse his interest and give him pleasure, if possible without His Highness being aware that it is to educate him and rectify his backwardness . . . two or three years traveling through Europe . . . Your Majesty, with your wisdom and experience, can either approve or reject my idea."[14]

The conversation ended inconclusively, but—and here we only have Godoy's word to rely on—Caballero intervened and persuaded the hesitant monarch to proceed with plans for finding a suitable consort.

The choice of bride was something of a surprise. Word that the Spanish monarchs were scouring the royal courts of Europe for an appropriate match soon reached the ears of the Bourbon branch in Naples. Relations between the two royal houses were strained due to personal antipathies (the Neapolitans once characterized their Hispanic cousins as "a worthless family . . . a family of cretins,"[15] with the latter responding in kind) and in part to the anglophile policies of the House of the Two Sicilies, whose foreign minister, John Acton, was English-born. In the light of later events, Godoy's defense of Carlos has a particularly hollow ring when he avers, "It is difficult to conceive the degree to which this monarch loved his brother the King of Naples."[16]

But dynastic alliances took precedence over other considerations. The customary haggling was complicated by the Italians' insistence that not only should Fernando marry the eighteen-year-old María Antonia, but that the heir apparent to the Neapolitan throne, Francisco Genaro, marry the Infanta María Isabel, now aged fourteen—a double wedding between first cousins. Francisco Genaro's sickly first wife was still alive, but, as anticipated, she cooperated with the plans under discussion and died on November 15, 1801. On March 24, 1802, an understanding Pope signed the necessary dispensation, thus removing the last obstacle. The final compact was witnessed the following month in Aranjuez; John Acton and the Duke of San Teodoro signed for the Neapolitans, and Godoy and Cevallos for the Spaniards.

Both queens were determined to make a success of the venture and, for the time being at least, were willing to forget past animosities. María Carolina, who on the basis of hearsay cordially detested Godoy, went out of her way to praise him to her sister-in-law in Madrid. On February 8, that is, in the middle of delicate negotiations on both sides, María Luisa gushed to Manuel, "I'm returning to you the letter from the Queen of Naples which gives us great pleasure. We hope that she will imbue her daughter with these excellent truths, as I have no doubt the results will have their effect on Fernando."[17]

The double betrothal necessitated a journey on both sides. On August 12 the royal party—which naturally included Manuel—left Madrid, and traveling in easy stages followed a leisurely route through Guadalajara and Saragossa and on to Barcelona. No details were overlooked; adequate drinking water was brought along, as was a conjugal bed, specially made by the cabinetmaker Hartzenbusch (the father of the dramatist). The court arrived in the Catalonian capital on September 11 to await the shipboard arrival of the Neapolitan relatives.

Also on board the *Reina María Luisa* was the recently crowned queen of Etruria, the monarchs' daughter Luisetta, as she was called within the family. Unlike her younger brother Fernando, she had always shown great affection for Manuel, in whom she often confided, as in a letter some months previously: "Florence, February 12, 1802. I cannot hide the fact that I have a slight suspicion that I may be pregnant. The first day I missed my period there was a ball, but I did not dance. I take great care of myself as that is God's wish. I ask you that if my parents go to Barcelona not to overlook the chance for me to see them, and I won't let my condition hold me back . . ." On April 20 she wrote Manuel: "If only we had such a faithful friend as my beloved parents have in you!" The following day, having learned that Manuel had obtained the royal permission for her to travel, she hastened to express her thanks: "Nothing will ever enable me to repay you for what you have done for me."[18] Her subsequent actions were to prove the emptiness of her protestation. But in the autumn of 1802 she meant every word of it.

As was customary with royal betrothals, the contracted parties took one another on trust. The prince's fiancée was, in fact, a forceful personality with a mind of her own. María Antonia, named for her aunt who as queen of France had perished on the guillotine, was as much Austrian as Italian, a vivacious girl despite the first ominous signs of consumption, which, of course, had never been mentioned in the correspondence. Though no classical beauty—the protruding Habsburg lips and Bourbon nose took care of that—she was intelligent and well educated, having already by the age of seventeen mastered several foreign languages. By way of contrast, Fernando had barely fathomed the rudiments of French.

Although portraits had been exchanged, far from being accurate likenesses, they called forth the painter's most flattering arts. The princess described to the Archduke of Tuscany the reaction she felt on first seeing her future husband. Her dismay was traumatic:

> I descend from the carriage and see the Prince: I thought I was going to faint. According to the portrait he was more ugly than handsome, but that made him out to be an Adonis; and how timid! You remember that San Teodoro [the Neapolitan ambassador in Madrid] had written that he was a good-looking fellow, very alert and kind. When one is warned in advance, the harm is that much less; but I, who had believed everything, was shocked to see that it was all just the opposite . . . A little later we were taken to our room and I began to weep, which lasted throughout the night. I cursed the moment I had deceived myself, but the harm had been done; there was no way out.[19]

On October 4 both weddings were celebrated amid great pomp and genuine popular enthusiasm. According to Godoy, "these fiestas and pleasures were the last to be enjoyed by Carlos IV and María Luisa . . . They never enjoyed them again for the rest of their lives."[20] The days and nights were devoted to a round of fireworks, balls, gala receptions—everything calculated to entrance the heart of María Antonia, who in her youth had danced away many a delirious evening at the palace in Schönbrunn. As usual on these joyous occasions, honors, medals, and promotions cascaded upon the numerous recipients to the tune of twenty-eight lieutenant generals, sixty-six division commanders, eighty-one brigadiers, a Captain-General of the Armada, and many others. In addition, there was a liberal sprinkling of Golden Fleeces and Grand Crosses, not to mention twenty-one Orders of María Luisa.

Manuel found himself in a particularly embarrassing situation. Many felt that he was attending the nuptials of his own flesh and blood, and perfectly innocent gestures, such as handing María Isabel a handkerchief when once she was close to tears, were interpreted as the concern of a father for his daughter. For his part, Fernando made no secret that he resented Godoy's opposition to his wedding. To the young prince, marriage hopefully meant freedom—freedom from irksome restraints, freedom from his domineering parents, and, above all, freedom at long last from the hated *privado*.

It was now time to bid an emotional farewell to the newly wed María Isabel and her husband Francisco Genaro, who were about to embark for Naples. The sorrow of the leave-taking was assuaged as the royal procession made its ceremonious way from Barcelona to Valencia, now happily reconciled to the Crown, and along the coast as far as Cartagena before turning inland and thence to Aranjuez. Outwardly, it was a prolonged triumph, each community vying with its neighbor to demonstrate its loyalty; inwardly, it was a disaster.

The letters of María Antonia to her mother tell a story of bitter disillusionment. Queen María Carolina, far from keeping the fiasco a family secret, gave intimate descriptions of Fernando's inadequacies to her ministers, who in turn passed these delicacies on to the diplomatic colony, which included Alquier, recently appointed French ambassador to Naples. To the Neapolitan representative in Paris, Gallo, the queen confided:

The Prince of Asturias has an ugly face, a tubby figure, round knees and legs, a piping delicate voice, and is utterly stupid. Though he is physically amorous, they are not yet husband and wife after sleeping together a week. He is disagreeable, dull, as lazy as his sister, and he never leaves his wife a single moment. He has no education, an unpleasant continuous giggle; and their existence is cramped, without comforts or amenities, and subjected to scandalous espionage. Poor Antoinette sends letters that make me weep. She writes: "Mother, you have been deceived. For you are too good a mother to have sacrificed me like this if you had known." She says again: "I shall not live, but I wish to behave well and deserve eternal life."

The day her brother left, she begged him sobbing: "I beseech you to take me away or kill me" . . . I think it monstrous that San Teodoro should have dared to deceive us so.[21]

Several other letters followed in a similar vein. In one unsparing moment, the queen referred to her son-in-law as "stupid, lazy, a liar, debased, and sly," adding that her daughter's letters "are breaking my heart."[22] Her pent-up fury attained such a pitch that she temporarily forgot all about Godoy. Not so María Luisa, who kept him *au courant* with vituperative notes such as: "We hate those from Naples more every day, likewise the one we have here . . . That rascally Court of Naples, and that snotty brat, my daughter-in-law, who keeps blowing on the fire . . ."[23] The delicate scrim of family rapprochement was fraying badly.

For the dejected princess, her future appeared a boundless expanse of unmitigated desolation in this alien land. She hated them all: the prying queen, the purblind king, and the conceited favorite. Nor had she a husband worthy of the name to whom to turn: "The Prince is a poor devil who has not been properly brought up; he means well, but has no education, no natural talent or liveliness. He is my very opposite, and I, to my great misfortune, do not love him at all."[24] Later, she bewailed, "He is as stolid as a young bull, utterly dull and stupid."

But bulls perform their duty; Fernando either could not or would not. Soon the bride was disclosing to her mother that a month after the wedding he was "completely silly, not even a husband physically and tedious into the bargain."[25] From Naples, the queen's reaction was incredulous:

Is what you tell me about your husband *possible?* I find it hard to credit and am filled with foreboding. Can it be that great booby is impotent? Heaven forbid! That would be the last straw. I do not know what to suggest. Of course it would be most indelicate for *you* to make the first move. You have done all you *decently* could. Words fail me. What a predicament! Six months married and still no consummation . . . I am very worried. I shall write to San Teodoro. You tell me that Fernando likes him and that he is now one of your little group. This should make things easier. I shall ask him to have a heart to heart talk with your husband and to tell him where his duty lies. People must be beginning to wonder. They may blame *you*.[26]

For her part, María Luisa made every effort to discover why her son was not performing his conjugal duty. In a letter to Manuel on February

3, 1803, she confided: "Father Fernando [the princess's confessor, provided by Godoy] has just seen me with the answer to the matter you know we entrusted him with. He was told some time ago that nothing had been done but he was not told the reason, and the good Father did not ask him, but only found him timid and cowardly. What do you think the Father and I can do?"[27] Manuel wisely did not wish to become involved in a matter best left to husband and wife. Even so, he does not escape that lightly. Izquierdo Hernández, after enumerating Fernando's shortcomings (including what he terms *debilidad orgánica*), lays part of the blame on his "distrust of the Prince of the Peace who had plunged him into such an obvious position of inferiority that the only action left to him was to adopt an attitude of enervated defense or passive resistance."[28] Eventually, the difficulties were overcome, "thanks to a beneficial lecture which San Teodoro gave him,"[29] and, to give substance to the latter's confidential report, the princess was soon expecting.

The news did little to reassure Manuel. In December 1803 the king suffered a recurrence of the apoplexy seizures which had felled him three years earlier. Again his recovery was slow, and for a time his life was despaired of. Even so, Manuel was further inundated with assurances from both monarchs of their undying affection and indebtedness toward him. Again the queen poured out the gratitude that she and her husband felt: "We do not know how to repay everything you have done for us, because up to now all we have done is to give you honors and a great deal of trouble; but it is very little to let you live in the way you deserve when we see the grandees with their millions in revenues and estates, some of them without merit, others traitors and disloyal."[30] It is difficult to envision precisely what the monarchs had in mind. Godoy's annual emolument— his salary as a councillor of state, his income from properties and titles, his acquisition of works of art, many received as gifts or bought at advantageous prices, his questionable revenue from favors granted and treaties concluded—what else could the *reyes* bestow on him short of the key to the state treasury? In the face of pandemic hunger and disease, his ostentatious wealth was more than unpardonable; it was insufferable.

Had Manuel's security depended solely on the sovereigns' continued favor, his future might have been assured. Yet, everywhere he cast his eye, he found cause for profound unease. Before long, María Antonia had gained complete ascendancy over her dullard husband; what hitherto had been sullen resentment was fanned into constant intrigue against the *privado* and the queen. Godoy complained bitterly:

> My position was no longer a happy one as far as feeling secure from enemy machinations behind my back was concerned. At that time the cruel party which was to ruin Spain began to take shape. To the despicable instigation which Canon Escoiquiz long ago had roused the Prince of Asturias against me was now added the fact that the Prince found out the counsel which I had given to Carlos IV to postpone the wedding . . . The Princess of Asturias was just as much against me, but assuredly she had no need of any such information to regard me with disfavor. Her mother, the Queen of Naples, always burned with hatred for France, and believed me to be an outspoken advocate of peace with the Republic. The first thing she charged her [María Antonia] with was to study and find out the best way to undermine my influence and to destroy it; never was a more obedient daughter ever born of a mother.[31]

The battle lines were now clearly drawn, no quarter asked or given on either side.

According to Godoy, not only did Escoiquiz visit the newly wed couple to offer his congratulations, but he used the occasion to give concrete form to an incipient conspiracy. For the first time, figures of the rank of the Duke of Infantado, the Duke of San Carlos, and especially the Count of Teba (later the Count of Montijo) thought seriously of a possible uprising. The Count of Teba was an old hand at the game, and as far back as 1794 had been banished to Ávila on Manuel's advice for the publication of a book critical of the royal power. His role in the Aranjuez upheaval was to prove decisive.

With Fernando now married, it was all but impossible to separate domestic from national considerations. María Antonia's loathing for her mother-in-law was exacerbated by the queen's habit of entering the princess's private apartments unannounced; even her books and underwear were subjected to the royal scrutiny. Nor was her affection increased when María Luisa morbidly insisted that the princess, now heavy with child, descend into the royal sarcophagus and contemplate the niches where she and the as yet unborn infantes would one day be laid to rest. How distant Naples and Vienna were from this cold, forbidding stone vault! A hostile country, a court still governed by rigid etiquette, a fumbling dolt for a husband, an insensitive mother-in-law dominated by a lascivious favorite—the cultivated princess hated each moment of her new life and those she held responsible.

In truth, Manuel's private life was no more serene. María Teresa had now turned hostile and openly resentful of her husband's ill-concealed liaisons with Pepita and other women. Lady Holland found the *privado* to be "large, coarse, ruddy-complexioned, with a heavy, sleepy voluptuous eye." She later noted in her journal, "The P. of the Peace passes a week alternately at the sitio [El Escorial] and here [Madrid]; one for the voice and support of the Queen, the other to secure the silence and obedience of his first and legal wife, the Tudó, whom he both loves and fears. In spite of the pains we have taken to get at the truth of the nature of those jarring connections, it is yet as much of a riddle as when I first heard of them, nor do I believe anyone has the key to the enigma. Recently the French thought themselves strong enough to displace him, but the Queen was roused, forgot his indignities towards her, and shielded him with her influence."[32] Manuel's conduct was such that the queen raised her eyebrows on more than one occasion. The immediate cause seems to have been some Andalucian maid-servants who had caught his fancy. María Luisa pronounced them to be "amusing but fatal" and went on to lecture him: "I very much regret this little tiff you are having with your wife because of the other women . . . Perhaps you would succeed better with your wife by showing affection and kindness, because that is the only way people of strong disposition can be won over."[33]

María Teresa's position at court was unenviable. Not only was she duty bound to her sovereigns as a liege subject and close relative, but even more so as the wife of their favorite. A further complication was the queen's fondness for Carlota, which exceeded any she had shown to her own children. Carlota and the Infante Francisco de Paula became inseparable friends, studying and playing together, which only gave malicious tongues additional grist for gossip. Scarcely a letter between the queen and Manuel went by without some mention of *la Mona* (the monkey, the cute one), as Carlota was dotingly called. When she was suffering from toothache and a swollen face, Manuel again assumed his self-appointed role of family doctor and reported to the queen: "*La Mona* is so pretty, and I have provided for cotton and oil; her mother remains silent but very plump, although gloomy as she washes, combs her hair, and dresses with the windows wide open; it seems to me she missed her true calling as from all this she should have been a huntress."[34] On another occasion in winter, Manuel wrote: "The little girl is feeling very well, though she hasn't gone for a walk due to the bad weather, but her mother walks enough for the two of them. Few human beings can be so pathetic and indifferent."[35] Manuel's misunderstanding of his wife's feelings did nothing to help the marriage; to no one's surprise, María Teresa left him at the first opportunity.

His attention was soon diverted elsewhere. Although Cevallos retained his position as First Minister, few believed the pretense for one moment, least of all the new French ambassador, Pierre de Beurnonville. Like his predecessor, Gouvion Saint-Cyr, he had exchanged his general's uniform for the attire, if not the manners of a diplomat. Beurnonville took up his post on January 4, 1803. His impression of the *privado* is as revelatory of his own duplicity as it is of Godoy's character.

> He is as friendly as possible in our social relationship, but I am dissatisfied with him as regards politics. He affects the greatest frankness towards me, no doubt so as to conceal the falseness I suspect in him. Every time I wish to discuss the vexations suffered by our commerce he maintains that he is not familiar with such details and that he wishes to confine his influence to larger political questions. Then he repeats to me what he has heard from the so-called scholars who surround him. He makes a pretense of being a great lord; however, once one has talked with him a couple of times and discovers the little education he has, one is amazed to see all of Spain at his feet. But he controls everything, and either we have him working in our interests or else we must overthrow him.[36]

Godoy did not have to wait long for the first unpleasant surprise. He had bested Bonaparte in Portugal, and the First Consul's retribution could not be deferred much longer. Without bothering to consult his Spanish partners, the French leader entered into secret pourparlers with the United States government of Thomas Jefferson regarding the sale of Louisiana in direct violation of the Treaty of San Ildefonso. The upshot was that Spain's former territory was relinquished for a paltry sixty million francs, not one centime of which accrued to His Most Catholic Majesty. Carlos was furious at Bonaparte's chicanery, and could only splutter ineffectually in a letter to Godoy dated May 27, 1803: "*Amigo* Manuel, you can see the knavery of the French in selling Louisiana to the Americans which gives us every right to remain neutral because they gave us their word not to transfer it and now they have done it in return for a mere trifle. We trust in you to get us out of all difficulties, because we have no other friend. I am, and shall always remain yours. Carlos."[37] Manuel did his best to placate the irate monarch, but as for positive measures there was nothing he could do.

The stage was now set for one of the most bizarre episodes in Godoy's extraordinary career. The story begins in 1801, when he was approached by an inspired fellow-adventurer named Domingo Badía y Leblicht, a native of Barcelona. Badía was born in 1767, a month before Godoy, and during a prolonged stay in Andalucía had acquired a profound interest in the Moslem faith and culture. He learned to speak Arabic with the fluency of a native, and Manuel was quick to perceive that he could utilize Badía's knowledge and dauntless spirit. Badía's idea was to pose as the Prophet's illustrious descendant who happened to be passing through Morocco on his way to the holy city of Mecca. Simply put, Badía was offering his services to the *valido* as a Spanish spy at the court of the sultan, an audacious plan that captured Godoy's imagination.

The future hadji laid his plans carefully. In Paris and London, he visited scholars to familiarize himself with Arab history, astronomy, mathematics, and general customs. A flowing beard, an impeccable genealogy, and lo and behold, Badía was metamorphosed into Ali Bey Ben Othman Bey, the last of the Abbasside line, which had once ruled in Spain. Having crossed the Straits of Gibraltar and landed at Tangier, he gained the trust of the Sultan Mulei Suleyman by correctly predicting a solar eclipse. Before long, the credulous ruler regarded Ali Bey as his closest confidant.

The artful Catalan quickly ascertained that the sultan was a fanatical autocrat so detested by his subjects that some were actively preparing a revolt against him. Moreover, the sultan was totally opposed to any alliance with the infidel Spanish which, of course, lay at the heart of Godoy's stratagem. Ali Bey gratefully declined the offer to lead a jihad against his native land; instead, he visited the principal rebel leaders, who, in return for Spanish help, promised to cede some of the wealthiest Moroccan provinces to King Carlos. Godoy saw his chance: "Would anyone say, in the conditions then prevailing in Europe, that the project was imprudent or extravagant? No; it is in times of peace that one settles differences and prepares oneself against future contingencies. With regard to France, the war in Morocco offered us a pretext to increase our forces without Napoleon suspecting us."[38]

Godoy was agreeably flattered when the Marquis de la Solana, the captain-general of Andalucía, depicted him as equaling Isabel la Católica in his breadth of vision: "Great minds that are privileged have a mutual understanding. Your Excellency, the real Maecenas of our young traveler, will not rest content merely to admire this great venture in detached fashion; you will also seek to lend it all your support."[39] This is exactly what Godoy had in mind. Using the transparent pretext that the sultan's forces were about to attack Spanish settlements along the coast, he concentrated an expeditionary force in Cádiz.

Such an invasion plan presupposed the king's support or at least his indifference. Carlos, however, was never quite the gullible monarch so often represented. When he contrasted the sultan's hospitality towards Badía with the treason now contemplated, he was aghast and resolutely forbade any such duplicity. In a letter to Manuel, he stated unequivocally: "No, this will never happen as long as I live. I approved of the war because it is just and advantageous to my subjects. I also gave my approval that an explorer scout the terrain, because this is the custom and sometimes necessary so as to wage war successfully; but I shall never consent to hospitality being turned to the detriment and harm of the one who offers it so graciously. I should be held responsible for such an act before God and the whole world."[40]

This incident may in turn have given rise to still another unsought title of Godoy. According to Lady Holland, "The people of Madrid call the Prince of the Peace, El Bonducani, the nickname of the Caliph at which all bow, obey, and tremble. On the day of the besamanos [the ceremony of kneeling and kissing the hands of the *reyes*], the ladies were all in the outer chamber, and were approaching the Queen's apartment, but in the center of the room stood the Prince of the P. playing with the Queen's little dog; the ladies did not venture to pass. The Queen, impatient and surprised at the delay, begged the King to look, who, seeing the impediment, said laughing, 'They won't pass the Bonducani!' "[41] Titles notwithstanding, on this occasion at least Carlos acted decisively. The orders for mobilization were countermanded, which was perhaps just as well; closer to home, Manuel's own political future and survival were at stake.

10

NAPOLEON

The Prince of the Peace was determined that Spain remain neutral despite the resumption of hostilities between France and England on May 18, 1803. Such a policy necessitated adroit handling of the respective ambassadors in Madrid. The English representative, John Hookham Frere (the translator of the *Poema del Cid*), went to great lengths to coax Godoy into an alliance against France. Frere, notwithstanding his profound knowledge of the Spanish language and literature, was less versed in tactful diplomacy and made little headway.

The French ambassador, however, was even more pressing than his English counterpart. Following instructions from the First Consul, Beurnonville requested Godoy, "as a token of friendship between the two nations," to return the sword of King François I taken by Emperor Carlos V at the Battle of Pavia, in 1525, and hinted that a refusal would be viewed with disfavor. Godoy replied: "I don't believe this trivial matter can cool such a good relationship; the proofs of esteem which the King has always given Bonaparte have their foundation in the common interest and glory of France and Spain, and precisely for this reason I am not of a mind that the King grant this petition as this sword recalls the ancient glories of our nation, and for that reason I shall always advise him not to accede."[1] When Fernando briefly ascended the throne in 1808, one of his first ignominious acts was to deliver the historic sword to the French.

Much as one may admire Manuel's independent spirit, his room for maneuver was severely limited. He might wriggle, protest, even strike back on occasion, but he was bound hand and foot by the terms of the Treaty of San Ildefonso, largely of his own making. The snare was contained in Article 3, which stated: "The First Consul consents that the obligations imposed on Spain by the terms of the Treaty which unites both nations may be converted into a financial subsidy of six million francs a month which Spain will give to her ally, counting from the renewal of hostilities until the end of the war."[2] Such an open-ended clause virtually made Manuel the prisoner of the Man of Destiny.

Godoy's fragile world was menaced on all sides. Frere was merely haughty and insistent; Beurnonville was downright impertinent and made scant effort to conceal his disdain of the favorite. An ex-minister of war during the Terror, his subsequent military and diplomatic—or rather un-diplomatic—career gave Manuel little cause for optimism. Bonaparte, de-termined that his new ambassador to Madrid be of far tougher mettle than Lucien, considered Beurnonville's gruff coarseness his principal virtue. In a note to Talleyrand, the French envoy ventured to shock his superior with a blunt account of Godoy's cupidity: "Not content with being Ge-neralissimo, the Prince of the Peace has just added the title of Chief of the Artillery and Engineer Corps. This new rank carries with it a re-muneration of 50,000 écus and places at his disposition all the armed forces of Spain. The indecency of such greed points up the progressive ambition of the Prince and sends a cold shudder down every spine."[3] Godoy countered with an equally forthright assessment of Beurnonville, portraying him as a "shameless military figure, unrestrained and determined in his arguments and intentions, a man of loose conscience, without any well defined political principles, adaptable to all systems . . . I had to confront this new man face to face who once again was changing the scene."[4] An open clash between the two was inevitable.

Admittedly, the Spaniards had given cause for complaint. Two French vessels had been seized by the English under the very guns of the fortress of Carnero without the Spanish garrison firing a shot to save their allies.[5] Bonaparte was further vexed by the rumor that England had encouraged Godoy to defect with a payment of £50,000, and, moreover, that Spanish troops had been mobilized close to the French border. In a violent al-tercation with the Prince of the Peace, Beurnonville assured him that the First Consul would not hesitate to send in an army of 100,000 men if the Spanish contingents remained at their frontier posts. Furthermore, Spain would suffer the same fate if she failed to pay the pledged subsidy.

As a final slap, the *privado* was given until September 7 to hand Frere his passports.

Manuel's respite was of brief duration. The southern provinces, which two years previously had been decimated by the plague, were now visited by yellow fever, ironically at the very moment that other yellow scourge—gold bullion—was beginning once again to flow in from the American colonies. Incessant floods and an earthquake in Valencia only made the situation more critical. The damaging rumor was propagated that the *cólera divina* (in Spanish the word means both anger and cholera) was directed by the Almighty against Godoy for his past interference in church matters.[6]

In many regions, the epidemic was accompanied by famine that devastated the larger cities, including Madrid. One day, Godoy was the recipient of a neatly quartered loaf of bread, a macabre warning to be taken to heart, and on another occasion his carriage was besieged by a hungry mob amid cries of "Peace and Bread!"[7] The ravages of pestilence, hunger, and attendant inflation required some explanation, and "as piety did not permit the Spaniards to reproach the Creator with these afflictions, and loyalty would not allow them to blame the king, a handy scapegoat was found in Godoy."[8] It mattered little that he brought in grain from abroad to alleviate the general suffering—quite the contrary, here was proof positive that the *choricero* was making a windfall profit while the nation agonized. In actual fact, many farmers who withheld their produce in hopes of raising the market price were furious that he forced them to distribute the food equitably. Even so, many people died of starvation. Such was the misery in Madrid that the *reyes* decided to forego their brief annual stay in the capital lest their presence provoke serious riots à la Esquilache. The fever raged throughout the summer and autumn of 1803 with recrudescences in the southern coastal cities the following year.

Against this troubled background, the king did his best to mitigate the cruel conditions of the subsidy, but to no avail. The royal temper was not improved when the French insisted on full payment, famine or no. Again, Manuel advised the king to stand firm in his determination to renegotiate the subsidy amount, an attitude which Carlos heartily endorsed in a note of August 29, 1803:

> *Amigo* Manuel: I very much liked your memorandum concerning the reply to the insolent note of the French, it is like all of yours. You are right when you say that now I'm getting to know my enemies, and don't think that just because things are calming down a bit and seem to be improving that

I am going to forget this incident and many others I have in mind. I hope it doesn't come to the critical point where they will declare war on us, but it would be well to prepare ourselves just in case, and you can make all the arrangements as we know from past experience how (as you put it) to exhort and get things done. But this would be the final resort. God be with you, Manuel, stay well, and depend on it that we are your constant friends.

Carlos.[9]

A brave letter, but unfortunately the initiative lay entirely with the French. Two days later, on September 1, Beurnonville struck at his quarry.

With matchless insolence, the ambassador presented his humiliating demands in the form of an ultimatum at the daily levee of the Prince of the Peace, thus making a public spectacle of what should have been a confidential discussion. Godoy makes no mention of the open diplomatic clash in his memoirs, but Beurnonville's account does conform in essence to the reports of witnesses present:

Godoy: It's an order, then? His Catholic Majesty cannot accept such from anyone, and therefore I will not accept your note.

Beurn: It is not my intention to harm you, Prince, but be advised that there are five hundred people in your salon; either accept, or I shall have them all witness that I am leaving with you an important communication for the King under your own personal responsibility.

Seeing that Godoy kept the note in his hand without offering a reply, Beurnonville continued:

Beurn: His Majesty is and always will be protected from all criticism. It is on your shoulders, Prince, that the reproof of the Spanish people will weigh; and you will be held responsible for all the calamities into which you did not hesitate to drag your country; and finally, in the eyes of Europe you will be considered the willing and guilty cause of the war.

Godoy: You wish me then to lose the public's favor?

Beurn: Prince, distrust adulation and an artificial popularity. Of all the flatterers who come to ask favors of you, you cannot depend on the attachment of a single one of them, and who might not be the instrument of public indignation the day that the First Consul, when he enlightens the King, will make you lose his confidence.[10]

According to Beurnonville, at this point tears welled up in Godoy's eyes. "I will come to receive my reply within twenty-four hours," the ambassador concluded. "His Majesty will be guided by your advice, and I trust sufficiently in your discernment to expect good news."[11] Whereupon the Frenchman stalked out of the startled assembly.

Faced with such a predicament, only one course of action was possible for the *privado:* to appeal directly to the king for help. Assuredly, Beurnonville's attitude was depicted as an egregious case of lese-majesty. Carlos was indignant. In ringing tones, he gave Manuel his instructions:

> Tell General Beurnonville that I have already dispatched my reply to the First Consul, and that I cannot depart from it. My financial situation will not admit of the sacrifice demanded, and I am determined not to enter into any engagement which I cannot fulfill . . . The crops have failed again this year all over Spain. If I declared war against England at this moment, I should expose my realm to the horrors of famine. However, the First Consul will be informed of all this through Azara, and I am satisfied that he will do me justice.[12]

Beurnonville, true to his word, insisted on seeing Godoy on September 3. By now Manuel had regained his composure and proceeded to read aloud the king's letter addressed to the First Consul. It was an astute move; the ambassador dared not interpose himself between the two heads of state. Rather lamely, the perplexed envoy divulged the contents of a communiqué received from Talleyrand that stated in part: "I hope to hear within a fortnight that you have opened the eyes of this prince [Godoy], who ought to know by this time that Bonaparte is the most irresistible man created by God." Pure bluster; Manuel remained unmoved. Disconcerted by his impassivity, Beurnonville adopted what was meant to be a conciliatory attitude. "Prince," he continued, "while it is yet time, abandon a policy which means your ruin. The First Consul will do justice to Charles IV, but he will call down the vengeance of France on his favourite. Be warned in time! The Spanish people are devoted to their sovereign, but they have no love for a favourite whose fortune is as great as the national debt."[13] Manuel came back with a suitable rejoinder, and the second confrontation between the two men ended as inconclusively as had the first.

By now, the First Consul was tired of Godoy's vacillations, convinced that this was the opportune moment to break the Spanish impasse once and for all. Accordingly, he sent a previous chargé d'affaires in Madrid, the Alsatian Herman, as his personal emissary with what amounted to yet another ultimatum. Talleyrand impressed on him that there was to be "no delay, no evasion, we want to finish," and that the forty-eight million francs a year were to flow into the French public treasury forthwith.[14] On October 3, 1803, there took place at the Escorial a discussion conducted in the bluntest language possible. Herman's tone was so belligerent that Godoy supposedly broke into tears and exclaimed; "How can it be that I'm being treated like this? This is not the way to treat a man who has married the niece of his King and who has rendered such services to his country!"[15] Once the weeping had subsided, he attempted to reduce the subsidy to a monthly payment of two million, only to be faced the following day with further demands. From all accounts, Herman used utterances and tactics not usually associated with diplomats (at least not of the nineteenth century), but Godoy refused to yield. Quite obviously, even more direct methods would have to be employed.

The Extremaduran mule had proved unexpectedly stubborn. Bonaparte, like Floridablanca on another occasion, was convinced that the king languished in ignorance regarding the true relationship between Godoy and the queen. Accordingly, Beurnonville was instructed to seek an audience with the king, during which he was to deliver a personal communication from the First Consul that provided irrefutable evidence of Godoy's misconduct. The ambassador, who in his frustration once referred to the *privado* as an *"âme de boue"* ("soul of mud"), was delighted to have been chosen as a conduit. Beurnonville's instructions from Talleyrand were explicit:

> You are forbidden to see or greet the Prince of the Peace who is the enemy of the French people. If he dares present himself or remain during the audience you are to have with the King, you will point out this audacity to the King as a clear sign of his dethronement. Should he be lacking in respect towards the King and France to the extent of speaking, you will confine yourself to saying that you cannot speak of the interests of France and Spain in the presence of the man who at Badajoz sold peace for eight millions and who, during the course of a far too long usurpation, has sold the honor of the ministry for 84 millions deposited in his coffers.[16]

Somehow, Manuel got wind of the content of the letter. Calling forth every ounce of his native intelligence, he hit upon an ingenious counterstroke. In a memorandum intended only for the king's eyes, he laid bare his scheme:

The French Ambassador is going to deliver to Your Majesty a letter from the First Consul. I have been able to learn of the terms: it is a violent ultimatum. The alternative is just as disagreeable if Your Majesty takes cognizance of it: to reject the demands of Bonaparte is to lose Spain, to accept them is to humiliate the Crown. Sire, accept the letter, but do not read it. By not opening it, you will avoid having to reply to the demands made upon you, and the meetings of Azara in Paris can continue without this direct communication doing any harm.[17]

On October 11 at a quarter past eleven in the morning, Beurnonville presented himself at the formal audience. The first sight was none too reassuring as Carlos, María Luisa, and Godoy appeared in their finery amid the impressive pageantry of the Spanish court. The ambassador, by now more than a little apprehensive, announced his purpose and then ceremoniously delivered Bonaparte's communiqué into the king's hands. Wonder turned to consternation when Carlos made no attempt to open the letter. Instead, with a disarming smile, he addressed himself to the thoroughly bewildered Frenchman and said: "Tell the First Consul that I esteem as much as I like him, and that I am much more attached to France than to England, and will do all that I can. I will tax my subjects, my clergy, I will tax myself; but I will not consent to the dismissal of Manuel, for no one can object to my liking for a man who acts properly and whose society is necessary to me. I accept, therefore, the Consul's letter, but I shall not open it, as Azara has this negotiation in hand."[18] A royal nod signified that the audience was terminated, leaving Beurnonville no alternative but to retire mouthing the diplomatic clichés best suited to the occasion.

Godoy had retained his post, whatever that was, but his bargaining strength had hardly improved. He did continue to meet with Hookham Frere, though the wrangling and interspersed threats on both sides scarcely merited the name of diplomacy. The favorite's tenuous position was not enhanced when he injudiciously revealed the substance of his confidential exchanges with His Britannic Ambassador to Beurnonville. To Manuel's embarrassment—not to mention Frere's chagrin—all was duly reported verbatim in the *Moniteur* on March 25, 1804.

That same year, two decisive events took place in France, neither of which boded well for Spain or Godoy. On March 14 a small French contingent crossed the German border and kidnapped the duc d'Enghien, a Bourbon prince, on the flimsy pretext that he was involved in a conspiracy against the First Consul. The young duke was brought to the fortress of

Vincennes, tried by a court-martial presided over by Bonaparte's brother-in-law, Joachim Murat, and shot by a waiting firing squad in the middle of the night. All Europe was shocked by this blatant murder of royalty. Only Carlos and Godoy remained silent; gone was the moral outrage of 1793 when Louis XVI was executed. The second event followed hard upon the first. When Napoleon proclaimed himself emperor, the Spanish monarchs—whatever their personal feelings—hurried to convey their felicitations to their fellow ruler. For Manuel, the only cheerful note that summer was the disfavor into which Beurnonville had fallen with his unpredictable taskmasters in Paris.

As so often during Godoy's career, an occurrence over which he had no control brought matters to a head. The English had already captured a Spanish vessel, the *Urquijo* (the bureaucracy took ample time to rechristen its ships), but Carlos, anxious to avoid war, told Manuel in his best paternal fashion, "I do not want my children to go to war." "But Sire," Godoy protested, "they have seized one of your ships!" To which the king rejoined, "The captain was drunk, one doesn't quarrel with that kind of people."[19] A subsequent outrage could not be dismissed so easily. On October 5, 1804, in total defiance of the laws of the sea, four Spanish frigates laden with treasure from the New World were set upon by a like number of English warships near Cádiz. One ship was sunk and the three others jubilantly brought to England as prizes. This flagrant act of piracy was protested in the House of Commons by Charles Fox (the uncle of Lord Holland) and was viewed with repugnance throughout Europe. Even so, Carlos hesitated to plunge his country into the unknown terrors of war. It was only on December 12, at the urging of Godoy, whose patience had run its course, that the peace-loving monarch signed the official declaration.

Whether the news of Napoleon's coronation in Notre Dame on December 2 played a decisive part in the favorite's *volte-face* is doubtful; the martial juices had begun to stir much earlier. Before long, he would be communicating with the emperor as "from one soldier to another," which must have made Napoleon wince more than any cannonade on the battlefield. In an effusive salutation, Godoy assured him that he was "ready to ride in person to Boulogne or anywhere else where the presence of Spaniards could further the Emperor's plans."[20] As for María Luisa, not one to be outdone in matters of rhetoric, she assured Manuel that "your memory and fame shall end only with the world."[21]

For better or worse, Godoy and Napoleon needed one another. With consummate cynicism, they bypassed their respective ambassadors in Madrid and Paris, leaving them to fulfill a purely decorative role. For the second time, Eugenio Izquierdo acted in the French capital as Manuel's personal representative. Godoy was flattered to have direct access to the emperor through Izquierdo's counterpart, the distinguished naturalist and confidant of Napoleon, Lacépède. Through this intermediary, Manuel humbly portrayed himself in a letter dated January 12, 1805, as "a soldier of few words but those truthful, a philosopher in his opinions, neither a boaster nor a groveler, modest but not timid, whose only ambition it is to preserve his country and merit the esteem of good men."[22]

In a demonstrative reply five weeks later, Napoleon addressed Manuel as "mon cousin," as if he were a ruling prince. Such a commendation obviously hid some ulterior purpose. The emperor, unwilling to accept the Prince of the Peace at his own face value, had instructed General Junot to visit him in Madrid and to report his frank assessment of the *privado*. The importance attached to Godoy's future role by the French leader is evident from the precise orders given to his envoy extraordinary: "You are to pay frequent visits to the Prince of the Peace; tell him that I have complete confidence in him, that I have observed with great pleasure the energy he has shown and that I believe he acts in good faith. Tell him I have set aside the bias which others had insinuated to his detriment, and that I recognize that he has more energy than the rest of the Court and the grandees." The emperor's true purpose soon becomes apparent: "[Tell him] that I will support him and use all my authority in his favor, that I expect from him just one thing, and that is that the Spanish fleet be ready for the great enterprise I have planned." The remainder of Napoleon's directive indicated the seriousness of the mission: "In no way are you to hint to General Beurnonville that you have been entrusted with an assignment relative to the Prince of the Peace. Tell the Prince that I intend to give him a present as proof of my consideration, that I hope that the Spanish squadrons will participate in glorious deeds so that the success of the same may be attributed to him and so that I may give him public testimonial of my high esteem."[23]

During the *reyes'* spring sojourn in Aranjuez, Godoy also received the full attention of Junot's wife, the Duchess of Abrantés, whose hawkish eyes directed her equally sharp quill:

I beheld a man at the other end of the apartment whose attitude and bearing appeared to me particularly ill suited to the audience-chamber of royalty. This man appeared to be thirty-four or thirty-five years of age [in

Manuel Godoy in Uniform by Goya, 1801. (Real Academia de Bellas Artes de San Fernando, Madrid)

fact thirty-seven]; his countenance was of that description which a fine, well-grown, hearty young man usually presents; but there was no trace of dignity in his appearance. The individual whom I am now describing was covered with decorations of all sorts . . . I might therefore reasonably suppose that this man was an important personage, and I was not wrong; he was the Prince of the Peace. I was struck with surprise at his free and easy manner. He was leaning, or rather lying, upon a console at the farther end of the apartment, and was playing with a curtain tassel which was within his reach.[24]

Not a flattering portrait, but, one must confess, of a piece with Goya's unsparing study of the puffed-up prince in uniform. The favorite's spiritual deterioration had set in. Gone are the earlier compassion and sensitivity toward others; all his energies are now bent on self-preservation.

If Napoleon had finally eradicated all potential rivals, Godoy's position was precisely the opposite. Fernando's marriage with María Antonia had introduced a Trojan horse into the Spanish court. The princess was regarded by many as little more than an English spy; her letters to her mother (sometimes written in a secret code) might well contain information useful to the enemy. Already Fernando had scented that some major naval operation was contemplated and immediately pressed Manuel for exact details. "I replied that the plans were on a vast scale and could easily be changed according to conditions; that Rochefort's squadron was to set sail for the East Indies, the Toulon fleet was headed for Egypt, leaving the remaining Spanish, French, and Dutch flotillas ready for a combined blow on Ireland when the time was ripe. As was only to be expected, Princess María Antonia wasted no time in extracting my reply [from Fernando] and sending it off to Naples."[25] Whether in fact she did so is open to question—no such letter has come to light—but undeniably Nelson was convinced that the main French fleet was bound for the eastern Mediterranean and acted accordingly. One of history's unresolved questions is what effect, if any, Godoy's brief conversation with Fernando played in Nelson's fruitless chase of the phantom fleet.

Manuel was clearly perplexed in his dealings with the heir apparent. He had once made Fernando a present of some magnificent Andalucian horses, only to see him return them on the grounds that his father had never kept his own stable before becoming king. Rumors abounded that the *valido* would take advantage of one of Carlos's incapacitating illnesses, declare Fernando unfit to rule on some pretext or other, and proclaim himself regent. Some indeed whispered that Godoy contemplated nothing less than a change of dynasty, citing his wife's royal lineage.[26] No concrete evidence supports such a serious charge, and, given his innate caution, so often in strange juxtaposition with his inordinate vanity, such daring aspirations seem unlikely. Pretentious he was, but a pretender to the throne—no.

As Manuel had feared, the presence of María Antonia at court had a profoundly unsettling effect. Soon *la Napolitana* was perceived as the rallying point of all those who hated the favorite—a goodly number. Under such circumstances, it is small wonder that the family correspondence took on an acrid tone. In a letter to San Teodoro, Queen María Carolina entreated him "always to distrust Godoy, her [María Antonia's] greatest enemy, also that of her husband, more especially of both of them in the future, for her to remain attached to her husband, the Prince of Asturias, to produce children, to look after her health, and to dissemble with the Queen . . ."[27] Unfortunately, one of the princess's more unguarded replies fell into Napoleon's hands. In a letter written in May 1805, she had referred to yet another of the king's illnesses, foolishly noting that "half an hour after Carlos IV's death, Godoy will be arrested; my husband and I are determined to take this step."[28] Within a few days, a copy of the original was in Manuel's possession, thoughtfully provided by the French emperor.

Godoy's expectations ran high that summer. Whether Napoleon kept him fully informed of his grandiose undertakings is doubtful—even the emperor's closest aides were often in the dark—but Godoy was deluded into believing that he was privy to the great plans afoot. The first jolt came on July 22, when a Spanish squadron was severely mauled by Admiral Sir Robert Calder in the fog off Cape Finisterre. The subsequent action at Trafalgar, fought on October 21, 1805, requires no further retelling. The Spaniards fought valiantly to a man, but to no avail. By the end of the day, Admiral Pedro Gravina and Dionisio Alcalá Galiano (the father of the essayist) among many others had joined Nelson in death. At one blow, Godoy's strongest card was plucked from his hand; Napoleon's award of the Grand Cordon of the Legion of Honor was scant compensation for the loss of the fleet.

As if defeat were not enough, Manuel also had to face an infuriated Fernando, who reproached the *privado* for having misled him. The exchange was far from pleasant:

> F. Look here, Manuel, I'll be frank with you. I've got to talk to you about these matters. Either they are deceiving you, or else you have deceived me. You told me the Toulon squadron was bound for Egypt.

G. But, Sire, I also told Your Highness that the plans might have to be changed according to events.

F. No, that won't do, because the Toulon squadron immediately set sail for the Atlantic.

G. But Your Highness no doubt remembers that the squadron left harbor twice. I can only infer that the first time it was to head for Egypt. But Nelson had prior intelligence and therefore that project had to be altered.

F. All right then, as far as Egypt is concerned, but none of the other things you have told me has turned out to be true. The fact is that in affairs of state I count for nothing in the palace and that I am treated like a downstairs servant. The Crown Prince is a reflection of his father and is deserving of the same respect. Have you ever lied to my father?

G. Sire, I have never lied to my King. One day Your Highness will be King, and may it please God that you will have servants as faithful and loyal as I am to your august father. Perhaps Your Highness sees things differently. To one who would sacrifice his own life to please Your Highness, nothing else counts. There is an easy solution: for some time I've been wanting to step down but have not been able to do so. Your Highness could help me by presenting my request at Court and which I beseech Your Highness to do with all my heart.

F. (with a wicked laugh) That way you would have me compromise myself, wouldn't you?

According to Manuel, before he could reply, Fernando turned his back on him and stalked out of the room.[29]

In temperate moments, Manuel truly wished to withdraw and be done with it, but the opium of public acclaim and the ephemeral glory that was his on the world's stage held him prisoner. Moreover, he had become so indispensable to the *reyes* that the choice was no longer his to make. Thus, the king of his own volition addressed himself to Napoleon on February 20, 1806:

Sire, my brother: The sentiments of affection and friendship that Your Imperial Majesty has shown in your letter to the Prince of the Peace require on my part the most hasty recognition and the most sincere friendship . . . It gave me the greatest satisfaction to note that Your Imperial Majesty agrees with me regarding the eminent merits of the Prince of the Peace whose virtues and talents honor my kingdom and oblige me to offer myself as a guarantor for whatever he undertakes; but he has experienced so much vexation in the painful conduct of this war . . . that I fear that he is thinking of giving up all his offices and asking me his retirement. For this reason I am turning to Your Imperial Majesty, beseeching you with all the sincerity I possess, that if there is some way we can agree on the means of keeping near me such a valuable person who is so essential for my happiness with the rank and distinctions he has deserved, that Your Imperial Highness will give me your opinion with the same frankness which I have shown.

Carlos[30]

María Luisa's approach was considerably more forthright. On August 14 she penned the following appeal from La Granja: "*Amigo* Manuel, you are right to say that now the moments count for more than in days previously, and that is why I feel sorry that you want to go your own way or to remove your hand from the helm, in which case we shall all be the losers. By living in peace, we shall be happy, the King, you and I, being the three of us the trinity on earth. If only you could see, Manuel, the fears I have that those French have played us another mean trick and that we shall come out the worse for it!"[31]

María Luisa was far less solicitous regarding her in-laws. She appeared totally unmoved when the Princess of Asturias suffered a premature delivery, which the queen described to Manuel with clinical detachment: "I have just been present at the miscarriage of my daughter-in-law. She had some pain and a little blood flowed, but not even as much as one day of my menstrual flow. The fetus was smaller than a grain of aniseed and the umbilical cord was as thin as a cobweb. The King had to put on his glasses to see it. . ."[32] On both sides, the voices became shriller, the insults more rancorous. Threats and fears of being poisoned abounded, all servants were presumed to be spies (on the merest suspicion two hundred Italians were arrested and fourteen of them banished), and the Neapolitan chargé d'affaires was sent packing.

None, however, could surpass the queen in outright vituperation. In one particularly abusive letter, she portrayed the princess to Manuel as "the spittle of her mother, a venomous viper, an animal filled with gall and poison in the place of blood, a half-dead frog and a diabolical snake" bent on encompassing the death of the reigning monarchs.[33] On another occasion—the mention of poison again provided the catalyst—María Luisa included her abject son in the defamatory tirade: "What are we going to do with this diabolical serpent of a daughter-in-law and cunning cowardly son of mine?" she asked Manuel. "If we don't restrain them by separating them from their advisers, I fear some upheaval, because I tremble at the thought of foreigners, and especially Italians, as they poison without any scruple, everything horrifies me, not so much for myself as I don't take anything for granted, and so then a close watch on all of them, especially in that room."[34] That both she and her husband were Italian-born, whereas the Borgias, those most proficient of poisoners, had their origins in Spain, seems to have escaped her attention.

Such dynastic bickering was the stuff Napoleon's dreams were made of. Exactly when he formulated the plan to replace the Bourbons in Spain is difficult to determine. Certainly he probed for weaknesses in the Spanish edifice by fomenting animosities that were only too evident. Thus, on June 28, 1805, he wrote to Godoy: "Quite independently of the Portuguese matter, wouldn't it be possible to make amends for the stupidity of letting a princess from Naples into Spain who, it would seem, will one day govern Spain despotically?"[35]

That Napoleon dared raise the delicate question is indicative of Spain's humiliating weakness (and this was four months prior to the disaster at Trafalgar). Implicit in his remarks to the Prince of the Peace is a low estimate of the moral worth of his correspondent. The record is dismally clear; in letter after letter to Napoleon, Godoy resorted to the most obsequious language. "My predictions have been fulfilled," he once enthused, "and the great actions of Alexander, Caesar and Charlemagne have turned to things of nought. History will be able to show nothing finer than Your Majesty's lofty deeds."[36] Worse still, in a fateful moment, he openly encouraged French intervention:

> The Queen of Naples has tried every means, but without success, to destroy the King and Queen of Spain; she also wanted to do away with me. The instrument of her crimes is her daughter. Their Majesties are in danger every day of being poisoned, just as I am. The keen perception of the Queen uncovered the plan and the conspiracy. . .The King has written to his brother, the King of Naples, threatening him with his vengeance if he does not dissuade his daughter from the abominable ideas she has conceived; but it rests, Sire, with Your Imperial and Royal Majesty to put an end to these dangers.[37]

Napoleon replied on February 2, 1806: "Nothing that the Queen of Naples does surprises me. I did, however, shudder at the mere reading of your letter. Rest assured of my concern for you and my wish to offer you proof of my protection."[38] The emperor did not tremble for long. He had already confided to Talleyrand, "At last I'm going to punish this hussy [María Carolina]. The outrages committed by this miserable queen increase with every courier."[39] On February 15 Joseph Bonaparte and General André Masséna entered Naples at the head of an army of 40,000 to be welcomed by the Duke of San Teodoro and the local *lazzaroni*. A few days previously, King Ferdinand and Queen María Carolina had judiciously fled to Sicily. The Neapolitan branch of the Bourbons had ceased to reign on the Italian mainland.

In view of Napoleon's boast that his dynasty would soon be the oldest in Europe, one might have expected the remaining Bourbons to close ranks. Not at all; if anything, the vicious personal attacks intensified. Fernando directly commissioned many of the quips aimed at his mother and Godoy. One such gibe said it all:

> An insolent old woman
> raised him out of the mud,
> poking fun at her good husband
> who is very accommodating.
>
> It's only fair it should happen like this,
> as from an old woman
> anything can be expected,
> except that she tell the truth.[40]

The barbs dedicated exclusively to the favorite came to the point even more succinctly. One such verse concluded not with the usual threats, but with a vivid depiction of his execution:

> As an assassin and traitor
> you'll see yourself burned alive
> in the Plaza Mayor.[41]

Fernando was doomed to a bitter disappointment; it was not Manuel who died, but his own wife, María Antonia.

The princess had been marked for the grave from the moment she disembarked in Barcelona. The harsh contrasts of the climate of the central plateau, repeated miscarriages and attendant illnesses, the mental stress of her unhappy marriage, her hatred of Godoy, the expulsion of her parents from Naples—it was all too much for the frail princess, whose health was already undermined by tuberculosis. She took to her sickbed during the third week of January 1806, and, despite occasional improvement, no hope for her recovery was entertained. Throughout the interminable vigil, Fernando remained at his wife's bedside, often reading a book or writing. For a brief moment, it appeared that she might yet confound the doctors (and her mother-in-law), but on May 20 the queen wrote to Manuel, "Perhaps tomorrow, before you receive this, you will have tidings of the princess' death. She is dying with considerable suffering and hard breathing, and her legs and hands are already cold."[42] The following afternoon, she breathed her last.

All too predictably, the premature end of the princess gave rise to more than the usual rumors and speculation. At the lighter end of the spectrum, María Antonia was reported to have reproached the queen before expiring: "I regret, Madame, to descend to the tomb without having had sufficient time to mould the heart of Fernando, whom Your Majesty failed to instruct."[43] Far more disturbing was the vehement reaction of Escoiquiz and others of the *partido fernandino*. The agitated prelate immediately set about consoling his former pupil. "Sire," he wrote, "I understand the tribulations of your pious heart, pierced by the arrow of misfortune. Irreparable loss! Console yourself, Sire, that the soul of your consort is now in the paradise of the just with the palm of martyrdom, as the wife of the Prince of Asturias died poisoned by Godoy. That is what the public is saying . . ." For once in his life, Fernando was governed by a sense of fairness. "The public is wrong and is slandering Manuel," he replied. "When I married María Antonia she was already consumptive."[44]

This vital fact was never widely reported. According to Alcalá Galiano, not only the masses thought the *choricero* responsible: "And don't think that such fantastic nonsense was only believed by the ignorant populace, just the opposite, since it was circulated as testified truth by people of superior rank and of good upbringing."[45] In his memoirs, Manuel could only shake his head in disbelief:

> I won't stop to refute the iniquitous suspicions spread by a few malicious people that she had died poisoned. It was well known throughout Spain that the Princess suffered from tubercular consumption dating back many years which, developing along natural lines, ended her days. The Neapolitan monarchs, showing little regard for their daughter's indisposition, and hiding it from us, arranged her marriage with wicked design and sacrificed her by sending her to a region like Madrid with a climate so different from that of Naples. The medical attention she received was conscientious; the seven professors of the King's chamber who attended to the Princess' health over a long period were able to lengthen her life even when all the resources of their art were exhausted, but her illness was incurable.[46]

Few wished to believe the unembellished truth, despite the publication of the official medical report in the *Gaceta de Madrid* on May 27. As bad luck would have it, the palace apothecary committed suicide a few months afterward, conclusive proof in the public mind that foul play was involved. For those tired of the poison theme, a variant had the *privado* place a scorpion in the princess's bed. Not to be outdone, the queen uncharitably hinted that syphilis might have been a contributory factor. On receiving the news in Paris, Napoleon pronounced one of the tersest funeral orations ever recorded: *"Il faut songer à la remplacer"* ("We'll have to think about replacing her").[47] It was far from being his last word on Spain.

11

PARRY AND THRUST

Manuel Godoy received the news of the princess's death with mixed emotions. To all outward appearances, he had cause for rejoicing. Nevertheless, he was assailed by gnawing feelings of uneasiness. A bold stroke was called for, one that would reinforce his hand at home. With uncharacteristic disregard for the law, he ordered five of Fernando's servants arbitrarily exiled to the Philippines and Puerto Rico. Their crime rang hollow enough; purportedly they had spoken of the favorite and the queen with gross disrespect. The blow, delivered more from weakness than strength, was aimed at throwing the Prince of Asturias off balance by serving as an oblique warning. Thanks to the war with England, the original sentence was changed to imprisonment in Spain—so much for Godoy's boast that the jails were free of political prisoners.

He was also giving thought to the future. Fernando had never fully shared his late wife's Francophobe sentiments; what if the young widower should seek a reconciliation with Napoleon? And what, in that case, if the French emperor should find the *privado* eminently dispensable? While kingdoms were being reapportioned with generous abandon, might this not be the best moment to approach the Corsican cartographer with a view to obtaining a modest demesne, say in Portugal?

Accordingly, Izquierdo was instructed to put the matter to Napoleon through the agency of Lacépède. Godoy's expression is hardly that of a coequal:

My gratitude to His Imperial Majesty is boundless. The hero who provides France with glory and happiness wishes to give me proofs of the concern with which he honors me. My security depends on his protection; I might undergo a great misfortune, the death of my sovereigns; I feel obliged, before that terrible moment comes, to secure for myself a way of life sheltered from any danger. . .Therefore I am ready to make myself the object of His Imperial Majesty's kindness and the recipient of his benevolence, and if it fits in with his views, to become one of the elements in the great political system which, by restoring peace to Europe, will affirm the freedom of the seas throughout the world. Any proposal of His Imperial Majesty will be accepted by our sovereigns.[1]

This letter was delivered by Izquierdo on March 1, 1806. For Spain and Godoy, the consequences were incalculable.

Manuel's personal envoy was kept waiting the best part of two weeks before receiving an unsatisfactory reply on March 13. The emperor's note acknowledged receipt of Godoy's communication but added curtly, "This is not clear enough; the Prince of the Peace ought to say what he wants."[2] Napoleon was determined to have him commit himself in writing with regard to Portugal. Throughout the summer of 1806, the unedifying haggling continued; the debate was no longer whether, but how Spain's neighbor was to be carved up.

On May 10 the irritant of the subsidy was settled once and for all. Though now at war with England, Spain had previously fallen into arrears to the amount of seventy-two million francs. Napoleon had been clamoring for the full payment, but Izquierdo managed to reduce the outstanding debt to a third of that sum. Lacépède, in the meantime, had been replaced as Napoleon's intermediary by General Michel Duroc, the Grand Marshal of the Palace and also a confidant of the emperor. Napoleon hastened to assure the favorite that he (Godoy) was a "sovereign individual, capable of great achievements, and one of the most extraordinary people of the century"[3]—a century, it should be noted, that had barely begun.

In a less exalted vein, Izquierdo urged his master to be more specific in his entreaties to the emperor: "Your Excellency stands on the banks of the Rubicon, like Caesar: you must either cross it and escape from the present situation, or else abandon everything. Unless the Emperor receives a firm proposal, unless one categorically answers his precise questions, any further negotiations are finished."[4] Godoy perceived the situation to be exactly the opposite; the more he proposed, the less the Olympian Frenchman disposed. With added urgency, Izquierdo warned:

The Emperor does not repeat the same things twice; he never takes a step which will not produce some result; he removes and bestows sovereignties; nobody influences his opinion; all the changes, all the agreements which he makes are nurtured in his mind, and his minister Talleyrand, his brother Prince Joseph, his generals and aides-de-camp, his retinue, his secretaries, even his wife, just like the public have no idea of the gestation until the news of the birth is published. If the Emperor felt like doing so, he could have Your Excellency named Infante, Prince, King, without anyone having the least foreknowledge.[5]

To emphasize the last point, Izquierdo concluded with the news that Murat had been named Grand Duke of Berg and Cleves with his capital in Düsseldorf, a broad hint that Godoy might also aspire to a similar rank—always assuming, of course, that he cooperated fully with the emperor.

To pique Godoy's vanity still further, Napoleon announced his intention of presenting him with an emblazoned sword. Izquierdo was requested to provide Manuel's coat of arms so that it might be engraved on the hilt. As a final touch, it was confirmed that Beurnonville would be retired as ambassador and Godoy consulted regarding a successor.

Buoyed by such earnests of the emperor's good intentions, Godoy (after considerable misgivings, to be sure) outlined his plans for the partition of Portugal. The unwitting victim was literally to be quartered: the Infante Don Carlos would rule in the north, then geographically in descending order, a province for Francisco de Paula, another for the Regent Juan and Carlota Joaquina, and finally in the south for one who "thanks to the benevolence of His Imperial Majesty and that of Their Catholic Majesties would be elevated to that rank."[6]

The *Memorias* pass over this disreputable correspondence in silence. By acquiescing in the annexation of Portugal, Godoy myopically countenanced the reprehensible practice of sundering territories against the will of the local population. That Napoleon might also have designs on Spain's northern provinces did not occur to him. Nor for that matter had he given any thought that the Bourbons might be called upon to make a sizable contribution to the furtherance of the emperor's "Italian System," little more than a euphemism for total French control.

The first intimation of such plans came during the night of June 13, when Izquierdo was summoned to Talleyrand's residence at eleven o'clock. The foreign minister immediately came to the point: "I received orders from the emperor to discuss with you a certain matter which requires the utmost reserve. His Imperial Majesty will make every endeavor to become master of the whole of Italy, and in the middle of the territories governed by him will not allow the Kingdom of Tuscany to be subject to another authority."[7] Naturally, fitting compensation would be offered; the queen of Etruria, the *reyes'* daughter, would rule in the north of Portugal, while the Prince of the Peace would govern in the south with the imposing title of King of the Algarve. Both halves would be placed under the protection of the newly proclaimed Emperor Carlos IV. As for the reigning House of Braganza, why, there was plenty of space in Brazil.

Izquierdo's letter outlining Talleyrand's shameless proposal came as a rude awakening to Manuel. Concern would have turned to dread had he known Napoleon's innermost thoughts as revealed to Metternich in a confidential moment: "The Spanish Royal House are my personal enemies; they and I cannot be on thrones at the same time."[8] Though the flattery continues unabated, henceforth Godoy's native distrust of the French, dormant the past two years, reasserts itself.

The *reyes,* excessively complacent in most matters, were thoroughly alarmed to see the thrones of their own daughters threatened. In light of these apprehensions, Godoy propounded to the monarchs a course of action similar to that taken in 1801, namely, a unilateral Spanish invasion and occupation of Portugal, but this time without notifying the French beforehand. Manuel made his position clear: "As we can now make ourselves masters of Portugal before [Napoleon] attacks it, and with Portuguese arms united with us against England, Bonaparte would have no pretext to interfere in the Peninsula, and it would remove the suspicions which he might still harbor against us."[9] Further, Spain's position at future peace talks would be strengthened as well as that of the royal couple in Portugal.

There were other sound reasons as well. Not only was Napoleon militarily beset in distant Prussia, but, should the French intervene (an unlikely occurrence), the Spanish Army could be depended upon to give a good account of itself. Anti-French feeling was running high; the subsidy payments had been widely resented, the disaster at Trafalgar was attributed to the pusillanimity of the Gallic ally, and rumors abounded that Napoleon coveted Spanish lands.

The martial excitement in the air did much to reassure Manuel. On September 29, he reported to María Luisa with evident self-satisfaction, "I declaimed to the soldiers without any predetermined theme, and I noticed with pleasure not only their great desire to fight but also that of the civilians to help them. The talk, together with the reception, lasted an hour and a quarter."[10] The following day, the queen in turn expressed her confidence to Manuel: "I have no doubt that all the military will fight against the French with plenty of spirit as they hate them, quite deservedly, and I hope you will deliver us from the afflictions and vexations they will cause us."[11] The stumbling block, as in the past, was the king's steadfast opposition to committing his nation to war. "Manuel," he admonished, "don't pester me, let's wait and take our time to think about it."[12]

Even so, Godoy remained undaunted. Throughout Spain, warlike preparations were evident. Beurnonville, a former general, would immediately have spotted what was afoot, but to his great annoyance had been ordered back to France that summer. In his place came Vandeul, something of a simple soul, an interim appointment until a permanent ambassador was selected. Vandeul accepted the vaguest of explanations for the battle array— even Gibraltar was mentioned as an objective—and saw no reason to press his inquiries.

On October 6, 1806, one of those bizarre incidents occurred that seek some rational answer in vain. In a magniloquent proclamation addressed to the nation, *mal escrita y peor pensada* (badly written and worse thought out),[13] Godoy summoned his fellow countrymen to arms. One specific detail was missing: at no point in the rambling manifesto was the identity of the enemy ever revealed. The declaration stated in part:

> In conditions less perilous than the present, the loyalty of Spaniards has sought to help their sovereigns with gifts and means advanced for the needs of the monarchy. Our present situation urgently requires these patriotic efforts . . . Come then, my beloved countrymen, come and enlist under the colors of the most beneficent of kings; I shall welcome you with the most intense gratitude, I promise all of you rewards if the God of our fathers through a victory assures us of a happy and lasting peace, the sole object of my prayers. No, do not let fear or treachery dissuade you; your hearts shelter nothing of the kind, nor can foreign seduction ever deprive them of their renown. Come then, and if things reach a point that we must cross swords with our enemy, let no one give cause to let his honor be besmirched or even be regarded as suspect for having seemed indifferent to this patriotic call . . .
>
> San Lorenzo, October 6, 1806.
>
> > The Prince of the Peace.[14]

To add consternation to confusion, Godoy's cumbrous prose was ordered to be read from the pulpit. No doubt he hoped that the congregations would grasp his intent, whereas Napoleon would be baffled by the murky syntax. Instead, a whole flood of questions arose in the mind of the average Spaniard. Given the apparent gravity of the situation, why had the appeal to the nation been signed by the *privado* and not by the king? Had Carlos approved of the text or, for that matter, even been consulted? If Godoy's purpose was to rally national support, he failed dismally.

Thirty years later, Manuel sought to silence his critics. In one of the least admirable passages of the *Memorias,* he attempts to exonerate himself at the expense of the king:

> Friends and enemies alike, nearly all have censured me for my proclamation of October 6. What is more, I myself knew that it was not the right time to launch it. But every moment I feared that the King would revoke his consent and that the whole purpose would be thwarted . . . Carlos IV made me change it and keep changing it, weaving and unweaving, and varying it in a thousand ways, but finally it was published. If I made a mistake acting this way, as I am told, I offer as my excuse my loyalty, my love for my king, my love of family and country faced with perils which, though perceived far off, filled my faculties and senses at all hours, day and night.[15]

Eight days after the declaration, at the twin battles of Jena and Auerstädt, Napoleon shattered Godoy's presumptuous hopes. If nothing else, the favorite could be grateful that his pompous language had been so cryptic. The news of the victories reached Madrid toward the end of October, filling everyone with apprehension. María Luisa was so distraught that she spoke in Italian to the French ambassador and in French to the Italian. To the Russian ambassador, Strogonoff, a discouraged Godoy confided: "If Emperor Alexander does not succeed in bringing down this [French] colossus . . . our turn will come and we shall be the last victims."[16] On October 23—the queen appears to have received an advance bulletin—Her Majesty wrote to *amigo* Manuel: "Soon you will be receiving the letters from Paris, they [the French] are beginning their victories like last year; it seems that the Devil is helping them." The next day, she expounded on the woes afflicting the troubled *trinidad*: "The picture you paint of our sad situation is accurate, much to our sorrow, and you have every reason to be ill-tempered as everything is closing in; it grieves me nonetheless, and I have no further word or wish than to have the sound judgment to place ourselves in your hands. The King says the same, and at the same time sympathizes with you for lacking sufficient means. You are our sole source of help . . ."[17] Carlos, in fact, lay prostrate at that very moment, overcome by the unwelcome reports from the battlefield.

Not so Godoy. Grasping the new reality, he sought out Vandeul to offer his congratulations on the emperor's masterly triumph: "Before proceeding to Germany," he assured the trustful chargé d'affaires, "His Imperial Majesty made known to me his projects. The forces prepared for him by his loyal ally, Spain, are always at his disposal. To which quarter does His Majesty wish they should be directed?"[18] Then, hypocritically, the *valido* berated the very persons at court who had supported his ill-advised utterances. "Your complaint is," he scolded them collectively, "that the Emperor of the French has too much power. But what use does he make of it? Is there another Sovereign as great as he? No. Can you point to a more liberal statesman? No. Was there ever a greater captain? No. You are rascals, more swayed by your passions than guided by concern for the public weal."[19]

Nevertheless, Godoy assures his readers that, despite the reverse suffered at Jena, he was still eager to launch a campaign against Napoleon. He stood alone: "No one hesitated to advise the king at that time to abandon the enterprise already embarked on. I found myself almost alone in my attempt to persuade Carlos IV against such weak advisers."[20] Yet, not only did Godoy pledge his "absolute devotion [to] the most perfect model of a hero that History has to show,"[21] but in addition hastened to dispatch two magnificent chargers to replace one killed in battle.

In Berlin, the Spanish ambassador, Pardo de Figueroa, made a brave attempt to defend Godoy's policy to Napoleon. He was immediately brushed aside by the irritated emperor:

> Have you read his proclamation? Do you know that he has ordered extraordinary armaments? . . . Spain is being flooded with lies . . . Among others the news is being spread that I envision the dethronement of the Bourbons, my allies, that I covet their Spanish kingdom, that I wish to get rid of them so as to give this crown to someone of my family . . . No one respects more than I do the personal character of Carlos IV, no one knows or esteems more highly the qualities and virtues of the Castillian people: we saw them at Trafalgar, without having to search further. Let's not talk about war.

Then, as a judicious afterthought, he added: "Also write to your friend the Prince of the Peace. His position, if he can keep it, is such that History will be able to dedicate a fine page to him for having protected his country from revolutions and wars which everywhere have afflicted nations . . . His fall is certain if he changes his policy."[22] As always, no amount of praise could hide the veiled threat.

Godoy was no doubt vastly relieved at the imperial display of moderation. For all that, the warnings were unequivocally clear. The favorite rightly judged that some token of amity was apropos. Joseph was recognized as king of Naples, a gesture that simply acknowledged a fact of life. Prince Masserano, a nullity of the first water, had already been appointed Spanish ambassador in Paris. On February 19, 1807, Godoy indicated that Spain would adhere to the Continental System, Napoleon's far-flung scheme to throttle England by means of an economic blockade.

Until now, these had been minor concessions that minimally affected Spain. Not so the emperor's request—a synonym for demand—for direct Spanish military assistance in northern Germany. Godoy hastened to comply, though he later boasted that he had reduced the original contingent from 25,000 men to 14,000.[23] The troops, under the command of his friend the Marquis de la Romana, were partially drawn from the Spanish garrison in Etruria—hardly a reassuring sight for Luisetta. By the late summer of 1807, the soldiers finally took up their occupation duties in Hamburg, more than a thousand miles from their homeland. With far greater alacrity, Manuel dashed off a congratulatory paean to the conqueror: "Sire, the events which today amaze the world do not increase the concept I had formed of the martial powers of Your Imperial Majesty. Of your enemies, what can I say? The enemies of the Continent have disappeared; formidable powers no longer exist . . . All that I desire now is the annihilation of the English, Your Imperial Majesty has only to wish it, and it will happen, as I see that everything is subject to your authority."[24]

Napoleon finally saw fit to appoint a permanent ambassador in Madrid. François de Beauharnais, who arrived in the Spanish capital on December 23, 1806, was the brother of the Empress Josephine's first husband, and as such the uncle of Eugène and Hortense, whom Napoleon regarded as his own children. The new envoy had just served as this country's representative in Etruria, and so was assured of a solicitous welcome from Luisetta's anxious parents. To Manuel's intense disappointment, the arrogant Beauharnais remained not only unimpressed with him but openly hostile to his overtures.

Mutual wariness soon turned to antipathy. In his report to the Foreign Ministry, Beauharnais did not hesitate to impugn Godoy: "Either due to a lack of manners or breeding, the deportment of this Prince seemed to me outrageous. I had hoped to find him natural and noble in his attentions, but instead I saw him as embarrassed, timid, and even fearful . . . This is a man who may be prevailed upon more by firmness than by reasoning or persuasion. I believe he has little moral courage; his talent is very ordinary and his sincerity suspect."[25] These final observations could just as easily serve as a self-portrait of the new ambassador.

For the truth is that Beauharnais, far from being the genteel diplomat, had come to Madrid to sow discord in the royal family and to further Napoleon's stratagems. The key to his scheming was Fernando. The choice of a second wife was crucial, and soon reports of an impending alliance filled the air. One potential bride was Antoinette-Marie, the niece of Murat, but Godoy gave Izquierdo instructions not to encourage such a match on the inscrutable grounds that "we must not make any proposals which could indicate a change of direction in our relationship with the Emperor."[26]

The favorite's true motivation was altogether more intriguing, nothing less than an audacious plan to make Fernando his own brother-in-law. As one might anticipate, Manuel vigorously denies that he furthered such a union:

> With even greater stupidity than malice my enemies sought to spread the rumor that, so as to affirm my authority and be able to retain my influence once Carlos IV was no more, I had inspired His Majesty with the idea of uniting in marriage the Prince of Asturias with the Infante Don Luis' second daughter, my sister-in-law. To anyone with any common sense I should like to ask what belief or hope there would have been that the Prince, once he had become my brother-in-law, would have changed his opinion, and from being a mortal enemy would have become my friend . . . I never gave this unfortunate project a moment's thought.[27]

Manuel's actual part in this murky matrimonial venture is obscure, but in a letter to Izquierdo dated November 11, 1806, he states, "I am considering and discussing with Their Majesties and the Prince of Asturias the wedding of my sister-in-law with His Highness."[28] Later, Fernando claimed that he rejected the idea out of hand with the scathing comment "I would rather remain a widower all the rest of my life—I would rather be a monk— than become the brother-in-law of Manuel Godoy!"[29]

This brave disavowal may be called into question, contradicted as it is by that unimpeachable source, Canon Escoiquiz. It seems that the heir apparent did in fact agree, albeit unwittingly, to marry Manuel's sister-in-law, yet another María Luisa. In a letter to his mother, Fernando signified his willingness to marry a Bavarian princess, but, incredibly enough, managed to confuse her name with Godoy's relative. Having committed himself in writing and terrified to admit his blunder to the queen, he wrote a pathetic letter to his former tutor in which he lugubriously accepted his fate. But Escoiquiz was not so willing: "I wrote to the Prince without delay, making quite clear to him the unfortunate consequences of such a marriage, and exhorting him to hasten his request for a private audience with the Queen and without waiting, as he had been advised."[30] Fernando replied abjectly that his mother had made up her mind, that he was to become related to Manuel, and that nothing would dissuade her. Only a belated appeal to the king at the earnest imploration of the canon saved the day.

Since his rustication to Toledo in 1800, Escoiquiz had maintained an inflammatory correspondence with his ex-pupil, of which the following letter is a fair sample:

> This lucky villain [Godoy] is trying by all means to impose himself as sovereign. Your kind father, following the perfidious advice of this stupid person, will not allow Your Highness to participate in the deliberations of the Council of State. Your Highness is a man of great talent and is not a child as the infamous favorite avers. He fears that the wise counsel of Your Highness might prevail and that the Prince of Asturias might discover the iniquitous tricks of his criminality and thus cast a cloud over his favor at Court. Your Highness must extricate himself from this fear which is unbecoming to royalty, so that you can express yourself courageously to your father, and so that a crown soon to be bestowed may be trained in the conduct of state affairs rather than be handed over as the monopoly of a parvenu.[31]

Escoiquiz's criticism of Godoy on this count is entirely unjustified. The *privado* had strenuously advocated Fernando's presence at council meetings; it was the king, and not Manuel, who objected.

Sometime during March 1807 Escoiquiz received an urgent letter from Fernando in which "he urged me out of fidelity to discuss with him and advise the most effective way of rescuing him from the machinations of that tyrant, to save the Kingdom, and even his own parents who, despite their blind affection for him [Godoy] would be his first victims."[32] Escoiquiz, demonstrating his fine sense of the theatrical, left immediately for Madrid in disguise.

In the capital, matters were coming to a head. Reportedly, Godoy's cronies (in particular his brother Diego) were spreading tales that the Prince of Asturias was mentally unfit to reign, that the other infantes were too young, and that a change of dynasty—or at the very least a regency—was necessary. No one in Madrid was more willing to give credence to such baseless rumors than Ambassador Beauharnais, who, through the intermediary of Escoiquiz, was anxious to ascertain Fernando's attitude toward Godoy. After considerable quibbling, the two schemers agreed that Fernando would casually drop the innocent question "Have you ever been to Naples?" to Beauharnais to indicate his approval of the parleys.

One hot summer day during the siesta hour, the ambassador and the canon met secretly in the sylvan seclusion of the Retiro gardens. Even this rendezvous was not without risk for they "had to pass under the windows of the residence of doña Josefa Tudó, the first wife or paramour of the Prince of the Peace, as the matter is still in doubt,"[33] and keep a sharp eye open for suspicious loiterers who might well be spies of the *privado*. Escoiquiz was wearing an artificial black beard in the searing heat, and to complete his impenetrable disguise was intent on reading the *Gaceta de Madrid*. The substance of the talks is clear enough. Fernando was anxious to have a French princess as his second wife, preferably a member of the reigning family. As luck would have it, Beauharnais had the ideal partner in mind: Marie-Stéphanie de la Pagerie, nineteen years of age, and both his cousin and that of the Empress Josephine.

By now, Beauharnais was more a fellow conspirator than a conventional ambassador. To forestall Godoy in case of the king's sudden death, Fernando was prevailed upon to sign an undated decree that appointed the Duke of Infantado Captain General of Castille with the responsibility of arresting Manuel. The duke, a grandee of Spain and the owner of vast terrains, was also a respected war hero and a sworn enemy of the *privado*. In an ill-considered moment, the latter had taken petty revenge on his foe by banishing him to provincial exile for a year and a half. From May 1807 onward, Infantado lent his full support to the complot.

One event, more than any other, lent support to the apprehensions of the *partido fernandino*. It began with hearsay, as Alcalá Galiano recalled in later years:

> Suddenly, while the Court was at Aranjuez, the word began to be whispered around Madrid that the Prince of the Peace had been named Admiral with the appellation of Most Serene Highness. The people did not admire any increase in court favors of one who already could be and was everything; but this new honor bestowed on the *valido* gave rise to gossip and suspicion. The address of Highness, as well as the addition of Most Serene, though at that time the word Royal was not added, not even for the Prince of Asturias, clearly indicated the resolve to place him on a par with the royal family, from whence successive and greater outrages were prophesied.[34]

Before long, rumor had become fact. On January 13, 1807, a grateful monarch appointed Manuel Admiral-General of Spain and the Indies, this despite his propensity for seasickness. More alarming from Fernando's point of view was the favorite's elevation to the unheard-of rank of *Alteza Serenísima,* by which accolade he was to be addressed in future. Revealing an unsuspected sense of dramatic timing, the king fell ill again, but to everyone's relief recovered fully.

The *reyes* were rapidly losing touch with reality. On January 3, 1807, they wrote the *privado* on the subject of his pending elevation:

> *Amigo* Manuel: The King and I are aware of your philosophy, your total indifference to gain, titles, and honors, for that you are well known to us and all the world; your deeds and opinions will remain immortal. You owe it to yourself more than anyone else, but the King is in your debt for what you have done and are doing for him and his realm. In light of his obligation as King, friend, and in consideration of the fact that you are married and united to our family, and indeed very closely, for that reason he must discharge his obligations as he should and wishes to. You too must give us this one more proof of friendship and admit what must be ... See, Manuel, we won't let you make any excuses.[35]

Recently, Godoy had acquired the magnificent townhouse of the Albas, the Buena Vista palace, presented to him by the city of Madrid. On the pretext that the rambling mansion required more than the assigned guard of fifty hussars, he secured a like number of grenadiers, and then, in July 1807, fifty-six more artillerymen and two cannons, a virtual private army.[36] As a further precaution, his brother Diego was appointed colonel of the Spanish Guards regiment while adding the titles of Grandee of Spain and Duke of Almodovar del Campo. Manuel, modesty itself, was content with the designation of Commandant Inspector of the King's Household, a post that afforded him every opportunity to keep Fernando under close surveillance.

Fernando's reaction, as recounted by Godoy, was completely in character. At a serenade given in the admiral-general's honor, Fernando's discordant notes rose clearly above the dulcet tones of the orchestra. Almost within earshot of his parents, the heir apparent could be heard discoursing to his brother Carlos about the latest honor accorded to the *privado.* "In this way," he quavered, "Godoy, a vassal of mine, is usurping from me the love and favor of my people. I count for nothing in the government; he is in charge of everything. This is intolerable." His brother responded, "Don't worry about it, the more they give him, the more you will soon have to take away from him."[37]

It is only too easy to believe that Godoy's outrageous rise to the most eminent rank was the final straw in the public mind. Such was not the case. Many perceived the moment opportune to seek special favors at one of the public audiences held by His Most Serene Highness, the admiral-general. As Alcalá Galiano, an eyewitness to such scenes, observes, "Despite the murmurings and discontent, nevertheless the desire was general to go and congratulate in the most obsequious way such a powerful personage on his new elevation."[38]

On a wintry day in January 1807, the eighteen-year-old Alcalá Galiano made the journey with his family from Madrid to Aranjuez for the express purpose of exchanging a few words with the potentate. The travelers were courteously received in the anteroom of Godoy's mansion by the inquisitor-general, Ramón de Arce, "a man who greatly enjoyed the protection of the *privado* of his monarchs."[39] The ecclesiastic disclosed that the first visitors that morning had been uncertain as to whether Godoy had in fact been elevated to royalty, and, rather than be found remiss, had gone on bended knee and kissed his hand, with the *privado* neither approving nor disapproving. Alcalá Galiano recalls, "The Prince of the Peace received us affably, but inattentively, with a haughtiness in keeping with his elevation, and without paying attention to me or to the apologies of my grandfather for not having offered his services."[40]

A few days later, the same family attended one of Godoy's public receptions in Madrid. Alcalá Galiano's description of the splendor surpasses anything he witnessed several years earlier:

A numerous assembly of important people and of the middle hierarchy filled the various rooms and even the recently built magnificent staircase of the house where, even more than in the palace of the monarchs, resided the supreme authority of the state. The Prince of the Peace arrived and passed through the crowd which was assembled to pay him homage, stopping but little. He was also entertained at two theatre performances, the first at the Cruz, the second at the Príncipe. He was very nearly accorded the treatment of royalty; doves were released into the air when he appeared in his box, and his bust was presented to him while a numerous chorus flattered him at the same time that an author complimented him in verses of little merit . . . The strange thing is that the public received him with handclapping, something to which he was not accustomed . . . This applause was detrimental to the person to whom it was accorded as it imbued him with the mistaken conviction that the wind of popular affection had turned favorable to him which up to now had constantly blown against his helmsmanship due to the tempestuous and dangerous sea of his favor at Court.[41]

Any assessment of Godoy's true strength during this critical period is weighted with imponderables. It was in his self-interest to minimize his influence on the king and thus by inference his responsibility for the later tragedy: "I was not the one who determined the King's volition; quite the contrary, his and that of others was imposed on me. Where is this level of power that has been attributed to me? Nowhere could it be seen more clearly that I was not a *valido*: if I had been, my advice would have triumphed or, to state it more accurately, the King would have listened only to my counsel."[42] Godoy argues that he was frequently overruled by the king, as when he wished to declare war on France even following the news of Jena. Carlos, regally assuming all responsibility, told him in words "which will never be erased from my memory" that "I am more your friend than you are to yourself. If I followed your advice and declared war which in turn brought about our downfall, I could charge you with having ruined me; but by subjecting your counsel to mine, and I being the one in command, if such an ill should befall us, I cannot blame you."[43]

The news of Napoleon's Pyrrhic victory at Eylau (February 1807) once again encouraged Godoy to persuade the king to declare war under advantageous conditions. As before, Carlos refused to give his assent. Furthermore, he was resolutely opposed even to a temporary occupation of Portugal. Manuel was disconsolate: "My fate would be different, had I been listened to. I was not, to my misfortune and that of Spain, and I bore the blame for what I did not do. Let no one accuse Carlos IV. The mischievous advisers overwhelmed him; among these, first and foremost, were the studious and cunning counselors of my enemies."[44] A new villain appears, none other than the king's younger brother, the Infante Antonio Pascual, who deserted his contemplative life in semiretirement to join the forces gathering around his nephew. In any case, Napoleon's decisive rout of the Russians at Friedland in June made any further talk of *una guerra justa* altogether irrelevant.

The emperor could now give undivided attention to his recalcitrant neighbor to the south. To attack Spain openly was unnecessary when the last of the Bourbons could, in effect, preside over their own demise. Napoleon's plan was of imperial proportions: Portugal was to be given a humiliating ultimatum, which, if rejected, would be followed by a joint Franco-Spanish invasion under French command. Again the Spanish ambassador in Paris, Prince Masserano, was kept in ignorance of the negotiations being conducted by Izquierdo and Duroc.

The weakness of Spain's position is all too apparent from a letter of María Luisa to Manuel a few months previously (October 19, 1806):

> We have seen all of Izquierdo's letters and what you wrote in the margin, which is very well put; but every day we are more in the dark and in a worse state. The King says that you are doing all that can be done which is what he wants, and that he approves of it and will support everything, he talks and thinks very clearly [an apparent reference to the king's illness]. He also says that Masserano should be asked where the Emperor is, and in that matter about America Cevallos says that if Talleyrand gets his hands on something we won't get off lightly as he wishes to rob us of Florida, and should that happen we would then lose Mexico. What they want in Paris is everything over there [in America], and everything you say is right.[45]

The Portuguese, under pressure from England, rejected the ultimatum presented on July 28, 1807; immediately, Napoleon proceeded with his alternative plan. Etruria (already occupied by French troops) was now to be exchanged for a solatium to be known as Northern Lusitania, ruled by Luisetta. The final reapportionment of the central sector between the Tagus and Douro rivers would await a formal peace settlement. For Manuel, the realization of his dreams was on the verge of fulfillment: the granting of a hereditary principality of his own, guaranteed by Napoleon. Two of the fourteen articles of the new treaty with France were entirely devoted to his future:

> II. The province of Alentejo and the Algarve will be given in full possession and sovereignty to the Prince of the Peace, who will enjoy them with the title of Prince of the Algarve.

> V. The principality of the Algarve will be a hereditary possession of the descendants of the Prince of the Peace in accordance with the laws of succession pertaining to the ruling family of His Majesty, the King of Spain.[46]

A few weeks later, when the favorite felt the principality within his grasp, he employed his obsequious pen to ingratiate himself with his benefactor: "Sire, expressions of gratitude wear a pleasing air, but do not always express the strength of feelings of him who has expressed them. A sword and a brave heart directing it in Your Imperial and Royal Majesty's service will ever be the worthiest tribute of gratitude open to those whom Your Majesty deigns to honor; your sincerest and most respectful admirer among them is myself."[47]

On the face of it, the Treaty of Fontainebleau did not involve the loss of a single clod of Spanish territory, an invidious achievement considering the fate of other nations. So far so good; but what of the seven secret articles appended to the original fourteen? Here, as might be expected, lay the *quid pro quo*. A French army of 25,000 men and 3,000 cavalry was accorded transit rights across Spain in order to strike directly at Lisbon, while a larger force of 40,000 was to be held in reserve in Bayonne, just north of the border; the supporting Spanish armies were to be placed under the command of General Junot.

On October 27, 1807, the treaty was formally signed by Duroc and Izquierdo, with Napoleon affixing his imperial signature two days later. Godoy's fondest ambitions were about to be fulfilled—or so it seemed. Fate decreed otherwise. The first of the two French armies had already crossed into Spain on the 17th, that is, ten days *before* the signing of the treaty. Soon, thousands of foreign troops were pouring into the northern provinces. This was not all. On the same day the treaty had been signed, Napoleon received a truly astounding letter from the Prince of Asturias. The real upheaval was to be reserved for the cold corridors of the Escorial palace, that austere repository of so much of Spain's history. At that very moment, a crucial event was in progress, nothing less than a palace revolt instigated by the heir to the throne. The hour of judgment was approaching for all the players in this drama, not least of all, Manuel Godoy.

12

THE ESCORIAL

AFFAIR

The rapid advance of Junot's army made it imperative that Beauharnais approach Fernando as soon as possible. During the course of a royal reception, after he had humored the king and queen with suitable small talk, he made his way across the crowded salon to where the Prince of Asturias was standing. Fernando casually asked Beauharnais if he had ever been to Naples and what he thought of the city, whereupon in reply the ambassador pulled out his handkerchief and blew his nose—the agreed-upon signal between the two men.[1] The heir to the throne, whether he realized it or not, was addressing a direct appeal to Napoleon to intervene in Spain's domestic affairs. However, the French ambassador was not content with mere words. The same evening, he stressed to Escoiquiz the need for a written commitment from the prince to convince the emperor of his sincerity. "The [oral] pledge is audacious," he declared, "I favor it and hereby offer to work in like fashion. But words are borne away by the wind, and that is why I think it necessary that Carlos IV's heir give some surety of his wishes so that he will be believed."[2] In brief, Napoleon was determined to extract the same damning type of document from Fernando that Godoy had already submitted relative to Portugal.

One minor problem remained. Napoleon preferred to peruse his correspondence in French, and it was suggested that, to achieve its intended effect, Fernando's letter to the emperor be written in that language. Escoiquiz and the ambassador between them composed an acceptable draft, but Fernando, before approving the text, first insisted that it be shown to the dukes of Infantado and Montijo, two of the leading conspirators. That men of such stature were privy to the contents makes the approach to Napoleon even more remarkable. The final version read in part:

> The state in which I have found myself for some time, and which cannot be hidden from Your Majesty's great perception, until now has been [an] obstacle which has withheld my pen from expressing my wishes. But now, full of hope in finding in Your Imperial Majesty's magnanimity the strongest possible protection, I am determined not only to evince the feelings in my heart towards your august person, but also to deposit the most intimate secrets in the bosom of Your Majesty as in that of a tender father . . . Filled as I am with respect and filial affection for my father (whose heart is the most upright and generous), I would not venture to tell Your Majesty what you do not already know better than I; that is, that these very same qualities often become instruments in the hands of astute and wicked people so as to obscure the truth in the eyes of the sovereign . . . With the utmost confidence I implore the paternal protection of Your Majesty, so that not only will you deign to bestow upon me as my wife a princess of your family, but will remove all the difficulties and obstacles which might hinder the sole object of my desires . . . Written and signed with my own hand and under my own seal, at the Escorial, October 11, 1807. The most devoted servant and brother of Your Imperial and Royal Majesty.
>
> Fernando[3]

Although Fernando had written his letter on October 11, the need to find a trustworthy courier delayed its journey northward until the 20th. Even using fresh relays, at least a week of hard riding was required to cover the distance between Madrid and Paris. Considering that the roads were clogged with soldiers and the impedimenta of war, all heading towards Spain in the late autumnal rains, the special messenger did extremely well to reach Napoleon at Fontainebleau on the morning of the 27th, a few hours before the secret treaty was officially signed. No one knows what immediate effect this demeaning letter had on the emperor, but it certainly demonstrated that Godoy's desire for a Portuguese kingdom was but one entrance to the Spanish labyrinth. Regarding the favorite, Napoleon could now state with assurance that "this faction [of Fernando] will not stop until they have thrown him into the abyss, and the day I wish, this faction will come over to my side."[4]

With each new report from the border provinces, Godoy grew more apprehensive. In the main, Junot's army had been well received; in fact, many of the citizenry were convinced that the French had really come to deliver them from the detested *privado* and perhaps even to place the Prince of Asturias on the throne. Godoy was gloomily aware that the euphoria engendered for a brief time by his elevation to admiral-general had completely dissipated. Near the end of 1807, Napoleon's personal observer of the Spanish scene, Count Tournon-Simiane, summarized Manuel's irredeemable plight in a dispatch to the emperor: "All classes of society hate him and accuse him of being the enemy of the country. The grandees, the nobility, the clergy, the merchants, the people, all see him as the country's oppressor. I have had the opportunity to seek the opinion of all sectors, and in all of them I found the same feelings expressed." To Tournon, only one solution was possible: "All eyes are now turned towards the Emperor. Spain in her misfortune regards His Imperial Majesty as the sole support who can save her, and dares hope that he will take the Prince of Asturias under his protection, give him a wife, and free him from the tyranny which oppresses him."[5]

Politically, Godoy was *in extremis*. Given such an atmosphere, no tale depicting his depravity could be scurrilous enough. Credulity knew no bounds as foul-mouthed raconteurs vied to cap each other's salacious anecdotes, while outright fabrications and gross distortions filled the air like flies in the local market. As each day passed, the virulence escalated; on good authority, it was known that the *choricero* had provided the queen with a succession of gigolos at the very moment he was seducing *la Tudó's* younger sister. It was accepted as incontrovertible fact that the favorite's mansions were little more than harems stocked with seductive odalisques for his perverted entertainment. Even more dastardly—this came from the usual unimpeachable sources—he was planning to poison both Fernando and the king so that he could marry the queen and usurp the Crown! Faced with such irrefutable "facts" and the advancing French armies, Godoy's position was hopeless. The only questions were how, and even more importantly, whether he could extricate himself.

Beyond a doubt, his dearest wish was to relinquish his ill-defined post and retire to his promised Portuguese domains. In one particularly troubled moment, he unburdened himself to Izquierdo: "I want to put an end to my career and have need of peace in the world at large to do it. Oh that I could make my name sound welcome to all and win in return a tear from posterity!"[6] Tears, it seems, came to Manuel and his generation almost at will. At his insistence, Pestalozzi's sentimental *Lienhard und Gertrud* had been translated into Spanish. Manuel noted, "Each time I received an installment of the manuscript I read it to Carlos IV. His spirit delighted in this work; not just once, but many times, I saw tears spring from his eyes as I read to him from the book."[7]

To all outward appearances, the pursuit of literature was the rage within the royal family. Most remarkable was Fernando's commendable industry, which had been so lacking as a pupil. Escoiquiz had suggested to Fernando that he translate into Spanish the *Histoire des révolutions arrivées dans le gouvernement de la République romaine* of the Abbé Vertot. The bulk of the work was probably undertaken by one of Fernando's more gifted servants in the small hours of the night; it was then read and edited by Juan Antonio Melón, a high official at the Printing Office who, like so many others, owed his post to Godoy. After some hesitation by Melón—works of such eminent authorship were supposed to be first sanctioned by the king—the translation was published under the initials "F. de B."

The prince's intention was to present a bound copy to his mother as a token of his affection. María Luisa, on discerning the subversive title, clutched her palpitating breast and exclaimed, "No revolutions, Fernando *mío,* you know how much we hate that name, and what has to be endured everywhere on account of revolutions." The king magnanimously allowed the offending volume to be preserved, but sternly warned that "he who is to reign must not expose himself to the contempt which might come his way if his work is not proof against criticism."[8] Instead, he recommended that his son translate Condillac's *Étude de l'histoire,* written for Mama during her childhood days in Parma. Fernando dutifully assented, and the matter was deemed closed.

On September 22, 1807, the court left the palace of La Granja to establish its winter residence at the Escorial. Fernando, in an access of apparent piety, voiced the wish to be lodged in the prior's old quarters, located close to the monks' cells. Again, the prince's labors appeared to be exemplary. A light was observed in his room until the early hours of the morning; doubtless he was working hard on his new translation to gladden the hearts of his parents. The king's consternation was therefore all the greater when he found an anonymous note on his desk with a melodramatic "Quickly! Quickly! Quickly!" scrawled at the top. The message read: "Prince Fernando is preparing a revolt in the palace. The crown of Your Majesty is in danger. The Queen runs the great risk of being poisoned. It is urgent to forestall this attempt without losing a moment. The loyal vassal who is giving this warning is not in a position to fulfill his duty in any other way."[9]

Predictably enough, the king's first reaction was to consult with his wife, Manuel being uncharacteristically laid low with fever in Madrid at the time. Contrary to some graphic tales, the monarchs did not fly into an uncontrollable passion on rereading the note; indeed, if anything, they rejected its contents as inconceivable. Not surprisingly, Godoy himself has come under suspicion as the author of the anonymous note, his convenient indisposition and absence from the Escorial being cited as supporting proof. The *reyes,* however, were prepared to dismiss the whole episode out of hand. Still another shock was required to jolt them back to reality.

The king was in the habit of informally visiting the infantes in their quarters unannounced. One evening, he was anxious to present Fernando with a bound volume of poems extolling the recent Spanish victories over the English in South America. The youth's perturbation was so evident that even his trusting father concluded that something was amiss. "The King," Godoy later recorded, "told me that he entered with the news and the book to receive his son's congratulations, and felt so well-disposed towards him that, had he seen some sign in his expression of that natural carefree spirit which an innocent person shows, he could never have decided on an investigation. But his son's confusion and embarrassment betrayed him, and his very own eyes revealed the whereabouts of the papers which were taken from him."[10] To make matters worse, Fernando adopted a disrespectful and peevish tone in answer to his father's questions. The accounts of this confrontation vary—some have the queen and her secretary Ballesteros present—but all agree that Carlos's fury became ungovernable on perusing the documents. Fernando was ordered to remain in his room incommunicado while the *reyes* and Caballero began a detailed scrutiny of the confiscated papers.

In his royal rage, the king neglected to post sentries at his son's door. That same evening, the Duke of Ayerbe, one of the conspirators, quite openly visited Fernando in the prior's cell. Escoiquiz tells the whole story somewhat differently. In his highly colored version, "the Prince of the Peace, tired of his secret and unproductive investigations . . . made use of his domination over the weak King, and helped by the Queen, filled him with terror regarding the Prince's [Fernando's] intentions and prevailed upon him to seize the papers unexpectedly."[11] The canon asserts that the queen immediately ordered the palace carpenters and locksmiths to secure the prince's door, but the guards were so attached to Fernando that the workmen were forced to desist and report back to a highly incensed María Luisa. As a result of this incident, the guard was disbanded and the soldiers posted to other regiments. According to Escoiquiz's suspect account, "the Queen, the Prince of the Peace, and the Minister of Justice, Marquis Caballero, busied themselves that evening and part of the next day examining the papers,"[12] the king being absent so as to be spared further anguish. It is an evocative scene of the trio around the fireside, except that Godoy, in one of the few points that everyone else agrees on, was in Madrid at the time (in fact his enemies are the first to insist on this detail, having thoughtfully provided him with yet another mistress).

The Duke of Ayerbe, himself in danger of imminent arrest, entrusted two messengers with notes from Fernando to the Duke of Infantado and Escoiquiz. At four o'clock on the afternoon of October 29, a rider dismounted at the canon's house and with understandable caution handed him the prince's message. The letter read: "Friend Escoiquiz: The latest news is that last night my parents got hold of all my papers, among them the cyphers and the codes, and of the statements against the Prince of the Peace, also your reply to my note regarding the message from the individual at the French embassy. I am warning you so that you will be on your guard. Also tell me what I should do. San Lorenzo, October 28."[13] Even though there was no signature and the handwriting was disguised, Escoiquiz felt certain that the letter came from Fernando. Immediately he penned a reply, urging the prince to be courageous and to maintain steadfastly that the intercepted papers stated only the truth, being directed not at the king but at a "tyrant," as he was pleased to designate Godoy. Just as importantly, Escoiquiz besought Fernando not to reveal the names of those involved in the undertaking. The note was never delivered; by the time the messenger reached the Escorial, it was already too late.

The agitation in the palace following Fernando's detention may easily be imagined. In Manuel's absence, Caballero took charge of the investigation in his capacity as minister of justice. To say the least, the confiscated papers made for dolorous reading. The further the *reyes* and their minister read, the more Caballero became convinced that the documents were treasonous and that Fernando merited the death penalty. In a highly emotional state, María Luisa shrieked her assent; had Manuel been present, he would certainly have discountenanced such irresponsible ravings.

This is not to minimize the significance of the sequestered documents. The most cursory examination convinced the king that Fernando was involved in a plot of alarming dimensions. Escoiquiz's narration to the contrary, only now were belated orders issued that the prince's cell be locked and a trustworthy guard be posted outside. A closer reading of the papers revealed the full extent of the conspiracy.

The first of the four lengthy documents was a diffuse letter addressed to the king in which the heir apparent warned his father of the dangers besetting the throne of Spain. Fernando—or rather Escoiquiz—urged the king not to consult with the queen because "some with their diabolic arts have managed to predispose her in their favor." Rhetorically, the prince asks the identity of their "presumptuous and principal leader," adding that "there is no more public knowledge. All the Court, all the nation, all of Europe knows it! Only my poor, adored father is unaware." And who is this execrable creature? The blunt answer left the incredulous *reyes* gasping for breath. "This man is Don Manuel Godoy, Prince of the Peace, General-issimo, Admiral, one who for each of these titles ought to kiss Your Majesty's footsteps; he who has been honored in the highest degree with your confidence, heaped with your favors, and who should be prepared to sacrifice himself in your service, in that of your hapless son, and that of all the royal family. This depraved man is the one who, having cast off all semblance of respect, clearly aspires to deprive us of the Throne and to do away with all of us."[14] The monarchs were horrified. There must be a mistake somehow. Surely Fernando could not mean their *querido* Manuel!

But this was only the beginning. Having dismissed the military preten-sions of the "most inept man in the world," Fernando warmed to his congenial task. The people are pained "by the anguish they feel on seeing a monster like Godoy" elevated to such a high position. Manuel a monster! One accusation followed hard on the other: his cupidity had already made him "the most opulent of vassals" and won him wealth and magnificent mansions far exceeding the amenities of the royal palaces, all at a time of widespread poverty and shortage of funds for the military.

Even this might be forgivable but for the *privado's* outrageous morals:

These, Sire, not only have reached the highest level of corruption and scandal, but also the most insolent effrontery. With his position of au-thority, his power, and his bribes, not only has he prostituted the flower of Spanish womanhood from the highest to the lowest classes, but his house on the occasion of private audiences, and the office of Secretary of State when he was in charge, were given over to open public festivities for prostitution, rape, and adultery in exchange for pensions, jobs, and honors, making use of Your Majesty's authority to gratify the sordid compliance of his unbridled lasciviousness and the obscene vices of his corrupted heart. These excesses, shortly after this shameless man became a minister, reached such a level of notoriety, that everyone knew that the only sure way of complying or getting promoted was to sacrifice the honor of a daughter, a sister, or his wife, to his insatiable and brutal lust.[15]

As for past misunderstandings, Fernando imputed them entirely to "such a contemptible monster," asking with a fine flourish: "And was I ever in doubt that my oppression, my misery, the gossip which has disturbed my quarters incessantly was the work of this pernicious man? Could I ever perchance attribute them to the tender and upright minds of Your Majesties? O Sire! I feared, I always feared the dark and gangrenous conscience of this tiger."[16] Godoy's "wickedness and heinous plans" went so far as to deny the prince any participation in the daily hunt for fear that he might confide in the king. Indeed, the favorite and his adherents were spreading the malicious falsehood that the heir to the throne was "a young man devoid of talent, without education, without application, in sum quite unfit, a dolt."[17]

Giving his poor father no time to catch his breath, Fernando went on to berate Manuel for having attempted to arrange the marriage with his sister-in-law. Clearly, he was aspiring to the throne, which he hoped to achieve in part by "placing me at the side of a lively and mischievous woman, whose unavoidable family relationship would provide him with the best means of corrupting her mind, perverting her habits, of dominating her and making her his spy and an enemy of mine, all the more pernicious for being inseparable and close to me."[18] Fernando only agreed to such a union because, were he to refuse, "this vindictive man would hasten to poison me"—presumably the same way Godoy removed all his other enemies.

Certainly, the next section of the memorandum was the most audacious and for Carlos the most painful. Fernando, setting himself up as judge and jury, proposed that the king sign a decree which "will be directed toward the sudden imprisonment of Godoy, his provisional transferral to a castle, where he will remain incommunicado until a new order is issued; the seizure of his homes, possessions, and papers with a very detailed examination, even of his own person so as to obtain those he is carrying; provisional incarceration of his servants . . . imprisonment of *la Tudó*, her family and servants . . . and various provisional confinements for all of Godoy's relatives."[19] Only thus could the kingdom be saved.

The second document took a more original approach, purporting to be a letter from a friar to his cousin. To safeguard the identity of the leading personages, they were cloaked in pastoral pseudonyms. The exposé was intended mainly for the queen's eyes:

> He [Godoy] is a depraved man, given over to all the vices, in whom arrogance, ambition, and ingratitude compete . . . He is exceedingly ignorant, and the little education and culture he possesses he owes entirely to your kind heart, you who have taken the trouble to give him some polish. His mind is only suited for intrigue and cunning at which he is a master. Finally, I am certain—and everyone sees it the way I do—that this man, in whose hands rest all the power, all the authority, and all the wealth, aspires to nothing less than sacrificing me, then my brothers and sisters, then my father, then you, so as to take possession of our home and fortune.[20]

For the first time, veiled mention was made of Napoleon (Don Marcos) and of Mademoiselle Stéphanie Tascher de la Pagerie (Doña Juliana). The consternation of the monarchs became more acute; Fernando's censure of Manuel had been painful enough, but had at least been kept within the bosom of the family, or so it was assumed. Now, everything was known to the emperor in unsparing detail. More immediately, the queen found herself directly challenged—by her own son no less!—if she insisted that he go through with the projected marriage to Godoy's sister-in-law: "Mother, you are tiring yourself in vain, I know everything there is to know about this man, and you know it even better than I, so it's pointless to insist."[21]

Nor could the third intercepted letter, dated Talavera, May 28, 1807, have proved any more reassuring. Again composed by Escoiquiz, it clearly revealed the secret interchanges between Beauharnais and Fernando through a third person, the author himself. Though couched in measured language—Godoy is even twice referred to as the *Príncipe Generalísimo Almirante,* a title Beauharnais steadfastly refused to accord him—the terrain is vaster, the implications more serious. True, the *reyes* are treated with respect, at least outwardly, but the usurpation of their powers in dealing with the head of a foreign state might well be regarded as the keenest insult of all.

By any criterion, the fourth letter must be accounted the strangest of the collection. As with the account of the anonymous note found on the king's desk, Godoy is the sole source. He states enigmatically, "There was one [letter] about which nothing has been said, because maternal love withdrew it in the middle of the proceedings, and it was not even shown to the judges."[22] Though unsigned, Godoy deemed it to be clearly the unaided work of Fernando and written the very day of its discovery. In an orgy of disconsolation, the Prince of Asturias fancifully compared himself with the Gothic figure of San Hermenegildo, a popular hero of legend. Hermenegildo (Fernando), in order to defend the Christian faith, is obliged to rebel against his father Leovigildo (Carlos) and invoke the protection of the Emperor Justinian (Napoleon). The despicable villains are the prince's stepmother Gosvinda (María Luisa reduced to a *madrastra!*) and Sisebuto (Godoy), who not only is the queen's lover but also presides over the execution of the sainted son.

According to the reconstruction of events by Manuel, who was still ailing in Madrid, the king, upon reading the letter, turned to Caballero and asked, "Tell me what such a son deserves!" "Sire," the minister replied, "without your royal clemency . . . the sword of the law could fall on his neck." This was too much even for María Luisa. "No more! No more!" she cried, "However badly he has acted, however ungratefully he has behaved towards me, don't forget he is my son! I still have some rights as a mother, and as such I will retain and keep from view this paper which condemns him. They have deceived him! They have ruined him!"[23] And, with that, María Luisa snatched the incriminatory document and hid it within her bosom.

In their pitiable confusion, both monarchs dispatched urgent letters to Manuel. The queen's plea was less hysterical and more considerate than might be imagined: "Manuel, consider our misfortune. I do not wish, and Carlos would never consent to your endangering your health; but I beg you, if you feel any improvement in your affliction, to take every precaution, because the King needs your counsel. Some punishment is necessary, and you will tell us how it is to be done, for the offense is grave and the full weight of guilt rests on the shoulders of a beloved one. We are anxiously awaiting your reply."[24] The recollection of Escoiquiz casts an entirely different light upon María Luisa's emotions: "It is impossible to describe the pleasure of the Queen and her favorite on discovering the individual names of the enemies to their tyrannical despotism. No less was their longing to imprison them so as to bathe in their blood."[25] Hyperbole aside, the charge is wildly inaccurate. Godoy (unlike Caballero) was opposed to the staging of a public trial and strongly advised from his sickbed that the family squabble be resolved amicably. No such letter has been found; because it had pleaded moderation and had shown him in a good light, Manuel believes that "this reply was removed by the hands of enemies who had sworn my complete ruin."[26]

The first interrogation of the prince was conducted largely by Caballero. Much to the latter's dismay, the royal mood was marked by parental understanding and an inclination to forgive. Quite inexplicably, Fernando turned truculent and scornful, resorting to transparent lies and elementary inconsistencies. Escoiquiz had instructed him to place the entire blame on María Antonia, his late wife, a convenient but unconvincing scapegoat. Caballero was quick to point out the discrepancy between the date of the princess's death and Godoy's appointment a year later to admiral-general, by which title he was twice referred to in the Talavera letter of May 28. Far from showing contrition, Fernando impudently retorted that "he and his wife knew that when it came to this letter he [Godoy] would already be Admiral, though at that time he was not."[27] With each contumacious insult the monarchs' patience wore thinner. By now exasperated with his recalcitrant son, the king left in a huff, unsure which course of action to follow.

Provoked by a fractious heir, assailed by his wife's lamentations, and egged on by Caballero, what was he to do? If only Manuel were there! He always had a ready answer to every challenge. But wait; what of Napoleon? Surely, the emperor would understand his predicament. Still governed more by emotion than sound judgment, the king dashed off the following:

Sire, my brother: At the moment that I was concerned with the best means of cooperating in the destruction of our common enemy, just when I thought that all the schemes of the ex-Queen of Naples had come to naught with the death of her daughter, I learn to my horror that the spirit of the most perfidious intrigue has penetrated into my palace. Oh, my heart is afflicted just having to refer to such a monstrous attempt! My eldest son, the heir apparent to my throne, had hatched the horrible plot to dethrone me, and had gone so far as to make an attempt on the life of his mother. Such an atrocious crime must be punished with the full severity of the law. The one which entitles him to succeed me must be revoked; one of his brothers will be more worthy to replace him in my heart and on the throne. I am now searching for his accomplices to find the thread of such incredible wickedness, and I do not wish to waste a single moment to inform Your Imperial Majesty, and I beg you to assist me with your counsel.

Carlos

San Lorenzo, October 28, 1807[28]

On the basis of the imprecise phrase "one of his brothers will be more worthy to replace him," Godoy has been designated by some historians as the moving spirit behind the pen. Was the Infante Carlos, the next in succession, about to be supplanted by Francisco de Paula? Godoy protests, "I was not told a thing about it. When I arrived at the Escorial a few days afterwards and saw the rough draft of that letter my bitterness redoubled; most of all I was pained that Bonaparte had been asked for his advice."[29]

Later that same day the irate monarchs, having perused the incriminating texts in more detail, decided that a second interrogation was called for. Accompanied by Caballero, they confronted the prince in his cell. The ensuing scene has been reconstructed from the queen's own lively account to Lord and Lady Holland during her later exile in Rome. By her own admission, the encounter was extremely tempestuous; voices were raised, dire threats uttered, and Fernando assailed from all sides. María Luisa was convinced that the cringing creature at her feet had even contemplated her own murder—matricide!—while the king and Caballero hurled vituperation at the tremulous prince, who tearfully admitted to everything, down to the last name. Only complete exhaustion on all sides brought down the curtain on this unedifying tableau.

The night of October 29 witnessed a chilling spectacle. At eleven o'clock, flanked by halbardiers of the royal guard, the Prince of Asturias was marched from his cell to a new place of confinement, the procession of soldiers and dignitaries eerily lit by the light of flickering torches held on high. The heir to the throne and his impassive father walked side by side, followed by four ministers and a retinue of locksmiths and stonemasons bearing the tools of their trades. The only sounds to punctuate the forbidding silence were the rhythmic echoes of footsteps resounding on the stone slabs and the doleful chant of the Hieronymite monks. Finally, the cortege halted at the monastery, where the terrified prince was unceremoniously thrust into a narrow cell.

The next morning, Caballero came to resume his bullying interrogation. Fernando's meager resistance now collapsed; exhausted by the satrap's incessant hectoring, he again confessed to all, in particular the part played by Escoiquiz and the Duke of Infantado. Orders were immediately issued for their arrest. Now that the full extent of the seditious plot was known, Caballero proposed that the king issue a manifesto to the nation. Some explanation was needed, but, given Fernando's widespread popularity, judicious phrasing was called for. Carlos, who had come to regret his haste in writing to Napoleon, insisted that the draft of any royal proclamation first be shown to Manuel, in Madrid. With a fine sense of the dramatic, the *privado* describes his agitated frame of mind upon receiving the copy of the proposed declaration: "It was the darkest hour of the night; the fever was burning me, my sight was blurred, my head was like a boiling sea; but notwithstanding my condition, an answer without the least delay was imperative, and that without being able to consult anyone or have anyone help me raise my pen."[30]

The precise authorship of the manifesto remains uncertain. Many of Godoy's detractors maintain that he rewrote Caballero's original draft, and that certain officials recognized his handwriting. Be that as it may, in its final form the proclamation was typical of what has been termed the "pretentious style of the period, both ridiculous and in poor taste."[31] Phrases abounded alluding to "atrocious deeds," an "unheard-of catastrophe," "the most enormous and bold plan" to dethrone the king, in which the Prince of Asturias and "several criminals" were involved. Thankfully, all had been arrested, including the king's own son and successor.[32]

If the purpose of the decree was to damn Fernando in the eyes of his countrymen, it achieved exactly the opposite effect. For the first time, here was proof positive that their beloved prince was taking measures to rid the country of the moral corruption at court; quite unintentionally, the royal proclamation became the rallying cry to Fernando's cause. In contrast to Godoy's shameful libertinage, he was perceived among the common folk as being devout, a paradigm of virtue. His main asset was precisely his enforced seclusion over the years, the very fact that he was unknown beyond a narrow circle. Ignorance was an essential ingredient of the myth.

On November 3 Manuel struggled out of his sickbed and, in his weakened state, made the journey across the Guadarrama Mountains to the Escorial. Predictably, the king was away on his daily hunt, which continued uninterrupted no matter how grave the crisis. As far as the stolid monarch was concerned, the contretemps was as good as over; Fernando had acknowledged his filial shortcomings, those responsible were under lock and key, and the nation had been duly informed. Furthermore, his wayward son had pledged to remedy his conduct and to "continue the esteem which is proper to a subject who is so useful and who has served the State so much as has the Admiral,"[33] taking good care to refer to Manuel by his latest title.

Most witnesses agree that the *reyes* were anxious to forgive and forget, though Godoy emphasizes that the parental wrath continued unabated. He unintentionally limns the distraught king as a maundering Lear, unable to comprehend his son's ingratitude: "I was so good to him! I, such a good father! To have deceived me thus! To have placed me in such a conflict! To have trampled all respect for me underfoot, to have compromised the good fortune of my realm by secretly asking a wife from the enemy of my royal house! To have thus opened the way so that he could subjugate us! And what would my subjects say of me if I were to pardon him?"[34] According to Manuel, it was only through his personal intervention that a reconciliation was brought about between father and son.

As he made his way to Fernando's cell, Manuel must have reflected on the irony of the situation; the Prince of Asturias, reduced to a whining, pathetic figure, was rapidly gaining strength throughout the land, whereas he, heaped with titles and honors unexampled in Spain's long history, could but count on the king and queen for support. No sooner had Godoy entered the prior's cell, he tells us, than Fernando threw himself into his arms amid cries of "Manuel *mío* . . . those scoundrels have deceived and ruined me. I have nothing against you, I wish to be your friend. You can get me out of the affliction in which I find myself." Fernando noted that Manuel was still feverish, whereupon the latter picked up the cue by exclaiming: "And I am also burning with love for Your Highness, the son of my monarchs, the one I have held so often in my arms, and for whom I would sacrifice a thousand lives if I had them." By Godoy's admission, "I wept even more than the Prince, true tears that welled up from my soul."[35] The upshot was that a contrite Fernando implored his parents' forgiveness with Manuel acting as intermediary.

Godoy, however, was not content with mere verbal assurances. He easily prevailed upon the remorseful prince to write letters to each of his parents. The preponderant opinion has been that the favorite either dictated the text or else brought two copies with him so that Fernando merely had to copy them in his own hand. Godoy bridles at such an insinuation and has Fernando ask him, "Wouldn't you like to dictate to me the words which would be best suited to move my parents' hearts?" To which Manuel unctuously replied, "The best words are those which inspire Your Highness' own feelings."[36] Fernando sat down and penned the following letters, which were reproduced in the *Gaceta de Madrid* on November 5:

> Dear Papa: I have transgressed, I have given offense to Your Majesty both as King and father; but I repent and promise Your Majesty the most humble obedience. I should not have undertaken anything without prior notice to Your Majesty, but I was taken by surprise. I have denounced the guilty,

and beg Your Majesty to forgive me for having lied the other night, and I ask permission for your grateful son to kiss your royal feet.

Fernando

To the queen he was no less submissive:

Dear Mama: I deeply repent the very great fault which I have committed against my parents and monarchs, and thus I implore Your Majesty with the utmost humility to deign to intercede with Papa so that his grateful son might be permitted to kiss his royal feet.

Fernando

San Lorenzo, November 5, 1807[37]

In a footnote, Godoy adds that the letters were actually written on November 3, but that in his agitation Fernando omitted to add the date, which was incorrectly inserted by Caballero two days later. On this slender basis, Fernando's partisans have claimed that he resisted Godoy's threats for two days before complying. Whatever the truth, the twin confessions opened the way to a royal pardon. Doubtless Manuel and the *reyes* hoped that, with Fernando suitably penitent, a public announcement including his two apologies and the king's pardon of his son would terminate the whole sorry business. Those who had conspired with the prince were to be brought to trial and face the full severity of the law. Technically, there could be little doubt as to their guilt, but the wisdom of pursuing such a course was very much open to question. In view of Fernando's recantation, the main purpose had been accomplished; surely, given the crucial reality of a foreign army entrenched in Spain's northern provinces, a general amnesty would have been more pertinent.

On November 3, at Manuel's instigation, Carlos wrote a personal letter to Napoleon. The *privado* bemoans the fact that no copy was made of the communication; practically alone of the documents exchanged, it never appeared in the *Moniteur*. To judge by the emperor's violent reaction, the contents must have been unusually blunt. Although Carlos had already decided to forgive his errant son, no mention of this was made in the letter, leaving the impression that the prince would still be brought to trial. Worse still, the king complained bitterly of Beauharnais's intolerable meddling in Spanish affairs. But the greatest audacity was to ask Napoleon point blank, in words undoubtedly suggested by Godoy, whether he knew about his ambassador's involvement. The thankless task of delivering the missive was left to Masserano, who handed it to the emperor on November 11.

The ensuing scene is familiar enough. Threats, curses, insults rained down on the startled Spanish delegation. The emperor blustered that never had a head of state been so insulted; such an offense usually called for an immediate declaration of war. At the very least, the Prince of the Peace would have to go, and every Spaniard in France must be arrested, including that scoundrel of an Izquierdo. Then, in a display of imperial magnanimity, Napoleon gave a thoroughly cowed Masserano one last chance:

> Send a courier to your Court immediately to say there is not a word of truth in your letter, that the Prince of Asturias has never written to me, and that my ambassador has never entered into any intrigue. Say that from this moment I am taking the Prince of Asturias under my protection, and that if he is touched, however little, or if my ambassador is insulted, or if the mobilized army does not leave immediately for Portugal in conformity with our agreements, I shall declare war on Spain, place myself at the head of my army to invade her, and recall my ambassador and throw you out of Paris . . . It's an outrage what is happening.[38]

The emperor's stratagem produced the desired effect. Wasting no time, Masserano sent a dispatch to the Escorial, whereupon Godoy and Carlos decided that any mention of French implication must be suppressed at the forthcoming trial. On November 13, in his own hand, Napoleon again assured his brother sovereign, "I owe it to Truth to inform you that I have never received a letter from the Prince of Asturias, and that I have never heard any mention made of him, either directly or indirectly, so that it would be true to say that I do not even know if he exists."[39] On November 15 a letter was received from Carlos IV confirming the royal pardon and the ratification of the treaty. From the outset, Godoy had opposed the arraignment of Fernando's accomplices. To strengthen the king's hand, Manuel now offered to relinquish all his offices and titles so that "father and son, finally united as I hoped they would be,"[40] could present a united front to the nation and the French. Carlos unhesitatingly refused, claiming that Manuel, rather than the accused faction, would appear to be the guilty party. The fact is the king needed his services more than ever, as he frankly admitted in a letter to *amigo* Manuel: "I have worries and deep afflictions which I cannot conceal. Once more I suspect Fernando of having a close relationship with your enemies and mine. Bonaparte is trying a double game, and I fear that by inciting war and winning Fernando over to his side he is seeking the ruin of my subjects . . . I never find out what is happening from the mouths of those who ought to perceive it and then give an account. I also observe a suspicious reserve in the ministers which I have never noted before. I don't know in whom I çan trust." Other than his unshakeable faith in God, he could only depend on the queen and Manuel: "If in spite of all some misfortune befall us, we shall share it together, and at least it will be of some comfort that we were not the cause of it or deserved it."[41]

Despite the king's entreaty, Manuel persisted in his petition to resign, adding that Fernando would forever remain convinced, however mistakenly, of his hatred and determination to humiliate him. In Manuel's telling, the king sent for his eldest son, and in a few dramatic sentences outlined the favorite's request. Fernando was aghast at the very thought. *"¡Padre mío! ¡Padre mío!"* he piped, "The man who returned me to your favor when I was so far from attaining it must never separate himself from us!" At this point, he grasped Manuel's hand fervently and pleaded: "If my papa will allow me, I ask only one sacrifice of you, and that is that you remain with us."[42] To no one's surprise, Manuel yielded.

The appointed day for the trial was now approaching. For the most part, the eleven presiding judges were men of impeccable probity. The impartial Don Arias Antonio Mon, governor of the Council of Castilla, was named to preside over the tribunal, and Simón de Viegas, reputedly beholden to the favorite, was appointed as the Crown prosecutor. Carlos, whatever his faults, had complete faith in the judicial process; not for one moment did it occur to him that in fact it was the *trinidad en la tierra* that was about to stand trial.

The case opened propitiously for the Crown as Viegas launched into a panegyric of Godoy, lauding him as "this illustrious personage . . . this Spanish hero, whose name will distinguish this period in history; in him the nation has had a perennial protector of the Throne, to whom is due the stability it enjoys; he has directed with prodigious ability the great and very important tasks entrusted him by the monarch's confidence."[43] Yet, barely three months later, he hastened to assure Fernando, "What I wrote at El Escorial was done out of fright and cowardice,"[44] and entirely due to his fear of the *privado*.

As to the trial itself, Godoy passes over the court proceedings in a sentence or two. The prosecution became ensnared in a trap of its own making; the charges of treason were so serious that Viegas was obliged to demand the death penalty for Escoiquiz and Infantado, a palpable absurdity in light of the withheld evidence. The Duke of Infantado protested his loyalty to the Crown and his wish to ensure a legitimate succession. Escoiquiz refuted the charges one by one, stressing the singular conditions prevailing in Spain; rather than being traitors, he contended that he and his codefendants were in fact patriots deserving of the nation's gratitude.

No longer on the defensive, the lawyers for the accused demanded their clients be set free. Escoiquiz maintains that Godoy did everything in his power to obtain a verdict of guilty: "The favorite left no stone unturned to seduce, bribe, intimidate, and make those intrepid and respectable jurors betray their duty. Not one of them wavered . . ."[45] More to the point, the roles played by Napoleon and Beauharnais having been excluded from the evidence, the Crown's case was totally unconvincing. One of the judges was literally on his deathbed, but before expiring was determined to sign the verdict. On January 25, 1808, all the defendants were declared innocent. The king was dismayed at the acquittal and at first could only exclaim, "My honor! My honor, before my crown!"[46] In his anger, Carlos was determined to publish all the relevant damning material, but Godoy successfully pleaded that national considerations were of paramount importance.

In a real sense, the monarchs and their favorite had been found guilty in the eyes of the nation. The enthusiasm of the masses knew no bounds; significantly, the lawyers in the case declined to accept their customary fees. Godoy's own brother-in-law, the Cardinal Archbishop of Toledo, had publicly declared that he would resign his high office (which he owed entirely to Manuel) if Escoiquiz were convicted. As a gratuitous insult, he professed to believe that Godoy was married to Pepita Tudó, and therefore would seek royal permission for his sister to retire to a convent in Toledo.

There was still time for one final folly. The general expectation was that the king—whatever his private feelings—would confirm the court's findings. Instead, he decreed that the defendants were to proceed immediately into provincial exile. The reversal of the verdict was received with indignation; as the ultimate bulwark of justice, the king was supposed to exercise clemency, not petty vindictiveness. Presumably, he hoped that, by dispersing the ringleaders, the back of the conspiracy would be broken. To the contrary, the Escorial affair grievously eroded the traditional respect in which the royal family had been held for centuries. But the most pressing reality was marching inexorably along the muddy roads of northern Spain: thousands upon thousands of French infantrymen pouring into the very heartland of the peninsula.

13

THE TIGHTENING

VISE

On November 30, 1807, the vanguard of Junot's army entered Lisbon, only to discover that the Portuguese royal family had embarked on English vessels the previous day and was now bound for Brazil. As the general surveyed the bedraggled remnants of his expeditionary force, he at least enjoyed the satisfaction of having attained the objective laid down by the emperor. Seemingly, the French involvement in the peninsula was now at an end.

Manuel and his monarchs welcomed the news of Junot's success with mixed emotions. Carlota Joaquina, the eldest daughter of the *reyes* and wife of the Portuguese regent, was now on the high seas, buffeted by winter gales; her throne appeared even less secure. For the *trinidad,* a minor compensation was that Junot's campaign seemed to be in accordance with the terms stipulated in the Treaty of Fontainebleau. But Godoy had good cause to worry. Why hadn't the treaty been published in Paris, thus giving him formal title to the Portuguese southern provinces? True, the Marqués de Solano had taken possession of the Algarve and the Alemtejo, but on the other hand the French had already occupied the remainder of the country.

Disturbing as was the French action, it was outdone by Junot's hypocritical invitation to the *privado* to visit his intended realm. The offer was meaningless, but in it Godoy saw one last opportunity to extricate himself from the closing gap by becoming, in effect, the prisoner of the French—

an ingenious solution to an intractable problem. Not for the first time, the Prince of the Peace did his best to turn adversity to his own advantage: "False, unstable, and vain as was the position that Junot proposed to me, in truth it was less exposed than that which I held at Court with no more foundation or efficacy than the good will of Carlos IV." So far, so good. At this point, Manuel's imagination takes flight: "Had I gone to the Alemtejo, at the first outrage committed by Bonaparte against my sovereigns and my country I could at least have roused Portugal and two-thirds of Spain, assembled a large army, entered into relations with many governments without hindrance, and in the last resort opened our ports to the English. The King would have had a safe place of refuge, and then Spain would have perceived in me not an ambitious person but a true friend and one who loved her."[1]

This assertion overlooks two salient facts: Spain was at war with England, not with France; and, in the country at large, Napoleon was still regarded as an ally. Further, it was widely believed that he would soon take personal command of the French armies and rid the nation of the *privado*. Indeed, by the turn of the year, the northernmost provinces of Spain were virtually under French military occupation. On December 24 General Dupont and an army of 25,000 crossed the Bidassoa, the rivulet near Irún which marks the border, and occupied Palencia and Valladolid, as well as penetrating deeply into Catalonia.

On February 1, 1808, another blow fell: Junot announced that henceforth he would administer the whole of Portugal in the name of the French emperor. Simply put, the House of Braganza had been dethroned at the stroke of a pen. Could not the same fate befall the Spanish Bourbons? As to Manuel's hopes of a principality to call his own, they had been revealed for what they were: ephemeral dreams, devoid of substance. Soon what had begun as a single thrust aimed at Portugal assumed the proportions of a full-scale invasion. In flat contravention to a secret clause in the Treaty of Fontainebleau, Napoleon did not bother to ascertain whether the English had landed troops—let alone consult with Godoy—before sending in four additional French armies at both ends of the Pyrenees.

Already Manuel had voiced his fears to the king that Napoleon might have designs on the Spanish Crown, but Carlos gently reproved him with the assurance that "an outrage of that sort must be judged nearly impossible nowadays. Let's wait a little; better to hold off until the Emperor explains himself than to demand it of him. He must offer some clarification, and I have no doubt that he will at any moment now."[2]

In sheer frustration, the *privado* urged the king to convene a special meeting of the council to discuss the options open to them. Although Godoy spoke for a full hour on the subject of Spain's treaty rights, given the king's attitude, it was a vain endeavor from the outset. "What you propose is just, proper, and what the honor of my crown demands," Carlos admitted, "but what could we do afterwards, if the Emperor insists that fresh troops enter?" "Sire," Manuel replied, "deny any entry with firmness, as long as there is now powerful reason envisioned in the treaty to justify it." "And if he orders their entry nevertheless," the king added plaintively, "what could be done?" "Defend ourselves, if he dares enter another's home without any sincere motive," Godoy answered, "and address the nation, explain what it is unaware of, trust in God, in our upright cause, and in Spain." "An heroic resolution!" the king exclaimed, "but a desperate one!"[3] Whether the exchange between monarch and favorite was quite as stirring as Godoy records it is open to doubt.

More certain is the fact that the privado failed to win any support from the other ministers. His proposed strategy of defensive action had in fact much to commend it; many of the French footsoldiers were raw recruits who had taken to pillaging; overextended supply lines had left the invading armies extremely vulnerable to attack in the mountainous terrain, and Dupont was a poor strategist. In addition, the frontier fortresses were still in Spanish hands.

But not for long. The citadel of Pamplona was the first to fall, the result of a contemptible ruse employed by General Darmagnac. Godoy, a mere two days earlier, had warned of the danger of allowing the French to encamp so close to the bastion. On February 16, in the early morning, a detachment of French soldiers staged a sham snowball fight outside the fortress gates. Suddenly, the retreating side spun round, surprised the unsuspecting guard, and seized the main bridge. Just as despicable was the trick two weeks later that delivered the castle of Montjuich, in Barcelona, to the invader. A contributory factor here was the irresolute action of the castle's governor, who lamely explained that the French were in need of protection from the enraged citizenry. The capitulation of San Sebastian, which could have been defended only at great cost to the civilian population, was on an altogether friendlier basis. Godoy had hoped that, in return, Murat would sound out his brother-in-law, the emperor, regarding the early replacement of Beauharnais in Madrid. Murat, in fact, did his best, but, by the time La Forest was appointed as the new ambassador, Beauharnais had completed his mischief.

Such was Napoleon's low esteem of the Spanish Bourbons and his confidence in their timidity that he had left for Italy on November 16, 1807. A week later, Luisetta was abruptly informed by the French minister, General d'Aubusson de la Feuillade, that she was no longer queen and was to leave for her new realm in Portugal forthwith. Unaccountably, her parents had never informed her of the secret clauses of the Treaty of Fontainebleau; if they had, her favorable opinion of *amigo* Manuel would have diminished considerably. In Milan, Napoleon received the deposed queen with the elaborate courtesies befitting her rank, but with little else; he could hardly tell her that he was browbeating his brother Joseph, happily ensconced as king of Naples, into becoming king of Spain, or that he had offered the Portuguese crown to Lucien if only he would divorce his wife. All Luisetta could do was continue her wintry hegira through France and Spain. At last on February 19, the convoy arrived in Aranjuez, where a melancholy family reunion took place.

It was galling enough that two daughters had been dispossessed within a matter of weeks—a third, María Isabel, was reduced to a toehold in Sicily—but Luisetta brought news that was potentially even more disturbing. During her conversation with the emperor, he had made some enigmatic references to the future by citing a past incident of doubtful historicity. A Spanish Christian king had supposedly once given Charlemagne a border province as a *cordon sanitaire* against the Moors and had even gone so far as to name the French hero his successor.[4] Presumably, the English were cast as the new infidel, but Godoy and his sovereigns had no difficulty in assigning the other roles or the contributions expected of them. Even if but indirectly, Napoleon was staking a claim to the lands north of the Ebro.

Godoy's despair is apparent in a letter of February 9 sent to Izquierdo, his personal emissary in Paris:

> The treaty you concluded no longer exists. The Kingdom is full of troops; the military posts in Portugal are being occupied by the same under the command of Junot. We have been requested to send the remainder of our units, and they have been ordered to march together with those of the Emperor. Everything is uncertainty, intrigue, and fear; public opinion is divided; the Prince [of Asturias] involved in a trial due to disobedience; the allied troops are living at our expense; the people are exhausted . . . You are disliked in Paris; the ambassador [Masserano] useless; what the devil does it all mean? Where will it all end? I have summoned you to give me a report; you have not come, and this raises further doubts in my mind.

If you know something, say it; if you do not, don't make a mystery of it, because the vital thing is to know.[5]

Further blows continued to fall in relentless succession. It was learned that Marie-Stéphanie de la Pagerie had married the Prince d'Arenberg on February 1 without so much as a word to Fernando—adieu, sweet princess! Other news from Paris was equally unsettling. Articles now began to appear in the *Moniteur* criticizing Godoy as an inept minister and a false friend. Such attacks never appeared by chance, but as part of a concerted campaign ordered by the emperor. In a note of March 8 to Jean-Baptiste Champagny, who had succeeded Talleyrand as foreign minister, Napoleon decreed that Fernando was to be declared innocent of any intrigue, but, for all that, was unfit to ascend the throne. As to the monarchs and their favorite: "The Queen must be painted the way she is, the King as well, as a good man, but without character or intelligence . . . One must stress the embezzlement of the Prince of the Peace and his immense wealth, and speak in detail about his criminal liaison with the Queen, first of all his calling with the title of favorite, and then as the favorite pandering to the shameful tastes of this princess, then about Malló and other lovers he has given to the Queen."[6] The evidence suggests that Napoleon intended the above to be distributed throughout Spain in the form of a pamphlet, but the onrush of events outstripped his intentions. Whatever the reason, the defamatory broadsheet was never published.

Part of Godoy's distress is easily traceable. Masserano, the Spanish ambassador in Paris, detested him and made little attempt to hide his feelings. Years later, Manuel still vividly recalled the envoy's antipathy: "From Paris, Masserano was not bashful when it came to writing his friends about the favorable things being said in the salons regarding the Prince of Asturias. He quoted words and expressions that appeared to come from the Emperor's lips, as appreciative of Fernando as they were disdainful of his father's government and, when it came to me, full of anger. He said that the coming visit of the Emperor to Spain would mark the end of my power, and with me would fall all those who reputedly were my henchmen."[7] By the spring of 1808, an extraordinary situation had arisen. Just as Masserano was actively working against the *privado,* in Madrid Beauharnais was confiding in Cevallos and Caballero behind Godoy's back. Anxious to return the favor, the Spanish ministers kept the French ambassador well informed of everything that transpired in the king's councils. Soon Izquierdo became Godoy's sole source of information, and even that trusted channel was showing unmistakable signs of dejection.

On February 20 Napoleon had appointed his swaggering brother-in-law, Joachim Murat, "Lieutenant of the Emperor in Spain," whom he once had characterized as *un héros et une bête* without specifying the exact proportions. As Murat left for his Spanish assignment, many thoughts crossed his ambitious mind. During his stay in Italy, he had made a favorable impression on the queen of Etruria, and his correspondence with the Prince of the Peace had always been most cordial. As Murat traveled through his native Gascony, he already envisioned himself as the next king of Spain.

The flamboyant cavalry general sounded an uncharacteristically cautious note in his first dispatches. Godoy had issued firm orders to prevent a repetition of the Pamplona incident; all units were to be constantly on their guard, the movement of the French troops was to be closely observed, and all Spanish detachments were to be ready to withdraw south of Madrid at a moment's notice. On February 29, even before he had entered Spain, Murat wrote to Napoleon: "Until the capture of the citadel of Pamplona we French were regarded without uneasiness or fear; but both sentiments have been awakened with that news, and today consternation is general in Spain. Supposedly the Prince of the Peace has said: 'As the French are acting that way, we can only regard them as enemies and get ready to fight them.' Even so, I believe that the Prince is incapable of such recklessness."[8] Two days later, he reported that "the Prince of the Peace is detested so much that if they [the Spaniards] did not believe he was supported by Your Majesty he would not last twenty-four hours. Isquierdo [sic] last night passed by hastily and said that he had been entrusted with an important mission from Your Majesty to take to his Court."[9]

Izquierdo was indeed on his way to Aranjuez. By now, Manuel and the *reyes* had not the slightest doubt they had been duped by Napoleon. The treaty, the sole legal basis for the French military presence in Spain, still had not been published. It is therefore all the more incredible that the king should again vacillate, still believing that there must be some explanation for the emperor's irregular conduct. Part of Carlos's faith in Napoleon's good intentions stemmed from a trivial gesture by the French head of state.

On January 10 Napoleon had ordered fourteen draft horses to be sent to the king of Spain and the Prince of the Peace as a token of his enduring friendship. The stalwart animals, not the fleetest of foot, reached the border on the last day of the month and continued their leisurely progress to Madrid in easy stages. Godoy was supposed to receive six of them, but Beauharnais, on his own initiative and perhaps to please Fernando, withheld those destined for the favorite. In any case, Napoleon had a change of mind and instructed Champagny to inform Beauharnais that "if the eight horses for the King of Spain and the six for the Prince of the Peace, which some time ago I ordered sent as a present, have arrived in Madrid, the Ambassador is to keep them in his stable, seeing that in the present situation it is hardly suitable to make gifts of horses to the King of Spain."[10] Carlos, blissfully unaware of Napoleon's retraction, twitted Manuel that his fears of the French emperor were exaggerated, citing the anticipated arrival of the horses as "proof" of good will.

Traveling considerably faster than the plodding animals, Izquierdo presented himself before his monarchs at the beginning of March. Indicative of Napoleon's changed attitude, Izquierdo had been instructed by Duroc to bypass Godoy and present the emperor's message directly to the *reyes*. However, Don Eugenio assured Manuel the contents were of so serious a nature that the king would certainly require his counsel. Godoy was now convinced that he was all that stood between Carlos and the joint perfidy of Fernando's *facción* and Napoleon. After so much anticipation, it turned out that Izquierdo had brought not so much a direct communication from the emperor, but rather a lengthy aide-mémoire which he had jotted down while Napoleon held forth on real and imagined grievances with regard to Spain. It was a chilly compilation. Not one to mince words, Napoleon stated it was his duty to maintain peace by opposing the English with "every type of means, ordinary and extraordinary, regular or irregular, violent or gentle."[11] Having thus arrogated absolute power to himself, the rest was easy. The frontier fortresses had been occupied by "pacific and innocent means" to protect the French rear. In addition, the emperor considered it necessary "to move and locate his armies, in combination with those of His Catholic Majesty, wherever circumstances might require their presence"[12]—a catchall phrase that needed no further elaboration.

Manuel and the king read on, fearing the worst. So as to prevent further outbreaks of violence, the French leader had felt obliged to fortify the Spanish border provinces. In fact, he could simply occupy them if he so wished since there were "historical antecedents and political reasons for adding them to the Empire,"[13] but as a generous ally he would exchange the provinces north of the Ebro for the whole of Portugal. His Catholic Majesty would do well to accept this proposal because the time might come when France would be forced to incorporate the northern provinces with nothing to offer in their stead.

Izquierdo's doleful report merely confirmed Luisetta's earlier warnings. Even so, Manuel and Carlos were stunned by its full impact. To the credit of those present, Napoleon's outrageous demands were immediately rejected. True, the Catalans and the Basques had not always proved to be the most amenable of subjects, but their ultimate loyalty had never been in doubt. Izquierdo, a native of Navarre, was incensed at the very thought of French hegemony over his homeland.

Clearly, the ultimatum called for an immediate reply. It was decided that Izquierdo should return to Paris with a firm but diplomatic refusal to accept the emperor's ignominious conditions. The issue was further confused when Luisetta proposed that the Ebro provinces be formed into a new kingdom for her infant son, Carlos Luis, in recompense for the lost Italian territories. Manuel was less than enthusiastic, and only with great reluctance agreed that the suggestion be submitted to Napoleon. Later, after Izquierdo had already left, Godoy reconsidered his action. Changing his mind, he sent a special rider after Izquierdo to recover the letter he had unwillingly written in support of Luisetta's plan. Whatever his own parlous state, he was determined that no province of Spain was to be broken off from the main body.

Of all the king's ministers, only the *privado* discerned Napoleon's true intentions. Yet, ironically it was his very presence which gave the emperor the pretext of "rescuing" Fernando from Godoy's "claws," to use Manuel's own expression. Once again, he offered to step aside if that would serve Spain's best interests. For Manuel, his exposed position offered more of a threat to his life than any security: "Wherever I was, I found myself surrounded by enemies; those who called themselves my friends were lukewarm and frightened, the entire Court and even the King were opposed to my advice. Yet the more difficult my position became, the more Carlos IV tied me to the foot of the throne about to collapse."[14]

For some time, Manuel had considered a bold course of action, namely for the court to abandon Aranjuez and to establish itself in Andalucía. From thence, should the need arise, the Spanish royal family could embark for Mexico or elsewhere in Latin America. Godoy has been severely criticized for advocating the withdrawal of the entire court—the kinder epithets range from "retreat" to "abandonment"—but he has also received acclaim from some surprising quarters. The Conde de Toreno, usually sparing in his praise for the *privado,* nevertheless believed that his idea was a masterstroke: "Now that we can be dispassionate judges and exercise a fine impartiality, it seems to us that the decision, considering the state of affairs, was both timely and correct . . . This resolution then, being the best adapted to the circumstances, demonstrates that by advising the journey Don Manuel Godoy was acting prudently, and posterity in this regard cannot censure his conduct."[15]

Besides the New World, another alternative was available. If Mexico was too far and Andalucía exposed to the French advance, what of the island of Mallorca? Here, on Spanish territory, protected by the British fleet, Carlos could have remained king, much as his brother reigned in Sicily. (Perhaps Manuel might also have bestirred himself on behalf of Jovellanos, who was languishing as a prisoner in Bellmer.) None of this happened. Cevallos, Caballero, and the other ministers, especially Gil de Lemos, the secretary of the navy, not to mention Fernando and his uncle Antonio—all were resolutely opposed to any move, especially one suggested by Godoy. Even so, the *privado* persisted in his plan, and ordered the Royal Guard to leave Madrid for Aranjuez to act as an escort should the decision still be taken to leave for either coast. As added protection, he instructed General Francisco Solano, the commander of the Spanish armies in Portugal, to redeploy his troops near Toledo, just to the west of Aranjuez.

Godoy had repeatedly advocated some direct action—resistance to the French, withdrawal from Aranjuez—but Carlos, indolent by nature and with a deep-seated fear of disorder dating back to the Esquilache days, preferred to await the course of events in the royal palace. Those around him noted that he had considerably aged that winter. Rather than be subjected to more unpalatable advice, he instructed Manuel: "I need a few days to get my house in order. Go to Madrid, do your weekly round as usual, take care of everything with common sense, and observe well the mood of the people. When you return, we will leave, unless some powerful reason should occur to make us change our minds."[16] Manuel had little doubt that the king would find such an excuse.

The palace of Buenavista, where Godoy held court one day a week, was in the Calle del Barquillo, at the corner of today's Plaza del Rey. According to him, the *madrileños* continued to go about their business as usual: "I can affirm that I did not observe any outward sign of the changes that were going on nearby. One day I walked over from my house situated in the Barquillo to the Admiralty, with no other retinue than my aides-de-camp, without a guard, and I paid the people of Madrid the same attentions with which they customarily honored me. As always, my house was open to everyone, the attendance was the same as before, comprising all classes of people . . ."[17]

This sanguine view is not corroborated by the many eyewitnesses who attended his last public audience. Far from acting as if nothing untoward were happening, he cautioned the assembly in a raised voice: "Gentlemen, the French advance fast upon us; we must be on our guard, for there is an abundance of bad faith on their side."[18] A more revelatory incident is recounted by Alcalá Galiano. Apparently the *privado* was discussing with two friars the Pope's treatment at the hands of the French. Suddenly, he posed the cryptic question: "How is it that the Holy Spirit of the dove has turned into a partridge?" His listeners were too embarrassed to reply, none having understood the allusion or what appeared to be a tasteless joke bordering on blasphemy. Godoy provided the answer, such as it was: "Yes, gentlemen, a partridge with colored feet." Then, before anyone could react, he added pathetically, "I am in such a sorry state that I should like to put on, not a habit such as you are wearing, but a sack and go into a corner."[19]

One of the last to see Godoy privately was Napoleon's personal emissary, the Count de Tournon-Simiane, a perceptive observer of the Spanish scene. Writing to his master, he noted: "The Prince of the Peace returned to Aranjuez at 3:00 p.m. on March 13. I took my leave of him at half past two, and I only spent ten minutes in his company. I was surprised how worried he was, everything about him revealed a profound unease."[20] As Godoy's coach rumbled along the rutted road to Aranjuez, from the curtained window he caught sight of an unaccustomed flow of people headed southward in the direction of the royal palace.

Manuel's relief upon arriving safely was short lived. During his absence, the king had found yet another anonymous note, the third in less than six months. In it, he was admonished not to trust Godoy and Izquierdo, and was reminded that the events in Naples and Portugal could easily be repeated in Spain. The king was specifically warned against leaving Aranjuez; indeed, it was his duty to remain there and receive the French emperor. Carlos discerned his eldest son's hand behind this latest machination, but, lacking any firm proof, he ordered Caballero to delve into the matter.

By the time Fernando had been summoned, Manuel was also present. The monarchs, in no mood for another exhausting bout with the heir apparent, adopted a conciliatory approach. Fernando was reminded that he had Manuel to thank for the royal display of moderation. In return, the Prince of Asturias expressed his boundless loyalty to his *padre divino* and to his mother, both of whom he would "follow to the end of the world, wherever they might command." Having kissed his parents' hands amid the usual effusion of tears, Fernando embraced Manuel before declaring: "You are my true friend, my heart is yours. I would be the most unjust of men were I to esteem you one whit less than my father. Who would dare come now and tell me that you wanted to deprive me of the succession to the Crown? You are the guardian angel of this royal house, you will save the kingdom, just as you have saved it so many times."[21]

The question now was whether Fernando, notwithstanding his strenuous assurances, would agree to accompany his parents to the coast. At Manuel's suggestion, another alternative was broached: the prince would remain behind as the king's lieutenant with a court of his own (from which Infantado and Escoiquiz would be excluded) while the ailing monarchs went south. Fernando appeared to welcome the idea, which, if nothing else, would have genuinely reconciled him to his parents and have presented a united front both to the nation and to the French. A day later, some of the *facción* (as Godoy termed Fernando's supporters) advised rejection of the plan on constitutional grounds. By now, Antonio Pascual, the king's brother, had become a leading voice among the dissidents, not so much out of love for his nephew, but rather out of hatred for María Luisa, who fully repaid the sentiment. She had once written to Manuel, "You have spoken to and advised Antonio very well, but I doubt that he will pay any attention as he is stupid and consequently stubborn."[22]

Still no final decision had yet been reached as to whether the royal family should remain in Aranjuez or not. Reports among courtiers, servants, and soldiers ran rife that an immediate departure was projected, and the palace grounds began to fill with citizens from every station of life, all united in their determination that none of the royal family was to leave. The mood of the council fluctuated from hour to hour; the majority of the members, like the judges in the recent Escorial trial, were convinced that Fernando would soon be king, thus making any action on the part of the *reyes* totally irrelevant. Cevallos, the nominal First Minister and cousin by marriage to Godoy, was at most lukewarm in his support of the favorite, and would soon disown him entirely.

Even so, Manuel managed temporarily to convince some council members of the need to withdraw to Andalucía. His success was mainly due to the fact that Caballero and Gil de Lemos, the secretary of the navy, were not present at the council meeting, having gone out for a walk. Caballero, on his return, was furious and refused to sign the necessary papers with the venomous remark, "The person who suggested such treachery and villainy was deceiving the King to the point of sacrilege." At this insult, Godoy unsheathed his sword, only to find Caballero's pistol already pressed against his ribs. Thereupon both men went to the king to arbitrate their quarrel. The minister of justice contended that, since there was nothing to fear from the French, the proposed evacuation was palpably absurd. Thus reassured, Carlos turned to Manuel and said, "When Caballero says that something isn't right, he knows what he's saying and can back it up." The council was called back into session, giving Caballero the opportunity to denounce Godoy as a traitor with the aspersion, "If you wish to go, be gone, you'll be doing the Kingdom a favor, you don't know what a Kingdom is, you only know how to enter and leave a palace."[23] Thus emboldened, the other ministers unhesitatingly turned against the *valido*. The king, already bewildered by the unseemly altercation, was advised by his confessor, Félix Amat, to give up all thought of flight, counsel he readily accepted.

In those days, Aranjuez was ordinarily a tranquil oasis centered around the *sitio*. As such, the resident population consisted mainly of royal retainers—courtiers, servants, and farmers—numbering no more than a few hundred at the most. By March 16 this was no longer the case. The troops of the Spanish and Walloon Guards had arrived from Madrid, and in some instances were already fraternizing with the swelling mass of tradespeople and ordinary citizens. As Manuel surveyed the scene from a distance, he could but wonder how loyal the soldiers would prove to be in a crisis. Interspersed in the crowd were spies and agents provocateurs, distributing money to the milling throng and spreading lurid tales of the *choricero's* iniquities. Gone was the traditional respect for the royal family; no longer was the king excluded from the ribald name-calling. By now, the *trinidad* was vilified as *el cabrón, la puta, y el alcahuete* (the cuckold, the whore, and the procurer),[24] a far cry from the earthly trinity María Luisa had in mind.

Such a hostile demonstration did not materialize without a guiding hand. As with the Esquilache riots of 1766, members of the aristocracy played a leading part in organizing the "spontaneous" outburst. Godoy is undoubtedly correct when he asserts that the groundwork for the *motín* (mutiny) of Aranjuez was carefully laid. Chief among the instigators was the Conde de Montijo, formerly Conde de Teba. Rumor—as insubstantial as most—averred that he had once been rejected by María Luisa as a lover and that from that day forth had vowed vengeance on the queen and her favorite. Another reason is far more likely: "On September 7, 1805, they exiled my mother in an offensive manner. Not only am I authorized, but I believe almost obliged to avenge her and free the homeland from the monster who was devouring her and who is betraying her through his ambition, ignorance, and political heavy-handedness."[25] Montijo himself had been living in Portuguese exile, but at the beginning of March returned to Madrid. Thence he went to Aranjuez, disguised as "Tío Pedro" in which peasant garb he was to play a leading role in the drama that was unfolding.

From the north, Murat's forces continued their march on Madrid. Any pretense that the capital was not their objective had been abandoned; indeed, there was now talk that the French armies might continue all the way to Cádiz, where part of the French Navy was being blockaded by the English. Murat, resplendent in his fine uniform, reckless on the battlefield, dashing with the ladies—the more thoughtful among the Spaniards began to anticipate his arrival with distinct apprehension. Yet, despite the violence between pillaging soldiers and enraged citizens, the French were still widely regarded as liberators and Godoy as the man single-handedly responsible for Spain's predicament.

By March 16 the king finally perceived that he must act lest the crisis erupt into revolution. Godoy prepared a tedious manifesto which, despite Carlos's signature, was never made public. In it, the favorite endeavored to explain the treaty with Napoleon, while at the same time acknowledging that there were differences of opinion with the French that would have to be resolved. The tract was overtaken by events, but Manuel's claim that, had the people been aware of its contents, "all the lies and intrigues of the conspirators would have been undone,"[26] is surely wishful thinking. Carlos, in desperate need of more practical advice, turned to Caballero, who prepared a more succinct proclamation that was posted at the palace gates.

The mob was now in an ugly mood, reminiscent of the Parisian throng which had sallied forth to Versailles to threaten the lives of Louis XVI and his family. Fortunately, the ringleaders paused long enough to read the official notice:

My dear subjects: Your noble agitation under these circumstances is yet another proof that assures me of the feelings in your hearts, and I who love you as an affectionate father, hasten to console you in the anguish which now lies heavily upon you. You may breathe freely; you should know that the army of my dear ally, the Emperor of the French, is crossing my Kingdom with peaceful and friendly intentions . . . Spaniards, calm yourselves; act towards the troops of your King's ally as you have done thus far, and within a few days you will see peace restored in your hearts, and I shall enjoy what Heaven has decreed for me in the bosom of my family and your love.

> Signed in my royal palace at Aranjuez,
> March 16, 1808. *Yo el Rey*.[27]

Surprisingly, no firm commitment was made to remain in Aranjuez, for in fact the monarchs, irresolute to the very end, still had not made up their minds. The announcement had an electrifying effect on the fickle crowd outside the gates. Shouts of joy rent the air, and, when the king and queen appeared on the balcony, they were acclaimed with huzzas. All seemed well under control as they returned to the royal apartments, the crisis as good as over.

As Carlos left for the hunt next morning, he appeared in especially good cheer. The quarry was cooperative as always, and the king returned to the palace invigorated and in high spirits. That evening, he found Manuel very depressed. Upon inquiry, he learned that his friend was fearful of an assassination attempt. Carlos good-naturedly told Manuel not to worry and bade him a good night's rest with the assurance, "Sleep in peace tonight, I am your shield, Manuel *mío,* and will be all my life."[28]

At ten-thirty, Godoy took his leave and was driven to his residence. Not a soul was stirring; the king was right, after all. The table was already set when Manuel arrived home to dine with his brother Diego and with Brigadier Jorge Truyols, commander of the Hussars. The three men enjoyed their leisurely meal together and then retired for the night. As Manuel undressed to go to bed, he saw little reason for undue concern. He was wrong. It was a night he would never forget.

14

MUTINY AT

ARANJUEZ

No one quite knows how it began. Some say that toward midnight a mysterious lady—perhaps Pepita Tudó, her features obscured by a mantilla—was seen emerging from Godoy's house accompanied by two guards. Whoever it was, the patrols of four to six men, muffled and armed with sticks, acting under the direct orders of *Tío Pedro,* were taking no chances. The carriage was halted, those who had just entered were bidden to disclose their identity. Somehow, in the darkness a pistol was inadvertently fired, and the carriage sped off. But then again the shot could easily have been a prearranged signal. Some claim they heard a rallying clarion call, while others were certain they saw the light of a candle flickering at the window of the Prince of Asturias. Whatever the stratagem, it signaled a concerted attack on Godoy's residence.

Memories tend to be highly selective. The *privado,* perhaps out of a sense of gallantry, denies that any woman left his house that night; his enemies, equally insistent, state flatly that he was in the arms of some mistress or other, whom he matter-of-factly sent away before retiring for the night. María Luisa never had any doubt as to who was responsible: "My son Fernando led the conspiracy; he had won over the troops; he placed a light at one of his windows as a signal for the riot to begin."[1] Manuel is more guarded: "But who gave the signal? For myself I cannot answer this question . . . If the signal were given from some location, it could not have been to warn that the *reyes* were about to depart [for the coast] as they had gone to bed and were sleeping, but only to indicate the assault on my house, the only heroic feat that was accomplished."[2]

One fact is certain: the attack on Godoy's life was premeditated. Pardo González states unequivocally that "the Aranjuez revolution was sedition on the part of the grandees of Spain, the nobles of Castilla, and the servants of the royal household."[3] Many of the rabble-rousers were in fact retainers of the king's brother Don Antonio; in some cases they did not even bother to change out of their livery. The assailants were marshaled into position, plied with wine and inflammatory tirades, and given sticks and stones as well as placards bearing the inscription, "Long live the King! Long live the Prince of Asturias! Death to that dog of a Godoy!"[4]

Even so, they hesitated to charge. Many believed that a strong detachment of guards was inside the *valido's* house ready to repel any onslaught—a sobering thought even to the most inebriated. Furious at their cowardice, the Conde de Montijo threw off his disguise for a moment and shouted, "What's holding you back? Hurry up, there's nothing to fear. What will people say of Spaniards if we lose this opportunity? Clear the way, I'm going to get on horseback seeing no one else is doing so. Quick, because we have to strike the blow before it dawns."[5] A squad of soldiers followed at his heels, and, finally seeing that no shots came from the building, the pressing mass thrust forward, intent on finding its prey.

Godoy's mansion was no fortress, and assuredly not designed to withstand the fury of an incensed mob. The ornate doors flew open at the first assault, the porcelain objets d'art shattered into a thousand fragments as they were swept aside, the frames of priceless paintings cracked as they were wrenched off the walls and hurled to the ground. In the frenzied search for its quarry, the bloodthirsty rabble trampled everything underfoot, overturning statuary, splintering mirrors and valuable glassware, ripping out pages from precious volumes, slashing the upholstered cushions with knives—all in a frantic attempt to discover the whereabouts of the *choricero*.

Yet, he was nowhere to be found. Instead the vandals came upon a terrified woman clutching a child to her bosom. This sight calmed them, for she was immediately recognized as the Countess of Chinchón. She was known to be of the royal blood and to detest her husband. The rowdies, in their anxiety to show the respect due her rank, harnessed themselves to a carriage they found in the coach-house, and amid cries of *¡Viva la inocente! ¡Viva la cándida paloma!* pulled the princess in triumph all the way to the palace. A few days later, she said of Manuel, "I hate him so much that I do not like that child because she is his."[6] She was never to see her husband again.

Word of the attack spread like wildfire. Diego, who but an hour previously had been dining with his brother, quickly ordered the troops under his command to open fire on the rioters. The guards refused to obey and struck him to the ground with their rifle butts. But for the timely intervention of Prince Castelfranco, colonel of the Walloon Guards, Diego might have been killed on the spot. His insignia were ripped off, a wound more to his self-esteem than to his person. He was immediately declared a prisoner and consigned to the proper authorities.

Meanwhile, the destruction at Godoy's house was continuing apace. Some of the despoilers were convinced that their prey had escaped in the guise of a woman, and so vented their fury all the more on the luckless mansion. Félix Amat, the king's confessor, hurried over to the house in an effort to disperse the crowd. Speaking with the full authority of his office, he admonished them: "This belongs to the King; it is not Manuel Godoy's. What you are doing shows a very serious lack of respect for our liege, the King. His Majesty has relieved Manuel Godoy of all his duties and offices. Return to your homes now. Don Manuel Godoy, the one you are looking for, is not here."[7] A calculated risk, indeed; if Godoy were not there (Amat had no way of knowing), then where was he? Fortunately, it did not occur to any of the crowd to ask, nor to verify that the *choricero* had in fact been dismissed by the king. As it was, some of the mob stayed in his house until seven in the morning before reluctantly giving up the search.

At the palace, Carlos and María Luisa paced up and down in an agony of uncertainty. Amid the shouts outside of "Death to Godoy!" no one felt inclined to sleep. For all the king's hand wringing, it was impossible to ascertain Manuel's fate. The ministers were evasive, even disrespectful, while the servants obeyed but grudgingly. Only Fernando seemed outwardly unmoved. In desperation, the *reyes* begged their son to step out onto the balcony and calm the agitated crowd. The heir to the throne pointed out that the people could only be appeased if Godoy were dismissed from all his posts. For a moment, the queen demurred, then acknowledged that there was no other way to save Manuel's life. Paper and pen were called for, and with a heavy heart Carlos signed the following decree:

> Wishing to place the army and the navy under my personal command, I have just relieved Don Manuel Godoy, Prince of the Peace, from his duties as Generalissimo and Admiral, granting him retirement to wherever he sees fit. Take note of this and communicate it to whom it may concern.
> Aranjuez. March 18, 1808.[8]

This decree was published at five in the morning, and half an hour later Fernando accepted the wild cheers of the crowd. Then, inside the palace, Carlos received the French ambassador at a special audience. So disconcerted that he saw nothing strange in the arrival of Beauharnais at daybreak, the king summoned the strength to say, "The Emperor can depend on me. I shall never leave the country. I give you my word of honor. Manuel has gone. I pity him. He has served me for twenty years, and I should be desolated if anything happened to him. I am done with generalissimos and shall march at the head of my troops myself. I will take no step without first consulting the Emperor. Let me know your ideas, my dear Ambassador, but for mercy's sake not just now; tonight has left me badly shaken."[9] And, with that, the king feebly motioned that the audience was over.

In their dejection, the monarchs found one ray of hope: Manuel had not been captured or . . . they dreaded to think of the alternative. Perhaps he had escaped and even now was headed for the coast and safety. From force of habit, the king sat down and, despite crippling arthritis in his right hand, wrote the following to Napoleon:

> For some time now in repeated petitions the Prince of the Peace has indicated to me his desire to be allowed to resign from his posts as Generalissimo and Admiral. I have acceded to this wish and have approved his resignation from the aforementioned positions; but as I can never forget the services he rendered me, above all that of working with me for the success of my constant desire to maintain the alliance with Your Imperial and Royal Majesty and the intimate friendship which binds us, I always wish to attest my consideration for this Prince.[10]

Even at this moment of supreme crisis, Carlos's first thought was for *querido* Manuel.

At the first light of dawn, the crowd still had not dispersed. At half past seven, the entire royal family, in a shaky display of solidarity, came out on the balcony to a frenzied reception from the populace below. The Infante Antonio threw his hat in the air in a fatuous display of enthusiasm, while Fernando had difficulty in suppressing his pleasure at the turn of events. The *reyes* did their best to smile bravely. So far, at least, Carlos and María Luisa seemed secure on their thrones. But what had happened to Manuel?

Of necessity, we are entirely dependent on Godoy's own account for the events that transpired. Thirty years later, he relived those convulsive hours:

It was midnight. My brother and Brigadier Truyols were retiring to go to bed, and I was beginning to get undressed when a shot was heard, then a trumpet call from someone mounted on horseback, and soon afterwards, a clamor in the distance which grew at every moment and seemed to be approaching. My brother, together with Truyols, went down to find out what was going on and to notify the guard. I took a cloak and went up to the top floor looking for a window from which I could see and make out the avenues of the palace and my house. The servant who helped me get ready for bed followed me. I entered the first room I found open, but as the window opened on to the inside court, I was about to leave and look for another room when my servant, affected by the noise and clamor inside my house, and without knowing what he was doing, closed the door on me and locked it, taking the key, and left me there shut up to the mercy of God and with no other protection.[11]

Quite likely the servant's action—conscious or otherwise—saved Godoy's life. By some quirk, the crowd rampaging through the house apparently took no notice of the upper room. For several hours, Manuel heard the sounds of wanton destruction below. At last the tumult ceased, to be replaced by an eerie stillness.

The garret in which Godoy found himself was the room of some servant. It contained a bed, three or four chairs, and a jug of water on a table; in the half-open drawer were some bread and a few raisins. Manuel ate and drank sparingly, hoping for the best but fearing the worst. As the hours went by, his hunger and thirst became more acute. Then, suddenly toward evening of the following day, he heard steps approaching and someone trying to open the locked door. It was a female servant who had come to collect her few belongings. "For heaven's sake!" Godoy heard her say to her male companion, "I haven't been able to find my husband all day, and probably he's got the key. Maybe he's a prisoner. How awful!" "Don't worry, and don't cry," came the reply, "We'll do the same to this one as with the others." So saying, he charged the door and broke the lock. Manuel vehemently denies the oft-repeated tale that he was hidden in a rolled-up carpet, claiming instead that he stayed motionless in a nook of the darkened room when the man and woman entered. As the servant girl reached into a trunk to gather her clothes, reportedly she could not refrain from reflecting on the fate of the Prince of the Peace. "Poor master! He was so good, and did so much for us! Where can he be now? I wonder how His Highness is faring!"[12]

Unfortunately, among the maid's possessions was the precious jug of water which she picked up on her way out. As soon as the coast was clear, Manuel tiptoed into an adjoining room. Although he does not mention it, he probably tried to escape through a secret passage to the neighboring house of the Duchess of Osuna, only to discover that he did not have the necessary key. Weak from the pangs of inanition, he lay down and fell asleep. When he awoke the next morning, thirty-six hours had passed since the mob had broken into the house. His thirst had now become intolerable, and so for the first time he ventured out of his hiding place. At the foot of the staircase sat an artilleryman smoking and counting his money. As Godoy, pallid and disheveled, made his way down the stairs, the soldier turned round in surprise, but Manuel bade him be silent with the inducement, "Listen, wait a moment, I'll be able to show you my gratitude . . ." At first, the soldier's reaction was positive—Godoy had always favored the artillerymen—but then, overcome by fear, he turned to his companions for help. With no other recourse available, the Prince of the Peace boldly addressed himself to the group: "Yes, it's me, my friends, I am yours. Dispose of me as you wish, but without abusing the man who has been like a father to you."[13] According to Manuel, not a hand was laid on him, and he was even able to walk around his house unmolested to inspect the damage. This delay may have proved his undoing, for, by the time he requested the soldiers to conduct him to the king, word of his discovery had spread and an angry crowd had gathered outside.

In a trice, the scene changed from the benevolent curiosity of the soldiers to the implacable hatred of the insurgents lusting after Godoy's blood. Only with the greatest of difficulty were the artillerymen able to protect their prisoner. The crowd, egged on by some of the Infante Antonio's retainers, struck the *choricero* with anything that came to hand—cudgels, knives, stones, not sparing the detested favorite from kicks and blows. Forced to run the gauntlet, Manuel bled profusely from wounds in his face and thigh as he desperately hung on to the saddle-trees of the horses on either side of him. Showing admirable presence of mind, one soldier held him by the collar while another threw a cloak over his head and shoulders. Thus protected, the picket and their prisoner made it to the barracks, where Godoy, more dead than alive, was thrust onto a pile of straw in a stable. Yet, even under the protection of an armed guard, there was grave risk that the ravenous mob might smash its way in and tear the favorite apart limb from limb. Only a miracle would save him. That miracle assumed shape in the most unexpected guise.

The news of Manuel's capture reached the palace almost immediately.

Relief quickly turned to anguish when harrowing accounts of the crowd's fury assailed the monarchs' ears. The king's first inclination was to rush over to the barracks in person and plead with the rioters. Thankfully, calmer counsels prevailed, and Fernando, exercising his newfound authority, agreed to intercede on Manuel's behalf. When the prince, accompanied by Montijo, arrived at half past ten, Godoy was being led up some stairs by his guards, possibly to be interrogated. The two men looked at one another for a moment in silence, at first unable to grasp fully the sudden turn in their respective fortunes. At the Escorial, it was Manuel who perhaps had saved the crown prince's life; now Fate chose to reverse the roles. Fernando was the first to speak. "I grant you your life," he declared, to which Godoy replied, "Is Your Highness then already king?" "Not yet, but I soon shall be."[14] Thereupon Fernando brushed aside Manuel's question regarding his parents and, turning to the crowd, assumed full responsibility for the prisoner with the assurance, "Gentlemen, I answer for this man. He shall be tried and his punishment shall fit the gravity of his offenses."[15] Sensing that he would indeed soon be king, Fernando doubtless felt it his duty to appear magnanimous in the eyes of his subjects.

The reaction of Carlos and María Luisa was decidedly mixed. Gratitude on the one hand was counterbalanced by resentment at their son's usurpation of the royal powers. It was evident that the *reyes* were now monarchs in name only. Carlos gave orders that his personal physician was to treat Manuel's wounds, but, instead, Capdevila, the regimental surgeon of the guards, was sent. Clearly, Godoy was not yet out of immediate danger. The rumor now spread that the king planned to spirit him away to Granada. Sure enough, a coach-and-six was seen to draw up outside the barracks, a sight calculated to rouse the mutinous mob to renewed violence. The traces were slashed, the carriage methodically destroyed, and one of the horses killed on the spot. Once again, Fernando's presence was needed to restore order. Unquestionably, the whole incident had been as carefully contrived as the original attack on Godoy's house. With suspicious spontaneity, voices were raised denouncing the king and praising Fernando.

On the evening of March 19, a special meeting of the Royal Council was summoned. Caballero informed the members that the monarchs had assented that Godoy be brought to trial. Throughout the day, squads of soldiers had conducted well-rehearsed maneuvers in the courtyard to intimidate the *reyes;* reports of a direct assault on the palace abounded. In his hour of need, Carlos found himself deserted by all save María Luisa; ministers faded away or else displayed an insolent nonchalance, no troop commander could be relied on, and outside the rabble kept up its incessant chant. Under such pressure, the king was reduced to a pathetic figure; without Manuel, life had no direction. Finally, toward seven o'clock that evening, an exhausted Carlos signed a letter of abdication which Caballero had taken care to draw up during the day:

> As the indispositions from which I suffer no longer allow me to bear the heavy weight of the government of my realms, and as it has become necessary for me to regain my health in a more temperate climate and in the tranquility of private life, I have decided, after due deliberation, to abdicate my crown in favor of my heir and beloved son, the Prince of Asturias. Therefore it is my royal wish that he be recognized and obeyed as King and natural lord in all my realms and dominions. So that my royal decree of free and spontaneous abdication may be carried out exactly and correctly, I am submitting it to the Council and to those whom it may concern.
>
> Signed at Aranjuez, March 19, 1808.
> Yo el Rey.[16]

The transfer of power from father to son was universally greeted with elation. As on all such joyous occasions, the poets were not found lacking in inspiration. The following gloating verses are a fair sampling of the jingles that flooded the country to celebrate Godoy's downfall:

> In this royal residence, then, a base tyrant
> without religion, stupid, arrogant,
> a traitor, iniquitous, lustful and vain,
> saw himself overthrown in an instant.
> Do you have any doubts who that insane monster is?
> Well, know then that it is the Admiral.[17]

It was left to a priest, Manuel Gil de la Cuesta, to compose the most defamatory attack on the *privado*:

> Because of you the persecuted Aranda died,
> Floridablanca lives in exile,
> Jovellanos in a living tomb,
> and many grandees languish in oblivion.
> Of mother, father, husband

you have besmirched the honor, and have profaned,
brutish polygamist, that sacred ground
where, unworthy, you have not deserved to tread.
Slander, murder, theft and assassinations
you have committed with insolent effrontery,
Oh, you most despicable of privados!
If admiral, if grandee you made yourself,
when you were the vilest of the wicked,
now Heaven will return you to what you were.[18]

The news of Fernando's accession to the throne reached Madrid within hours of the proclamation. Godoy's town house was sacked with meticulous thoroughness: the furniture was thrown out the window to provide kindling for a huge bonfire, into which were thrown tapestries, paintings, and even doors wrenched from their hinges. Alcalá Galiano witnessed the wanton destruction of the house of Diego Godoy in the Paseo del Prado: "Soon under the windows appeared the light of a bonfire. At once one could see at the same windows men of the very worst possible aspect who were tossing everything they could find into the fire. This action was accompanied by furious shouts, hurrahs when they saw the destruction and vows of death to the objects of the public hatred." The houses of anyone connected with the favorite, no matter how tenuous the relationship, were subject to fire and pillaging. "The shouts of 'Death to the *privado*' continued unabated, now he was called by his last name of Godoy which had been forgotten for many years . . ."[19] Only when the rioters became hopelessly drunk and started releasing prisoners from jail as well as looting foodstores and taverns did the government institute night patrols to restore order.

As the news of Godoy's overthrow spread to other cities, bells were rung, Te Deums chanted, and fiestas celebrated. Unable to lay their hands on the original culprit, most towns and villages had to content themselves with the destruction of his official portraits (one was dragged out of a church where it had been placed in appreciation of the Prince of the Peace). Often the frenzied conduct of the crowd assumed xenophobic forms. The botanical gardens in Sanlúcar de Barrameda were uprooted—so much for Godoy's efforts to introduce cinnamon and indigo into Spain—and, to leave nothing undone, the lifeboats built in Cádiz on his instructions were all destroyed. During the sacking of his library in Aranjuez, Arab texts sent by Badía were found, incontrovertible proof that the *choricero* was in league with a foreign power and was planning to make Moslems of them all.

On March 21 a decree was issued in Fernando's name ordering the confiscation of "all the goods, assets, common stock, and rights of Don Manuel Godoy."[20] That he had not yet been brought to trial was irrelevant; his guilt was assumed from the beginning. Throughout Spain, his supporters and appointees went into hiding. Pedro Cevallos, in his ambivalent position, thought it prudent to submit his resignation, but Fernando declined to accept it on the extenuating grounds that "even though he is married to a cousin of the Prince of the Peace, Don Manuel Godoy, he has never shared the unjust ideas and design which may be taken for granted in that man."[21] Orders were issued for the release of Urquijo, Cabarrús, Floridablanca, and Jovellanos from their respective exile or imprisonment. By royal command, the bullfights were reinstated, the price of tobacco lowered, and henceforth the people were to receive a freer flow of wine, which the hated *privado* had reduced during the course of the war.

In the wake of his immense popularity, Fernando began to adopt a condescending attitude toward his parents. Very well, if they wished to spend their remaining days in seclusion, what better place than Badajoz, the birthplace of their *querido* Manuel: that the province of Extremadura has one of the harshest climates in Spain was none of Fernando's concern. Nor for that matter was the disrespect shown the ex-monarchs by their entourage, as for example when the Conde de Fernán-Núñez waited in attendance on Carlos during a meal. A servant entered and, ignoring the seated sovereign, whispered a message into the count's ear. When Carlos indignantly protested this gross breach of etiquette, Fernán-Núñez impudently replied, "Sire, the King is calling me."[22] More than anything else, these calculated insults rankled in the elderly monarch's mind. Perhaps he had acted too hastily in renouncing his throne.

María Luisa and Luisetta were even more resentful of Fernando's attitude. The ex-queen of Spain bitterly reproached Carlos for his precipitate action, taunting him for not having demanded Manuel's release as a quid pro quo. Luisetta, who had just been deposed herself, was in no mood to address her impertinent brother as king and decided upon direct action. If Manuel were to be saved, French intervention was required. Accordingly, Luisetta sent a confidential letter to Murat at his headquarters in El Molar imploring his help. The Grand Duke of Berg immediately grasped the import of the message and ordered his aide-de-camp, General Bailly de Monthion, to ride *ventre à terre* to Aranjuez and apprise him of the situation.

That night, Monthion rode his horse so hard that he arrived at the palace at eight in the morning. First Luisetta was awakened, then her parents. "I was forced to abdicate my crown," Carlos assured the Frenchman, "so as to save my life and that of the Queen, otherwise we would have been assassinated that night. The conduct of the Prince of Asturias is even more reprehensible as he fully knew that it was my wish to transfer the crown to him as soon as he was married to a French princess, a marriage which I have ardently desired."[23] More immediately, Manuel had to be rescued from what promised to be certain death. "They have just taken away the Prince of the Peace and wish to kill him," Carlos lamented. "His only crime is having been faithful to me all his life. His death will be mine, I won't survive it. My position is very sad."[24] Carlos and María Luisa both expressed their wish to spend the rest of their days in retirement with Manuel. Luisetta added: "The poor Prince of the Peace, covered with wounds and bruises, is languishing in prison, and never ceases to invoke the terrible moment of his death. The only person he remembers is his friend the Grand Duke of Berg, and says that he is the only one he trusts and who can accomplish his salvation."[25]

Murat quickly realized the potential for mischief in Carlos's statement and sent the saddle-weary Monthion back to Aranjuez with a rough draft penned by Murat himself retracting the abdication of a few days ago. To lend spontaneity to the declaration, it was antedated to March 21. The letter to Napoleon read in part:

> Sire, my brother . . . I was forced to abdicate; but encouraged now by the complete confidence I entertain in the magnanimity and genius of the great man who has always shown himself to be my friend, I have resolved to comply with everything that this great man will decide for us, my fate, that of the Queen, and of the Prince of the Peace. I hereby lodge my protest with Your Imperial and Royal Majesty against the events at Aranjuez and against my abdication, and I place my trust entirely in the affection and friendship of Your Majesty.[26]

For good measure, Carlos also signed a formal protest declaring his abdication invalid.

Murat now found himself in a quandary. With the knowledge of the *reyes'* retraction uppermost in his mind, he was about to enter Madrid, where no doubt, he would meet formally with Fernando, considered by his countrymen to be the new king of Spain. With what title should he address the prince? Then there was the question of Manuel Godoy. A report had circulated that he was to be tied to a cart and left to the mercy of the crowd. For any number of reasons—military, political, or common humanity—Murat was determined to deny the rabble its prey. Without delay, he contacted Francisco Negrete, the captain-general of Madrid. The vehemence of Murat's protest may be inferred from a letter Negrete wrote to Caballero:

> When I went this morning to the general headquarters of Prince Murat to congratulate him, he asked me whether it was true that Don Manuel Godoy was to arrive that day in Madrid as a prisoner. I replied in the affirmative, whereupon he broke out in anger, saying that it was not right that on the very day he was to present himself at Court there should be insulting scenes which would disturb the public order and force him to draw his sword and wage war. Despite my opinions, he handed me the enclosed letter, and with considerable intensity made me verbally responsible for the arrested man's safe arrival. As time is of the essence, I have dispatched two officers to ride flat out [*matando caballos* in the more picturesque original] to the escort to make them wait somewhere for His Majesty's orders, as the Grand Duke of Berg told me that, should the case arise, he would use the armed force he had at his disposal.[27]

A Captain Marbot, instructed by Murat to keep a watch on the captive, was shocked to see his deplorable condition: "I came across Godoy some two leagues from the outskirts of the capital. Even though this ill-fated man was terribly wounded and completely covered with blood, his guards had the cruelty to attach shackles to his feet and hands, and to tie him by the body to a wretched uncovered cart, exposed to the burning rays of the sun and to thousands of flies, attracted by his open wounds . . . Since being wounded, he has not even been attended to. His shirt, soaked with his coagulated blood, had stuck to his skin; he only had one shoe, no handkerchief, he was half naked, and devoured by fever."[28] As a result of Murat's timely intervention, the procession bearing Godoy to certain dismemberment was stopped a few miles short of its objective. The fallen favorite was taken instead under heavy guard to the village of Pinto, there to await further orders.

On the morning of March 23 the French army, numbering 40,000 men, made its triumphal entry into Madrid. Leading his troops was the flamboyant Grand Duke of Berg, twirling his marshal's baton. Long black curls falling to his shoulders, attired in a doublet of green velvet with red silken sash and leather boots to match, the whole surmounted by a crimson shako from which protruded a white plume, Murat certainly was not lacking in panache. As he made his way along the spectator-lined streets, enthusiastic cries of "Long live Napoleon!" and "Death to Godoy!" rent the air.

Originally, it had been planned that Murat be lodged in the Palacio del Buen Retiro, the residence Pepita had vacated in her escape to the south. However, the grand duke protested that he had no wish to live in the "recently pillaged rooms of the mistress of the Prince of the Peace,"[29] and so with fine logic he transferred to Godoy's former palace of the Admiralty.

So Manuel was not to be lynched by the crowd. The following day more than made up for any thwarted expectations. Fernando's entry into the capital was a sustained acclamation as the throng went delirious. On his way to the royal palace, he was besieged by a frantic mass of men and women, strewing flowers in his path and cheering itself hoarse. Yet something was missing. Murat, on the shallow pretext of reviewing his troops, at first made no effort to welcome Fernando. When the two later met to exchange courtesies, the Spaniard was irritated that Napoleon's representative merely addressed him as "Your Royal Highness" instead of the anticipated "Your Majesty." His treatment at the hands of Beauharnais was even more summary. The ambassador, already roundly scolded by Murat for allowing Fernando to leave Aranjuez, in turn censured the prince for having been too eager to grasp the crown. "I was forced to do so by the circumstances,"[30] was all the young man could stammer in reply.

The new king—if indeed such he was—became desperate to shore up his position. He could settle accounts with Manuel later, but the immediate need was to gain full recognition from the French. The first opportunity for a conciliatory gesture came on March 31, when Murat requested that the sword of King François I taken by the Emperor Carlos V in 1525, which Godoy had declined to relinquish, be restored to the French. Fernando unhesitatingly complied, making Murat an additional gift of six horses. Perhaps Fernando's worst miscalculation was of a tactical nature. A few weeks earlier, the *privado* had instructed the Marqués del Socorro to transfer his troops from the Portuguese frontier to Madrid so as to strengthen the capital's defenses; in a craven act of appeasement, Fernando countermanded Godoy's directive and ordered the Spanish troops to return to their original base.

Meanwhile, Manuel had remained a prisoner at Pinto, uncertain as to his fate and cut off from news of the outside world. Still suffering from his open wounds, he was debilitated by fever and loss of blood, his face obscured by several days' growth of beard. His jailers taunted him that he had won but a temporary reprieve. Godoy's only comfort was that some French contingents had established their quarters nearby, though he had no way of knowing what this might presage.

From Aranjuez, María Luisa made it her personal crusade to free

Manuel. Hardly a day went by without an impassioned plea—sometimes two or three letters before nightfall—being sent to Murat. One theme predominates throughout: Manuel's safety and the eventual reunion of the *trinidad*. There is always the fear of assassination as Manuel lies helpless in his cell: "We always dread they are going to kill or poison him, if they know he is going to be rescued. Can't some measures be taken before they resolve to do it? If only the Grand Duke could order his troops to go there, without saying why, and then slip them in to where the poor Prince of the Peace is, without giving the others a moment to fire a pistol shot or do anything else."[31] Did the emperor know what was being contemplated by Fernando? He must be informed at once, "so that he will not be prejudiced by the lies which day and night are being hatched against us and the poor Prince of the Peace, whose good fortune we prefer above our own. But those two pistols kept loaded to kill him make us tremble, and that is on my son's orders which shows what sort of a heart he has."[32]

Just in case Murat were still in the dark regarding Fernando's true character, María Luisa conceived it her duty to pass on some maternal observations: "My son is very evil-minded, his nature is bloodthirsty, he has never shown his father or me any affection, his advisers thirst for blood . . . They wish to do us all the harm possible but the King and I have more interest in saving the life and honor of our innocent friend than ourselves."[33]

More letters followed in the same vein. Here was an open invitation to Murat to take advantage of the split in the Spanish camp. For this, María Luisa, spurred by her obsession to see Manuel live, must be held largely to blame. All the while, Fernando was unaware that his parents were denigrating him and plotting Manuel's release behind his back and, far more importantly, that they had retracted their abdication.

It was not until March 27 that Napoleon received news of the momentous events in Aranjuez. For the first time, Murat was given precise instructions regarding the *trinidad*: "You must prevent any harm being done to the King, the Queen, and to the Prince of the Peace. Until the new King has been recognized, act as if the old one were still reigning. If there is any talk of bringing the Prince of the Peace to trial, I should be consulted. Tell Beauharnais that it is my wish that he intervene to make sure that such a trial is not carried out."[34] On March 31 Napoleon received the letter from Carlos maintaining that his abdication had been forced from him and therefore was invalid. This was all the French emperor needed; better to deal with an exhausted Carlos than an ambitious Fernando. The following day, Murat was directed to "get the Prince of the Peace out, even if he has to be a prisoner. It doesn't matter how, the thing is to get him out of Spain."[35] At the same time, the emperor ordered General Jean-Marie Savary, a man known for his unswerving loyalty, to go posthaste to Spain and assess the situation firsthand.

On April 1 Manuel was transferred from Pinto to Villaviciosa, still under twenty-four hour supervision by the Spanish guards who in turn were surrounded by a larger contingent of French soldiers. His condition had improved to the point that at times he was even impertinent toward his captors. He regained his spirits sufficiently to complain about his food, the demeaning conditions, the treatment to which one of his rank was subjected. In vain he requested his clothes and servants on the grounds that the village of Villaviciosa was his by virtue of his title of Conde de Chinchón! Godoy was highly indignant when informed that he was no longer to be addressed as generalissimo or admiral as a result of a royal decree of March 18; moreover, as a subject of King Fernando VII, he was now also that sovereign's prisoner. Most galling of all, he found himself under the direct surveillance of Don Ramón Patiño, the Marqués de Castelar. Like so many others, Castelar owed his position entirely to the *privado*, but now was only too anxious to prove his loyalty to the new king by acting harshly toward his old benefactor.

These were hardly considerations that concerned Murat. The real question was whether the life of one man was worth the certain resentment and possible violence which would follow. Still, he had received direct orders from the emperor, and he was used to obeying without hesitation. Accordingly, he replied to Napoleon on April 5:

> Freeing the Prince of the Peace won't be difficult, but given the state of public opinion against him, one has to fear the results . . . The Queen of Etruria informed me yesterday that legal proceedings against him had been instituted; I immediately called upon the Minister of Justice to suspend the proceedings. From him I also found out that they had placed shackles on his feet. At once I voiced my complaints to the Prince of Asturias. An hour later he told me that he would order the trial against the Prince of the Peace to be suspended and ease the harshness to which he was subjected; if all these things are not done at once, I will get the Prince out of prison by force and send him to Bayonne.[36]

On April 9 Carlos and María Luisa left Aranjuez for the Escorial, where they came under Murat's direct protection. The grand duke had already assured them that "the trial of the Prince of the Peace won't take place, and that I answer for his life; his enemies, no matter who, will not dare go against this decision . . . the Prince of the Peace is in Villaviciosa." María Luisa refused to be comforted: "Does the Grand Duke know that yesterday Fernando ordered the Prince of the Peace to be placed in chains and that they are beginning to take statements from him? There's no doubt they wish to put him on trial. Perhaps one day they'll do it, so as to kill him before the Emperor can save him."[37] Then followed the repeated fervent supplication to rescue Manuel "from this horrible situation." With little else left to him, Carlos presented Murat with a horse, which "although a little on the old side, will still provide good service, at least I hope so." By way of apology, the queen added that "he has a small protuberance on his ear, he's about fourteen or fifteen years old, but still good for another four or five years; he's for the purpose of war, seeing that he is the best charger and trotter we have. Right now he's limping a bit, because they hurried too much when they cured his hoof, but this doesn't mean anything. Needless to say, he's the best the King has, and that's why he's presenting him to the Grand Duke of Berg."[38] There is no record of the dashing Murat having led a cavalry charge mounted on this latter-day Rocinante.

And so the *motín de Aranjuez,* which should have settled everything, in fact settled nothing. Fernando was king—up to a point, for so preponderant was the French presence that, without firm recognition from that quarter, the title was meaningless. A fierce debate ensued among Fernando's advisers whether he should leave Madrid and meet Napoleon, who supposedly was journeying to Spain, or simply await events in the capital. But Carlos and María Luisa also had plans of their own; they were now determined to be the first to speak to the emperor and inform him of their son's treachery. And then there was Manuel, manacled and left lying in his tomblike cell, wondering if each new day might be his last. Time was of the essence, and, whatever their differences, each saw his salvation in Napoleon. With so much at stake, all hopes were turned to the north and a possible meeting with the French emperor.

15

JACTA EST ALEA

Seldom has a popular monarch endured such frustration as did King Fernando VII. The rancorous dissension among his entourage is typified by an incident involving Escoiquiz, the leading proponent of the journey to meet the emperor. Among the many opposed were two advisers, José Hervás and the Marquis de Sardoval. At a dinner given by Cevallos, Escoiquiz threatened to expose Hervás to the French generals present. Sardoval was so incensed that he bitterly reproached Escoiquiz afterward, saying, "Your attempt to denounce my friend Hervás is infamous; the only reason I won't punish you is out of consideration for your ecclesiastic habit and tonsure." Escoiquiz tried to remonstrate, but Sardoval continued: "If you carry out this vile action, I shall go to the nunciature and shout that Archdeacon Escoiquiz has a nude Venus in his home to gratify his senses." "Please lower your voice," the canon pleaded. Sardoval still had a final thrust to deliver. "And I shall add that in Valladolid he has two children whose mother, Robustiana Infante, bewails his frailty and desertion."[1] Despite this and other altercations, Escoiquiz's counsel prevailed, and on April 10 Fernando set forth from Madrid with a large retinue. He was not to see his capital again until six years later.

Among those accompanying Fernando were Cevallos, the dukes of San Carlos and Infantado, and the omnipresent Escoiquiz. Yet, more in keeping with reality, the key figure was Napoleon's myrmidon, General Savary, recently created Duke of Rovigo. He assured Fernando that Napoleon had already departed his quarters in Bayonne; what he failed to mention were his orders to arrest Fernando should the prince (as the emperor termed him) show signs of turning back.

At Burgos, there still was no news of Napoleon's anticipated arrival; indeed, from all reports, he had not even crossed the frontier. Much against his ministers' better judgment, Fernando, encouraged by Escoiquiz, decided to press on to Vitoria. Here they were met, not by the emperor or his representative, but by a figure from the past, Mariano Luis de Urquijo, who added his urgent plea not to cross the frontier to that of the ministers, the local dignitaries, and the citizenry, all united in their resolve to safeguard Fernando. For the first time, Savary's advice to continue was not heeded. Consequently, he suggested that he ride on to Bayonne and return with a clarification from the emperor.

The digressive letter he brought back from Napoleon was surprisingly tactless, containing the famous admonition that "any approach of an heir-apparent to a foreign sovereign is a criminal act." Not only did the emperor reprimand Fernando for his recent conduct, but inexplicably went on to defend Godoy:

> It would not be in the interests of Spain to persecute a Prince who has married a Princess of the royal family and who has governed the kingdom for such a long time. Now he has no friends; neither will Your Highness if one day you should be so unfortunate. The people willingly take revenge on the respect with which they pay us homage. Besides, how can formal charges be brought against the Prince of the Peace without doing the same to the monarchs, your parents? This trial would foment hatred and seditious passions, and the result would be damaging to your Crown. Your Highness has no more right to it than what your mother has transmitted to you. If the trial stains the honor of your mother, Your Highness destroys your own rights. Disregard weak and treacherous counsel. Your Highness does not have the right to judge the Prince of the Peace. His transgressions, if they charge him, disappear in the rights of the Throne. I have often expressed my wish that the Prince of the Peace be kept away from affairs of state; if I have not insisted any further, it has been due to my friendship for King Carlos, setting to one side the frailty of his affection [for Godoy]. Oh, miserable humanity! Weakness and error; that is our emblem. But all this can be reconciled; let the Prince of the Peace be exiled from Spain, and I will offer him asylum in France . . .
>
> Bayonne, April 16, 1808. Napoleon.[2]

Napoleon's letter was disappointing, hardly that of one monarch to another. Yet, at no point did it flatly withhold recognition, but rather kept it at a tantalizing distance—say, that between Vitoria and Bayonne. Savary gave Fernando the ultimate in assurances when he declared: "I shall allow my head to be cut off if within a quarter of an hour after Your Majesty's arrival in Bayonne the Emperor has not recognized you as King of Spain and the Indies. Just to remain consistent he will probably begin by addressing you as 'Your Highness,' but after five minutes he will be calling you 'Your Majesty,' and after three days everything will be arranged and you will be able to return to Spain immediately."[3]

Even so, most doubted Napoleon's sincerity. Again, it was Escoiquiz who tipped the scales in favor of the journey. On the morning of April 19, the citizens of Vitoria made one last attempt to dissuade their beloved monarch. A few went so far as to cut the harnesses of the royal mules while others formed a human barricade across the road. Only some hasty repairs and a direct appeal to the crowd by Fernando made the journey at all possible. The travel party spent one last night in Spain at the border before, in Escoiquiz's fatuous words, "*Jacta est alea* [the die is cast]: on the 21st we crossed the Rubicon, I mean the Bidassoa. We entered France."[4] Ahead lay Bayonne, Napoleon, and deepest degradation.

Despite considerable French pressure, Godoy remained a prisoner in Spanish hands. Only on April 8 was he informed of the charges brought against him, but on the same day he learned that the *reyes* were alive and well, and about to take up residence in the Escorial. Ironically, he found a certain reassurance in the 578 Spanish guards assigned to watch over him, distrustful as he was of the French as allies. He felt extremely depressed; of course, he had no way of knowing that, but for Murat, he would have perished at the hands of the Madrilenian mob. He readily convinced himself that he was in constant danger of assassination, and, fearing the traditional *bocado,* suspected everyone from the Marqués de Castelar, his insensitive custodian, to the doctor and guards who brought him his food. Then sometimes he would perk up, assuring Castelar that his official papers would one day exonerate him from charges that he had a fortune salted away in a London bank. In one expansive moment, the forty-one-year-old prisoner admitted that his main defect in the past had been his attraction for the fair sex, "as happens to all up to the age of forty."[5] With light-hearted nostalgia, he touched upon an affair with Maria Michel, a lady recommended to him by none other than Murat. Some comfort was allowed upon being able to receive his daughter, Carlota, who did not then share her mother's sentiments and who later rejoined the *reyes* at the Escorial.

At Villaviciosa, Manuel was kept prisoner in the castle chapel, his dark, damp *capilla-calaboza,* as he wryly termed it. The three guards constantly observing him were instructed to withhold all news of the outside world; no books were allowed, no fork, toothpick, or even bones in the meat, for fear the prisoner might use them as a weapon. Such was the pettiness of his captors that, despite the incongruous presence of an altar in his cell, he was not permitted to receive the sacrament or confess, even though it was Easter. At no time was he given a change of clothing. Evincing understandable bitterness, he later commented, "When I left the hands of my illustrious jailors, my cloak and bloodstained clothes were my only apparel. I had no other."[6]

Thanks to his sound Extremaduran constitution, his health gradually improved. Castelar was more immediately concerned over the possible armed intervention of the Swiss Guard quartered at nearby Getafe. These mercenaries had remained loyal to King Carlos and had been heard to shout, "Long live Godoy, death to Bonaparte and all his soldiers!"[7] Others were also intent on securing Godoy's release. An anonymous writer, perhaps one of the guards, wrote to María Luisa: "Madame, a faithful vassal who remembers past benefits warns you that if the French attack Villaviciosa, the governor has orders to kill his prisoner. Let Murat invite the chiefs from the palace to his house and hold them as hostages."[8] The queen exerted even more pressure on Murat to ensure Manuel's safety. As a result, General Belliard and Ambassador Beauharnais were sent to the members of the *Junta Suprema de Gobierno* to hasten Godoy's release. In reply, the Infante Antonio asserted that, as the head of an interim government during the king's absence, he was not empowered to make such an important decision.

But the Grand Duke of Berg refused to give up so easily. A courier was dispatched posthaste to obtain a favorable judgment from the young king. Fernando sought to temporize by offering half rather than the whole loaf: "In view of my obligation to administer justice to my people, I have issued orders to the most respected tribunals in my kingdom that Don Manuel Godoy be judged according to the law of the land . . . But if Your Honor is interested in the life of Don Manuel Godoy I give you my royal word that, in case he is condemned to death after the most thorough inquiry, I shall pardon him out of consideration for your mediation."[9]

No full pardon was ever contemplated. By throwing a sop to the French,

Fernando hoped for the best of all possible worlds: Murat would desist from making further demands; and Godoy would be tried in public and found guilty, thus giving a magnanimous king the opportunity to commute his death sentence to solitary confinement in a fetid dungeon or perhaps a lifetime in the rotting hulk of a galley-ship. Annoyingly, Murat persisted in his strong request that Godoy be placed under French surveillance. Finally, on April 20, under the direct threat of violence from Murat, grudging assent was given to place Godoy at the disposal of the French emperor.

Only one problem remained: the actual transfer of the prisoner. At two o'clock in the morning of April 21, the French General Exelmans and Colonel Rosetti, Murat's aide-de-camp, rode to Villaviciosa with the requisite papers. Even so, Castelar was extremely loathe to release Godoy and for a moment thought of armed resistance; only the signatures of Fernando and Cevallos convinced him of the order's authenticity. Later, Murat, on the basis of an eyewitness report, asserted that Godoy was found in prison "without a shirt, without clothes, barefoot, without having washed, with his beard grown and filthy, and his wounds still open."[10] The two officers explained their mission to the Prince of the Peace. He donned slippers and military capote, then in complete silence accompanied the soldiers across a plowed field to a waiting carriage. It was early morning now as they rumbled toward the French camp at Chamartín. Rosetti later wrote that "such was the Prince's terror of being recognized that he sat hunched up at the back of the carriage, and we had difficulty in persuading him that he had nothing to fear and in getting him back to his seat. And this was the man who had, as caprice and pleasure directed, governed Spain and the Indies for twelve years."[11] Six years later, Napoleon, spared the wounds and spittle that Godoy had endured from the mob, was no more courageous as he traveled in a closed carriage to his first exile.

For the *reyes,* Manuel's deliverance was more welcome than had it been their own. Carlos told Murat that the news "gave him back life, for he would beyond question have died, had he been condemned to continue for any time separated from his dear Manuel."[12] Overjoyed, the monarch dashed off a letter to the favorite which in his haste he forgot to seal. Murat declined to see Godoy in person, but nevertheless took care that the royal message was delivered. Carlos's effusive letter read: "Incomparable friend Manuel. How much we have suffered these last few days, seeing you sacrificed by these godless men just because you are our only friend! We have never ceased to importune the Grand Duke and the Emperor, the ones who extricated you and us. Tomorrow we set out to meet the Emperor, and there we shall conclude everything as best we can for you in the hope that he will let us live together until death. We will always be your constant friends, and we will sacrifice ourselves on your behalf, just as you have sacrificed yourself for us. Carlos."[13]

Not all were delighted at the news of Godoy's release. Even as he was being rushed to Bayonne under a heavy French guard, the Infante Antonio vented his spleen in a hateful letter to Fernando:

> The vermin [his ungallant designation of his sister-in-law, María Luisa] is corresponding to her heart's content with the Grand Duke of Berg and has obtained the release of the *choricero;* but it is your sanctimonious father who insisted with the greatest fervor that he be freed and not have his head chopped off . . . Why wasn't he hanged as I advised you? Luisetta of Etruria claims that it was in your quarters that you gave your word of honor to Murat. Do you think that she has some vices? Those who asked for Godoy's freedom are my brother and the vermin. She was ready to burst into tears, even to go on her knees. So the Frenchman agreed to save the prisoner. The bodyguards, who are real gentlemen, refused to surrender him themselves, which was left to the provincial grenadiers. Get this! I like this bit! The guards would only have handed him over to the hangman. Well, our fellow is now in the hands of [Colonel Manhès], and soon you'll be seeing him in Bayonne.[14]

The style here is indeed the man; any commentary would be superfluous.

Fernando and his entourage were now firmly inside French territory. The reception, to say the least, was discouraging, hardly in keeping with the official pomp accorded visiting royalty. Any lingering optimism was dispelled by the approach of Fernando's younger brother, the Infante Carlos, and three grandees who had preceded the main group to Bayonne. Their report was wintry clear; the previous day Napoleon had declared that the Bourbons were no longer to rule in Spain.

The Hotel Dubrocq, assigned to the Spaniards in Bayonne, was as unprepossessing as their welcome. About an hour after their arrival, the emperor alighted from his horse to pay a courtesy call on his visitors. Fernando, in a demonstrative display, gave the startled emperor an *abrazo* and attempted to plant a kiss on both cheeks; Napoleon's greeting was considerably more restrained. At a second meeting that afternoon at the castle of Marrac, there was an interchange of pleasantries, significant by their very insignificance. It was depressingly clear that Napoleon had no intention of recognizing Fernando as king.

As Escoiquiz was about to take his leave with the others, the emperor bade him remain behind to exchange a few words. Napoleon quickly came to the point; henceforth the Bourbon dynasty was to be replaced by his own. Escoiquiz assures us that he protested vehemently, but with equal energy he denounced Godoy as being single-handedly responsible for Spain's recent misfortunes. Thus, the "only too famous conspiracy of the Escorial" was entirely caused by the "malice of the Prince of the Peace, supported by the Queen's passion for him and the weak credulity of Carlos IV." As for the events at Aranjuez, "the people's revolt, in truth, had no other impulse than a sudden and general increase in the hatred which for so long had been gathering against the Prince of the Peace."[15] By Escoiquiz's own admission, he went too far in his execration of the "despicable, treacherous favorite." Napoleon gently rebuked the canon, saying "You are not giving me a fair picture of the man. He has not conducted himself so badly in his administration."[16] A few minutes later, with a disarming tweak of Escoiquiz's ear, the emperor indicated that the meeting was at an end.

Godoy was now fast approaching the French border. His military escort timed the headlong dash through the open countryside so as to traverse the larger cities under cover of darkness. Burgos was reached two hours after midnight, but the detachment pressed on for fear that Godoy might be recognized. His arrival in Bayonne was preceded by heartfelt letters of gratitude from the *reyes* to Napoleon. "We do not know," María Luisa wrote, "where to begin to show Your Imperial and Royal Highness our thanks . . . Your letter has brought us such an abundance of happiness that words fail me to express it. I shall always be your friend." To which Carlos added: "The news of which Your Imperial Highness apprises me in your amiable letter, that within two hours you will have the Prince of the Peace within your power, has filled both of us with joy."[17] Immediately thereafter, the aging monarchs set out on the same journey northward.

On April 26 Godoy crossed the Bidassoa. It was the last time he set eyes on Spain. In a letter to Talleyrand, the emperor voiced his indignation at the harsh treatment meted out to one who, until very recently, had been the most powerful man in Spain:

The Prince of the Peace arrives this evening. This unfortunate man arouses pity. For a whole month he lingered between life and death, always threatened with perishing. What would you say to the fact that during this period he has no change of shirt and has a seven-inch beard? There the Spanish nation has shown an unheard-of inhumanity. They impute to him the most ridiculous things. They say five hundred million francs were found on him. Just yesterday the ringleaders were saying: what has he done with his money? All we found was the regular expenses of a large household! Have some articles written, not to justify the Prince of the Peace, but which depict in strokes of fire the misfortune of the popular events and which inspire pity for this unfortunate man.[18]

For once, Napoleon manipulated the press to another's advantage.

Godoy was lodged by Savary in a small house on the main road between Bayonne and Biarritz. True to form, Cevallos and the others in Fernando's entourage completely shunned the erstwhile favorite. The following day, on April 27, Napoleon and Godoy met face to face for the first time at Marrac. They spoke together for an hour on a variety of subjects. Manuel recounts that he more than held his own in repartee with his formidable disputant. Granted the *privado* was a man of spirit and blessed with great resilience, but after his injuries, confinement, and breakneck journey—not to mention his rudimentary French—it is doubtful that he could have addressed the self-assured emperor on an equal footing.

For better or worse, the *Memorias* contain the only detailed record of the encounter. Napoleon was indignant when he saw the open scar on Godoy's forehead: "This is cruel and an outrage, even more to the sovereign you served than to yourself!" he began. "At last you are free and can see that I was not your enemy."[19] In an affable tone, the emperor chided his interlocutor for having mistrusted French intentions over the years and especially for having rejected the advantageous exchange of the lands north of the Ebro for six Portuguese provinces. "How much glory you would have garnered if you had placed yourself at my side, instead of having wished to declare war on me!" At this, Manuel extolled the fierce national sentiment in the breast of every Spaniard and so admirably embodied by Carlos IV. Napoleon interrupted the favorite's disquisition by saying, "You are mistaken. If I wanted to, one smile from me in favor of the Prince of Asturias would suffice to add these provinces to my Empire, without giving up anything in return."[20] A sobering truth.

And the Prince of the Peace? As a fellow player in the mounting drama, he had excited Napoleon's interest, even sympathy, but now he had outlived his purpose and was therefore to be dispensed with. The emperor concluded the dialogue as quickly as it had begun. Soon afterward, he confided to Talleyrand, "The Prince of the Peace has the look of a bull with something of Daru thrown in [Count Pierre Antoine Daru, the intendant-general of the army]. He is beginning to recover. They have treated him with unprecedented barbarity. It is good that he should be free of all false imputation, but it is just as well to leave him shrouded in a slight veil of contempt."[21] Godoy was to be raised up—but not too high.

Finally, at two on the afternoon of April 30, Carlos and María Luisa drove up in their ornate coach pulled, as usual, by a a team of imported French mules. Godoy's daughter, Carlota, rode with them, while following behind was an extensive caravan laden with trunks, household goods, and all manner of timepieces. The gout-ridden king suffered from a legion of infirmities that had made the long journey an extended agony; only the thought of being reunited with Manuel enabled him to bear the pain with fortitude. In sharp contrast to the indifferent reception accorded Fernando, the *reyes* were received in Bayonne with a guard of honor, a salute of sixty cannon, and the pealing of church bells. All in all, it was a welcome fit for a king and queen—reigning monarchs at that.

For the two elder infantes, already browbeaten by Napoleon, the reunion with their parents was especially painful. With some effort, the king bade his second son, Don Carlos, a perfunctory "Good day," but the sight of Fernando advancing was too much. The king refused to speak to him and waved him off, though María Luisa went through the motions of greeting both sons. All the royal affection was reserved for Manuel, whom the king and queen alike pressed to their bosoms amid tears of heartfelt thankfulness.

The entire assemblage of Spanish courtiers, including Escoiquiz and the Duke of Infantado, went through the empty formality of kneeling and kissing the hands of the king and queen. Afterward when Fernando attempted to follow the royal couple to their apartments, Carlos turned and cried out in anger, "Have you not outraged my white hairs enough?"[22] Fernando stood as if thunderstruck.

Then, at five o'clock, the emperor arrived. Napoleon immediately addressed Carlos as "Your Majesty," even as he assured the senescent king that the best years of his reign still lay ahead of him. Carlos wearily confessed that the time had come to lay down "the crown truly that of thorns borne so many years,"[23] and signified his intention to abdicate in favor of his eldest son, notwithstanding their mutual antipathy. The emperor pointed out that Fernando was immature and inexperienced, lacking in the right qualities, all of which could produce civil strife that in turn would require French intervention. This could easily be prevented if "Your Majesty, on your full and absolute authority, were to call your son and require him to terminate his government and to renounce his guilty pretentions by returning his crown to you through a written act signed by his own hand."[24] Carlos was readily persuaded to accede to Napoleon's suggestion.

Godoy emphasizes that he was not present during the above meeting, nor did he witness the violent altercation with Fernando that followed. "It is well known what my conduct was at Bayonne in that sad and strange situation in which father and son found themselves."[25] Napoleon, a practiced hand at the verbal assault, was nevertheless taken aback by the insults and crude threats that issued from the *reyes*. On May 1 he wrote to Talleyrand: "I saw the King and Queen receive their son very badly; they would have been at blows for several hours and all have died if the King had not accepted the abdication ... King Carlos is a good man. I don't know if it is rank or due to circumstances, but he has the look of an honest and kind patriarch. The Queen wears her heart and her past on her face, which says quite enough. It surpasses anything one may imagine."[26] The deplorable family quarrel merely confirmed the wisdom of an earlier decision; Napoleon had already ordered Murat to send the Infante Antonio and the remaining royal children to France.

The following day, the emperor invited Carlos and María Luisa to dinner at the Marrac palace. Manuel noted that his sovereigns, accustomed to being slighted in their own land, proved only too susceptible to Napoleon's solicitude. At one point, Carlos had trouble mounting the staircase unaided and turned to the emperor for support. "I don't have any strength, that's why they wanted to get rid of me," he confessed. To which Napoleon gallantly responded, "We'll see. Just lean on me, I have enough strength for the two of us." "That I can well believe, I'm basing all my hopes on that," a grateful Carlos replied.[27]

That Godoy originally was not invited to the banquet seems clear enough. The king is said to have looked around the table for his friend and finally asked Napoleon, "And Manuel, where's Manuel?" Godoy heatedly denies this unregal episode and states that it was the emperor who sent for him without any prompting. In any case, Carlos attacked the sumptuous meal with gusto. "Luisa," he said, pointing to a succulent dish, "take some of this, it's particularly good." Napoleon, the perfect host, beamed with approval. Without a trace of embarrassment, Carlos described his former life for the emperor: "Every day, whatever the weather, winter or summer, I used to leave after breakfast, and after having heard Mass I went off hunting until nightfall. In the evening Manuel took care to tell me whether things were going well or badly. Then I went to bed, to start all over again the next morning unless some important ceremony forced me to remain."[28]

Napoleon, who supervised every detail of government even when on his most distant campaigns, must have listened incredulously to this singular admission.

For Godoy, the days in Bayonne passed pleasantly enough. No longer at the center of power, he was now more the observer than active participant. Thanks to Murat's mediation, he had been joined not only by Carlota but by Pepita and their two sons. Before long, the entire ménage had moved in with the *reyes*. The exact part played by the Prince of the Peace during the days that followed is uncertain. By his own testimony, he avoided the company of the other Spaniards, mostly his enemies, nor was he further consulted by Napoleon. For the first time in sixteen years, he was reduced to a subordinate role, more the king's comforter than counselor.

Carlos's need for solace is no more evident than in the interchange of letters between father and son that followed. Fernando, with some justice, was puzzled by his father's insistence that he give up the crown, for in the same breath the king declared his reluctance to reign over or even to live in Spain. Reasonably enough, Fernando, at Escoiquiz's direction, penned a suggestion that all return to Madrid. There, before a specially convened Cortes, the prince would renounce his immediate claim to the throne or, should his father so wish, govern in his name as viceroy. The sole proviso was that "Your Majesty will not take with you persons who quite justly have incurred the hatred of the nation."[29]

Within minutes, Napoleon's police had intercepted Fernando's letter. The emperor, not endowed with endless patience, by now had had enough. In all probability, he dictated the content of Carlos's intransigent reply, the tone of which was set by the coldness of the opening sentence: "My son: The perfidious advice of the men surrounding you has led Spain into a critical situation; only the Emperor can save her." Incredibly, Carlos was forcing his son to renounce his rights to the succession so that the Spanish crown might be handed to Napoleon! But, first of all, Fernando was subjected to an avalanche of reproaches concerning his participation in recent events: "And what has your conduct been under these circumstances? That of having brought disorder into my palace and having roused the bodyguards to mutiny against me. Your father was your prisoner; my First Minister whom I elevated and adopted into my family, was taken covered with blood from one prison to another. You have tarnished my grey hairs and deprived them of a Crown covered with glory by my parents and which I preserved without blemish."[30] The remainder of the letter was a model of clarity: Carlos was king by divine right, the abdication had been wrung from him by force and was therefore invalid, so any further discussion was at an end.

Quite unexpectedly, Fernando stood his ground. But Napoleon's unremitting pressure soon began to tell. Fernando, mindful of the fate that had befallen the duc d'Enghien, began to waver in his resolution. As for Carlos, he was prepared to sign practically any document placed before him. On May 4 he consented to a decree making Murat Lieutenant-General of Spain, in effect president of the junta in place of the Infante Antonio, his own brother. His signature was immaterial; by then the damage had already been done.

Napoleon had in fact previously issued orders that Don Antonio, Luisetta, the ex-queen of Etruria, and her young brother, the Infante Francisco de Paula, were to be brought to Bayonne. At half past eight on the morning of May 2, two carriages drew up outside the royal palace in Madrid to conduct the remaining members of the royal family to France. Reports of Fernando's humiliation in Bayonne had seeped back to the Spanish capital, where the mood was one of barely contained hatred toward the oppressor. And now the *gabachos*—yet another derisive term for the French—were about to snatch away the last of the ruling house, including the fourteen-year-old Francisco de Paula. Luisetta's carriage had already driven off, but, when the crowd saw the young prince emerge from the palace with tears in his eyes, they were determined to prevent his leave-taking.

The rousing events of the *Dos de Mayo* have been recounted many times; the fury of the *madrileños,* the attack on the French soldiers, Murat's vicious reprisals—the story is well known to anyone who has marveled at Goya's two magnificent canvases commemorating the heroic sacrifices of the populace. One detail is usually overlooked. It is generally agreed that it was the appearance of Francisco de Paula, pale and overcome by emotion, that touched off the spontaneous uprising. Yet this is precisely the prince who supposedly was Godoy's son. In other words, the citizenry gave their lives to rescue the bastard son of the *choricero,* or so we are asked to believe. Izquierdo Hernández answers his own question: "For Godoy's son? What better proof is there that the child was not the son conceived in adultery? Would the people have behaved the way they did if they had perceived the 'indecent similarity' in the Infante about which we have spoken?"[31] Assuredly not.

No sooner had Murat brought the rioters under control than a courier was dispatched to the emperor. The 330 miles from Madrid to Bayonne were covered in a little over two days, the messenger stopping only to change horses. Napoleon was out riding with Savary in the afternoon of May 5 when he received Murat's news. It was all he needed. Seething with contrived fury, he rode immediately to Carlos's lodging and thrust the report into the hands of the startled monarch. The king read a paragraph or two, turned to Godoy and said, "Manuel, have Fernando and Carlos brought here."[32] The end could be delayed no longer.

Godoy has left a lively account of Napoleon's anger. Why, the emperor fulminated to Carlos, hadn't Fernando yet replied to the king's letter or, better still, renounced his claim to the throne once and for all? The rebellion in Madrid was all Fernando's fault, therefore he must be made to answer for it. "We've got to put an end to these crimes this very day!" he shouted. "Have your son called. No more putting things off! No more delay!" Having sent for the two princes, Godoy judged the moment expedient to retire to his room upstairs and therefore did not witness the "lamentable scenes which followed, nor was I summoned to them."[33] Nor was Savary present when Fernando arrived. This has not prevented his claiming that he and Godoy took turns to listen at the keyhole, a charge Manuel indignantly denies.

None of the participants in the encounter that followed—Napoleon, Carlos, María Luisa, and Fernando—has left a firsthand account of what transpired. A dramatic reenactment of the scene by that consummate actor, the French emperor, has been recorded by the Abbé de Pradt, a close friend of Escoiquiz. Upon returning to Marrac, Napoleon summoned those present. According to the Talma *manqué,* "Carlos accused his son of conspiring against him, of outraging his white hair . . . he was like the King of Priam. The scene was becoming more and more impressive when the Queen burst in and interrupted it with a wealth of threats and invective. After reproaching her son for having dethroned his parents she asked me—yes, me—to send him to the scaffold. What a woman! What a mother! She horrified me. I felt sorry for the Prince at that moment." The emperor added: "There is only one man with any imagination in that lot, the Prince of the Peace. He wanted the monarchs to go to South America. That would have been splendid, and no doubt he would have brought it off if the Aranjuez uprising had not occurred."[34] Splendid indeed; but for whom?

Napoleon accused Fernando openly of having fomented the Madrid uprising—a highly doubtful thesis—and on this flimsy basis declared that only the father came into question as king of Spain. Whereupon Carlos shouted at his terrified son, "The blood of my subjects has been shed and the blood of the soldiers of my great friend Napoleon! You are in part responsible for this slaughter!" Once more the queen ranted on about the death penalty, only to be interrupted by the emperor's ultimatum to the two princes: "If between now and midnight you have not recognized your father as your lawful King, and do not so inform Madrid, you will be treated as rebels."[35] Fernando stammered a few incomprehensible words, enough to make Napoleon deliver the coup de grace: *"Prince, il faut opter entre la cession ou la mort"* ("Prince, you must choose between abdication or death").[36] Whatever his past difficulties with the French language, Fernando had no trouble understanding the emperor's purport. With a nod he signified his assent.

One final act now remained. Interlarding his badinage with compliments in Italian, a language common to the Spanish monarchs and the French emperor, Napoleon easily convinced Carlos that it was in everyone's best interests that a prince from the Bonaparte dynasty reign in Madrid. No sooner had the emperor taken his leave than the *reyes* summoned Manuel. Gradually, they realized what they had done. The king's face was flushed, his eyes bloodshot, and the queen was sobbing as she declared, "The king has renounced the crown to Bonaparte!" Godoy was flabbergasted but, before he could protest, Carlos interrupted with a passionate outburst of self-justification. "No, I haven't given anything away . . . I was no longer King . . . My crown! My crown! They took it away from me in Aranjuez!" Manuel attempted to console the distraught monarch, asking whether or not Napoleon had gone back on his word to restore him as king. Carlos admitted he had not, but added, "He wants me to enter my realm through fire and blood. You know me well . . . Never! I will never have blood spilled for my cause! I will never be the executioner of my people! I will never reign through the help of foreign troops!"[37]

At this point, Godoy offended the irascible monarch by having the temerity to ask whether he or Napoleon had suggested the idea of abdication. According to Carlos, the emperor had told him in uncompromising language that neither Fernando nor his uncle Antonio was fit to rule in Spain, and therefore, "If Your Majesty does not wish or dare not take part in this enterprise, I will grant you asylum in my realm and Your Majesty will renounce yours in my favor."[38] Dire threats followed; even as the old king recounted his ordeal to Manuel, tears rolled down his cheeks. Godoy— and the reader is entirely dependent on his account—still was unwilling to surrender abjectly to the Corsican bully. "But, after all," he pointed out, "a conversation is not a treaty, and maybe there still is a way out." But Carlos was a defeated man. "I have given my word, and the Emperor is not a man who releases his prey." At this, María Luisa turned to Manuel and said, "That is true. What a predicament! What a horrible outcome! What will they say about us in Spain?"[39] Spain, the proudest of nations, had submitted at the nod of a tired head. A correction: her rulers had surrendered, but not her people. Napoleon never grasped the essential difference.

Godoy still had one minor service to perform before passing into oblivion. Marshal Duroc was announced; he entered bearing a document of abdication already drawn up that merely required an official Spanish signature to attest to the fait accompli. Carlos insisted on two conditions only: one, that the prince, whom the emperor was to name king of Spain, would respect the country's territorial integrity, and, secondly, that only the Catholic religion would be tolerated. Even at such a sorrowful moment Manuel was not forgotten. The final paragraph stated expressly that "any actions taken against our faithful subjects since the Aranjuez revolution are null and void, and their property is to be restored to them."[40] With a heavy heart, Manuel signed his name on behalf of the king and left the world's stage to others.

Only some minor tidying up now remained. Fernando was readily prevailed upon to give his assent to the renunciation. His ministers, almost to a man, threw in their lot with Napoleon and served his brother Joseph Bonaparte, derided as *el rey intruso* upon his assumption of the crown of Spain. Talleyrand had been notified to prepare his castle at Valençay to receive Fernando, his brother Carlos, and their uncle Antonio, where that worthless trio spent the next six years in comfortable exile while Spain bled in their name. The *reyes* were assigned the Château de Compiègne, well known for the excellence of its game preserve. For Napoleon, Godoy had served his purpose. The emperor's instructions concerning his future were insulting in their matter-of-factness: "As far as the Prince of the Peace is concerned, he can live in Paris or wherever he likes, because he is harmless enough."[41] There was never any question where Manuel would go. Along with Pepita, their children, her family, and his daughter, Carlota, he willingly accompanied the venerable monarchs on their journey into exile.

In his memoirs, Godoy valiantly tries to absolve Carlos of all blame. Even the great Napoleon abdicated twice, he reminds his readers, and yet has not suffered the obloquy of history that has forever stained the reputation of the Spanish monarch. A good debating point, but sadly irrelevant. Napoleon remained in stature an emperor to the very end. Yet, ironically, he was the ultimate loser at Bayonne as he indirectly admitted later: "Bayonne was not a snare but a tremendous, brilliant *coup d'état*. A little bit of hypocrisy would have saved me, or if only I had agreed to abandon the Prince of the Peace to the fury of the people. But the idea struck me as terrible and would have appeared to have been obtained at the price of blood."[42] His argument fails to convince. By throwing Godoy to the wolves, he would have gained a short-lived popularity, only to incur the same pack's rancor the moment he entrapped Fernando. As for Carlos, it was his tragedy that he was better suited to the congenial role of country squire than to the demands of kingship. Few monarchs—Shakespeare to the contrary—have exchanged their kingdom for a horse, much less for a hunting gun. Carlos was one of them.

16

EXILE

A few more demeaning documents to sign, an annual subsidy for the deposed *reyes,* some travel arrangements to be made, and the Bayonne debacle was over, at least for the Spanish Bourbons. On May 9, 1808, the ex-monarchs, accompanied by Manuel, his extended family, and a numerous retinue, set out from Bayonne on their long exile. No farewells were wasted on Fernando and his brother; the parents and sons never saw one another again.

The trip was made in easy stages; Fontainebleau was reached on May 25, and their destination, the ancient Château de Compiègne to the northeast of Paris, in mid-June. Carlos and María Luisa found that only one of the palace wings had been placed at their disposal, as the main royal apartments were inadequately furnished for such distinguished guests. "The King will thus get used to the quarters provisionally assigned to him," Napoleon reasoned, "and I shall not be deprived of the château and park in the hunting season."[1] The poor accommodations were the first of many disappointments. To those attuned to the dry climate of the Castillian plateau, the weather of northern France was depressingly damp and inimical to rheumatism. Worse still, the hunting in the surrounding forests fell below expectations. And already the emperor had fallen into arrears with the promised monthly payments.

This augured ill, for the expenses of the royal exiles were considerable. They were reluctant to curtail their opulent life-style—when en route two liveried footmen stood stiffly at attention at the back of the lumbering carriage whatever the weather—but in addition the host of courtiers, servants, and other attendants far exceeded earlier calculations. Besides the Infante Francisco de Paula, there was also Carlota, who, in view of her title of Marquesa de Boadilla del Monte, obviously needed her own lady-in-waiting. Then there were Pepita and the two young boys, Manuel *hijo* and Luis. Thanks to Murat, Pepita's two unmarried sisters, Magdalena and Socorro, as well as their mother, had also escaped from Spain, as had Manuel's brother Diego, all of whom joined the royal party.

One member was unexpectedly absent. Luisetta had tried in vain to reach a separate accord with Napoleon. Her hope was to be restored as queen of Parma; instead, because of her intransigence, she was placed under the scrutiny of Fouché's agents in Nice. Twice she attempted to escape to England, thereby incurring the further wrath of the emperor, who finally packed her and her daughter off to a nunnery in Rome. Her young son, Carlos Luis, was taken from her and added to the already numerous family surrounding Carlos and María Luisa.

With the onset of autumn, the royal thoughts turned to a warmer clime. Napoleon raised no objection to the transfer. On September 20 the itinerant court of some two hundred persons set out towards the Mediterranean. Aix-en-Provence was briefly considered, but Manuel found the price of suitable property beyond the group's means; the widespread rumor that the *trinidad* had made off with a vast fortune was as baseless as the others. Seemingly affluent, in actual fact the royal refugees were forced to practice an unwonted frugality. The caravan reached Marseilles on October 18 and settled into a large house near the center of the city. For the next four years, it was to be their home.

General Antoine Thibaudeau, the prefect of Marseilles, had frequent occasion to observe his guests. He found that "the King was a tall and handsome old man, paralyzed with gout; a good, honest man, he was simple, unaware of things, and resigned to his fate. The Queen was small and ugly; she had a lot of black, curly hair, and was bedecked with many jewels, chains, and feathers. Her skin was coarse, but she showed off her beautiful arms with pleasure, though she hid her fat legs. She was not lacking in talent and dignity. As for the Prince of the Peace, he was a man of average height, strongly built, and broadshouldered. He did not leave a very distinguished impression. His small eyes had a certain sharp aspect."[2] One day the king, accompanied as usual by the queen and Manuel, with his habitual frankness asked Thibaudeau's wife, "Madame, how many children have you had?" "Three, sire," she replied. "What's that?" Carlos said, taken aback, "Why, my Luisa has given me twelve. She is a good mother and a good wife. She has never caused me the slightest trouble."[3]

Beginning November 1, 1809, Napoleon further reduced the subsidy from 500,000 francs a month to less than half that amount on the specious grounds that "until order has been reestablished in Spain and payments from there are forthcoming, my finances do not permit me to pay more than 200,000 francs a month."[4] But for some contributions sent by the ever-faithful Izquierdo and, quite unexpectedly, by Manuel's brother-in-law, the Marquis of Branciforte, the émigrés would have found themselves obliged to further restrict their style of living. Even so, their plight required surreptitious visits to the pawnshop to sell off some family jewels and silver plate.

In Napoleonic France, the disposal of such valuables did not go unnoticed. The fact is that a large number of the Spanish crown jewels had simply disappeared without a trace. Napoleon had ordered Joseph Fouché, his efficient minister of police, to investigate the mystery. Godoy's reputation was such that it was widely assumed that he had somehow spirited the jewels, and especially a priceless pearl known as *la perilla,* out of the country. Yet, many questions remained unanswered. The *privado,* of course, was the ideal villain, but given the suddenness of the Aranjuez uprising and his close supervision in prison, he appeared to lack the opportunity. Then what of the *reyes,* especially María Luisa? Here was a woman who had the time, the means, not to mention the depraved character, to purloin the nation's heritage. At Compiègne, Fouché had kept the *trinidad* under constant surveillance, only to draw a blank. Perhaps he might be more fortunate in Marseilles. Accordingly, he instructed Thibaudeau to make further inquiries and, if possible, to closet himself with the king at a suitable moment.

Wagging tongues had gone so far as to place an approximate value on the missing gold and diamonds at between thirty and forty million francs. For Thibaudeau, the trick was to separate the king from his constant companions and then discover what he knew about their activities. Only the first part went according to plan. As bad luck would have it, María Luisa and Godoy appeared just as the questioning began. Thibaudeau had shown the king a letter from Fouché suggesting that any valuables be placed with the proper authorities for safekeeping. "Ah," exclaimed the queen, "the Duke of Otranto [Fouché] is one of our friends." "He is afraid," Carlos interjected, "that thieves could rob us of our diamonds." "Our diamonds! My goodness, but we don't have any! You, *monsieur le préfet*, have seen me wearing some jewels. But that is all I possess and is my personal fortune. We did not bring any of the Crown jewels."[5] The queen was speaking no less than the truth; Napoleon might have done better to investigate his own brother-in-law, the Grand Duke of Berg.

If life in exile varied but little, in the outside world momentous changes were afoot. Aided by the English under Wellington, the Spanish guerrilla forces were slowly gaining the initiative, while in Cádiz a patriotic Cortes had drawn up a liberal constitution in 1812. The exiles were largely oblivious to these events. Carlos and Manuel enjoyed distributing alms among the poor of Marseilles during their morning walks, followed by a substantial midday meal, a deserved siesta, and then a late afternoon drive with the queen in one of their venerable carriages. The evenings were devoted to soirees, receptions, and the occasional concert with the king setting the pace as first violinist. All in all, a pleasant but empty life.

In view of Luisetta's presence in Rome and their own childhood memories of Parma and Naples, the monarchs now wished to settle permanently in Italy. Napoleon, preoccupied with the impending invasion of Russia, readily gave his permission. There followed the usual travel preparations, official farewells and private leave-takings, the laborious packing and other vexing details that each move necessitated. Finally, on July 16, 1812, the richly wrought carriages, incongruously drawn by teams of wheezy mules, trundled into the Eternal City. The monarchs and their retinue installed themselves temporarily in the Borghese Palace, one of the most magnificent residences in the city. Four years of exile had already slipped by. The children were growing up, while the adults were growing corpulent. Manuel had become unmistakably middle-aged and stout, less the nimble-minded minister of yore than the ponderous attendant at some minor court, which is indeed what he had become. The colony also received new additions. Two of Godoy's relatives, his sister Antonia, the Marchioness of Branciforte, and his cousin Carmen, now both widows, joined the expatriates in Rome.

Spain, which called forth conflicting memories, was all but forgotten. The news of Wellington's triumph at Vitoria and the final expulsion of the French from the peninsula aroused only passing interest. Fernando would soon return to Spain as *el rey deseado,* but as late as October 1, 1813, all that Carlos could write to his son in Valençay was that "incomparable Manuel is giving lessons to Francisco Antonio and loves you as much as ever,"[6] probably true enough. Rarely did the exiles pause to consider their future position as subjects of King Fernando VII.

One day the sovereigns sought to impress a visiting French dignitary. With some difficulty, Manuel was prevailed upon to dress up in his old finery. As in some midnight revelry at Madame Tussaud's, the ex-*valido* displayed himself successively in his dusted-off uniforms as generalissimo, grand admiral, and councillor of state to the delight of the onlookers. María Luisa was thrilled at this vision of yesteryear. "Walk, Manuel, walk!" she ordered the strutting mannequin, "How handsome he is!" Carlos dutifully echoed his wife's sentiments, and, seizing their cue, the entire court enthused with one voice, "How handsome he is, my goodness, how handsome!"[7]

Exile in Rome consisted of little more than rounds of boring receptions, strolls along the Corso, the monthly visit to Luisetta permitted by the French authorities, and, every so often, an evening concert attended by Manuel, Pepita, and the others. The king, dressed in a frilled shirt and a nankeen wine-colored jacket with matching breeches, white stockings, and shoes with silver buckles, would give his fellow players the signal to begin. Invariably, Carlos was the winner, if such is the correct term. "There you see," he panted to María Luisa and Manuel as he wiped the perspiration from his brow with a red handkerchief, "you heard it yourselves, they can't keep up with me. Oh, if only I had my cellist Dupont here! Now *he* could keep up with me! The Romans can't do it, they're not up to it!"[8] No one dared point out that His Majesty had skipped at least four bars.

If the *reyes* had given up all thought of returning to Spain and occupying positions of power, Manuel still entertained hopes. In 1812 he was barely forty-five years old, an age when most statesmen had the better part of their careers before them. Yet, here he was, an outcast in a foreign city, living in reduced conditions with his mistress and their two children—already a forgotten figure. The essayist Mariano de Larra later was to characterize him as "Don Manuel Godoy, condemned to be a spectator of the fallen Prince of the Peace."[9]

But changes were in the air. Napoleon's empire was visibly crumbling. In January 1814 Pope Pius VII began the first stage of the return journey that was to bring him back to Rome after an enforced absence of nearly five years. Three months later, on March 22, Fernando set foot once more on Spanish soil to the wild acclaim of his subjects. At the urging of Escoiquiz and the Duke of Infantado, he turned against the liberals and, with the enthusiastic support of the church and the nobility, declared himself an absolute monarch. In short order, the Cortes were dissolved, moderates imprisoned or exiled, and the Inquisition reinstated. Godoy's last hopes of returning to Spain were irretrievably dashed. Seemingly, the nation preferred reactionary rule to the reforms of the *privado*. Fernando understood the people; Manuel never had.

The effects of Fernando's restoration were soon felt in Rome. His dislike of Godoy had not diminished with the passage of time; rather, it had grown into an obsessive hatred. As Spanish ambassador to the Holy See he sent Antonio Vargas Laguna. The new envoy, like Manuel, had been born in Badajoz, and owed his political advance entirely to the favorite. He was now to prove himself a worthy representative of his new king: deceitful, cunning, and utterly unscrupulous, determined to destroy the unity of the *trinidad*, with especial attention being paid to Godoy.

To achieve his purpose, Vargas enlisted the help of the increasingly senile Carlos. On October 1, 1814, the old king was prevailed upon to sign an irrevocable act of abdication in favor of Fernando. Closer to home, the ambassador bribed the servants and even induced the personal attendants, including Ramón de San Martín, the majordomo of the royal household, to spy on their masters. Nor was the immediate family immune. Manuel's cousin, Carmen Alvarez de Faria, recently appointed lady-in-waiting to the queen, sent in regular reports on her mistress's activities, while Carlota's governess was paid to inform on Godoy.

The pressures soon began to tell. Despite Manuel's pleas for economy, the king bought timepieces with a profligacy that strained the exiles' budget to the breaking point. Financial exigencies had forced a move to the comfortless Barberini Palace, and now, following Napoleon's abdication, Fernando held all the purse strings. Life soon became unbearable for the inmates: lack of adequate heating, bickering caused as much by unfounded tales as by the cramped quarters, all led to mutual distrust. On Vargas's instructions, all correspondence was intercepted by the Spanish embassy, with the connivance of the local police, and copies forwarded to Madrid.

Little did the queen and the others know that Carlos, now a dyspeptic old man given to maundering outbursts, was in secret communication with his vengeful son. At the direct instigation of Fernando, the Pope reluctantly ordered Manuel and his family to leave Rome for Pesaro, on the Adriatic, in effect a second exile. Fortunately, the separation was brief. During the Hundred Days following Napoleon's escape from Elba, Murat, king of Naples since 1808, inadvisedly marched on Rome in the emperor's name. The *reyes* fled to Verona, where they were joined by Manuel. By chance, Lord Holland happened to be in the same city. With his customary solicitude, he proposed that Godoy reside permanently in England, an offer that

Fernando VII in Royal Robes by Goya, 1814. (Museo del Prado, Madrid)

was gratefully declined. After news of the emperor's defeat at Waterloo, the royal convoy of five coaches bearing the monarchs as well as Pepita and her children returned to Rome. Manuel alone was denied permission to accompany the party and so retraced his steps to Pesaro. Murat, after some reckless ventures, ended his days in front of a firing squad in Calabria before the year was out.

If Vargas fancied he had broken up the *trinidad,* he failed to reckon with the queen's determination. Pope Pius VII, a compassionate man who had himself known the pangs of exile, was so impressed by María Luisa's many qualities, including her generosity towards the poor, that he was moved to declare: "I admire this lady. If she were a sinner, she would be like Mary Magdalene and would save herself. . . . In the rim of her eyes are not the vices which have been imputed to her, but her tears. How many she must have shed which have never been seen or guessed!"[10] For her part, the queen had resolved if need be to appeal to the Pope for Manuel's return. She had quickly seen through Vargas's duplicity, and had even upbraided him in the king's presence, much to the latter's embarrassment.

Now was the time to act decisively. In a letter to Vargas, she implied that he was acting on his own, contrary to the wishes of his sovereign:

> It is not my son Fernando who denies his parents the consolation to have at their side the only man who has been loyal to them. You are the one who is directing the clique [*camarilla*] which they have formed in Madrid, you who owe Manuel everything you ever have been or are now. You never fooled me. When I saw you vent your fury on Aranda, I told Manuel your zeal seemed exaggerated and that you were merely ambitious, and that you would behave the same way towards him, were he to fall from power. The King thought the same, but Manuel defended you. Now you are paying him back, just as expected.

No doubt it was the queen who persuaded her husband to add a note, though the comment regarding Pepita—perhaps an afterthought to lend an aura of respectability—seems to be the king's own: "You must write to my son and see the Pope, and tell them from me that once Tudó and her children are out of the palace I want Manuel to return to our company. I will also ask the Pope to intercede with Fernando, as Manuel has to accompany us. He attends me with respect and affection, he helps me get up and sit down, as you can see I cannot do it except with great difficulty . . . In other words, Vargas, Manuel is essential for the Queen and myself."[11]

On August 27, 1815, one day after arriving back in Rome, both monarchs visited the Pope, who, true to his word, pleaded Godoy's case with His Catholic Majesty, King Fernando VII. Pius's letter placed the newly restored monarch in a dilemma. Resorting to dissimulation, his instinctive reaction when on the defensive, Fernando wrote an ingratiating reply to the pontiff: "Concerning Don Manuel Godoy, he may return to the company of my august parents. Your Holiness knows as I do the reasons for keeping them apart. However, my dear parents desire his companionship, and Your Holiness is interceding to see that this is carried out. Could I possibly deny the wishes of my dear parents and the intercession of Your Holiness? Neither the tender affection which I entertain for them, nor the sincere regard I have for Your Holiness would permit it. I am therefore allowing Godoy to return to the company of my august parents."[12] Manuel came back to Rome on October 7, and four days later expressed his gratitude in person to the Pope at Castel Gandolfo.

Sadly, the matter did not rest there. Carlos, torn between a quarter century's dependence on Manuel and an awakening fondness toward Fernando—further evidence that the old king's memory was slipping—suffered an agony of indecision as he tried to placate both of them. In an incautious moment, he had taken out a loan from an aristocratic Roman banker with little prospect of repayment. Thanks to Vargas's mediation, Fernando agreed to settle his father's debt, which only served to bind the dotard more closely to his calculating son. As for the ambassador, his communications to Fernando often verged on the impertinent, as in his letter of October 15, 1816: "When the *reyes padres* are no longer living and Your Majesty no longer has to pay their allowance, it will be the time to see what justice can be meted out to the favorite." Vargas, posing as a patriot, objected to any direct payment to Godoy, "a request Your Majesty must flatly deny given the deplorable financial state of the nation."[13] When Fernando wrote a conciliatory statement to his mother regarding Manuel, Vargas commented: "His Majesty affirmed that the Queen showed the greatest appreciation for the new assurances you have given with regard to Godoy. One can see in Their Majesties' faces how pleasing Your Majesty's promises were. Their *creature [hechura,* underlined in the original] does not disguise the fact that he is full of confidence."[14] If so, it was entirely misplaced; neither Vargas nor Fernando had the slightest intention of alleviating Godoy's penury.

Financial need was only one of several vexations facing Manuel. His equivocal private life, cheerfully tolerated in France, was less so in the capital of Catholicism. María Luisa long ago had taken Pepita and her progeny to her heart, but Carlos, more straitlaced, had often frowned on the irregular domestic arrangement. For better or worse, Godoy was married to María Teresa and not to Pepita. Divorce was out of the question, indeed nonexistent, but annulment remained a distant possibility. To facilitate such a course of action, Pepita settled in Genoa with the two boys until the case was concluded.

With her customary resolve, the queen made the first approaches to the Pope. At the same time, she tried to enlist the support of Fernando as Manuel's temporal overlord. Fernando evasively countered that such matters lay within the province of the church and not the Crown. To reiterate the point, on June 15, 1817, Vargas wrote a memorandum to Carlos: "Sire: Your Majesty understands that there are certain areas in which sovereigns cannot and ought not to involve themselves . . . As the worthy son of Your Majesty does not have the authority to determine such a matter, how do you expect him to write to the Queen approving the separation of Godoy and his wife, either directly or indirectly?"[15] Carlos readily acceded, and that was the end of it.

Manuel's dislike of his wife in no way lessened his affection for his daughter. Carlota Luisa Manuela de Godoy y de Borbón was now seventeen years old. When she was just three, her father had persuaded King Carlos to create the Duchy of Sueca for her, and, after their exile in 1808, she had been given the title of Marquesa de Boadilla del Monte, a name associated with the Chinchón side of the family. Imperceptibly, the youthful delight she and Francisco de Paula, six years her senior, took in one another had grown into a deeper emotion. Manuel and especially María Luisa favored the betrothal of their respective offspring. That such a union was seriously contemplated should effectively dispel the allegation that Godoy had fathered both children.

Fernando was determined that the marriage never take place. Tales were circulated that Carlota was with child, rumors shown to be baseless when María Luisa presented her to Roman society. Undaunted, Vargas stated flatly that Carlota could never return to Spain with her prospective husband, citing the need to "protect" her from the "fury" of the indignant Spanish populace, which remembered the *privado* so well. From Madrid, Cardinal Bardaxí wrote to María Luisa on November 14, 1816, explaining the hostile popular sentiment: "Here there is endless talk about the return of the Infante Don Francisco and that of Godoy's daughter. Everyone is happy about the first one . . . About the second one they murmur out loud and without restraint."[16] Behind his wife's back, Carlos had advised Fernando to refuse Carlota any part of her father's claim for restitution of properties, to which Vargas added: "Your Majesty need not fear that Carlotita will have nothing to eat if she does not regain those possessions. Her father, if he remembers that he is, can leave her those which he still has."[17] Vargas was hopelessly inconsistent in his reports, at times claiming that Godoy was *sin camisa* (shirtless) and then complaining about the wealth to be left to his "bastard children." At all events, when Fernando withheld his royal consent, the proposed marriage was called off.

Frustrated at every turn, Manuel looked to new horizons. María Luisa had assiduously cultivated the friendship of Prince Kaunitz, the Austrian ambassador to the Vatican, the scion of a distinguished family, and more importantly, the brother-in-law of the Austrian chancellor, Metternich. The queen was anxious to help Manuel carve out a new diplomatic career for himself in Vienna, even if it meant separation from her dearest friend. Kaunitz proved most receptive to her request. Somehow, not a word of the project had reached Vargas's ears. On July 25, 1817, Kaunitz confirmed a diplomatic post in a personal letter to Godoy: "His Majesty the Emperor [Francis II] has given the order that you, Prince, as well as your family, be welcomed to his states whenever you wish to go there. I have full authorization to deliver to you the passports you may require. I take this opportunity to renew the assurance of my highest consideration. Kaunitz. To His Most Serene Highness, the Prince of the Peace."[18]

Isolated in Genoa, Pepita was delighted at the prospect of a settled life in the Austrian capital. On her own initiative, she hurried to Lucca, where she knew that Metternich planned to take the waters. The meeting was a great success. As was his custom with attractive ladies, the chancellor welcomed her cordially and readily confirmed Godoy's appointment. In a letter dated August 29, Pepita informed Manuel that he would have a post as secret advisor to the emperor and be able to wear a magnificent uniform with all his old orders: "Well, then, everything has been taken care of, all that remains is to praise God, because you are now secure, recognized, appreciated, and presented to the public the way you deserve, which is no trifle in itself . . . I am overjoyed and am only worried about Luis' illness. I hope that God will also favor us in this. Farewell. At another time receive an embrace from your trusted friend, Pepa."[19]

Only a few formalities now remained. Metternich immediately agreed to Pepita's request that Don José Martínez, a Spanish official, go in person to Vienna to obtain the necessary passports. It was a fatal mistake. Martínez was a spy in the employ of Vargas and hastened to inform his master of the scheme afoot. Vargas was convinced that Godoy had indeed stolen the Spanish crown jewels, including the famous *perilla;* doubtless the favorite planned to sell them and buy property in Austria with the proceeds. Fernando was more perturbed at the prospect of Godoy being reinstated with his former honors in Vienna, well beyond the reach of Bourbon control. Accordingly, he sent Pedro Cevallos to Rome to investigate Godoy's intentions. Not only had the favorite furthered the careers of Vargas and Cevallos as early as 1793, but both men had later married sisters who were his first cousins. At Bayonne, Cevallos had taken special care to avoid Manuel; now, nine years later, he greeted his relative with an effusive *abrazo.* Once he had ascertained the situation, he journeyed on to Vienna to prepare further mischief.

Manuel's imminent departure threw the queen into alternate fits of depression and euphoria. A hurriedly scribbled note of September 25 shows her delight at an honor bestowed by the Roman guards on Manuel: "You have no idea the pleasure it has given me. Is this the beginning of a regeneration? I would go mad with happiness were everything to come to light and be respected the way it should be. How envious people would be! What pleasure to see everyone burst! And what civility they'd show! And how much bending of the knee! Social life! Crowds! People! And always the same!" A scant two days later, the queen's mood had changed entirely. Once more, Pepita's younger son Luis was showing signs of serious illness: "I cannot rest, nor will I until he is well and can embrace me, until we are all together and never separated until I die."[20] Increasingly, the specter of approaching death pervaded the queen's thoughts. Only Manuel's new lease on life provided grounds for fleeting optimism.

And still no news from Vienna. The little community knew that their mail was being intercepted; Luisetta had once complained to her brother in Spain that his ambassador was hardly more than a spy. With Pepita in Genoa were her mother, her sister Socorro, and the two adolescent boys, Manuel *hijo,* "nearly as tall as I am and the picture of his father," and Luis, of a sweet disposition, intelligent, but always ill. At times their father was remiss in writing, causing Pepita to reproach him that "the boys and I only live and are calm when you give us a token of your affection and we know you are well." Naively, Godoy believed that he had found a way to circumvent the censorship. In an unguarded moment, he wrote to Pepita, "I suppose that Martínez has worked out a way with you to continue the correspondence in safety so that the villains won't enjoy taking away the letters."[21] Little did he suspect that Martínez had gained the confidence of

Pepita's mother, Catalina Catalán, and that Luis's bedridden state gave him and an unprincipled doctor ample opportunity to snoop around in their search for the missing crown jewels.

Cevallos, on his arrival in Vienna, was instructed to inform Metternich that it was the express wish of King Fernando VII that residency be refused to a common criminal like Godoy. Yet, far more damaging to his cause was a mendacious letter to the Austrian emperor drawn up by Vargas but willingly signed by Carlos. No single action attests more clearly to the degree of senility and deviousness to which the aged king had fallen. The letter to Francis II, of which Manuel never learned the contents, reads in part:

My dearest brother and nephew:

Your Majesty is aware of the hatred of the Spanish nation for Godoy, as well as the resolution for my own part, the King my son, and the Cortes of the Kingdom have taken against him. Whatever might have been my excessive kindness towards him, these facts cannot remain hidden from Your Majesty, inasmuch as they are known throughout Europe. If he has come to reside near me, and if no thought has been given to renewing his trial and demanding his presence, this can be attributed to my benevolent mediation and to the boundless love and respect which the King, my son, shows me. Such proofs of kindness should instill in Godoy's heart the sincerest recognition and prevent him from undertaking any action without my careful approval. Nevertheless, he has paid little heed to such considerations and has permitted himself to approach Your Majesty without my knowledge, hiding from me the fact that he has obtained not only Austrian naturalization for himself but also for his concubine and bastard children, titles, positions, and honors which sovereigns are accustomed to reserve in order to reward outstanding merit in their own subjects . . . I would by no means tolerate it for Godoy to continue living in Rome from the moment he acquired naturalization in a foreign country or even the right of asylum in any state of Europe . . . I hope that Your Majesty will willingly agree with what I have outlined so that I can finish my days in peace and on the other hand avoid the consequent unpleasantness with a son whom I love with all the tenderness which is right and proper in the light of the respect and attention with which he treats me.

Carlos.[22]

Cevallos arrived in Vienna on October 13, 1817, and met with Metternich the following day. At a subsequent meeting, the chancellor argued that Godoy's naturalization was in Spain's best interests for he could then be placed under close surveillance. Finally, "as regards honors, there is no discussion as he will not be given any; but as for the rest, there is no need to change the slightest thing already agreed upon. On the contrary, I confirm everything."[23] Cevallos was told that Godoy had expressed a desire to remain in Rome and serve the *reyes,* but as an Austrian citizen; moreover, the original request had come from King Carlos himself in a personal appeal to Francis II, no matter what he stated in his latest letter. Such was Metternich's spirited defense of Manuel that Cevallos became convinced the wily chancellor had acquired the famous *perilla,* no doubt from Godoy.

By December, Pepita knew all about Cevallos's duplicity. On December 5 she wrote to Manuel from Pisa a hasty note "just for your eyes, read it, then destroy it," which obviously he did not do: "Manuel *mío:* I don't know how I haven't gone crazy these last few days what with the terrible particulars of this business, but I think things are falling into place. If only you knew who our enemy was in this affair! You would be horrified to know there was so much wickedness and falsity in this world, and quite rightly you would say we have to flee from the living . . . I believe these are Cevallos' wicked deeds, but I am surprised that Metternich has let himself be deceived . . . Farewell. Once more, silence and courage. Your true love, Pepa."[24]

Godoy had good cause to worry. Harassed by the police, spied on by Vargas and his minions, rebuffed by King Carlos—and still no reassuring word from Vienna. On December 18 he made one last desperate plea to Metternich: "Prince, what are the new transgressions imputed to me? . . . I beg you to examine the matter and take advantage of the most opportune moment to submit it to the decision of His Imperial Majesty. It is my honor and sense of justice which solicit your mediation."[25] As was her wont, María Luisa added her urgent voice to Manuel's in several letters to the chancellor and the emperor. To Francis II she wrote: "Your Imperial Majesty and Apostolic King will consider it no less than an act of duty on my part recommending to you the most unfortunate of persons but also the most worthy of his sovereign's esteem, both on account of his loyalty and his gratitude . . . No doubt Your Majesty will recognize that this is the Prince of the Peace about whom I am speaking."[26]

It was all to no avail. Even though Kaunitz was favorably impressed by Godoy and Metternich once referred to him as "my colleague," it was not enough. The Emperor Francis wrote to Carlos on February 2, 1818, informing him that, since Fernando was opposed to Godoy's plans and was still his sovereign, he had no choice but to accede to the Spanish king's expressed wish. Lamentably, despite his earlier stance, Metternich gave in to Cevallos on every point, assuring him that henceforth Godoy would be regarded as persona non grata. Similar pressure was brought to bear on the ruler of Tuscany. The Spanish ambassador there was instructed to "see and procure that the Grand Duke not allow Don Manuel Godoy into his states or at least not receive him at Court in his presence should he try to do so."[27] In Paris, Count Fernán-Núñez received orders to persuade the restored Bourbon monarchy not to grant Godoy asylum and even to revoke the Legion of Honor bestowed on him by Napoleon. To their credit, the French refused to give in. Similarly, when the Swiss Confederation was requested to bar Manuel and Pepita from settling in Geneva, the federal president, J. Ch. Amrhyn, countered that "the constitutional forms of a federation of republics are hardly compatible with the action of a secret police state."[28]

These were minor consolations. The spying had become so blatant that Pepita occasionally penned letters containing false information, confident that Vargas would act on the intelligence gleaned. With a single-mindedness bordering on obsession, Vargas was prepared to hound Godoy and *la Tudó* throughout Europe if need be to recover the diamonds. Eventually, the ambassador recognized the futility of his methods and, all else having failed, turned to the law. Not satisfied, he pressured Carlos to get rid of Godoy and have Pepita arrested and sent to Spain. The king's reply was characteristically spineless: "*Amigo* Vargas: There is no sacrifice I would not make for Fernando, but though it is certain what you say, it would make me the Queen's executioner . . . As far as *la Tudó* is concerned, Fernando can do what he wishes, but if the order is given for this man to leave, you and Fernando are overlooking something, because the Queen will finish me off with her afflictions."[29] Manuel, now relegated to "this man," was entirely dispensable, but not so the king's peace of mind; hence, he could remain on sufferance.

Life in exile had placed a severe strain on Pepita's usual outgoing nature. Separation from Manuel, the dragged-out Vienna affair, the continued aspersions on the paternity of her children, and Luis's prolonged illness— by early 1818 Pepa was close to a nervous collapse. In desperation, she permitted her valuables to be compared with an official list of the crown jewels. When the package was opened in Vargas's presence, Carlos laughed aloud, for he immediately recognized a gift he had made to Pepita years ago in Spain.

Both monarchs suffered constantly from the afflictions of the elderly.

Carlos was now seventy. Contrary to a lifetime's habit, he ate sparingly and had trouble falling asleep. The queen, three years younger, was weakened by nervous fatigue, which caused her to spend long hours in bed. They still managed to live in a grand style, surrounded by lackeys, grooms, and all manner of servants. Thanks to a regular subsidy from Fernando, the *reyes* had been able to purchase a country home in Albano, a couple of miles from the Pope's summer residence in Castel Gandolfo. There, as in olden times in Aranjuez, the crowds would cheer them whenever they drove past in their carriage. To most of the spectators they appeared as figures from a bygone age.

The years had also caught up with Manuel. Now past the watershed of life, he too lived in a world of memories. Often Pepita would chide him for his silence, and from Genoa she bitterly complained: "For four years now I have led the most miserable life in the world. I have a child at death's door, and all I need is peace, a lot of peace, tranquility."[30] Luis's illness had been diagnosed as advanced consumption with no hope of recovery. Pepita, deeply affected by the little boy's affliction, wrote to Manuel: "My strength is failing me, and I also thought I was going to die. I am old and full of grey hairs; these last few days have added twenty years to me."[31] She was sustained by a flow of letters from María Luisa praying for *Luisito de mi alma* and bemoaning his "three years of suffering without any improvement! Three years of martyrdom!"

And now both of the *reyes* fell seriously ill. Carlos only recovered thanks to an application of Spanish fly (cantharides, five of them) and to massive doses of quinine. The queen, despite some brief improvement, never fully regained her health. Manuel also was confined to a sickbed, the result of severe depression brought about by news of Luis's decline and the daily tensions of the Barberini Palace. To Pepita he confided: "I'm so tired of gossip, I can't wait for the moment to get out of this fire. All that keeps me here is the state of health of Their Majesties and the determination to serve them until the last drop. For this single pleasure of gratitude and friendship I would sacrifice all that I possess of the world's kindness."[32]

By February 1818 it was evident that the end was near for Luis. On the 23rd Pepita wrote to Manuel: "Last night he did not even rest two hours, and of course I was holding him. Poor soul! He now has all your letters with him in bed. He doesn't read them, he kisses them with his dog at his side, motionless. He seems to know the state he is in and that he must not be disturbed. I love him more than anyone else."[33] On March 18, at the age of twelve, Luisito breathed his last, ten years to the day after the *motín* at Aranjuez. Manuel and the queen were heartbroken at the news. Both felt that the death of the young boy presaged their own.

The king's recovery had surprised everyone, none more than the patient himself. So much so, that he decided on his own to visit his younger brother, King Fernando IV of the Two Sicilies, irreverently dubbed *Nasone* (Big Nose) by his subjects. Carlos was glad of the respite from his wife's tears, Vargas's constant scheming, and the increasing day-to-day tensions with Manuel. Moreover, it would be the first time since his youth that he had seen Naples.

Carlos's visit to his brother in the autumn of 1818 was not without a definite purpose. Since 1802 the *reyes'* daughter María Isabel (widely reputed to be Godoy's daughter) had been married to her cousin and heir to the throne, Francisco Genaro, the Duke of Calabria. Carlos now conceived the idea of marrying off his son, Francisco de Paula (also reputedly Manuel's progeny) to Luisa Carlota, the eldest daughter of María Isabel and her husband. Such a consanguineous alliance—that of an uncle to his niece—would require the Pope's sanction and the visit of the Neapolitan relatives to Rome.

Whether Fernando IV in between visits to the theater and Pompeii touched on the supposed relationship between María Luisa and Godoy is no more than conjecture. But it was during the weeks away from Rome that a noticeable change occurred in Carlos's attitude toward his partners in the *trinidad*. In a spiteful moment, he discussed with his brother means of getting rid of Manuel and even of divorcing María Luisa should she stand in the way! When Fernando IV, along with his mistress, the Princess of Partana, and the others descended on Albano on October 24 before proceeding to Rome, Godoy was abed with a bout of malaria and thus was spared any direct confrontation.

The highlight of the visit was the celebration of Carlos's seventieth birthday on November 4. Also in attendance was Luisetta, now the Duchess of Lucca. From Spain, Fernando magnanimously authorized his father to dispense a Grand Cross of Carlos III or two, and, in a display of regal evenhandedness, María Luisa was allowed to bestow the Banda de Damas Nobles on the daughter of the Princess of Partana. Only Manuel failed to make the honors list; instead, Vargas renewed his complaint that the French still had not removed the favorite's name from the recipients of the Legion of Honor. Finally on November 6, the royal visitors returned to Naples. With unseemly alacrity, Carlos seized the opportunity to accompany them. He was never to see María Luisa and Godoy again.

Manuel's full recovery took a further three weeks. The queen, despite her own infirmities, nursed him back to health. She owned to Pepita that "it will be a long convalescence requiring much care. Let us all contribute towards his life. You need never have any doubts as to me. I don't know how it was that I didn't die! I would willingly give my life, I beg God that he won't have to suffer again, a small tribute to his gratitude and friendship!"[34] At the height of his illness, he had been administered the last rites and had written his will, leaving nearly everything he possessed to Carlota. Understandably, Pepita resented the discrimination against Manuel *hijo*, and, though Godoy soon rectified the omission, the damage was done.

Even as Manuel's health improved, the queen's declined. The winter was unusually severe, with freezing temperatures extending as far south as Naples. Already on October 22 (that is, two days before the Neapolitan relatives arrived), the queen complained to Pepita: "It won't stop raining. I live in utter solitude. Now old and crippled, my nerves torture me, and I can see that my days are numbered."[35] During the visit, she was bedridden for days at a time. A week later, she wrote, "Here it is so lonely, so cold, so quiet, so melancholy, that it is like the antechamber of Death. Everyone has a cold, is ill or dead; my mood has become so black that all I wish to know is that people don't exist."[36] Manuel, back on his feet again, informed Pepita on October 31 that "the Queen's health has deteriorated quite a bit, and this concerns me because, as you know, outside this lady and my family nothing has a claim on my regard and friendship."[37]

The end was fast approaching. María Luisa complained of the cold in her bones and often felt depressed. More specifically, she suffered from headaches, blood pouring from her nose, incessant sneezing, and stomach cramps. Her letters to Pepita chronicle the fluctuations of her last illness. On December 1: "Having pains in my legs, but today at least my nerves are better." December 4: "Here one only talks about sudden deaths." Then on December 18: "I am still bedridden. I'm feeling better, but I feel so very old that if you saw me, you would not recognize me."[38] She now had difficulty breathing and falling asleep, complicated by frequent thirst and a fast pulse rate.

Incredibly, despite the alarming symptoms, her personal physician, Dr. Soria, failed to note the gravity of her condition. Not so Manuel, destined to play the family doctor to the very end. By the final days of the year, her state was critical. On December 31 Manuel dashed off a letter to Pepita:

> For more than a month now I have been telling Soria to withdraw some blood with leeches as is the custom, but the scoundrel kept saying that he

could not see anything wrong and so lost a great deal of time. So five days ago Her Majesty fell ill. I took her pulse and found that she was very feverish. I kept haranguing the doctor, but did not get anywhere. Finally, Her Majesty took to her bed the day before yesterday, but despite her coughing and expectoration, *the doctor still saw nothing wrong* [underlined in original] and was satisfied to give her orange water. In such a state, angry at his ignorance or malice, I called in my own doctors . . ."[39]

Two days later, the queen was failing rapidly:

Her Majesty the Queen is in the greatest danger . . . Today she will receive the sacraments. This last proof of friendship was reserved for me. Everyone was afraid of the just reproach of public opinion, and no one could make up his mind to tell her of the need to hurry. Nor did I want the doctors to come as this would mean the death of her. Finally, with a lot of trouble I managed to persuade her, and she confessed at once yesterday. Today she will take Communion, and this completed will rest quietly. I hope that His Majesty the King will come in a couple of days, because in the second letter he was told of the danger.

In a postscript, Manuel added: "I have carried out the duties of friendship. Her Majesty has confessed and made her peace with Our Redeemer."[40]

A few hours later, María Luisa's terrestrial sufferings were over. The *trinidad en la tierra* was no more. Manuel wrote: "My protectress no longer lives. Her Majesty the Queen died at a quarter past ten at night on the second of January. His Majesty the King did not arrive."[41] Present at the bedside were both daughters, several grandchildren, Carlota, and the man who had made it his lifetime duty to serve his queen until the moment of death. Luisetta and María Isabel kissed him and thanked him for his devotion to their mother. Such was his desolation at the queen's passing that he again fell gravely ill. On January 7 he wrote to Pepita:

I have concentrated all my thoughts on the precepts of our holy religion, and I only think of my soul which soon will appear before its Creator. I confess that I have committed many errors in this world; but never for a moment have I neglected my duties toward those who depended on me. With my own eyes I have seen the falsity of these people who, because they thought I would never overcome my illness, have shown me an extraordinary and insulting indifference, if I compare their conduct with the consideration with which they should treat me. I have complained to them in the words of a moribund; but though I know them for what they are, I shall not cease doing good towards them . . .[42]

Among the mourners, grief soon gave way to greed. Had the queen written a will and, if so, to whom had she left everything? Vargas, that prince of priers, could only guess, and was forced to admit lamely to Fernando: "Up to now I don't know if the Queen made out a will before dying; but this is something we will find out when Don Carlos comes and goes through her papers."[43] In fact, it was Vargas himself, through his incessant bullying of the queen in the matter of the diamonds who, quite unwittingly, had helped her reach a decision. According to Godoy—certainly no dispassionate observer—the king was so furious at Vargas's outrageous conduct that both he and the queen determined to make Manuel their sole beneficiary. This line of reasoning would be highly suspect but for the date of the will, signed September 24, 1815. Manuel had been exiled from Rome by Pope Pius VII in 1814 on petition from Fernando, and was only permitted to return on October 7, 1815, that is, *after* the will had been drawn up. What pressures—if any—he brought to bear on the *reyes* from such a distance is unknown. More illuminating is a letter that Carlos wrote to Manuel on the subject: "Before your arrival from Pesaro, the Queen asked me to authorize her to make out a will in your favor, leaving you the few possessions remaining to her as remuneration for your services and as a small indemnification on our part for all you have lost on our account. I gave her permission, the will was drawn up and signed by me, and I hand this document over to you. Keep it, perhaps as the last testimonial of affection we have felt for you and of the appreciation you deserve. Things are happening in such a way, Manuel, that I do not know if the Queen and I can survive these outrages."[44]

Essentially it was a nuncupative will, despite the written form. After a religious prologue and thanks to God, followed by a request for 2,000 Requiem Masses for their souls and a small bequest to the hospital of Sancti-Spiritus, both monarchs recommended themselves to Fernando and their beloved family. The key section read: "These dispositions having been made, we hereby resolve and name as our universal heir to all that might belong to us at the moment of our death, with all rights pertaining, without exception, Don Manuel Godoy, Prince of the Peace, to whom for the satisfaction of our conscience we owe this indemnification for the many and great losses he has suffered obeying our orders."[45] The rest of the family were asked to accept the blessings from heaven which, while most welcome, were less tangible than the benefits given to Manuel. Finally, all were adjured to observe the wishes expressed in the will as "an act of Christian justice."

The queen's death came undoubtedly as a great shock to Carlos, who, on his doctors' orders, nevertheless remained in Naples. Clearly, the terms of the 1815 will were very much on his mind. And so, on January 4 he wrote Vargas a letter disassociating himself from his late wife's action, claiming that "as I was so ill, I was weak enough to sign it; and so I declare that, far from assenting to it, I disapprove of it as being contrary to our laws. Tomorrow I shall write you at greater length, because right now I don't even know where my head is."[46] In fact, Carlos never sent the second letter, but, on the basis of the first, Vargas assured Fernando that the queen's will was invalid. Vargas could have spared himself the trouble; later Manuel voluntarily renounced his rightful claim rather than submit to endless litigation. To no one's surprise, a vicious family quarrel ensued. In the end, Fernando received the lion's share and Manuel was left penniless.

María Luisa's funeral, even in her husband's absence, was on a magnificent scale with twenty-one cardinals in attendance. Pope Pius VII insisted on a service befitting a queen, and to that end paid a share of the expenses from his own treasury. Carlos, who was beginning to enjoy the relaxed life at his brother's court in Naples, saw no further need to maintain the Barberini Palace, in Rome. Accordingly, he wrote to Godoy on January 7:

Friend Manuel. You cannot imagine how much I have felt the terrible blow of the loss of my beloved wife after fifty years of happy marriage. I have been quite overwhelmed; but, thanks to God, I feel much better now. I have no doubt that you tended her during her illness with all possible attention, but now that the Queen is no more it is not seemly for Carlota to live in my residence. I am granting her a thousand duros a month, so take her to live with you and kindly do it before I come to Rome. This in no way prevents you from coming to see me as often as you wish. I remain, as always, the same. Carlos.[47]

The same? Surely not; ever since Bayonne, the king had evinced a senescent peevishness in his dealings with others, a petty distrust toward his own flesh and blood, and a marked ambivalence as far as Manuel was concerned.

And now Carlos himself lay dying. He had taken care to make a new will, one excluding that same Manuel who had served him so faithfully for close on thirty years and who later would tenaciously defend his ungrateful monarch in his memoirs. On January 14 the king was laid low by an attack of fever and took to his bed for the last time. Servants were immediately sent to inform his brother, who, true to family tradition, was out hunting.

With impeccable logic, he observed, "Either my brother will die, or he will get well. If he dies, what can it matter to him whether I give up my hunting or not? If he gets well, he who is so good a sportsman himself will be delighted to see me return with a good bag to cheer his convalescence."[48] King Carlos IV was granted his quietus at 1:20 in the morning of January 19, just seventeen days after his wife. He had died in the city of his birth, home at last.

Now that both monarchs were no more, Vargas could search the royal apartments to his heart's content. He failed to discover any of the crown jewels for the simplest of reasons: they had never been in Godoy's or the *reyes'* possession at any time. On receiving news of the death of his parents, Fernando ordered their remains to be brought to Spain for burial in the mausoleum below the Escorial. By royal decree, the queen was declared to have died intestate. That being the case, her personal jewelry and other belongings were to accompany their late mistress. All that was left to Manuel were memories. Those were beyond Fernando's power to take away.

17

THE LONG LAST

YEARS

*F*or the first time, Manuel was truly independent, free to lead his own life. Yet, freedom brought challenges he had never been called upon to face before. He held no position, his financial resources were pitiable, but his responsibilities to kith and kin were greater than ever. His only alternative was to move in with the families of Pepita's two sisters, Socorro and Magdalena. Both were married and had numerous children. Years ago, when Socorro had become the Countess of Stefanoni, Manuel had generously presented her with the small Villa Campitelli. Now, almost penniless, he installed himself with Carlota in two small rooms by the main entrance, each cluttered up with furniture, and bitterly cold. His plight moved Socorro to write to Pepita, "I am very sorry to see what people are, because the first to despise him are his own relatives who owe everything to him, and then all the others. Suffice it to tell you that of all the family that went to Naples, not one has come to see him. We are very much concerned about the arrangement in the house, but what can we do, we the only ones left to him? We are still waiting to see what happens to the report made in Spain, and if he wants to remain in this house which is his, we shall pick up our moveables and go wherever God intends us to."[1]

Others were less understanding. Luisetta, the Duchess of Lucca, saw that Manuel could now safely be discarded, whatever the deathbed wishes of her mother. The future clearly lay with Fernando. Two days after the queen's death, Luisetta wrote to her brother: "The day before she died she called me to her bedside and said to me: 'I am going to die. I commend Manuel to you; you may rest assured, you and your brother Fernando, that you could not find a person more affectionate.' I kissed her hand and told her that I loved her with all my soul. This was the last time I was able to speak to her . . . Poor little one, she will never be forgotten in my heart. My brother, for my guidance, what am I to do if Manuel asks to come to Lucca, as he has already indicated he would like to?"[2]

For his part, Fernando had no qualms whatsoever in regard to the former *privado*. Through Vargas, he bluntly informed Manuel and Pepita that any discussion concerning a pension was now terminated; furthermore, neither of them was ever to return to Spain. The fifty-one year-old Manuel was emotionally drained by the rebuffs from all sides. Sixteen persons were now living in the Villa Campitelli, including a contingent of shrieking infants who, in all innocence, sorely tried his frayed nerves. During the day, he rested his exhausted body as well as he might, only emerging toward evening to take a brief walk with Carlota.

Over the years, Manuel's relationship with his daughter had undergone many vicissitudes. When her plans to marry Francisco de Paula fell through, Carlota had set her sights on the son of Prince Chigi, a family of papal lineage. From Spain, Manuel's estranged wife, María Teresa, was opposed to an alliance with a "descendant of the nepotists of Pope Alexander VI" and, more persuasively, refused to provide a dowry. As Manuel was pinched for every penny and King Carlos had voiced his disapproval of the match, Carlota's prospects for matrimony appeared slender indeed. For a time, she was openly hostile to her father—Vargas had convinced her that Godoy wanted to marry her off quickly so that he could leave what little he had to his bastard children—but on the death of Luisito she had wept unashamedly and there had been a family reconciliation. Carlota's fortune improved almost at the same time that Vargas left Rome, surely no coincidence. In 1820 she married Count Camilo Rúspoli, a scion of the old Roman aristocracy. To Manuel's regret, Carlota and her husband left soon afterward to settle in Spain. Quite rightly, he feared that once there she would come under the influence of her mother.

It was a challenging time for Carlota to return to the country of her birth. Fernando's tyrannical reign had resulted in the stifling of all progressive thought at home and in the humiliating loss of the American colonies, including that of Florida, to the United States. On January 1, 1820, Lieutenant Rafael de Riego launched a successful *pronunciamiento* against the obscurantist regime. The jails were emptied of political prisoners, the

Inquisition abolished, and freedom of the press reinstituted—all, it should be noted, aims that Godoy had advocated while in office. On March 20 King Fernando VII was obliged to swear allegiance to the 1812 Cádiz Constitution. To heal past wounds, many of the *afrancesados* and other exiles were pardoned. Perhaps the Prince of the Peace might also be able to return . . .

Tragically, the liberals fell to squabbling among themselves. Manuel, who might have won their favor by castigating Fernando, chose to maintain a dignified silence; he had promised the late king that he would not reprove his son, and he kept his word. But his forbearance was not reciprocated by others. For reasons best known to himself, Lucien Bonaparte, now living near Rome, saw fit to snub his old partner of the War of the Oranges. To Luisetta, Godoy was plainly an embarrassment. Only Lord Holland evinced any kindness by renewing his offer of asylum in England. Manuel was touched by the consideration shown, but had set his heart on returning to his native land. Again, he was doomed to disappointment.

By October 1823 Fernando was riding a broad wave of popular reaction against the liberals. Backed by a French army now welcomed as liberators, he exacted a terrible revenge on his enemies. Had Godoy returned to Spain, he might well have suffered the same fate as Riego: first, dragged through a delirious crowd on a charcoal-burner's cart drawn by a donkey, then executed in public, and finally quartered with each severed part consigned to a separate grave.

The Spanish dream had ended in a nightmare. Manuel, helpless to play any meaningful part, remained in Rome, a pathetic suppliant. The years passed by, each a milestone to oblivion. Napoleon had died in 1821, leaving the legend in other hands. Three years later, Luisetta breathed her last in Lucca. Although Manuel did not suspect it, he was to outlive most of his contemporaries and their children as well.

Occasionally a happier moment relieved the gloom. With the concurrence of Pope Leo XII, on September 7, 1824, Manuel *hijo* was legitimatized, even though Godoy's lawful wife, María Teresa, was still alive in Toledo. This kindly act opened the way for the *valido's* son to marry Miss Mary Crowe, an English girl, on December 10, 1827. Both lived long lives, and their children assured the continuation of the direct family line. And then came the most helpful news of all. María Teresa died on November 24, 1828, thus finally enabling Manuel and Pepita to regularize their union. The wedding took place on February 7, 1829, effectively countering the long-endured charges of bigamy. Manuel was sixty-two, his bride fifty.

At about the same time, Fernando wedded his fourth wife, María Cristina of the Two Sicilies. As the king still remained childless, this marriage was of crucial importance to Spain. Fernando's bride was the daughter of Francisco Genaro and María Isabel, the groom's own sister. The fact that the king had chosen to marry his niece was not as remarkable as the popular supposition that the monarch's mother-in-law, his sister, was Godoy's illegitimate daughter by the late Queen María Luisa. One particular stands out from the rest: Fernando's hatred of Manuel to the contrary, he simply did not credit the defamatory tales in circulation, otherwise he most certainly would never have taken as his bride one who, in effect, would have been the favorite's granddaughter. For reasons best known to himself, on May 14, 1825, Fernando generously ordered that "ten thousand *ducados* be paid annually to the aforementioned Marquesa de Boadilla [Carlota] as an allowance from the goods confiscated from D. Manuel Godoy,"[3] and even went out of his way to insist that Manuel's daughter be paid on time.

Godoy's title of Prince of the Peace continued to rankle with Fernando. Manuel's first wife had at least been a princess of the royal blood, but why should the Tudó woman now be raised to the same exalted station as *la Princesa de la Paz*? It was shameful enough that Carlos IV had created her the Countess of Castillofiel, but there were limits. His royal father, in a most unpropitious moment, had also granted Godoy his outrageous title; Fernando, on his own, was powerless to deprive him of it. He could, however, threaten, importune, and bully him into exchanging it for a less offensive one. The services of Pope Pius VIII were discreetly called upon. Manuel, in a vulnerable position, was unable to withstand the combined pressure exerted upon him. To please His Holiness, he reluctantly agreed to give up his proud title for that of Prince of Bassano, a modest estate near Sutri to the north of Rome, which he had bought for 70,000 piastres.

But reactionary Italy offered no viable future to Manuel. A liberal by instinct, he was more attracted to the France of Louis Philippe, the Citizen King. And so in 1832 Manuel and Pepita sold their property and made the long journey to Paris, where they arrived on April 11 amid a cholera epidemic. They rented rooms on the Boulevard Beaumarchais near the spot where the Bastille had once stood. Pepita opened a salon, which at first enjoyed considerable social success, even attracting the Austrian ambassador among its habitués. Within a few months however, mismanagement and lack of means put an end to the ambitious enterprise.

Not even the news of Fernando's death in 1833 helped the two exiles. In Spain, Godoy was all but forgotten, a remote figure whose name cropped up once in a while when older folk reminisced about the Corsican *Malaparte* and his treachery. Carlota, now living in Valencia with her family, wanted nothing further to do with her father. Practically destitute, Manuel appealed to the sense of justice of various ministers in Madrid. To Francisco Zea Bermúdez, the First Secretary of State, he wrote from Paris on September 8, 1833:

> My necessity increases, yet it does not seem right that I should be placed in a situation to have to beg abroad. I am not asking for alms; I am asking for the fulfillment of sacred duties. The will of the Queen Mother, which I enclose, will let Your Excellency see just one part of the innumerable vicissitudes which characterize my misfortune. I refused to claim it at the time, and King Fernando VII was free to dispose of his inheritance . . . After the unfortunate Aranjuez mutiny the people did not rob me of anything. Jewels, documents, money, funds, clothes, furniture, and even the cinnamon and sugar in my larder, the lime for my Buenavista palace, stones, bricks, everything—everything was sold off, and the proceeds went to the royal treasury. I left Spain with the shirt of my King on my back . . . since then I have not received anything![4]

Equally moving is the plea addressed to Francisco Martínez de la Rosa, famous both as a playwright and politician, and who, like Godoy, had also known the pain of exile:

> My need grows, and I have to be importunate as what I claim is just . . . I know the world, I have governed, I have lived among all types, I know men moved by their passions, and I believe that, steeped in history, I am at some advantage in judging them. For a long time Spain has been living in error and blaming me with silence. It is an eloquent silence and for me a great sacrifice as proof of my obedience to my King and friend! The time will come and is not far off when I will prove that in my writings. It is late; but truth and reason never grow old.[5]

Godoy received a courteous reply, no more.

Poverty was not the cruelest blow he was forced to endure. Pepita, whose foolish extravagances were dragging them both further into debt, now deserted the man who had stood by her for more than forty years. She returned to Spain and found lodgings in Madrid. Manuel, still barred from his homeland, could only pour forth a piteous flow of letters imploring the restitution of his titles and fortune. But the politicians in Spain had far weightier matters to consider. On his deathbed, Fernando had vacillated until the last moment as to the validity of the Salic law that excluded female succession. In the resultant confusion, his brother Carlos had asserted his right to the throne. The subsequent Carlist wars may well be regarded as Fernando's baleful legacy to his country. A final irony: had he upheld the 1812 Cádiz Constitution, his daughter Isabel would have succeeded him without question, for one of the articles expressly reaffirmed the right of a queen to rule over Spain.

With the government in Madrid pressed for every peseta, Godoy's claims were given short shrift. Spurned by his wife as well as his relatives and fellow countrymen, he turned for assistance to Louis Philippe. The French king well remembered the dark days of the revolution, when his mother had been unable to find asylum anywhere in Europe. Godoy, then at the height of his power, had allowed the Orléans prince's mother to settle in Barcelona after the other nations had turned their backs on her. Louis Philippe had not forgotten; out of gratitude, he granted Manuel an annual pension of five thousand francs. Not a fortune, to be sure (the Citizen King was of a parsimonious nature), but enough to ensure a genteel poverty.[6]

Manuel now gave his full attention to the project alluded to in his letter to Martínez de la Rosa, namely, the compilation of his memoirs. In all probability, he had done some of the preliminary work during the years in Rome. The purpose was twofold: to vindicate himself before the public, and to provide some additional income. The unstated hope was that the resultant sympathy would enable him to return to Spain and recover his due. Despite the caviling of his detractors, there is no reason to doubt that Godoy wrote the bulk of the first draft unaided. The extent of the later contribution of Colonel Jean-Baptiste Esménard, his collaborator and trans-lator, is less certain. Some scholars have claimed to perceive the editorial hand of the abbés Siccard and Sicilia. Whatever assistance he may have received, Godoy's imprint is clearly discernible on every page: the self-exculpatory tone, the encyclopedic approach so dear to the eighteenth century, the fierce protestations of loyalty to king and country, the eagerness to quote any source or voice that conceivably might lend support.

With few exceptions, his critics have seriously questioned the veracity of the *Memorias*. Typical is the indictment of Fugier: "Godoy's [memoirs] are nothing but a continuous lie, and so impudent that they border on the unconscionable."[7] (Nevertheless, like so many others, he has not hesitated to avail himself of this source.) There is no arguing the fact that Manuel is inaccurate at times, that entire speeches are recalled verbatim to his own advantage, and many unwelcome details—whole episodes for that matter—are transmuted or simply ignored. A more serious criticism is his contention that at all times he was merely carrying out the king's express orders. He could hardly claim otherwise. As the sole source of his power and legitimacy, he was obliged to defend the memory of Carlos IV to the very end, however strained that relationship may have been at times.

In Paris, Manuel had come briefly into contact with several resident Spaniards as well as the occasional visitor. None of them, however, could be termed a close friend. One passing traveler was the poet and essayist José Mor de Fuentes. Later, he recalled an incident that occurred on Ascension Day in the year 1834:

> I was going through the middle of the woods so as to make good time to the Tuileries. On one of the inside paths I came across a Frenchman named Esménard who had lived a long time in Madrid and who spoke Spanish like a native. In his company was an individual of some age, on the stout side but still agile, and with regular features. He was wearing a blue frockcoat and a ribbon of some insignia in his buttonhole. I surmised that he must be one of the many retired French generals in these parts, and on joining them, so as not to fall into the very bad habit then so common of speaking a language which those present did not understand, I greeted them and began to speak in French. I then noticed that the stranger turned away a little, and as his company did not interest me that much, I soon took my leave. As I bade them farewell, Esménard said to me in Spanish, "We will have to get together." "Whenever you wish," I replied, and we agreed to meet the next morning at my house.
>
> Hardly had we met when Esménard asked me: "Didn't you recognize the man who was with me yesterday afternoon?" "Not at all," I replied, "I suppose some French general." "General, my foot, that was Godoy! Now you'll see what happened afterwards," he added. "When he heard us speaking Spanish he said to me: 'That man seems to be a Spaniard.' When I explained who you were, he replied: 'I'm sorry I didn't get to speak with him. I thought my presence displeased him.' The fact is," Esménard then said, "when he sees a stranger, he is startled, and even more so if the person happens to be a Spaniard." "You mean he still feels the effects of Aranjuez?" I said. "It seems so," and we went on to other matters.[8]

Sad to relate, the four volumes of memoirs that appeared between 1836 and 1837 in Esménard's French translation were a commercial failure. Instead of titillating revelations of sexual misconduct, the author offered a long-winded vindication of his ministry. Undaunted by the lack of success of the French version, he set about preparing a Spanish edition, which was published soon afterward in Madrid. Other than fleeting curiosity, the main reaction was surprise that the septuagenarian was still among the living.

Spain was now embroiled in a bloody civil war between the partisans of the late king's brother, Don Carlos, and the government forces that rallied round Fernando's widow, the Regent María Cristina, on behalf of her infant daughter Isabel. Was the Queen Mother, in fact, Godoy's grand-daughter? Madol, among others, believed that she was: "In truth, the Regent María Cristina had no reason to remember her grandfather in Paris. She had enough to do with the domestic struggles in Spain. It is highly likely that Godoy's petitions never reached her hands. Was it possible that, despite everything, she was unaware of her relationship to Godoy? But, when one considers the actions of her daughter Isabel in later years, there can be no doubt that María Cristina was well informed and had passed on to her daughter the secret of her origin."[9] Madol's conclusion is based on Queen Isabel's later decree allowing Godoy to return to Spain. It is not a convincing thesis.

If the public at large remained unmoved by the plight of the former *privado,* an increasing number of highly placed officials became convinced of the merits of his case. General Campuzano, the Spanish ambassador in Paris, visited him in his cheerless rooms, and, as a result, wrote to his government on March 11, 1837: "The Prince of the Peace is reduced to misery. I recommend to you, as a gesture of national generosity, that as compensation for the injustices committed against him he be given back the lowly remnants of his former opulence which he humbly requests."[10] Since 1808 no court action or legal decree of any sort had ever been directed against Godoy, nor had there been a formal indictment, and certainly no hint of a trial.

One of Manuel's most welcome visitors was Lord Holland. Old friends, they met in a Paris hotel on September 19, 1838. The English aristocrat has left a sympathetic word portrait of the favorite:

> I saw the Prince of the Peace much altered in appearance, but still the same character of countenance. Good-humored, self-satisfied, somewhat jovial and hearty, in his bad French and chuckling voice, and an arch expression in his eyes, he complained much of the ingratitude of the world . . . He complained bitterly of the Tudó, to whom he said he had been attached from his youth, to whom he had sacrificed everything, and for whom he had incurred the (I think he said ludicrous or absurd) imputation of bigamy, and whom all the world knew he had actually married after the death of his first wife, for the purpose of legitimating her son. He had

settled on her all he had in the world out of Spain, and she had left him and taken the whole, so that he was reduced to absolute penury, and lived entirely on the small pension *Luis Felipe* allowed him . . .[11]

According to Lord Holland, Godoy particularly resented the manner in which his estates had been expropriated and portioned out, among others to the Duke of Wellington. No law had ever been passed to confiscate his property legally; now that it had been given to others, there was scant prospect of recovering any part. Lord Holland thought the ex-*privado* generous in his appraisal of Napoleon, and, more surprisingly, in his opinion of Fernando, though he was quick to censure the king's brother, Don Carlos. "He said he had been reduced to great distress and degradation; but I found his spirits less depressed and his conversation more natural and frank than I expected. I asked if he saw Don Francisco [de Paula], and his manner of saying "no" convinced me that the Prince, who is notoriously his son, had made no advances to him, for he somewhat earnestly explained that it did not become him to seek his protection . . ."[12]

No sooner had Lord Holland taken his leave when, quite by chance, he came across a lady of Mediterranean complexion being aided up the stairs by some servants. To his surprise, he learned that she was none other than the Duchess of Sueca, Godoy's own daughter. Carlota was prematurely enfeebled in body, and, though now living close to her father, some of whose property in Spain she had at long last inherited, steadfastly refused to help him in his misery. Lord Holland could only muse:

> She is married to a Roman prince; but his royal consort's children and connections seem to treat him with the same insensibility, harshness, and cruelty as his mistress and wife, the Tudó, and all that depend on her. She is living in comparative splendor at Madrid, while her husband is training a miserable existence as a pensioner or almost beggar in Paris, surrounded by relations, acknowledged or unacknowledged children, grandchildren, and what not—Infants, Princesses, Duchesses, etc., etc., not one of whom condescends to take the slightest notice of him, or show the least tenderness, regard, or interest about one to whom some owe their station and riches, and all, more or less, their very existence! A strange name and fate "To point a moral or adorn a tale."[13]

As the years passed, Godoy's bitterness increased. All the political figures, all the friends he had helped in the past had deserted him. And now his own family. Pepita only bothered to write when in need of money to settle her debts. In the meantime, Manuel was barely scraping together an existence in a garret on the Rue Neuve des Mathurins. Somehow he managed to send her small sums of money he could ill afford. The unkindest blow, however, was dealt by Carlota. Unwilling to believe that his own daughter could turn against him, Godoy vented all his scorn in a letter to his heartless son-in-law, Count Camilo Rúspoli: "Just give me, at the very least, the consolation to see the law punish the dishonor of a foreigner introduced into my family to sow discord and feed the ingratitude of a daughter. The weight of such infamy is hastening the days of my life; it is not the misery, nor the shame to which so many faithless traitors have reduced me."[14]

Now, in typical Balzacian fashion, the most likely knock at the door was that of the pitiless creditor, the pressing bill-collector, or finally that of the police to convey him to the debtors' prison. To one lawyer he wrote in desperation in 1840: "I cannot, nor do I wish to intervene in the money matters of the Princess, my wife. I cannot intervene, because I lack the means to put an end to such misfortune. Nor should I, because my peace of mind, which was destroyed by numerous reverses of fortune, the result of bad business transactions by the Princess, would be further reduced through the persecution of her creditors who would simply descend on me."[15] All that Manuel could do was transfer to even more modest quarters on the fourth floor at 20 Rue de la Michaudière, near the Opéra.

It was in such straitened circumstances that Godoy received the visit of the gifted Spanish essayist, Ramón de Mesonero Romanos. Only six years old at the time of Godoy's fall, the author nevertheless had retained a keen interest in his subsequent fate. Together with a friend, Mesonero went to pay his respects to the Prince of the Peace:

> He welcomed us with great courtesy, and when Melón told him the object of my wish and also that I was a writer, though not a politician, he seemed pleased and spoke to me of his misfortunes and the injustice with which he had been treated by certain historians . . . He asked me if I had read his *Memorias* and what opinion the younger generation had formed of him. I tried to show him that we retained none of the passionate hatred and biases of our parents, and rather that, having suffered under the rule of Fernando VII, even felt somewhat envious of those who had lived under more enlightened and tolerant governments. I spoke with approval of his beneficent measures to promote science and the national culture, of the protection he extended to the talented men of that period, of the voyages he entrusted to Rojas Clemente and Badía . . . All of this seemed to gratify

him, as he expressed his thanks to me in an idiom whose phrases and pronunciation reminded one very much of Italian which he had spoken habitually over some thirty years. He repeated that his most ardent wish was to return to Spain and take a walk round the Prado, but that the government and the courts, by delaying his rehabilitation, were completely denying him that pleasure.[16]

All that Godoy sought was acknowledgement of the justice of his cause and the integrity of his lawyers. Mesonero, deeply moved by the old man's entreaty, promised to do his best upon his return to Madrid. He was one of the few to keep his word.

And now, thanks to Mesonero's good offices and the exertions of others, fortune began to smile on Manuel, if rather wanly. Carlota, who had once declared before the Cortes that her father had died, relented insofar as to grant him an annual pension of 12,000 duros. On April 30, 1844, his former property was restored to him, that is, the remnant which had not been irretrievably lost. In the wake of the First Carlist War, the government could never have restituted the full debt to Godoy, even if so inclined. Far more significant was Queen Isabel's decree of May 31, 1847, allowing the eighty-year-old ex-favorite to return to Spain and regain his former titles; only that of the Prince of the Peace (because he was not of royal blood) and the ranks of generalissimo and grand-admiral were denied him. To make up for the loss—supreme irony!—he was awarded the Grand Cross of the Royal and Military Order of San Hermenegildo, founded by Fernando VII in 1815. In any case, the decrees and honors were largely meaningless, for Manuel was far too elderly and set in his ways to travel. With its strange sights and sounds, his homeland, which he had not seen for nearly forty years, had become another foreign country.

Sometimes news of a different nature reached the ears of the *anciano*. More royal alliances were contemplated, some of which, if all the old scuttlebutt were true, would have linked Manuel with many of the ruling houses in Europe. Alquier, that inveterate court chatterbox, once claimed in Naples that "Queen María Carolina is informed of everything, and told me that the young Infanta, whom the Prince [Francisco Genaro] had just married, is the daughter of the Prince of the Peace whom she resembles in her features."[17] Later, as we have seen, Francisco de Paula married Luisa Carlota, the eldest daughter of this union. In the end it comes down to this: to accept the loose tattle at face value is likewise to admit Godoy as the progenitor of two royal lines.

But the matter does not end there. As already noted, Fernando VII in turn took his niece María Cristina as his fourth wife. Again accepting rumor as fact—which millions were only too delighted to do—not only was Godoy Fernando's grandfather-in-law, but now through the birth of Isabel in 1830 was also the founding father of the nineteenth-century Spanish Bourbons. Nor is that all. When Isabel, since 1833 Queen Isabel II of Spain, was sixteen years old she married her cousin Francisco de Asís, the son of Francisco de Paula and Luisa Carlota. In other words, if what Manuel's and María Luisa's detractors allege is true, the inescapable corollary is that the *privado* was related to the reigning queen on both sides of the family. For good measure, Louis Philippe's son, Antoine, the Duke of Montpensier, married Queen Isabel's sister Luisa, thus giving Godoy entrée into the French royal family as well. To have direct descendants reigning in Spain, France, and Italy is no mean achievement for a once destitute bodyguard from Extremadura. In this matter, there is no middle ground; either Manuel is innocent of the charges, or else every Spanish ruler after Fernando VII must acknowledge him as a forebear.

None of this, however, concerned Godoy. For more than half a century, he had steadfastly disavowed the misconduct imputed to him. As he sat alone on many a long evening, what memories must have flooded the mind of the man who once had enjoyed wealth and titles beyond compare, who had dared measure himself against the great Emperor Napoleon himself! Such thoughts also suggested themselves to Mesonero Romanos years later as he penned his own memoirs. With forgivable hyperbole, he recalled:

> We saw that Colossus whom our parents had seen direct with absolute power the destinies of the monarchy and the treasures of the New World for fifteen years, reduced to a sad annuity of six thousand francs, living poorly on the fourth floor. Apparently he was so resigned to his fate and to the amazing vicissitudes of life, that he could easily be found seated on a chair in the gardens of the Palais Royal or the Tuileries. He seemed amused by the children who played around him, picking up their hoops and tops, lending them his stick to ride on, and sitting them on his knees to accept their childish affection . . . Others took him to be a retired actor or a veteran theatre-goer. By all he was simply known as Monsieur Manuel, without anyone suspecting that a Prince's crown had once graced that beautiful head, that those shoulders, now stooped, had once borne a truly royal mantle, and that the ring which still sparkled on his finger was the marriage ring placed there by a granddaughter of Felipe V and Louis XIV.[18]

Some solace from loneliness was afforded the former Prince of the Peace when the children of his and Pepita's son Manuel would sometimes visit their grandfather. Once their artless laughter had faded away and he was left on his own, his thoughts would turn again to Pepita. With a trace of self-pity and the usual complaint regarding his precarious finances, on March 14, 1846, he wrote to his wife in Madrid: "All that remains, then, to put an end to my lament, is to tell you that our grandchildren, brought up in the wise precepts of our sacred religion, have left the convent to be educated at boarding school in accordance with the demands of society and the customs of our age. The first expenses of their move are costing me 2000 francs; the two college students and the rent of the house will more or less amount to a like sum. I am receiving four thousand francs a month. What will I have left over, then, for family expenses at home?"[19]

In truth, despite Carlota's grudging contributions, Godoy's financial position remained desperate. Once, his creditors threatened to take away his furniture, and by July 1848 he could no longer afford to pay his servants' scanty wages. By February 1850 his credit was exhausted: "If the loan doesn't come through I won't know how to extricate myself from the cart which is crushing me. Is it possible that by March they won't even have paid me my allowance for January?" Clearly his energies were fast ebbing. In the same letter to Pepita, he plaintively writes: "This will be the last letter penned by me, the final light of my life has been extinguished." In a pathetic postscript, he adds: "Please don't waste a moment in getting me a short-term loan, otherwise they won't have anything with which to pay for my burial unless it arrives soon."[20]

And now, in the gathering twilight of life, there returned a last flicker of Godoy's one great love. He had always loved Pepita, and, though his letters were often filled with reproach, she had never relinquished the claim to his heart. Could they not meet once more and perhaps even be reunited? In the summer of 1850, he dashed off a note to her: "I've been told that you are thinking of coming to Paris, please let me know in time as, lacking the money, I won't be able to buy a mattress for you."[21] She never came. Yet, with a tenacity that had marked his entire life, Manuel clung to his dream. On March 15, 1851, now aged eighty-four, he wrote: "Dear Pepita. I am looking for the necessary means to cover the house expenses as I can't make ends meet with what I get. If I succeed, I shall provide myself with all that is required for my trip, and I shall arrive in Madrid in time to complete my business."[22] No doubt like Goya a quarter century earlier, the octogenarian would have made the arduous crossing of the Pyrenees, but fate willed otherwise.

On April 10, weighed down by inescapable debts, Manuel penned his *apologia pro vita sua.* In it, he poured out his heart to Pepita:

> Dear Pepa. I am replying to your letter of the fourth of last month. I appreciate in my very soul the feeling of affection you express in it. Over the long period of forty-five years that I have known you and over such a large part of the world, neither misfortune nor the envy of your enemies pledged to destroy you has been able to alter the confidence which the sincerity of your young years once impressed on me . . . I have been liberal and frank towards you, generous to a fault and have kept silent. Least of all has the absence which events since 1835 forced on us persuaded me to change my first impression of you. My wretchedness, poverty, necessity—all of that counts for little, and what I possess I dedicate it all to you. Now that not only my own sufferings but also those of a family that honors me with its name are involved, I propose, even if it imperils my life (as an old man) to reestablish myself in Spain, as I am convinced that without my personal intervention and my knowledge of how much is my due, the restoration of my interests would not be complete, nor would the privileges on which it is based in accordance with my rank and services be accorded me.[23]

It was not to be. Manuel was slipping away, not from any identifiable illness—he had remained remarkably healthy for most of his life—but simply from old age. Or perhaps he was affected by what the Portuguese term *fado,* an indefinable sense of melancholy and nostalgia. Probably his letter dated September 3 was his last communication with Pepita: "Yesterday Manuel left, having received a letter from his wife informing him of the precarious state of her health. As he did not have sufficient funds for the journey, to make it possible I humiliated myself before the banker Ulibarren. In such circumstances the nobility has to demean itself . . . I am an old man, lacking in strength, and I don't know if I'll be able to undertake the journey as soon as I would like to . . . I'm taking advantage of my grandson to write to you as the trembling of my old age won't permit me to do so."[24]

The end came quietly a month later on October 4, 1851. Few noticed his passing. In Spain, the Prince of the Peace had long since been consigned to a historical footnote, overlooked amidst the civil wars and political scandals that beset the country. A cursory paragraph or two, and Spain's most powerful figure of the century had been disposed of. Nor was France in any mood to pay heed to trifling matters. Stirring events were afoot in Paris, the glories of the Napoleonic Empire were about to be revived in the person of the emperor's nephew—of what concern was the death of an old man when the future seemed to hold such promise?

Five days after Manuel's death, a simple funeral service was held in the parochial church of Saint Roch. His casket was temporarily placed in the crypt pending final burial. On January 16, 1852, Manuel Godoy, the Prince of the Peace, Duke of Alcudia, First Minister to King Carlos IV of Spain and the Indies, was laid to rest in the Père Lachaise cemetery. He still lies there today, but no longer alone. In 1880 his daughter-in-law, Mary Godoy, née Crowe, was buried in the same tomb, and a few years later he was joined by two of his grandchildren. A fading inscription, a medallion of indifferent workmanship, a general aura of neglect—nothing more remains of this once all-powerful man.

Godoy is deserving of a more fitting epitaph. Again, we turn to Mesonero Romanos:

> Surely the singular fate of this man, as much his rapid and amazing rise as his profound fall and protracted agony, is most remarkable and perhaps unique in the annals of history . . . Don Álvaro de Luna and Don Rodrigo Calderón, perishing on a scaffold in the squares of Valladolid and Madrid, concluded their tragic history in logical fashion . . . The Conde-Duque de Olivares and the Duke of Lerma, the first seeking refuge in his estates and the other in the sacred purple of a cardinal, barely survived their disgrace. Father Nithard, Don Fernando Valenzuela, Alberoni, Ripperdá, the Princesse des Ursins, the Marquis de Esquilache, all died far from the scene of their triumphs, but have not been forgotten or completely deprived of their political greatness.
>
> Godoy alone for more than half a century has dragged out an obscure and miserable existence in the presence of great European events but without figuring in any of them. He has outlived his own history, he has heard the judgment of posterity, he has attended his own obsequies, and has looked with indifference on the oblivion of three generations. Only his death at the age of eighty-four, and forty-four years after his fall, has made his name ring again for a moment and revealed his existence in the neighboring capital. A few Spaniards, witnesses to those respectable remains, accompanied his body to the vault of Saint Roch, pending transferral to the homeland. Only the present lines have been thought worthy by the Spanish press to honor the memory of the Prince of the Peace.[25]

Mesonero Romanos wrote the above in 1852. He was entirely too optimistic that, with the waning of past animosities, Manuel might yet be buried in Spanish soil. Later, he added: "On my last trip to Paris in 1865 I visited, as is my habit, the cemetery of Père Lachaise, and especially the enclosure extending to the left of the chapel which, on account of the number of our fellow countrymen who rest there, is known as the Spaniards' Island. There, among many other graves, may be found those of Moratín, Urquijo, Fernán Núñez . . . There is a small area surrounded by a railing, and at the head of it is a humble gravestone inscribed: 'Here rest the remains of Don Manuel Godoy,' that prodigy of fortune and also the amazing exemplar of human misfortune."[26]

The story has one further chapter. On July 31, 1884, a royal decree issued in Madrid authorized the construction of a *Panteón de Hombres Ilustres* in the San Justo cemetery.[27] Among those deemed worthy of burial there was Godoy's old friend, the poet Juan Meléndez Valdés, who had died as a lonely exile in Montpellier as long ago as May 24, 1817, and who, since then, had been interred four times in as many locations. Others to receive a state funeral were the dramatist Moratín, who had died in Paris in 1828, and his friend Francisco Goya, who succumbed in Bordeaux a year later. Not until 1889 was the artist's coffin finally brought back from France to be buried in the church of San Antonio de la Florida, which he had decorated a century earlier. The exiles have all returned to Spain—all, that is, except for Manuel Godoy.

Manuel's longevity was shared by many of his family. Pepita even lived to witness the revolution of 1868, in which Fernando's daughter, Isabel II, *la de los tristes destinos,* was driven from her throne after a turbulent reign debased by tawdry love affairs that put anything attributed to María Luisa to shame. Shortly before Pepita's death, the future historian Pérez de Guzmán attended a performance in the Teatro de la Zarzuela of a popular light operetta entitled *Pan y toros.* The story concerned a romance of a bygone age, that between the attractive Pepita Tudó fresh from Cádiz, and the court favorite, Manuel Godoy, the Prince of the Peace. During the intermission, two elderly ladies were discussing the merits of the zarzuela. To his surprise, Pérez de Guzmán recognized one as the Countess of Castillofiel, the selfsame Pepita Tudó. A few months later, on September 7, 1869, she died in a fire that broke out in her apartment. She was ninety years old.

The following generation also lived to a respectable age. Manuel *hijo,* born in Madrid in 1805, died on August 24, 1871, his Englishborn wife seven years later on December 4, 1878. Their children in turn inherited the Bassano title and went on to adopt diplomatic careers, admittedly with middling success. On the other side of the family, Carlota, the Countess Rúspoli, born in the first year of the century, lived until March 13, 1886, when she finally expired in Florence. Her two sons retained the Alcudia title inherited from Godoy and those of Chinchón and Boadilla del Monte from their mother. Adolphe, the elder grandson of Manuel and María Teresa, died in Paris on February 4, 1914, and a great-grandson lived until the outbreak of the Civil War in 1936. There is every reason to believe that the descendants of the *privado,* scattered over at least three countries and possibly more, are justifiably proud of their common ancestor. It is to be hoped that one day the good name of Manuel Godoy will likewise spread far beyond the confines of the Pyrenees. Surely he has waited long enough.

18

CODA

Our tale is now ended. The questions, however, persist. Was the appointment of a *privado*—any *privado*—itself an invitation to disaster? Was Godoy's rise and fall as preordained as in any ancient Greek tragedy? What mistakes could he have avoided, or was Spain's position vis-à-vis Napoleon hopeless from the beginning? Or could another First Minister—Floridablanca, perhaps—have been more effective? Is there a moral to the story? And if so, what?

To answer these questions requires an impartial assessment of Godoy. It is essential to regard him as a historical figure, to set emotions to one side, and to judge him dispassionately. Rarely has he been given a fair trial based on unassailable facts alone. Julio Burell has stated the case succinctly: "On the Prince of the Peace there has weighed—and God only knows how much longer will continue to weigh—the legend which hate and popular disdain have forged and which nothing can destroy. Joseph Bonaparte still remains *Pepe Botellas,* squint-eyed and a drunkard; Don Manuel Godoy, a distinguished man, *hidalgo extremeño,* enlightened enough for his era, will continue to be the *choricero* who by some repugnant aberration inspires love in the heart of a lascivious Queen with his castanets and his guitar."[1]

So much for the legend. Yet one overriding question is not disposed of so easily: can a monarch and his minister hope to rule effectively in the face of widespread acceptance of such stories? Had Godoy married Pepita Tudó when he first met her—better still, had he found a wife before becoming First Minister—at least the aspersions of bigamy and the charge that he was marrying into the royal family for self-advancement could never have been raised. More importantly, had he maintained a judicious detachment from the queen at the outset, his enemies would have found themselves obliged to judge him as a politician, not as a philanderer. González Ruiz observes: "Our beloved, severe, and terrible Spain has never been indulgent towards frivolity, especially when seen enthroned in the highest places."[2] Such being the case, Godoy's ministry had faint hope of gaining popular support. The wonder is not that he ultimately failed, but that under such conditions he remained in power for sixteen years.

Given the above, could Godoy have strengthened his position and have become, say, a Conde-Duque de Olivares, feared, obeyed, even grudgingly respected? Probably not; he simply was not cast in a heroic mold, or, to put it another way, showed little taste for the exercise of naked power. For this reason, among others, he has been dismissed as "an elusive, somewhat enigmatic character, perhaps more of pasteboard than steel."[3] Godoy really had little option. He is far from being Madol's "first dictator of our times." He is an intermediate figure, even something of an anachronism, caught between the domineering *valido* of the Habsburg seventeenth century and the military officers brought into power by the innumerable *pronunciamientos* of the nineteenth.

Nor had he overthrown a regime that was manifestly corrupt or had alienated itself from the people. Quite the contrary; he owed everything to his monarch who, whatever his faults, most certainly could not be termed an oppressor. Godoy, then, is the victim of two quite distinct perceptions in the public mind: "A parvenu who attains the rule in a state by the gun and adventure easily becomes the hero of legend, and popular favor never abandons him. But if we are dealing with a bed, literally or figuratively, bad reputation and repudiation take over; the effort is too soft, and in a country of frowning and libidinous men, it is condemnable."[4] Anathematized during his own lifetime, Godoy has not recovered to this day.

In foreign policy, the Prince of the Peace cannot escape his share of criticism. Certainly, he erred grievously: the disadvantageous alliances with the French, his greed following the War of the Oranges, his injudicious manifesto to the nation on the eve of the Battle of Jena, and his vacillation in the crucial early months of 1808 may be cited, to name but a few. Napoleon on St. Helena made the disparaging remark of Godoy, "He was far from being a clever man. He should never have allowed a foreign army to cross the Pyrenees."[5] Yet whose was the greater error? Napoleon himself admitted that it was the "Spanish affair" that brought about his ruin. But the emperor's downfall has a heroic quality about it, an appeal to the imagination and the emotions that Manuel's does not. The *privado's* career is too much of a patchwork, lacking in bold vision. There is a certain dinginess about it all; frequently he is reduced to a struggle for mere personal survival.

But, having conceded as much, one cannot ignore the vast stage on which Godoy's tragedy is played out. He was, in sum, First Minister to a monarch whose realms extended the length and breadth of the Americas to the distant Philippines, an empire which remained intact during a stewardship that encompassed the second presidency of Washington, that of John Adams, and both terms of Jefferson.

The fact is that Spain, by comparison with other European nations, has not received the attention commensurate with her true importance. To a large extent, Godoy has suffered from this general neglect. From Felipe II and the Armada (these remembered mainly because both impinged on England) to the Civil War of the present century, there is a gap of four and a half centuries during which the average foreigner would be hard pressed to name a single event or Spaniard, for that matter. Even the war of liberation against Napoleon is best known as the Peninsular War, in which the Duke of Wellington is the hero; the Spaniards are there to provide scenery and a supporting cast.

The defense rests. Godoy's case has been presented and pleaded; the jury is still out. In the final analysis, it is not Manuel Godoy the favorite or the statesman who stands trial, but Unamuno's "man of flesh and bone, who is born, suffers and dies—especially who dies—who eats and drinks and plays and sleeps and loves, the man who is seen and heard, the brother, the true brother."[6] Godoy could easily have lived out his life in comfortable·exile in England; instead, he chose to devote himself to the *reyes,* wherever that path might lead him. He had made that decision many years earlier in the country he loved so well. In a letter dated September 22, 1799, that is, at the height of his power, he wrote to his friend Miguel Cayetano Soler, the minister of the treasury: "The gratitude I feel towards the Queen does not leave me a moment of peace. My friend, I cannot abandon her, I must accompany her as far as the urn where her ashes are placed, and then beweep her loss on her grave."[7] A sentimental style, perhaps faintly embarrassing to the modern ear. Twenty years later, Manuel, true to his word, afforded the queen her last solace on earth. Need more be said?

Notes

Preface

1. Geoffroy de Grandmaison, *L'Ambassade française en Espagne pendant la Révolution (1789–1804)* (Paris: Librairie Plon, 1892), p. 73. "La reine, plus âgée que lui de dix ans . . . Il mourut à Rome en 1823."

2. Richard Ford, *A Handbook for Travellers in Spain and Readers at Home, 1845,* 3 vols. (Carbondale: Southern Illinois Press, 1966), II, p. 785.

3. Segundo Serrano Poncela, *Formas de Vida Hispánica* (Madrid: Editorial Gredos, 1963), p. 124. Only the third essay deals with Godoy.

Introduction

1. The best edition of Godoy's *Memorias* is that published in two volumes in the *Biblioteca de Autores Españoles* (B.A.E.) series, vols. 88, 89 (Madrid: Ediciones Atlas, 1956). The preliminary study to the *Memorias* by Carlos Seco Serrano entitled *Godoy: El hombre y el político* is an excellent introduction to the subject.

2. Ibid., 88, p. 4.

3. Ibid., p. 8.

4. Ibid., p. 10.

5. Actually what Godoy read was Muriel's translation into French of William Coxe's uncomplimentary work which he entitled *l'Espagne sous les rois de la Maison de Bourbon* (Paris, 1827). Muriel, an *afrancesado,* had been living in France since 1814. Godoy refers to both Coxe and Muriel with considerable asperity in his *Memorias,* which in turn partially prompted Muriel to write his own *La Época de Carlos IV* in Spanish shortly before his death, in 1840.

Chapter 1

1. Hans Roger Madol, *Godoy* (Madrid: Alianza Editorial, 1966), p. 44.

2. Carlos Corona Baratech, *Revolución y reacción en el reinado de Carlos IV* (Madrid: Ediciones Rialp, 1957), p. 273.

3. Ibid.

4. Grandmaison, *L'Ambassade,* p. 202.

5. Carlos Pereyra, *Cartas confidenciales de la reina María Luisa y de Don Manuel Godoy* (Madrid: M. Aguilar, n.d.), p. 185. The letter is undated.

6. Cándido Pardo González, *Don Manuel Godoy y Álvarez Faria, Príncipe de la Paz* (Madrid: Imprenta de la Viuda de A. Álvarez, 1911), p. 9. Written by a professional soldier, the work emphasizes military events.

7. Madol, *Godoy*, p. 24.

8. This certainly is the opinion of the majority of historians. Against this must be weighed a letter from Floridablanca to Carlos III quoted by Manuel Izquierdo Hernández in his *Antecedentes y comienzos del reinado de Fernando VII* (Madrid: Ediciones Cultura Hispánica, 1963), p. 46. The minister writes: "Your Majesty has admitted the prince to all the official communications, and you have placed confidence in him regarding commercial affairs to a degree hitherto unknown in the annals of the monarchy and without precedent in other nations . . ." How much of this is standard flattery and how much truth is difficult to establish.

9. Izquierdo Hernández, *Antecedentes*, p. 11.

10. Ibid., p. 37.

11. Ibid., pp. 14–15. A detailed list with dates of all the children born to Carlos IV and María Luisa.

12. Jacques Chastenet, *Godoy, Master of Spain, 1792–1808* (London: The Batchworth Press Ltd., 1953), p. 20.

13. Izquierdo Hernández, *Antecedentes*, p. 41.

14. Juan de Escoiquiz, *Memorias de Tiempos de Fernando VII*, B.A.E. 97 (Madrid: Ediciones Atlas, 1957), p. 14.

15. Madame Junot, Duchesse d'Abrantès, *Memoirs*, 3 vols. (New York: Scribner and Welford, 1883), II, p. 375.

16. Escoiquiz, *Memorias*, p. 14.

17. Andrés Muriel, *Historia de Carlos IV*, B.A.E. 114, 115 (Madrid: Ediciones Atlas, 1959), I, p. 137. Pro-Aranda, anti-Godoy, and devastating to the queen. Carlos Seco Serrano protests, "The portrait of María Luisa of Parma which [Muriel] offers us in these pages is so lamentable that she is reduced to a symbol of corruption, an inhuman creature; her pitiless detractor does not attribute to her one single positive quality."

18. Quoted at length by Pereyra, *Cartas*, p. 24.

19. Junot, *Memoirs*, II, p. 383.

20. José Blanco-White (pseudonym: Leucadio Doblado), *Letters from Spain* (London: Henry Colburn & Co., 1822), p. 332.

21. Edmund D'Auvergne, *Godoy, the Queen's Favourite* (Boston: The Gorham Press, 1913), p. 26.

22. Richard Herr, *The Eighteenth-Century Revolution in Spain* (Princeton: Princeton University Press, 1958), p. 317.

23. Gabriel H. Lovett, *Napoleon and the Birth of Modern Spain*, 2 vols. (New York: New York University Press, 1965), I, p. 10.

24. Blanco-White, *Letters,* p. 360.

25. Chastenet, *Godoy,* pp. 23, 25, and especially Madol, *Godoy,* pp. 60, 61: "It is very likely that for some time the King had no doubts as to the relationship between Manuel and María Luisa. But he could not separate himself from the favorite. It is certain that his inclination for Manuel, as seems clear from later documents, was not without some erotic character. Godoy, endowed with certain feminine traits and a very feminine vanity, appeared quite capable of playing the part of a *mignon.*" This is the same Madol who decries the "exaggerations of the journalistic art" (p. 77) and who insists that "documents are more exciting than false inventions. The true events of life are full of adventure and more fantastic than poetic imagination" (p. 79). Where, then, are these documents?

26. Izquierdo Hernández, *Antecedentes,* p. 45.

27. Pereyra, *Cartas,* p. 29.

28. Ibid., p. 31.

29. Ibid., p. 36.

30. Ibid., pp. 49, 50. Pereyra quotes the letter in its entirety.

31. John D. Bergamini, *The Spanish Bourbons* (New York: G. P. Putnam's Sons, 1974), p. 100.

Chapter 2

1. Antonio del Solar y Taboada and José de Rújula y de Ochotorena, *Godoy, Príncipe de la Paz* (Badajoz: Tipografía Viuda de Antonio Arqueros, 1944), p. 19.

2. Pardo González, *Don Manuel Godoy,* p. 17.

3. Godoy, *Memorias,* I, p. 13.

4. Muriel, *Historia,* I, p. 138.

5. Pardo González, *Don Manuel Godoy,* p. 8.

6. Blanco-White, *Letters,* p. 334.

7. D'Auvergne, *Godoy,* p. 35.

8. Ildefonso Antonio Bermejo, *Historia anecdótica y secreta de la corte de Carlos IV,* 2 vols. (Madrid: Casa Editorial de la Viuda de Muñoz, n.d.), pp. 40–42.

9. Izquierdo Hernández, *Antecedentes,* p. 54.

10. Chastenet, *Godoy,* p. 24.

11. Izquierdo Hernández, *Antecedentes,* p. 59.

12. Escoiquiz, *Memorias,* p. 15.

13. D'Auvergne, *Godoy,* p. 38.

14. Izquierdo Hernández, *Antecedentes,* pp. 52, 53. These pages contain a detailed list of Godoy's promotions and other dates.

15. Pardo González, *Don Manuel Godoy,* p. 12.

16. Herr, *Revolution,* p. 240.

17. Grandmaison, *L'Ambassade,* p. 62.

18. Blanco-White, *Letters,* p. 337.

19. Rafael Olaechea and José Ferrer Benimeli, *El Conde de Aranda*, 2 vols. (Saragossa: Librería General, 1978), II, p. 24. The authors claim that "the conclusion to which one comes . . . is that Masonry did not exist in any organic form in the Spain of the eighteenth century."

20. Ibid., p. 47.

21. Izquierdo Hernández, *Antecedentes*, p. 65.

22. Muriel, *Historia*, I, p. 90.

23. Chastenet, *Godoy*, p. 54.

24. Godoy, *Memorias*, p. xviii of Seco Serrano's Introduction, quoting Juan Pérez de Guzmán, *La reina María Luisa, esposa de Carlos IV*, p. 76.

25. Jean-Louis Jacquet, *Les Bourbons d'Espagne* (Lausanne: Éditions Rencontre, 1968), p. 200.

26. Herr, *Revolution*, p. 439.

27. Godoy, *Memorias*, I, p. 159 fn.

28. Ibid., p. 15.

Chapter 3

1. Madol, *Godoy*, p. 46.

2. Godoy, *Memorias*, I, p. 25; Madol, *Godoy*, p. 49.

3. Blanco-White, *Letters*, p. 337.

4. Godoy, *Memorias*, I, p. 18.

5. Ibid., I, p. 35.

6. Ibid., I, pp. 15, 18.

7. Herr, *Revolution*, p. 287.

8. Muriel, *Historia*, I, pp. 198–203.

9. Godoy, *Memorias*, I, pp. 70–79.

10. Muriel omits this speech entirely. Nor, so far as I know, has any other historian alluded to it.

11. Muriel, *Historia*, I, p. 203.

12. Ibid., p. 204. Godoy makes no mention of this reply, which is frequently quoted.

13. Godoy, *Memorias*, I, p. 80. This is his version. Muriel, as Aranda's defender, has him reply to the king: "Sire, I bow my head to the authority of Your Majesty"— quite a different rendition of what purportedly is the same occasion. Godoy, of course, was a participant, whereas Muriel came by his information secondhand. This does not vouchsafe for the greater accuracy of either version.

14. Madol, *Godoy*, p. 64.

15. Godoy, *Memorias*, I, p. 95.

16. El francés le trata hoy
    al español de collón
    por consentir la nación

la gobierne ¿quién? Godoy.
¿Pero qué admiración le doy
si la Reina por su lujuria
le enamoró—¡oh qué furia!—
y le sacó del cuartel,
para joderse con él
Señor Duque de la Alcudia?

Iris M. Zavala et al., *Historia ibérica. Economía y sociedad en los siglos XVIII y XIX* (Madrid: A. G. Ibarra, S.A., n.d.), p. 43. A detailed account of the Picornell conspiracy.

17. Ibid., p. 45.

18. Ibid., p. 53.

19. Madol, *Godoy*, pp. 71, 72.

20. Jean Sarrailh, *L'Espagne éclairée de la seconde moitié du XVIIIe siècle* (Paris: Imprimerie Nationale, 1954), p. 607 fn.

21. Blanco-White, *Letters*, p. 338.

22. Godoy, *Memorias*, I, p. 123.

23. Madol, *Godoy*, pp. 68, 72, fn. 10. "Godoy intended to marry her," he states flatly. This is not the generally held opinion.

24. Del Solar y Taboada, *Príncipe*, p. 57.

Chapter 4

1. Pereyra, *Cartas*, p. 187.

2. Izquierdo Hernández, *Antecedentes*, pp. 193, 194.

3. Grandmaison, *L'Ambassade*, p. 103.

4. Godoy, *Memorias*, I, p. 143.

5. Quoted by Pereyra, *Cartas*, p. 107.

6. Pardo González, *Don Manuel Godoy*, p. 52.

7. Grandmaison, *L'Ambassade*, p. 123.

8. Pereyra, *Cartas*, p. 204.

9. Godoy, *Memorias*, I, p. 153.

10. Ibid., p. 123.

11. Madol, *Godoy*, p. 90.

12. Grandmaison, *L'Ambassade*, p. 178.

13. Lovett, *Napoleon*, I, p. 10.

14. Muriel, *Historia*, I, pp. 178–79. Malaspina's voyage of 1789–93 has never been given the credit it deserves. Had his intended account been published, his reputation today might be quite different. In a real sense, he is a tragic figure, remembered, if at all, for his part in the attempted coup against Godoy.

15. Godoy, *Memorias*, I, p. 155.

16. Muriel, *Historia*, I, p. 302. Muriel, quite rightly, points out that Godoy had

no need to fudge the details of this incident in his *Memorias,* for the unadorned facts do him credit. On occasion, Godoy needlessly "improved" the record.

17. Julián Marías, *Los Españoles* (Madrid: Revista de Occidente, 1962), p. 45.

18. Godoy, *Memorias,* I, p. 191 fn.

19. Blanco-White, *Letters,* p. 344.

20. Francisco Martí, *El proceso de El Escorial* (Pamplona: Ediciones Universidad de Navarra, S.A., 1965), p. 74.

21. Ibid., p. 73.

22. Corona Baratech, *Revolución,* p. 288.

23. Lord Henry Richard Holland, *Foreign Reminiscences* (New York: Harper & Brothers, 1851), pp. 94, 95.

24. Bermejo, *Historia,* p. 17 of *Prólogo,* by Julio Burell.

25. Escoiquiz, *Memorias,* p. 6 (both quotations).

Chapter 5

1. Godoy, *Memorias,* I, p. 253.

2. Martí, *Proceso,* p. 99.

3. Escoiquiz, *Memorias,* p. 5.

4. Juan de Escoiquiz, *Idea sencilla de las razones que motivaron el viaje del rey don Fernando VII a Bayona,* B.A.E. 97 (Madrid: Ediciones Atlas, 1957), p. 205.

5. Corona Baratech, *Revolución,* p. 329.

6. Godoy, *Memorias,* I, p. 254.

7. Ibid., p. 257.

8. Escoiquiz, *Memorias,* p. xvii of the *Estudio preliminar,* by Miguel Artola.

9. Del Solar y Taboada, *Príncipe,* p. 83.

10. Godoy, *Memorias,* I, p. lii fn. of Introduction, by Seco Serrano.

11. Pereyra, *Cartas,* p. 111.

12. Godoy, *Memorias,* I, p. 246.

13. Madol, *Godoy,* p. 97.

14. En daros Excelencia o bien Alteza
    la pública opinión no se ha fijado,
    dúdase, gran señor, si sois casado,
    y cual es vuestra esposa con certeza.
Martí, *Proceso,* p. 87.

15. Jacquet, *Bourbons,* p. 203.

16. Madol, *Godoy,* p. 97; Chastenet, *Godoy,* p. 84.

17. Grandmaison, *L'Ambassade,* p. 138.

18. Chastenet, *Godoy,* p. 81.

19. Pereyra, *Cartas,* p. 119.

20. Martí, *Proceso,* p. 77 fn.

21. Chastenet, *Godoy,* p. 86.

22. Miguel Artola, *Antiguo Régimen y Revolución Liberal* (Barcelona: Editorial Ariel, 1979), p. 147.

23. Josep Fontana, *La quiebra de la monarquía absoluta (1814–1820)* (Barcelona: Ediciones Ariel, 1971), p. 152.

24. Antonio Domínguez Ortis, "La Sociedad Española en el Tránsito del siglo 18 al 19," in *España a finales del siglo XVIII,* Gonzalo Anes et al. (Tarragona: Hemeroteca de Tarragona, 1982), p. 48.

25. Herr, *Revolution,* p. 397.

26. Julián Juderías, *Don Gaspar Melchor de Jovellanos* (Madrid: Jaime Ratés Martín, 1913), p. 43.

27. Serrano Poncela, *Formas,* p. 151.

28. Muriel, *Historia,* II, p. 49.

29. Godoy, *Memorias,* I, p. 251.

30. Ibid., p. 252.

31. Herr, *Revolution,* p. 441.

32. Corona Baratech, *Revolución,* p. 280.

Chapter 6

1. Godoy, *Memorias,* I, p. 258.

2. Grandmaison, *L'Ambassade,* p. 169.

3. Escoiquiz, *Memorias,* p. 10.

4. Godoy, *Memorias,* I, p. 289.

5. Ibid., p. 290.

6. Pereyra, *Cartas,* p. 189.

7. Hans Buisman, *Spanien* (Darmstadt: Wissenschaftliche Buchgesellschaft, 1972), p. 32.

8. Pereyra, *Cartas,* p. 191.

9. Ibid., p. 222.

10. Ibid., p. 227.

11. Izquierdo Hernández, *Antecedentes,* p. 58.

12. Pereyra, *Cartas,* pp. 243, 251, 259.

13. Ibid., p. 289.

14. D'Auvergne, *Godoy,* p. 127.

15. Madol, *Godoy,* p. 116.

16. Chastenet, *Godoy,* p. 95.

17. André Fugier, *Napoléon et l'Espagne,* 2 vols. (Paris: Librairie Félix Alcan, 1930), I, p. 96.

18. Izquierdo Hernández, *Antecedentes,* p. 198.

19. Ibid., p. 199.

20. María Teresa, born at Aranjuez, February 16, 1791, died at El Escorial, November 2, 1794; Felipe María Francisco, born at Aranjuez, March 28, 1792, died in Madrid, March 1, 1794.

21. Pereyra, *Cartas,* p. 157.

22. Guillermo Díaz Plaja, *Epistolario de Goya* (Barcelona: Editorial Mentora, 1928), p. 85.

23. Antonina Vallentin, *This I Saw: The Life and Times of Goya* (New York: Random House, 1949), p. 156.

24. Díaz Plaja, *Epistolario,* p. 82.

25. Vallentin, *This I Saw,* p. 181.

26. Lord Kenneth Clark, *The Romantic Rebellion* (New York: Harper & Row, 1973), p. 75.

27. Pierre Gassier and Juliet Wilson, *The Life and Complete Work of Francisco Goya* (New York: Reynal & Co., 1971), p. 152.

28. Pereyra, *Cartas,* p. 233.

29. Elizabeth du Gué Trapier, *Goya and His Sitters: A Study of His Style as a Portraitist* (New York: Hispanic Society of America, 1964), p. 19.

30. Pereyra, *Cartas,* p. 284.

31. Ibid., p. 304.

32. Ibid., p. 310.

33. Joaquín Esquerra del Bayo, *La Duquesa de Alba y Goya* (Madrid: Librería de Ruiz Hermanos, 1928), p. 226.

34. Ibid., p. 229.

35. Pereyra, *Cartas,* p. 288.

36. Ibid., p. 341.

37. Vallentin, *This I Saw,* p. 195.

38. Esquerra del Bayo, *Duquesa,* p. 230.

39. Godoy, *Memorias,* p. xxxv fn. of Introduction, by Seco Serrano.

Chapter 7

1. Pereyra, *Cartas,* p. 173.

2. Grandmaison, *L'Ambassade,* p. 194.

3. Madol, *Godoy,* p. 107.

4. Godoy, *Memorias,* I, p. 291.

5. Ibid., p. 236.

6. Serrano Poncela, *Formas,* p. 156.

7. El poder no en violencia se asegura,
   ni el horror del suplicio le sostiene,
   ni armados escuadrones;
   pues donde amor faltó, la fuerza es vana.
   Tú lo sabes, señor, y en tus acciones

ejemplo das. Tú la virtud oscura,
tú la inocencia amparas. Si olvidado
el mérito se vio, tú le coronas;
las letras a tu sombra florecieron,
el celo aplaudes, el error perdonas,
y el premio a tus aciertos recibiste
en placer interior que el alma siente.

Godoy, *Memorias,* I, p. 235.

    8. Ibid., p. 221.

    9. Serrano Poncela, *Formas,* p. 154.

    10. Y aquí, malgrado que en su diestra lleva
La suma del poder, miro del dardo
También herido de la atroz calumnia
De mi príncipe el seno; da a los pueblos
La dulce paz por que llorando anhelen,
Y esta dichosa paz en un delito
Que, estúpida, le increpa la ignorancia.

Leopoldo Augusto Cueto, ed., *Poetas líricos del siglo XVIII,* B.A.E. 63 (Madrid: Ediciones Atlas, 1952), pp. 213–14.

    11. No lo sufráis, señor, mas, poderoso,
el monstruo derrocad que guerra impía
a la santa verdad mueve envidioso.

Ibid., p. 200.

    12. Acaso vuestra gloria,
Por aliviarme, vivirá en la historia
Con duración eterna.

Ibid., p. 301.

    13. Serrano Poncela, *Formas,* p. 161.

    14. Entró en la Guardia Real
y dio el gran salto mortal.
Con la Reina se ha metido
y todavía no ha salido.
Y su omnímodo poder
viene de saber . . . cantar.

Corona Baratech, *Revolución,* p. 308.

    15. Como miró por su casa
fué Príncipe de la Pasa.
Que a España e Indias gobierna
por debajo de la pierna.
Es un mal bicho al que al cabo
habrá que cortar el rabo.

Ibid.

16. William Beckford, *The Travel Diaries of William Beckford of Fonthill,* 2 vols. (Cambridge: Cambridge University Press, 1928), II, p. 248.

17. Ford, *Handbook,* II, p. 784.

18. Lord Byron, *Childe Harold's Pilgrimage* (Boston: Ticknor & Co., 1886), Canto I, Stanza 48.

19. Antonio Alcalá Galiano, *Recuerdos de un anciano,* B.A.E. 83 (Madrid: Ediciones Atlas, 1955), p. 24.

20. Ibid.

21. Ibid., p. 25.

22. D'Auvergne, *Godoy,* p. 82.

23. Lovett, *Napoleon,* I, p. 22 fn.

24. Lord Holland, *Reminiscences,* pp. 92, 93.

25. Madol, *Godoy,* p. 112.

26. Ibid., p. 120.

27. Ibid., p. 121. Also Chastenet, *Godoy,* p. 71.

28. Ibid., p. 86; Chastenet, *Godoy,* p. 71.

29. Ibid., p. 87.

30. Godoy, *Memorias,* I, p. 343.

31. Lovett, *Napoleon,* II, p. 768 fn.

Chapter 8

1. Fugier, *Napoléon,* I, p. 87.

2. Godoy, *Memorias,* I, p. 319.

3. Chastenet, *Godoy,* p. 104.

4. Pereyra, *Cartas,* p. 167.

5. Ibid., p. 366.

6. Marqués de Lema, *Antecedentes políticos y diplomáticos de los sucesos de 1808* (Madrid: Librería de F. Beltrán, 1912), p. 68. An invaluable source up to 1803, but unfortunately never completed.

7. Pereyra, *Cartas,* p. 374.

8. Ibid., p. 388.

9. Ibid., p. 174.

10. Lema, *Antecedentes,* p. 69.

11. Grandmaison, *L'Ambassade,* p. 213.

12. Nicolás González Ruiz, *Dos Favoritos: Potemkin, Godoy* (Barcelona: Editorial Cervantes, 1944), p. 97.

13. Grandmaison, *L'Ambassade,* p. 202; D'Auvergne, *Godoy,* p. 83.

14. Madol, *Godoy,* p. 133.

15. Chastenet, *Godoy,* p. 103.

16. Pereyra, *Cartas,* p. 175; Grandmaison, *L'Ambassade,* p. 202.

17. Jacquet, *Bourbons,* p. 213.

18. Lema, *Antecedentes,* p. 104.

19. Madol, *Godoy,* p. 126.

20. Godoy, *Memorias,* I, p. 314.

21. Jacquet, *Bourbons,* p. 213.

22. Ibid., p. 149.

23. Chastenet, *Godoy,* p. 107. Also, Lema, *Antecedentes,* p. 160; Jacquet, *Bourbons,* pp. 213–14.

24. Lema, *Antecedentes,* pp. 150–51.

25. Ibid., p. 162.

26. Izquierdo Hernández, *Antecedentes,* p. 81; Muriel, *Historia,* II, p. 237.

27. Lema, *Antecedentes,* p. 178.

28. Madol, *Godoy,* p. 136.

29. Pío Zabala y Lera, *España bajo los Borbones* (Barcelona: Editorial Labor, S.A., 1945), p. 80.

30. Lema, *Antecedentes,* p. 158.

31. Fugier, *Napoléon,* I, p. 156.

32. Chastenet, *Godoy,* p. 109.

33. Lema, *Antecedentes,* p. 187.

34. Godoy, *Memorias,* I, p. 331.

35. Lema, *Antecedentes,* p. 165.

36. Godoy, *Memorias,* p. lxxv fn. of Introduction, by Seco Serrano.

37. Lema, *Antecedentes,* p. 219.

38. Ibid., p. 205. Suvarow was the brilliant Russian general who fought against the French in Italy and Switzerland.

39. Grandmaison, *L'Ambassade,* p. 226.

40. Lema, *Antecedentes,* p. 231.

41. Pardo González, *Don Manuel Godoy,* p. 73.

42. D'Auvergne, *Godoy,* p. 138.

43.　　Príncipe, duque, conde
todo lo es ya, y espera
ser Rey de los Algarves,
pero será lo que la suerte quiera.
　　Pues ya la Providencia
oye el llanto y gemido
que por tu culpa has envilecido.
Corona Baratech, *Revolución,* p. 309.

44. Ibid., p. 307.

45. Pereyra, *Cartas,* p. 318. Letter of August 1, 1800.

46. Izquierdo Hernández, *Antecedentes,* p. 82.

47. Lema, *Antecedentes,* p. 292.

48. Fugier, *Napoléon,* I, p. 178.

49. Lema, *Antecedentes,* p. 259.

50. Pardo González, *Don Manuel Godoy,* p. 89.

51. Francisco Martí, *El motín de Aranjuez* (Pamplona: Ediciones Universidad de Navarra, S.A., 1972), p. 22.

52. Lema, *Antecedentes,* p. 290.

53. Ibid., p. 291.

54. Ibid., p. 271; Madol, *Godoy,* p. 140.

55. F. Soldevila, *Historia de España* (Barcelona: Ediciones Ariel, 1964), VI, p. 101. Soldevila claims that Godoy never wrote his own memoirs on the tenuous grounds that "the *Memorias* cannot be the work of the same author as these tasteless, pretentious, and declamatory letters" (p. 102).

56. Godoy, *Memorias,* p. liii of Introduction, by Seco Serrano.

Chapter 9

1. Izquierdo Hernández, *Antecedentes,* p. 78.

2. Ibid., p. 81.

3. Godoy, *Memorias,* II, p. 69.

4. Bergamini, *Bourbons,* p. 112.

5. Madol, *Godoy,* p. 143.

6. Lady Elizabeth Holland, *The Spanish Journal of Elizabeth Lady Holland* (London: Longmans, Green, and Co., 1910), p. 91 fn.

7. Esquerra del Bayo, *Duquesa,* p. 244; Lema, *Antecedentes,* p. 312.

8. D. B. Wyndham Lewis, *The World of Goya* (New York: Clarkson N. Potter, Inc., 1968), p. 147.

9. Esquerra del Bayo, *Duquesa,* p. 246.

10. Eunice Smith Beyersdorf, "A Rediscovered Portrait of Godoy, Minister to Carlos IV," in *The Burlington Magazine,* No. 717, Vol. CIV, December 1962, pp. 536–39.

11. Godoy, *Memorias,* II, p. 83.

12. Esquerra del Bayo, *Duquesa,* p. 267.

13. Lady Holland, *Journal,* p. 75.

14. Godoy, *Memorias,* I, p. 360.

15. Fugier, *Napoléon,* I, p. 301.

16. Godoy, *Memorias,* I, p. 360.

17. Lema, *Antecedentes,* p. 297.

18. Izquierdo Hernández, *Antecedentes,* pp. 85, 86.

19. Martí, *Proceso,* p. 112.

20. Godoy, *Memorias,* I, p. 363.

21. Harold Acton, *The Bourbons of Naples* (London: Methuen and Co. Ltd., 1959), p. 461.

22. Fugier, *Napoléon,* I, p. 301.

23. Ibid., p. 302.

24. Martí, *Proceso,* p. 112.

25. Izquierdo Hernández, *Antecedentes,* p. 209.

26. Nina Epton, *The Spanish Mousetrap* (London: Macdonald & Co. Ltd., 1973), p. 68.

27. Izquierdo Hernández, *Antecedentes,* p. 210.

28. Ibid., p. 210.

29. Fugier, *Napoléon,* I, p. 303.

30. Lema, *Antecedentes,* p. 307.

31. Godoy, *Memorias,* I, p. 382.

32. Lady Holland, *Journal,* pp. 74, 113.

33. Lema, *Antecedentes,* p. 318 fn. Letter of November 27, 1803.

34. Esquerra del Bayo, *Duquesa,* p. 264. Letter of September 13, 1804.

35. Esquerra del Bayo, *Duquesa,* p. 264.

36. Grandmaison, *L'Ambassade,* p. 241. Also D'Auvergne, *Godoy,* p. 152; González Ruiz, *Favoritos,* p. 103.

37. Pardo González, *Don Manuel Godoy,* p. 95; Godoy, *Memorias,* p. lxxvii of Introduction, by Seco Serrano.

38. Godoy, II, *Memorias,* p. 32.

39. Madol, *Godoy,* p. 160.

40. Pardo González, *Don Manuel Godoy,* p. 113. Godoy, *Memorias,* II, p. 34, repeats the spirit of the letter.

41. Lady Holland, *Journal,* p. 117.

Chapter 10

1. Pardo González, *Don Manuel Godoy,* p. 121.

2. Soldevila, *Historia,* VI, p. 121.

3. Grandmaison, *L'Ambassade,* p. 242.

4. Godoy, *Memorias,* I, p. 384.

5. D'Auvergne, *Godoy,* p. 154.

6. Pardo González, *Don Manuel Godoy,* p. 106.

7. Fugier, *Napoléon,* I, p. 300.

8. D'Auvergne, *Godoy,* p. 172.

9. Godoy, *Memorias,* p. lxxviii of Introduction, by Seco Serrano.

10. Grandmaison, *L'Ambassade,* p. 258.

11. D'Auvergne, *Godoy,* p. 157. This version closely adheres to the preceding account by Grandmaison. Also cf. Madol, *Godoy,* pp. 150–51.

12. D'Auvergne, *Godoy,* p. 157.

13. Ibid., p. 158.

14. Fugier, *Napoléon,* I, p. 230.

15. Ibid., p. 233. Godoy's wife was the king's first cousin. Probably out of deference to the king and the thirty-two year age difference, María Teresa was referred to as the monarch's niece.

16. Ibid., p. 231.

17. Grandmaison, *L'Ambassade,* p. 268.

18. D'Auvergne, *Godoy,* p. 163.

19. Fugier, *Napoléon,* I, p. 325 fn. Also D'Auvergne, *Godoy,* p. 169.

20. Chastenet, *Godoy,* p. 122; Fugier, *Napoléon,* I, p. 321.

21. Chastenet, *Godoy,* p. 122; Fugier, *Napoléon,* I, p. 325.

22. Chastenet, *Godoy,* p. 124.

23. Madol, *Godoy,* p. 166.

24. Junot, *Memoirs,* II, p. 379.

25. Godoy, *Memorias,* II, p. 44.

26. Corona Baratech, *Revolución,* pp. 332–33. The author quotes contemporaries, including Escoiquiz, Alcalá Galiano, and García de León Pizarro, who inclined toward this view, shared in part by Fugier and Lema among later historians. Seco Serrano (p. lxxxix of his Introduction to Godoy's *Memorias*) voices a contrary opinion.

27. Fugier, *Napoléon,* I, p. 367.

28. Madol, *Godoy,* p. 168.

29. Godoy, *Memorias,* II, p. 48.

30. Pardo González, *Don Manuel Godoy,* p. 146.

31. Ibid., p. 127.

32. Izquierdo Hernández, *Antecedentes,* p. 217.

33. Fugier, *Napoléon,* II, p. 32.

34. Godoy, *Memorias,* p. lxxxvii of Introduction, by Seco Serrano; also Martí, *Proceso,* p. 125. A minor discrepancy exists between the two versions, but the basic thrust is identical.

35. Fugier, *Napoléon,* I, p. 371.

36. Chastenet, *Godoy,* p. 145.

37. Godoy, *Memorias,* p. xci of Introduction, by Seco Serrano.

38. Madol, *Godoy,* p. 170.

39. Fugier, *Napoléon,* II, p. 33.

40. Una vieja insolente
    le elevó desde el cieno,
    burlándose del bueno
    del esposo, que es harto complaciente.
    Justo es que así suceda,
    pues de una vieja loca
    todo puede esperarse,
    menos que diga una verdad su boca.

Martí, *Proceso,* p. 146.

41. Por asesino y traidor
    Te has de ver tostado vivo
    Sobre la Plaza Mayor.

Ibid.

42. Izquierdo Hernández, *Antecedentes,* p. 221.

43. Bermejo, *Historia,* I, p. 103.

44. Izquierdo Hernández, *Antecedentes,* p. 222.

45. Antonio Alcalá Galiano, *Memorias,* B.A.E. 83, 84 (Madrid: Ediciones Atlas, 1955), I, p. 312.

46. Godoy, *Memorias,* II, p. 89 fn.

47. Fugier, *Napoléon,* II, p. 266.

Chapter 11

1. Martí, *Proceso,* p. 79.

2. Godoy, *Memorias,* p. xciv of Introduction, by Seco Serrano.

3. Madol, *Godoy,* p. 172.

4. Fugier, *Napoléon,* II, p. 48.

5. Pardo González, *Don Manuel Godoy,* p. 147.

6. Godoy, *Memorias,* p. xciv of Introduction, by Seco Serrano.

7. Ibid., p. xcv.

8. Chastenet, *Godoy,* p. 160.

9. Godoy, *Memorias,* II, p. 99.

10. Fugier, *Napoléon,* II, p. 145.

11. Pardo González, *Don Manuel Godoy,* p. 156.

12. Ibid., p. 157.

13. Martí, *Proceso,* p. 139.

14. Godoy, *Memorias,* II, p. 510, Appendix IV. Godoy, composing his memoirs in exile, did not have access to the original text, but reconstructed the Spanish version from foreign translations. His inclusion of this unflattering document does him credit.

15. Ibid., p. 89.

16. Fugier, *Napoléon,* II, p. 157.

17. Godoy, *Memorias,* p. xcviii of Introduction, by Seco Serrano.

18. D'Auvergne, *Godoy,* p. 203; Chastenet, *Godoy,* p. 153.

19. Chastenet, *Godoy,* p. 153; Fugier, *Napoléon,* II, p. 157.

20. Godoy, *Memorias,* II, p. 90.

21. Chastenet, *Godoy,* p. 153.

22. Fugier, *Napoléon,* II, pp. 151–52.

23. The exact number and quality of the contingent is in dispute. See Fugier, *Napoléon,* II, pp. 168–74, for a detailed discussion on this point.

24. Martí, *Proceso,* p. 140 fn.

25. Ibid., p. 178.

26. Fugier, *Napoléon,* II, p. 163.

27. Godoy, *Memorias,* II, p. 194 fn.

28. Izquierdo Hernández, *Antecedentes,* p. 228.

29. D'Auvergne, *Godoy,* p. 222.

30. Escoiquiz, *Memorias,* p. 20.

31. Bermejo, *Historia,* I, p. 99.

32. Escoiquiz, *Memorias,* p. 18.

33. Ibid., p. 28.

34. Alcalá Galiano, *Memorias,* I, p. 317.

35. Godoy, *Memorias,* p. lxii of Introduction, by Seco Serrano.

36. Fugier, *Napoléon,* II, p. 185.

37. Godoy, *Memorias,* II, p. 100 fn.

38. Alcalá Galiano, *Memorias,* I, p. 317.

39. Ibid.

40. Ibid., p. 318.

41. Ibid.

42. Godoy, *Memorias,* II, p. 92.

43. Ibid., II, p. 93 fn.

44. Ibid., II, p. 105.

45. Pardo González, *Don Manuel Godoy,* p. 129.

46. Godoy, *Memorias,* II, p. 184. Godoy gives the full text both of the treaty and of the secret articles.

47. Chastenet, *Godoy,* p. 157.

Chapter 12.

1. Escoiquiz, *Memorias,* p. 25.

2. Bermejo, *Historia,* I, p. 112.

3. Martí, *Proceso,* p. 191.

4. Fugier, *Napoléon,* II, p. 284.

5. Godoy, *Memorias,* p. ciii of Introduction, by Seco Serrano.

6. Chastenet, *Godoy,* p. 160.

7. Godoy, *Memorias,* II, p. 138.

8. Ibid., pp. 191–92.

9. Izquierdo Hernández, *Antecedentes,* p. 234. Godoy, *Memorias,* II, p. 189, gives the same note.

10. Godoy, *Memorias,* II, p. 192.

11. Escoiquiz, *Memorias,* p. 33.

12. Ibid.

13. Ibid., p. 34.

14. Izquierdo Hernández, *Antecedentes,* p. 240. The documents are reproduced almost in their entirety on pp. 239–49, also in Martí, *Proceso,* pp. 211–30.

15. Izquierdo Hernández, *Antecedentes,* p. 241.

16. Ibid., p. 243.

17. Martí, *Proceso,* p. 216.

18. Izquierdo Hernández, *Antecedentes,* p. 244.
19. Ibid., p. 222.
20. Martí, *Proceso,* p. 220.
21. Ibid., p. 222.
22. Godoy, *Memorias,* II, p. 193.
23. Ibid., p. 195.
24. Bermejo, *Historia,* I, p. 151.
25. Escoiquiz, *Memorias,* p. 36.
26. Godoy, *Memorias,* II, p. 197.
27. Izquierdo Hernández, *Antecedentes,* p. 250.
28. Ibid., Martí, *Proceso,* p. 240.
29. Godoy, *Memorias,* II, p. 202.
30. Ibid., p. 201.
31. Izquierdo Hernández, *Antecedentes,* p. 251.
32. Ibid., p. 250.
33. Ibid., p. 254.
34. Godoy, *Memorias,* II, p. 205.
35. Ibid.
36. Ibid., p. 206.
37. Izquierdo Hernández, *Antecedentes,* p. 260.
38. Fugier, *Napoléon,* II, p. 298.
39. Ibid., p. 299.
40. Godoy, *Memorias,* II, p. 213.
41. Pardo González, *Don Manuel Godoy,* p. 176.
42. Godoy, *Memorias,* II, p. 226.
43. Martí, *Proceso,* p. 291.
44. Izquierdo Hernández, *Antecedentes,* p. 279.
45. Escoiquiz, *Memorias,* p. 53.
46. Izquierdo Hernández, *Antecedentes,* p. 278.

Chapter 13

1. Godoy, *Memorias,* II, p. 244.
2. Ibid., p. 241.
3. Ibid., p. 243.
4. Ibid., p. 268.
5. Izquierdo Hernández, *Antecedentes,* p. 290.
6. Fugier, *Napoléon,* II, p. 423.
7. Godoy, *Memorias,* II, p. 254.
8. Izquierdo Hernández, *Antecedentes,* p. 291.
9. Ibid., p. 292.
10. Martí, *Aranjuez,* p. 65.

11. Godoy, *Memorias*, II, p. 271. Godoy reproduces the memorandum in its entirety (pp. 271–77). Izquierdo Hernández gives an excellent summary on pp. 293–95 in *Antecedentes*.

12. Ibid., p. 275.

13. Ibid., p. 276.

14. Ibid., p. 244.

15. Conde de Toreno, *Historia del levantamiento, guerra, y revolución en España*, B.A.E. 64 (Madrid: Ediciones Atlas, 1953), p. 20. Seco Serrano, on p. cxviii of his Introduction to Godoy's *Memorias*, echoes the same sentiments.

16. Godoy, *Memorias*, II, p. 289.

17. Ibid., p. 290.

18. Blanco-White, *Letters*, p. 399.

19. Alcalá Galiano, *Memorias*, p. 324.

20. Izquierdo Hernández, *Antecedentes*, p. 298.

21. Godoy, *Memorias*, II, p. 298.

22. Izquierdo Hernández, *Antecedentes*, p. 231.

23. Martí, *Aranjuez*, pp. 117–18.

24. Jacquet, *Bourbons*, p. 238.

25. Martí, *Aranjuez*, p. 115 fn.

26. Godoy, *Memorias*, II, p. 310.

27. Izquierdo Hernández, *Antecedentes*, p. 303.

28. Godoy, *Memorias*, II, p. 316.

Chapter 14

1. Escoiquiz, *Memorias*, p. 145. This excerpt and others that follow in this chapter are not from the actual memoirs but from the correspondence that Escoiquiz appended. This in turn was taken from the *Moniteur*.

2. Godoy, *Memorias*, II, p. 317 fn.

3. Pardo González, *Don Manuel Godoy*, p. 209.

4. Martí, *Aranjuez*, p. 141.

5. Ibid., p. 148.

6. Junot, *Memoirs*, p. 381.

7. Martí, *Aranjuez*, p. 155.

8. Izquierdo Hernández, *Antecedentes*, p. 312.

9. Chastenet, *Godoy*, p. 191.

10. Madol, *Godoy*, p. 200.

11. Godoy, *Memorias*, II, p. 317.

12. Ibid., p. 318.

13. Ibid., p. 321.

14. Ibid., p. 322.

15. Chastenet, *Godoy*, p. 192. This account, among others, varies slightly from that of Godoy, but not in its essentials.

16. Pardo González, *Don Manuel Godoy,* p. 219; Izquierdo Hernández, *Antecedentes,* p. 317.

17. En este sitio, pues, un vil tirano,
    sin religión, estúpido, arrogante,
    traydor, inicuo, lujurioso y vano,
    se miró derrocado en un instante,
    ¿y dudáis quién será tal monstruo insano?
    pues sabed que lo es el Almirante.
Martí, *Aranjuez,* p. 164.

18. Por ti murió el de Aranda perseguido;
    Floridablanca vive desterrado;
    Jovellanos en vida sepultado,
    Y muchos grandes yacen en olvido.
    De la madre, del padre, del marido
    Arrancaste el honor, y has profanado,
    Polígamo brutal, aquél sagrado
    Que indigno tú pisar no has merecido.
    Calumnias, muertes, robos y atentados
    Con descaro insolente cometiste
    ¡Oh, tú, el más ruin de los privados!
    Si almirante, si grande te creaste,
    Cuando eras el más vil de los malvados
    Hoy el cielo te vuelve a lo que fuiste.
Ibid., p. 207.

19. Alcalá Galiano, *Memorias,* p. 327.

20. Martí, *Aranjuez,* p. 211.

21. Pardo González, *Don Manuel Godoy,* p. 221.

22. Izquierdo Hernández, *Antecedentes,* p. 340.

23. Ibid., p. 341.

24. Madol, *Godoy,* p. 207.

25. Izquierdo Hernández, *Antecedentes,* p. 343.

26. Pardo González, *Don Manuel Godoy,* p. 220.

27. Ibid., p. 229.

28. Georges Roux, *Napoléon et le Guêpier Espagnol* (Paris: Flammarion, 1970), p. 36.

29. Izquierdo Hernández, *Antecedentes,* p. 329.

30. D'Auvergne, *Godoy,* p. 294.

31. Escoiquiz, *Memorias,* p.140. Again, not from the memoirs but from the appended correspondence.

32. Ibid., p. 144.

33. Ibid., p. 145.

34. Madol, *Godoy,* p. 209.

35. Pardo González, *Don Manuel Godoy,* p. 248.

36. Martí, *Aranjuez*, p. 264.
37. Madol, *Godoy*, p. 212.
38. Ibid.

Chapter 15

1. Pardo González, *Don Manuel Godoy*, p. 227.
2. Martí, *Aranjuez*, p. 313; Izquierdo Hernández, *Antecedentes*, p. 379.
3. Pedro Cevallos, *Exposición de los hechos y maquinaciones que han preparado la usurpación de la corona de España*, B.A.E. 97 (Madrid: Ediciones Atlas, 1957), p. 161.
4. Escoiquiz, *Memorias*, p. 67.
5. Pardo González, *Don Manuel Godoy*, p. 244.
6. Godoy, *Memorias*, II, p. 332.
7. Pardo González, *Don Manuel Godoy*, p. 250.
8. D'Auvergne, *Godoy*, p. 299.
9. Martí, *Aranjuez*, p. 326.
10. Ibid., p. 360.
11. Chastenet, *Godoy*, p. 202.
12. Ibid.
13. Godoy, *Memorias*, II, p. 364.
14. Jacquet, *Bourbons*, p. 223.
15. Escoiquiz, *Memorias*, pp. 121–22.
16. Ibid., p. 135.
17. Madol, *Godoy*, p. 220.
18. Roux, *Guêpier*, p. 49.
19. Godoy, *Memorias*, II, p. 366.
20. Ibid., p. 367.
21. Madol, *Godoy*, p. 224; E. Ducéré, *Napoléon à Bayonne* (Bayonne: E. Hourquet, 1897), p. 83.
22. Ducéré, *Bayonne*, p. 81.
23. Godoy, *Memorias*, II, p. 384.
24. Ibid., p. 385.
25. Ibid.
26. Roux, *Guêpier*, p. 51; Ducéré, *Bayonne*, pp. 82, 83.
27. Ducéré, *Bayonne*, pp. 84, 85.
28. Ibid., p. 88.
29. Godoy, *Memorias*, II, p. 389.
30. Ibid., p. 392. Also Izquierdo Hernández, *Antecedentes*, p. 402.
31. Izquierdo Hernández, *Antecedentes*, p. 425.
32. Martí, *Aranjuez*, p. 407.
33. Godoy, *Memorias*, II, p. 407.

34. Soldevila, *Historia*, p. 303; Ducéré, *Bayonne*, p. 94.

35. Ducéré, *Bayonne*, p. 95.

36. Cevallos, *Exposición*, p. 167.

37. Godoy, *Memorias*, II, p. 408.

38. Ibid., p. 409.

39. Ibid., p. 410.

40. Izquierdo Hernández, *Antecedentes*, p. 415.

41. Madol, *Godoy*, p. 235.

42. Jacquet, *Bourbons*, p. 245.

Chapter 16

1. D'Auvergne, *Godoy*, p. 314.

2. Madol, *Godoy*, p. 235.

3. Ibid., p. 238; Chastenet, *Godoy*, p. 214.

4. Madol, *Godoy*, p. 236.

5. Ibid., p. 237.

6. Izquierdo Hernández, *Antecedentes*, p. 530.

7. Jacquet, *Bourbons*, p. 230.

8. Ibid., p. 229; also Madol, *Godoy*, p. 240.

9. Godoy, *Memorias*, p. cxix of Introduction, quoted by Seco Serrano.

10. Pardo González, *Don Manuel Godoy*, p. 261.

11. Ibid.

12. Ibid., p. 262.

13. Ibid., p. 263.

14. Ibid., p. 266.

15. Juan Pérez de Guzmán, *Estudios de la vida, reinado, proscripción y muerte de Carlos IV y María Luisa de Borbón* (Madrid: Imprenta de Jaime Ratés Martín, 1909), p. 16. Despite a confusing chronology, this work is an invaluable guide to the years in Rome. Godoy's *Memorias* unfortunately end with the events in Bayonne.

16. Ibid., p. 254.

17. Ibid., p. 258.

18. Ibid., p. 35.

19. Ibid., p. 40.

20. Ibid., p. 61.

21. Ibid., p. 71.

22. Ibid., p. 105; D'Auvergne, *Godoy*, p. 318.

23. Pérez de Guzmán, *Estudios*, p. 108.

24. Ibid., p. 116.

25. Ibid., p. 139.

26. Ibid., p. 140.

27. Ibid., p. 155.

28. Ibid., p. 156.

29. Ibid., p. 179.

30. Ibid., p. 194.

31. Ibid., p. 202.

32. Ibid., p. 204.

33. Ibid., p. 214.

34. Ibid., p. 300.

35. Ibid., p. 198.

36. Ibid., p. 199; Chastenet, *Godoy*, p. 224.

37. Pérez de Guzmán, *Estudios*, p. 200.

38. Ibid.

39. Ibid., p. 305.

40. Ibid.; Chastenet, *Godoy*, p. 225.

41. Pérez de Guzmán, *Estudios*, p. 305.

42. Madol, *Godoy*, p. 250.

43. Pérez de Guzmán, *Estudios*, p. 337.

44. Ibid., p 327.

45. Ibid., p. 331.

46. Ibid., p. 338.

47. Ibid., p. 282; Chastenet, *Godoy*, p. 225.

48. Chastenet, *Godoy*, p. 226; Jacquet, *Bourbons*, p. 233.

Chapter 17

1. Pérez de Guzmán, *Estudios*, p. 283.

2. Godoy, *Memorias*, p. cxxi of Introduction, by Seco Serrano.

3. Ángel Ossorio, *La agonía del Príncipe de la Paz* (Madrid: Establecimiento tipográfico Anónima Mefar, 1923), p. 23.

4. Pérez de Guzmán, *Estudios*, p. 340.

5. Ibid.

6. Ossorio (*La agonía*, p. 33) questions whether Godoy did in fact receive a regular pension or merely a single payment on September 21, 1834. He certainly was paid some meager annuity, whether from the French government or Carlota is not clear.

7. Fugier, *Napoléon*, I, p. xxvii of Introduction.

8. José Mor de Fuentes, *Bosquejillo de su vida y escritos* (Granada: Universidad de Granada, 1951), pp. 147–49.

9. Madol, *Godoy*, p. 265.

10. Pérez de Guzmán, *Estudios*, p. 341.

11. Lord Holland, *Reminiscences*, p. 204.

12. Ibid., p. 207.

13. Ibid., p. 208.

14. Madol, *Godoy*, p. 264.

15. Ibid., p. 265.

16. Ramón de Mesonero Romanos, *Memorias de un setentón*, B.A.E. 203 (Madrid: Ediciones Atlas, 1967), pp. 10–11.

17. Madol, *Godoy*, p. 258.

18. Mesonero Romanos, *Memorias*, p. 11.

19. Ossorio, *La agonía*, p. 26.

20. Ibid., p. 29.

21. Ibid.

22. Ibid., p. 30.

23. Godoy, *Memorias*, p. cxxvi of Introduction, by Seco Serrano.

24. Ossorio, *La agonía*, p. 32.

25. Mesonero Romanos, *Memorias*, p. 11.

26. Ibid., p. 12.

27. William E. Colford, *Juan Meléndez Valdés* (New York: Hispanic Institute, 1942), p. 136.

Chapter 18

1. Bermejo, *Historia*, p. 17 of *Prólogo,* by Julio Burell.

2. González Ruiz, *Favoritos*, p. 8.

3. Lewis, *Goya*, p. 93.

4. Serrano Poncela, *Formas*, p. 125.

5. Quoted by Lewis, *Goya*, p. 159.

6. Ángel Del Río, *Antología general de la literatura española*, 2 vols. (New York: Holt, Rinehart & Winston, 1960), II, p. 483.

7. Martí, *Aranjuez*, p. 417 fn.

Glossary of Foreign Terms

abrazo: embrace, hug

afrancesado: Spanish sympathizer with the French, especially during the Napoleonic invasion (1808–13)

alcoba: bedroom

alma; Luisito de mi alma: soul, heart; Luisito my love, dearest

Alteza Serenísima: Most Serene Highness

amante: lover, sweetheart

amorío: love affair

amor propio: self-esteem

anciano: elderly man

autor: author

bailío: knight commander of the Order of Malta

bocado: (as used here) poison given in food

caballero: gentleman; nobleman, cavalier

calabozo: dungeon, cell

calumnia: slander

camarista: (as used here) maid of honor to the queen of Spain

canción de gesta: ancient ballad relating stirring deeds

cándida paloma: innocent dove

capilla: chapel, small church

caprichos: fancies, whims

cara; muy mala cara: face; real ugly face

casa de corrección: reformatory, approved school

castizo: of good breed, pure, very Spanish

choricero: sausage-maker or seller, term of derision for Godoy

ci-devant (Fr.): former; royalist, aristocrat

Conde: Count

condottiere (It.): leader of mercenary troops

Consejo de Estado: Council of State

corazón; mi afligido corazón: heart; my grieving heart

corrida: bullfight

cortejo: gallant, beau, paramour

Cortes: Parliament, Legislative Assembly

cuesta abajo: downhill

debilidad orgánica: physical, organic weakness

demasiado bueno: too good, kind

ducado: (as used here) ducat, a former gold coin

enemigo capital: chief enemy

Extremeño: citizen of Extremadura, province of western Spain

franchute: frenchy, froggy, contemptuous term for the French

gaditano: citizen of Cádiz in southern Spain

godo soy: I am a Goth

guerra justa: justified war

hidalgo: one of impoverished nobility

hijo: son, junior

infante: child of the Spanish monarchs

jornada: one-day journey; king's stay in a royal country residence

lazzaroni (It.): slackers, beggars

letras humanas en toda su extensión: the humanities in all branches

levantamiento: revolt, uprising

leyenda negra: literally the "black legend," defamatory stories about Spanish cruelties, spread by enemies of Spain.

luces, las: the Enlightenment, the eighteenth century

madrastra: stepmother

madrileño: citizen of Madrid

maja: elegant, well-dressed young lady as depicted by Goya

marido cornudo: cuckold husband

mariscal de campo: field marshal

memorias: memoirs

mignon (Fr.): pretty, dainty, darling, favorite, pet

ministro confidente: trusted minister

modiste (Fr.): milliner

mort, la (Fr.): death

motín: mutiny, uprising

muerto, el rey ha muerto: dead; the king is dead (has died)

octava: eight-line stanza

Oficio Santo: Holy Office, Inquisition

pantalón y botas: trousers and (riding) boots

papel insultante: insulting document

partido fernandino: group supporting Fernando, future King Fernando VII of Spain

paz: peace

pecador, un gran: a great sinner

pegadito en el estómago: a little plaster on the stomach

Pepe Botellas: Joe Bottles, disrespectful name given by Spaniards to Joseph Bonaparte when he was king of Spain (1808–13)

Pintor de Cámara: Royal Painter

populacho: crowd, rabble, mob

príncipe: prince
privado: royal favorite
pronunciamiento: military revolt, especially during the nineteenth century
pueblo sin rey, sin ley, y sin Dios: nation without a king, no law, and without God
pundonor: point of honor
querido: dear, beloved
real: royal
reino: kingdom, realm
rey deseado: the Desired One, name given to Fernando in exile by his supporters
reyes: Spanish monarchs, king and queen
rey intruso: the Intrusive King, yet another term of derision for Joseph Bonaparte
santa trinidad en la tierra: holy trinity on earth
siglo: century
sitio: royal residence
tertulia: social gathering, club, salon
valido: royal favorite
voz popular: voice of the people
Yo el Rey: I the King (formal phrase)
zarzuela: light comic opera, operetta

Bibliography

Acton, Harold. *The Bourbons of Naples*. London: Methuen and Co. Ltd., 1959.

Alcalá Galiano, Antonio. *Memorias*. Biblioteca de Autores Españoles (B.A.E.) 83, 84. Introductory essay by Jorge Campos. Madrid: Ediciones Atlas, 1955.

——. *Recuerdos de un anciano*. B.A.E. 83. Introductory essay by Jorge Campos. Madrid: Ediciones Atlas, 1955.

Altamira, Rafael. *A History of Spain*. Princeton: D. Van Nostrand Company, Inc., 1962.

Anes, Gonzalo. *Economía e Ilustración en la España del siglo XVIII*. Barcelona: Editorial Ariel, 1981.

—— et al. *España a finales del siglo XVIII*. 2nd ed. Tarragona: Hemeroteca de Tarragona, 1982.

Artola, Miguel. *Antiguo Régimen y Revolución Liberal*. Barcelona: Editorial Ariel, 1979.

Atkinson, William. *A History of Spain and Portugal*. London: Penguin Books, 1960.

Beckford, William. *The Travel Diaries of William Beckford of Fonthill*. 2 vols. Cambridge: Cambridge University Press, 1928.

——. *Un inglés en la España de Godoy*. Translation and prologue by Jesús Pardo. Madrid: Taurus Ediciones, 1966.

Bergamini, John D. *The Spanish Bourbons*. New York: G. P. Putnam's Sons, 1974.

Bermejo, Ildefonso Antonio. *Historia anecdótica y secreta de la corte de Carlos IV*. Prologue by Julio Burell. 2 vols. Madrid: Casa Editorial de la Viuda de Muñoz, n.d.

Beyersdorf, Eunice Smith. "A Rediscovered Portrait of Godoy, Minister to Carlos IV." *The Burlington Magazine*, No. 717, Vol. CIV, December 1962, pp. 536–39.

Blanco-White, José (pseudonym: Doblado, Leucadio). *Letters from Spain*. London: Henry Colburn & Co., 1822.

Breunig, Charles. *The Age of Revolution and Reaction, 1789–1850*. New York: W. W. Norton & Company, 1970.

Buisman, Hans. *Spanien*. Darmstadt: Wissenschaftliche Buchgesellschaft, 1972.

Byron, Lord. *Childe Harold's Pilgrimage*. Boston: Ticknor & Co., 1886.

Cabarrús, Conde de. *Cartas sobre los obstáculos que la naturaleza, la opinión y las leyes oponen a la felicidad pública*. Madrid: Imprenta de Burgos, 1820.

Cevallos, Pedro. *Exposición de los hechos y maquinaciones que han preparado la usurpación de la corona de España*. B.A.E. 97. Madrid: Ediciones Atlas, 1957.

Chastenet, Jacques. *Godoy, Master of Spain, 1792–1808*. London: The Batchworth Press Ltd., 1953.

Clark, Lord Kenneth. *The Romantic Rebellion*. New York: Harper & Row, 1973.

Colford, William E. *Juan Meléndez Valdés*. New York: Hispanic Institute, 1942.

Connelly, Owen. *The Gentle Bonaparte*. New York: The Macmillan Company, 1968.

Cook, John A. *Neo-Classic Drama in Spain: Theory and Practice*. Dallas: Southern Methodist University Press, 1959.

Corona Baratech, Carlos. *Revolución y reacción en el reinado de Carlos IV*. Madrid: Ediciones Rialp, 1957.

Cox, Ralph Merritt. *Juan Meléndez Valdés*. New York: Twayne Publishers, 1974.

Cueto, Leopoldo Augusto, ed. *Poetas líricos del siglo XVIII*. B.A.E. 63. Madrid: Ediciones Atlas, 1952.

D'Auvergne, Edmund. *Godoy, the Queen's Favourite*. Boston: The Gorham Press, 1913.

Defourneaux, Marcelin. *Pablo de Olavide*. Paris: Presses Universitaires de France, 1959.

Del Río, Ángel. *Antología general de la literatura española*. 2 vols. New York: Holt, Rinehart & Winston, 1960.

Del Solar y Taboada, Antonio, and De Rújula y de Ochotorena, José. *Godoy, Príncipe de la Paz*. Badajoz: Tipografía Viuda de Antonio Arqueros, 1944.

Díaz Plaja, Guillermo. *Epistolario de Goya*. Barcelona: Editorial Mentora, 1928.

Doblado, Leucadio. *See* Blanco-White.

Ducéré, E. *Napoléon à Bayonne*. Bayonne: E. Hourquet, 1897.

Elliott, J. H. *Imperial Spain, 1469–1716*. New York: Mentor Books, 1966.

Epton, Nina. *The Spanish Mousetrap*. London: Macdonald & Co. Ltd., 1973.

Escoiquiz, Juan de. *Idea sencilla de las razones que motivaron el viaje del rey don Fernando VII a Bayona*. B.A.E. 97. Madrid: Ediciones Atlas, 1957.

———. *Memorias de Tiempos de Fernando VII*. B.A.E. 97. Preliminary study by Miguel Artola. Madrid: Ediciones Atlas, 1957.

Esquerra del Bayo, Joaquín. *La Duquesa de Alba y Goya*. Madrid: Librería de Ruiz Hermanos, 1928.

Fontana, Josep. *La quiebra de la monarquía absoluta (1814–1820)*. Barcelona: Ediciones Ariel, 1971.

Ford, Richard. *A Handbook for Travellers in Spain and Readers at Home, 1845*. 3 vols. Carbondale: Southern Illinois Press, 1966.

Fugier, André. *Napoléon et l'Espagne*. 2 vols. Paris: Librairie Félix Alcan, 1930.

Gassier, Pierre, and Wilson, Juliet. *The Life and Complete Work of Francisco Goya*. New York: Reynal & Co., 1971.

Glover, Michael. *Legacy of Glory*. New York: Charles Scribner's Sons, 1971.

Godechot, Jacques. *Napoléon*. Paris: Editions Albin Michel, 1969.

Godoy, Manuel. *Memorias*. B.A.E. 88, 89. Preliminary study by Carlos Seco Serrano. Madrid: Ediciones Atlas, 1956.

González Ruiz, Nicolás. *Dos Favoritos: Potemkin, Godoy*. Barcelona: Editorial Cervantes, 1944.

Grandmaison, Geoffroy de. *L'Ambassade française en Espagne pendant la Révolution (1789–1804)*. Paris: Librairie Plon, 1892.

Hargreaves-Mawdsley, W. N. *Spain under the Bourbons, 1700–1833*. Columbia: University of South Carolina Press, 1973.

Harris, Enriqueta. *Goya*. London: Phaidon Press Ltd., 1969.

Herold, J. Christopher. *The Horizon Book of the Age of Napoleon*. New York: American Heritage Publishing Co., Inc., 1963.

Herr, Richard. *The Eighteenth-Century Revolution in Spain*. Princeton: Princeton University Press, 1958.

Hills, George. *Spain*. New York: Praeger Publishers, 1970.

Holland, Lady Elizabeth. *The Spanish Journal of Elizabeth Lady Holland*. London: Longmans, Green, and Co., 1910.

Holland, Lord Henry Richard. *Foreign Reminiscences*. New York: Harper & Brothers, 1851.

Hume, Martin. *Spain: Its Greatness and Decay (1479–1788)*. Cambridge: Cambridge University Press, 1899.

Izquierdo Hernández, Manuel. *Antecedentes y comienzos del reinado de Fernando VII*. Madrid: Ediciones Cultura Hispánica, 1963.

Jacquet, Jean-Louis. *Les Bourbons d'Espagne*. Lausanne: Éditions Rencontre, 1968.

Jovellanos, Gaspar Melchor de. *Obras escogidas*. 3 vols. Introductory essay by Ángel del Río. Madrid: Espasa-Calpe, S.A., 1955.

Juderías, Julián. *Don Gaspar Melchor de Jovellanos*. Madrid: Jaime Ratés Martín, 1913.

Junot, Madame, Duchesse d'Abrantès. *Memoirs*. 3 vols. New York: Scribner and Welford, 1883.

Kany, Charles E. *Life and Manners in Madrid, 1750–1800*. New York: AMS Press, 1970.

Lema, Marqués de. *Antecedentes políticos y diplomáticos de los sucesos de 1808*. Madrid: Librería de F. Beltrán, 1912.

Lewis, D. B. Wyndham. *The World of Goya*. New York: Clarkson N. Potter, Inc., 1968.

Livermore, Harold. *A History of Spain*. London: George Allen and Unwin, Ltd., 1958.

Lovett, Gabriel H. *Napoleon and the Birth of Modern Spain*. 2 vols. New York: New York University Press, 1965.

Lucas-Dubreton, J. *Napoléon devant l'Espagne*. Paris: Librairie Arthème Fayard, 1946.

Madariaga, Salvador de. *Spain: A Modern History*. New York: Frederick A. Praeger, 1960.

Madol, Hans Roger. *Godoy*. Madrid: Alianza Editorial, 1966.

Marañón, Gregorio. *El Conde-Duque de Olivares*. Madrid: Espasa-Calpe, S.A., 1959.

Marías, Julián. *Los Españoles*. Madrid: Revista de Occidente, 1962.

Markham, Felix. *Napoleon*. New York: New American Library, Mentor Books, 1963.

Martí, Francisco. *El motín de Aranjuez*. Pamplona: Ediciones Universidad de Navarra, S.A., 1972.

———. *El proceso de El Escorial*. Pamplona: Ediciones Universidad de Navarra, S.A., 1965.

Martínez Friera, J. *Godoy, Príncipe de la Paz. Biografía novelada*. Madrid: Afrodisio Aguado, S.A., 1944.

Mesonero Romanos, Ramón de. *Memorias de un setentón*. B.A.E. 203. Madrid: Ediciones Atlas, 1967.

Mor de Fuentes, José. *Bosquejillo de su vida y escritos*. Granada: Universidad de Granada, 1951.

Muriel, Andrés. *Historia de Carlos IV*. B.A.E. 114, 115. Preliminary study by Carlos Seco Serrano. Madrid: Ediciones Atlas, 1959.

Olaechea, Rafael, and Ferrer Benimeli, José. *El Conde de Aranda*. 2 vols. Saragossa: Librería General, 1978.

Orieux, Jean. *Talleyrand*. New York: Alfred A. Knopf, 1974.

Ortis, Antonio Domínguiz. "La Sociedad Española en el Tránsito del siglo 18 al 19." In *España a finales del siglo XVIII*. Gonzalo Anes et al. 2nd ed. Tarragona: Hemeroteca de Tarragona, 1982.

Ossorio, Ángel. *La agonía del Príncipe de la Paz*. Madrid: Establecimiento tipográfico Anónima Mefar, 1923.

Pardo González, Cándido. *Don Manuel Godoy y Álvarez Faria, Príncipe de la Paz*. Madrid: Imprenta de la Viuda de A. Álvarez, 1911.

Peers, E. Allison. *A History of the Romantic Movement in Spain*. 2 vols. New York and London: Hafner Publishing Co., 1964.

Pereyra, Carlos. *Cartas confidenciales de la reina María Luisa y de Don Manuel Godoy*. Madrid: M. Aguilar, n.d.

Pérez Galdós, Benito. *El 19 de marzo y el 2 de mayo*. Madrid: Viuda e Hijo de Tello, 1898.

Pérez de Guzmán, Juan. *Estudios de la vida, reinado, proscripción y muerte de Carlos IV y María Luisa de Borbón*. Madrid: Imprenta de Jaime Ratés Martín, 1909.

Polt, John H. R. *Gaspar Melchor de Jovellanos*. New York: Twayne Publishers, 1971.

Reglá, Juan, and Alcolea, Santiago. *El Siglo XVIII*. Barcelona: Editorial Seix Barral, S.A., 1957.

Rojas, Carlos. *Diálogos para otra España*. Barcelona: Ediciones Ariel, 1966.

Roux, Georges. *Napoléon et le Guêpier Espagnol*. Paris: Flammarion, 1970.

Salas, Xavier de. *Goya*. Trans. G. T. Culverwell. New York: Mayflower Books, 1981.

Sánchez, José, ed. *Nineteenth-Century Spanish Verse*. New York: Appleton-Century-Crofts, 1949.

Sarrailh, Jean. *L'Espagne éclairée de la seconde moitié du XVIIIe siècle*. Paris: Imprimerie Nationale, 1954.

Schickel, Richard. *The World of Goya*. New York: Time-Life Books, 1968.

Schop Soler, Ana María. *Las relaciones entre España y Rusia en la época de Carlos IV*. Prologue by Carlos Seco Serrano. Barcelona: Publicaciones de la Cátedra de Historia General de España, 1971.

Serrano Poncela, Segundo. *Formas de Vida Hispánica*. Madrid: Editorial Gredos, 1963.

Smith, Rhea Marsh. *Spain: A Modern History*. Ann Arbor: University of Michigan Press, 1965.

Soldevila, F. *Historia de España*. Vol. VI. Barcelona: Ediciones Ariel, 1964.

Thomas, Hugh. *The Spanish Civil War*. New York: Harper and Brothers, 1961.

Toreno, Conde de. *Historia del levantamiento, guerra, y revolución en España*. B.A.E. 64. Madrid: Ediciones Atlas, 1953.

Trapier, Elizabeth du Gué. *Goya and His Sitters: A Study of His Style as a Portraitist*. New York: Hispanic Society of America, 1964.

Vallentin, Antonina. *This I Saw: The Life and Times of Goya*. New York: Random House, 1949.

Villa-Urrutia, Marqués de. *La Reina María Luisa y Bolívar*. Madrid: Francisco Beltrán, n.d.

Zabala y Lera, Pío. *España bajo los Borbones*. Barcelona: Editorial Labor, S.A., 1945.

Zavala, Iris M., et al. *Historia ibérica. Economía y sociedad en los siglos XVIII y XIX*. Madrid: A. G. Ibarra, S.A., n.d.

Index